SUZUKA

4

Kouji Seo

TRANSLATED AND ADAPTED BY
David Ury

LETTERED BY
North Market Street Graphics

BALLANTINE BOOKS · NEW YORK

Suzuka volume 4 is a work of fiction. Names, characters, places, and incidents are the products of the author's imagination or are used fictitiously. Any resemblance to actual events, locales, or persons, living or dead, is entirely coincidental.

A Del Rey Trade Paperback Original

Suzuka volume 4 copyright © 2004 by Kouji Seo
English translation copyright © 2007 by Kouji Seo

All rights reserved.

Published in the United States by Del Rey Books, an imprint of The Random House Publishing Group, a division of Random House, Inc., New York.

DEL REY is a registered trademark and the Del Rey colphon is a trademark of Random House, Inc.

Publication rights arranged through Kodansha Ltd.

First published in Japan in 2004 by Kodansha Ltd., Tokyo.

ISBN 978-0-345-49049-0

Printed in the United States of America

www.delreymanga.com

9 8 7 6 5 4 3 2 1

Translator/adapter: David Ury
Lettering: North Market Street Graphics

Contents

A Note from the Author iv

Honorifics Explained v

Suzuka, Volume 4 1

Bonus Manga 182

Translation Notes 184

Preview of Volume 5 188

A Note from the Author

LATELY I'VE BEEN SO DAMNED BUSY THAT I NEVER ACTUALLY GO TO SLEEP. I JUST PASS OUT! I NEVER EVEN MAKE IT TO MY FUTON. THAT KIND OF MAKES ME SOUND LIKE I'M A BUSY, BESTSELLING AUTHOR OR SOMETHING, BUT THE TRUTH IS, I'M JUST ALWAYS LATE FOR MY DEADLINES.

Honorifics Explained

Throughout the Del Rey Manga books, you will find Japanese honorifics left intact in the translations. For those not familiar with how the Japanese use honorifics and, more important, how they differ from American honorifics, we present this brief overview.

Politeness has always been a critical facet of Japanese culture. Ever since the feudal era, when Japan was a highly stratified society, use of honorifics—which can be defined as polite speech that indicates relationship or status—has played an essential role in the Japanese language. When addressing someone in Japanese, an honorific usually takes the form of a suffix attached to one's name (example: "Asuna-san"), is used as a title at the end of one's name, or appears in place of the name itself (example: "Negi-sensei," or simply "Sensei!").

Honorifics can be expressions of respect or endearment. In the context of manga and anime, honorifics give insight into the nature of the relationship between characters. Many English translations leave out these important honorifics and therefore distort the feel of the original Japanese. Because Japanese honorifics contain nuances that English honorifics lack, it is our policy at Del Rey not to translate them. Here, instead, is a guide to some of the honorifics you may encounter in Del Rey Manga.

-san: This is the most common honorific and is equivalent to Mr., Miss, Ms., or Mrs. It is the all-purpose honorific and can be used in any situation where politeness is required.

-sama: This is one level higher than "-san." It is used to confer great respect.

-dono: This comes from the word "tono," which means "lord." It is an even higher level than "-sama" and confers utmost respect.

-kun: This suffix is used at the end of boys' names to express familiarity or endearment. It is also sometimes used by men among friends, or when addressing someone younger or of a lower station.

-chan: This is used to express endearment, mostly toward girls. It is also used for little boys, pets, and even among lovers. It gives a sense of childish cuteness.

Bozu: This is an informal way to refer to a boy, similar to the English terms "kid" and "squirt."

Sempai/
Senpai: This title suggests that the addressee is one's senior in a group or organization. It is most often used in a school setting, where underclassmen refer to their upperclassmen as "sempai." It can also be used in the workplace, such as when a newer employee addresses an employee who has seniority in the company.

Kohai: This is the opposite of "sempai" and is used toward underclassmen in school or newcomers in the workplace. It connotes that the addressee is of a lower station.

Sensei: Literally meaning "one who has come before," this title is used for teachers, doctors, or masters of any profession or art.

[blank]: This is usually forgotten in these lists, but it is perhaps the most significant difference between Japanese and English. The lack of honorific means that the speaker has permission to address the person in a very intimate way. Usually, only family, spouses, or very close friends have this kind of permission. Known as *yobisute,* it can be gratifying when someone who has earned the intimacy starts to call one by one's name without an honorific. But when that intimacy hasn't been earned, it can be very insulting.

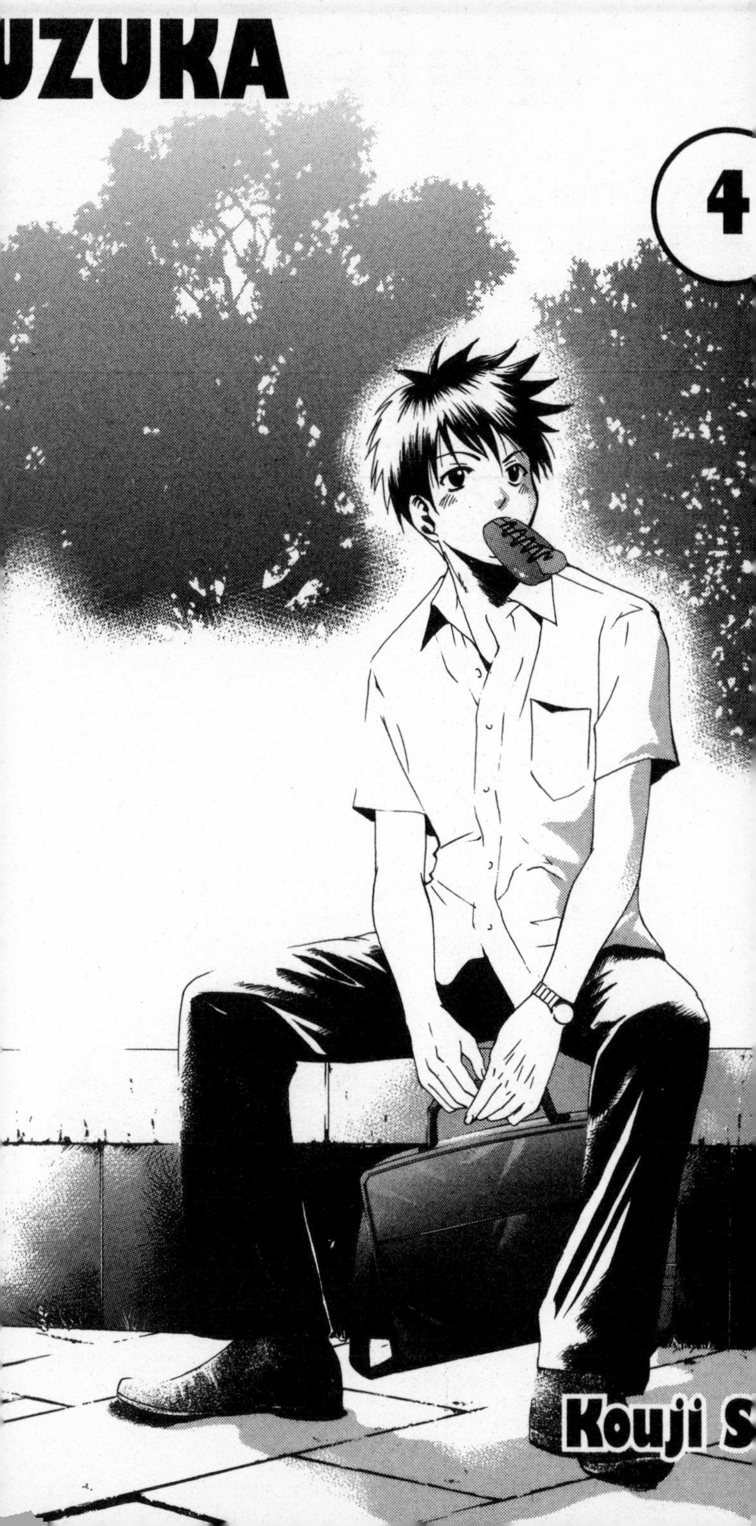

UZUKA
4
Kouji S

CONTENTS

#23 Kazuki.................................3
#24 Fool.................................23
#25 Provocation.................................43
#26 The Target.................................63
#27 The Showdown.................................83
#28 Results.................................103
#29 An Upswing.................................123
#30 Line of Focus.................................143
#31 Fireworks.................................163

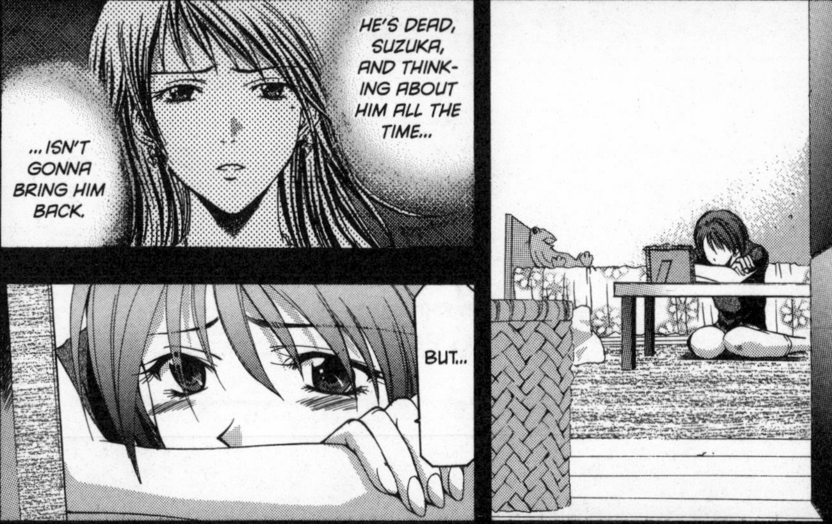
HE'S DEAD, SUZUKA, AND THINKING ABOUT HIM ALL THE TIME...
...ISN'T GONNA BRING HIM BACK.
BUT...

SUZUKA

#23 KAZUKI

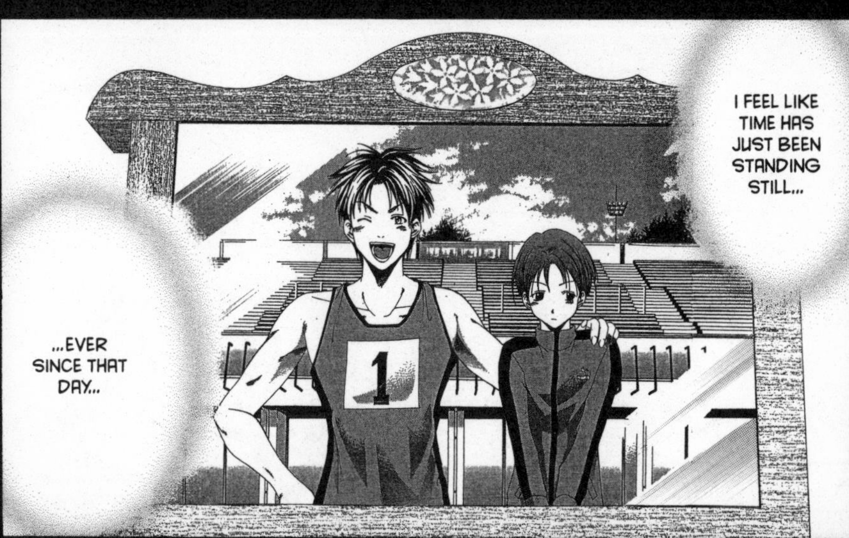
I FEEL LIKE TIME HAS JUST BEEN STANDING STILL...
...EVER SINCE THAT DAY...
1

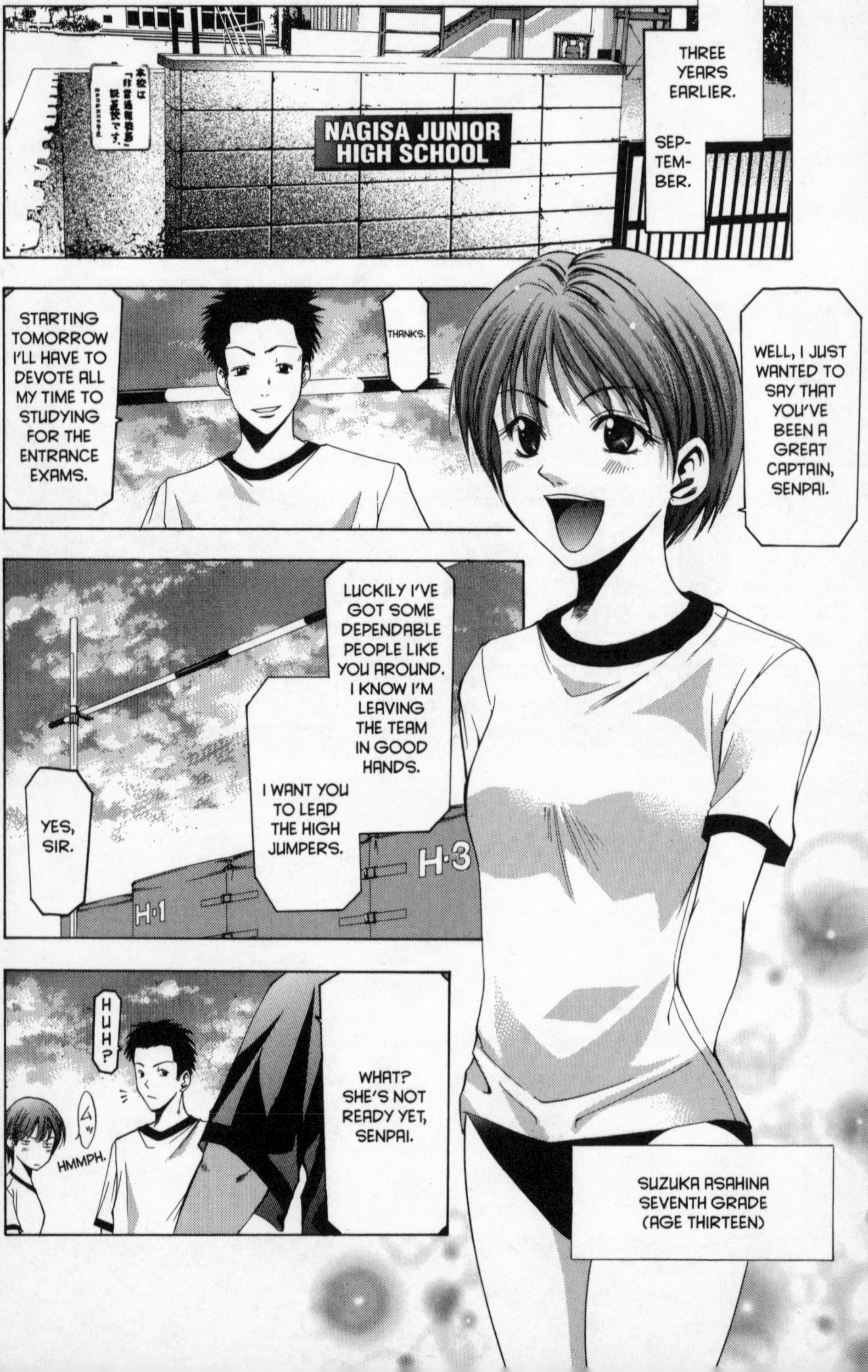
THREE YEARS EARLIER.
SEPTEMBER.
NAGISA JUNIOR HIGH SCHOOL
WELL, I JUST WANTED TO SAY THAT YOU'VE BEEN A GREAT CAPTAIN, SENPAI.
SUZUKA ASAHINA
SEVENTH GRADE
(AGE THIRTEEN)
THANKS.
STARTING TOMORROW I'LL HAVE TO DEVOTE ALL MY TIME TO STUDYING FOR THE ENTRANCE EXAMS.
LUCKILY I'VE GOT SOME DEPENDABLE PEOPLE LIKE YOU AROUND. I KNOW I'M LEAVING THE TEAM IN GOOD HANDS.
I WANT YOU TO LEAD THE HIGH JUMPERS.
YES, SIR.
H-3
H-1
WHAT? SHE'S NOT READY YET, SENPAI.
HUH?
ムッ
HMMPH.

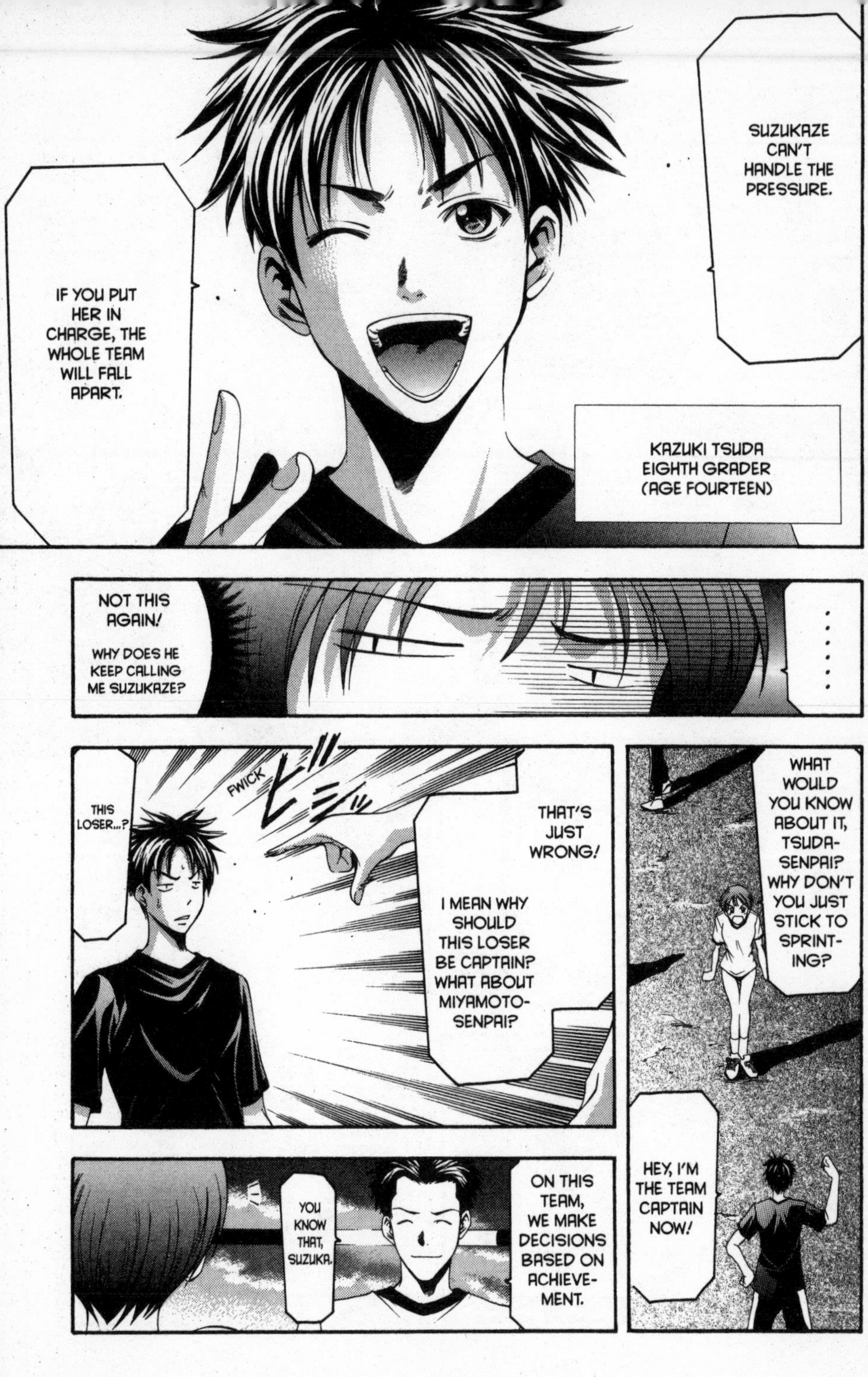
SUZUKAZE CAN'T HANDLE THE PRESSURE.
IF YOU PUT HER IN CHARGE, THE WHOLE TEAM WILL FALL APART.
KAZUKI TSUDA EIGHTH GRADER (AGE FOURTEEN)
......
NOT THIS AGAIN!
WHY DOES HE KEEP CALLING ME SUZUKAZE?
WHAT WOULD YOU KNOW ABOUT IT, TSUDA-SENPAI? WHY DON'T YOU JUST STICK TO SPRINTING?
THAT'S JUST WRONG!
I MEAN WHY SHOULD THIS LOSER BE CAPTAIN? WHAT ABOUT MIYAMOTO-SENPAI?
FWICK
THIS LOSER...?
HEY, I'M THE TEAM CAPTAIN NOW!
ON THIS TEAM, WE MAKE DECISIONS BASED ON ACHIEVEMENT.
YOU KNOW THAT, SUZUKA.

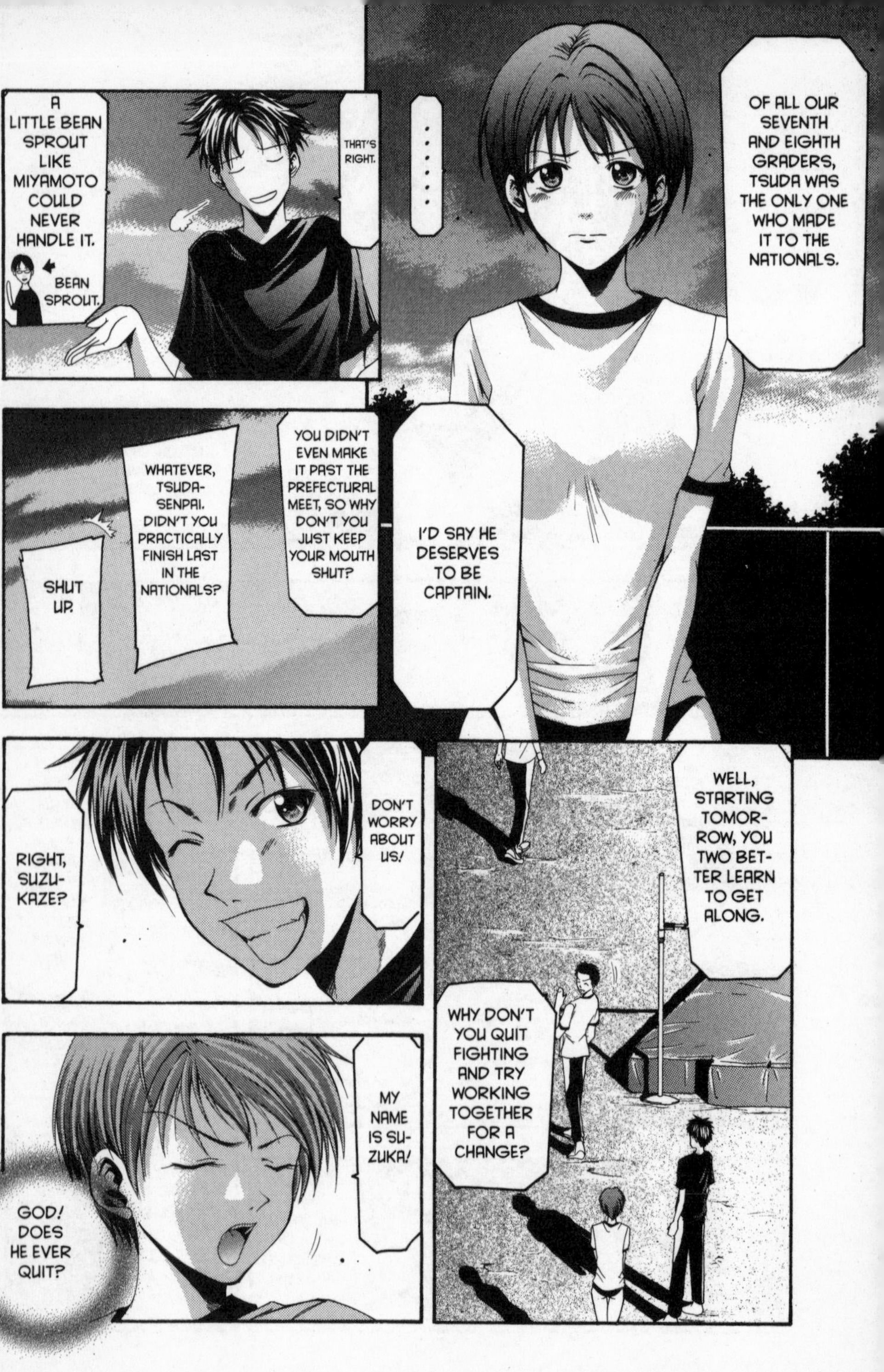
OF ALL OUR SEVENTH AND EIGHTH GRADERS, TSUDA WAS THE ONLY ONE WHO MADE IT TO THE NATIONALS.
......
I'D SAY HE DESERVES TO BE CAPTAIN.
THAT'S RIGHT.
A LITTLE BEAN SPROUT LIKE MIYAMOTO COULD NEVER HANDLE IT.
BEAN SPROUT.
YOU DIDN'T EVEN MAKE IT PAST THE PREFECTURAL MEET, SO WHY DON'T YOU JUST KEEP YOUR MOUTH SHUT?
WHATEVER, TSUDA-SENPAI. DIDN'T YOU PRACTICALLY FINISH LAST IN THE NATIONALS?
SHUT UP.
WELL, STARTING TOMOR-ROW, YOU TWO BET-TER LEARN TO GET ALONG.
WHY DON'T YOU QUIT FIGHTING AND TRY WORKING TOGETHER FOR A CHANGE?
DON'T WORRY ABOUT US!
RIGHT, SUZU-KAZE?
MY NAME IS SU-ZUKA!
GOD! DOES HE EVER QUIT?

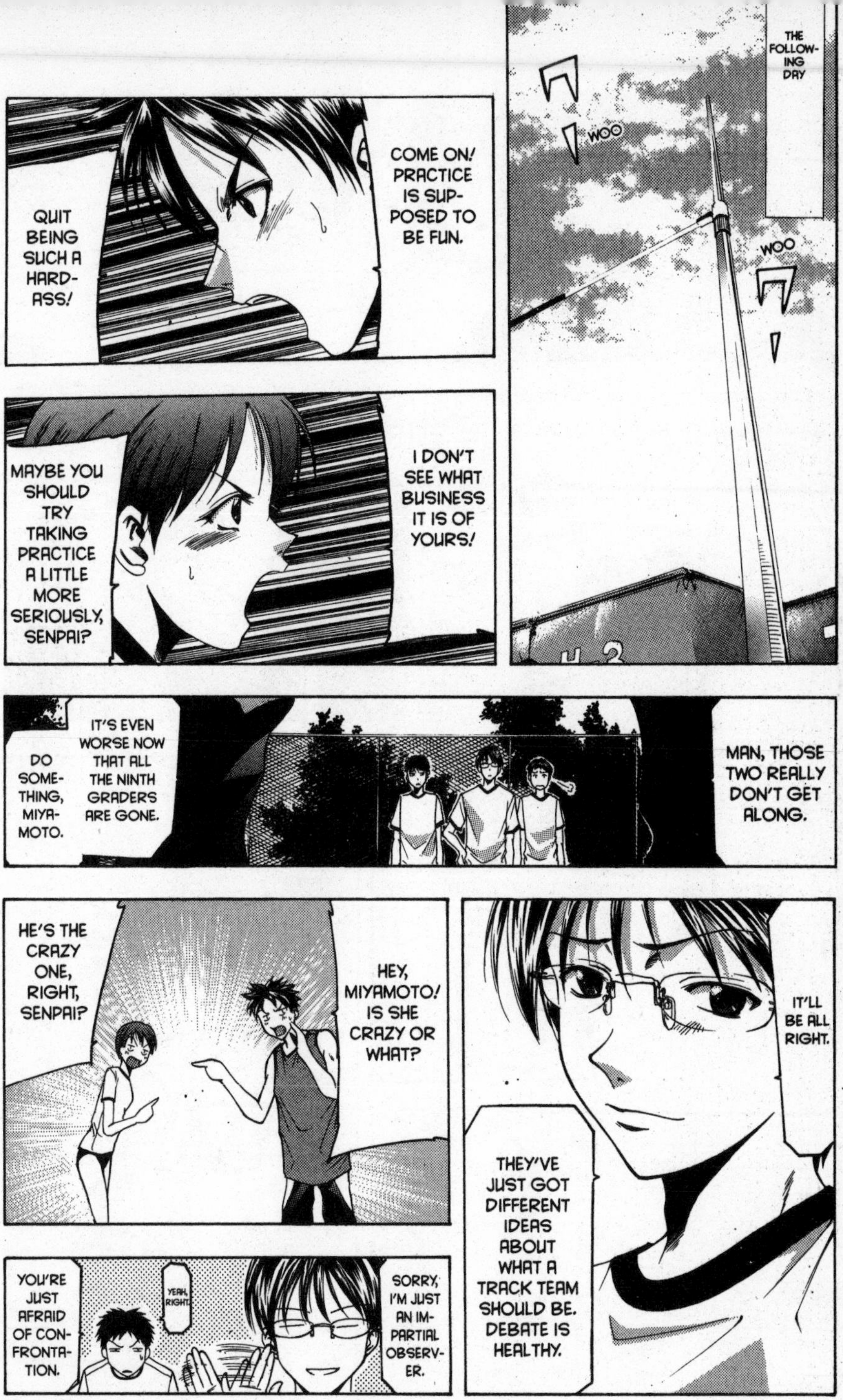
THE FOLLOWING DAY
WOO
WOO
COME ON! PRACTICE IS SUPPOSED TO BE FUN.
QUIT BEING SUCH A HARD-ASS!
I DON'T SEE WHAT BUSINESS IT IS OF YOURS!
MAYBE YOU SHOULD TRY TAKING PRACTICE A LITTLE MORE SERIOUSLY, SENPAI?
MAN, THOSE TWO REALLY DON'T GET ALONG.
IT'S EVEN WORSE NOW THAT ALL THE NINTH GRADERS ARE GONE.
DO SOMETHING, MIYAMOTO.
IT'LL BE ALL RIGHT.
THEY'VE JUST GOT DIFFERENT IDEAS ABOUT WHAT A TRACK TEAM SHOULD BE. DEBATE IS HEALTHY.
HEY, MIYAMOTO! IS SHE CRAZY OR WHAT?
HE'S THE CRAZY ONE, RIGHT, SENPAI?
SORRY, I'M JUST AN IMPARTIAL OBSERVER.
YEAH, RIGHT.
YOU'RE JUST AFRAID OF CONFRONTATION.

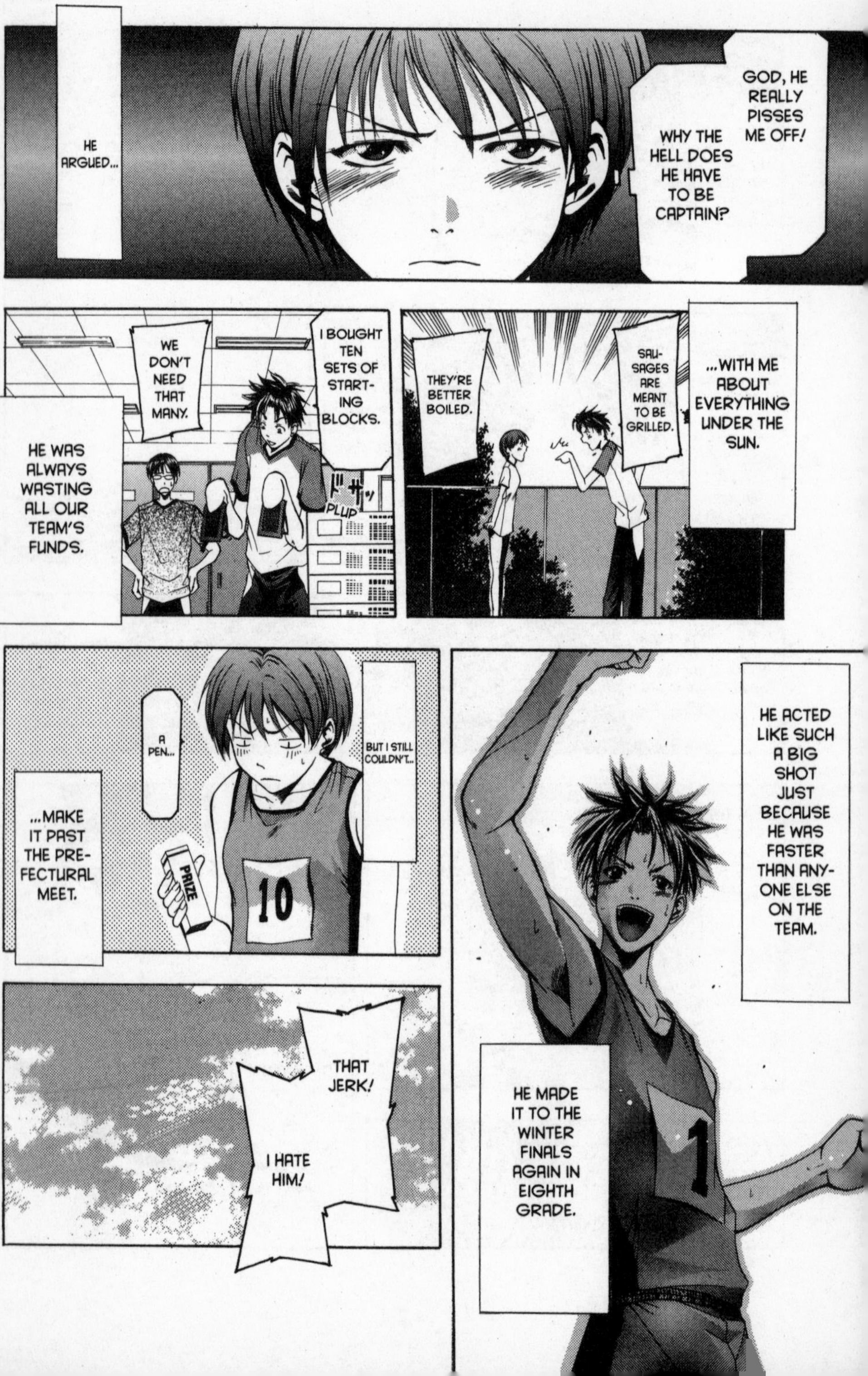
GOD, HE REALLY PISSES ME OFF!
WHY THE HELL DOES HE HAVE TO BE CAPTAIN?
HE ARGUED...
...WITH ME ABOUT EVERYTHING UNDER THE SUN.
SAUSAGES ARE MEANT TO BE GRILLED.
THEY'RE BETTER BOILED.
I BOUGHT TEN SETS OF STARTING BLOCKS.
WE DON'T NEED THAT MANY.
ドサッ PLUP
HE WAS ALWAYS WASTING ALL OUR TEAM'S FUNDS.
HE ACTED LIKE SUCH A BIG SHOT JUST BECAUSE HE WAS FASTER THAN ANYONE ELSE ON THE TEAM.
HE MADE IT TO THE WINTER FINALS AGAIN IN EIGHTH GRADE.
1
BUT I STILL COULDN'T...
A PEN...
PRIZE
10
...MAKE IT PAST THE PREFECTURAL MEET.
THAT JERK!
I HATE HIM!

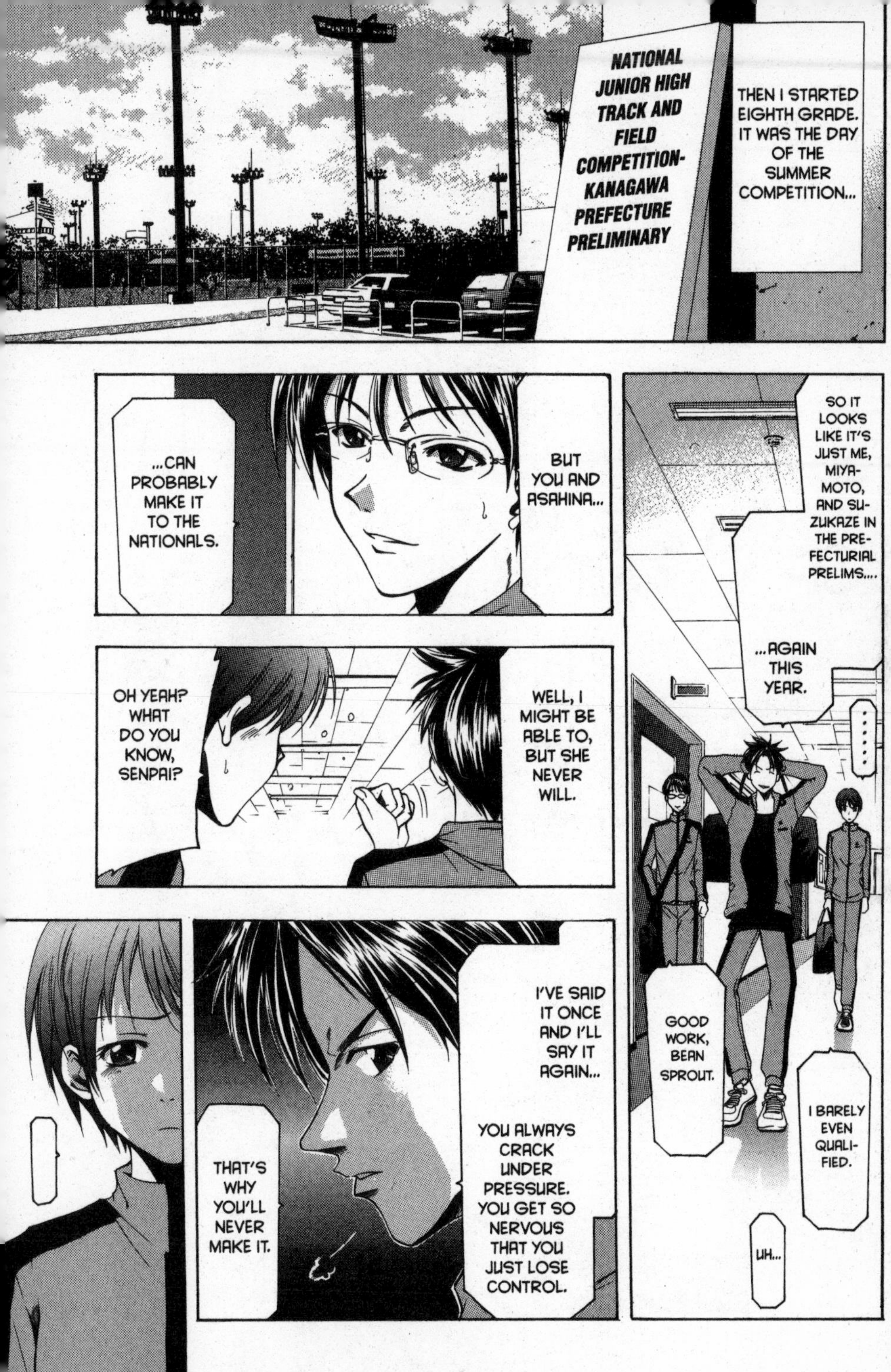
THEN I STARTED EIGHTH GRADE. IT WAS THE DAY OF THE SUMMER COMPETITION...
NATIONAL JUNIOR HIGH TRACK AND FIELD COMPETITION- KANAGAWA PREFECTURE PRELIMINARY
SO IT LOOKS LIKE IT'S JUST ME, MIYA-MOTO, AND SU-ZUKAZE IN THE PRE-FECTURIAL PRELIMS....
...AGAIN THIS YEAR.
......
GOOD WORK, BEAN SPROUT.
I BARELY EVEN QUALI-FIED.
UH...
BUT YOU AND ASAHINA...
...CAN PROBABLY MAKE IT TO THE NATIONALS.
WELL, I MIGHT BE ABLE TO, BUT SHE NEVER WILL.
OH YEAH? WHAT DO YOU KNOW, SENPAI?
I'VE SAID IT ONCE AND I'LL SAY IT AGAIN...
YOU ALWAYS CRACK UNDER PRESSURE. YOU GET SO NERVOUS THAT YOU JUST LOSE CONTROL.
THAT'S WHY YOU'LL NEVER MAKE IT.
...

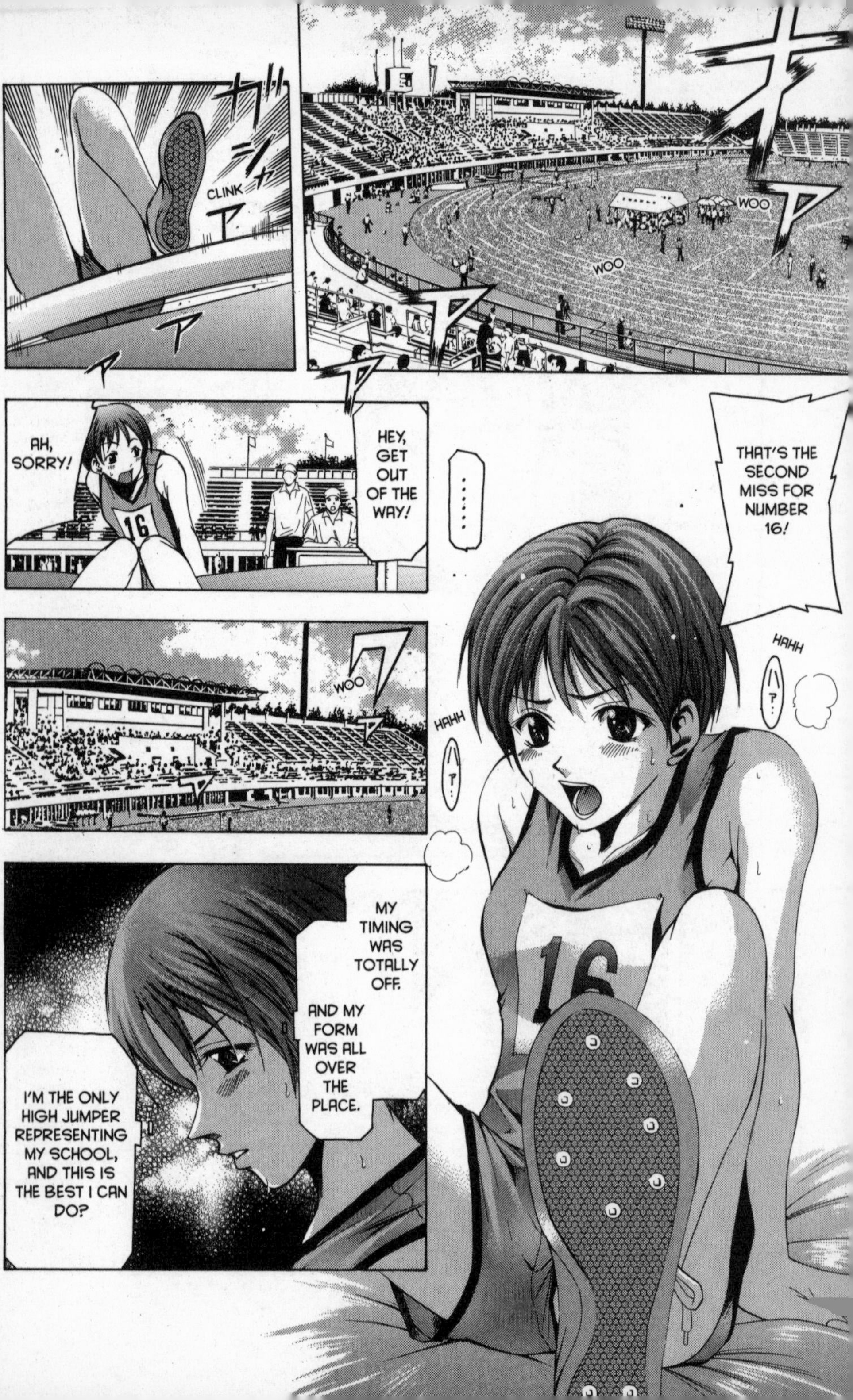
WOO
WOO
CLINK
THAT'S THE SECOND MISS FOR NUMBER 16!
HAHH
HAHH
......
HEY, GET OUT OF THE WAY!
AH, SORRY!
WOO
MY TIMING WAS TOTALLY OFF.
AND MY FORM WAS ALL OVER THE PLACE.
I'M THE ONLY HIGH JUMPER REPRESENTING MY SCHOOL, AND THIS IS THE BEST I CAN DO?

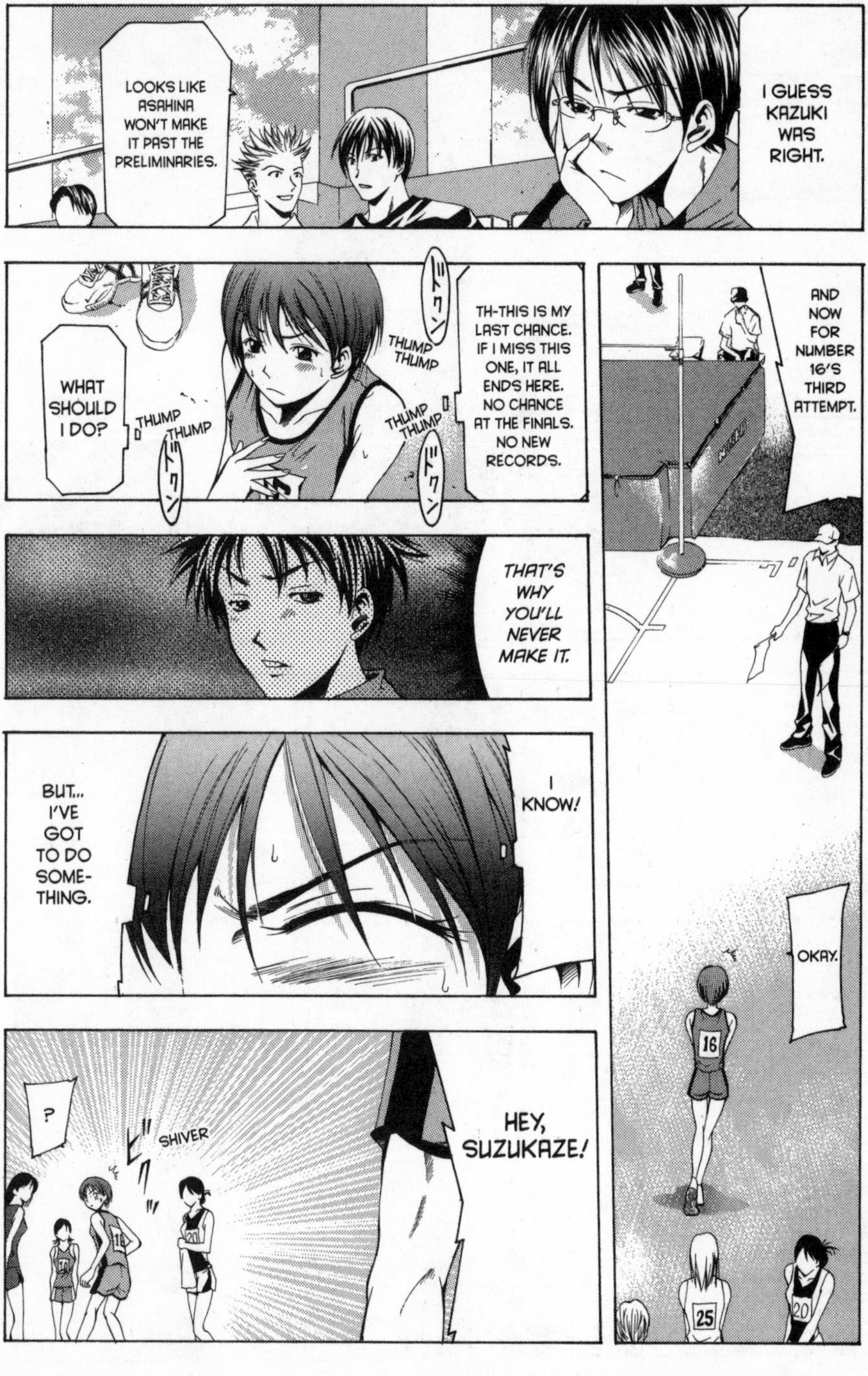
LOOKS LIKE ASAHINA WON'T MAKE IT PAST THE PRELIMINARIES.
I GUESS KAZUKI WAS RIGHT.
AND NOW FOR NUMBER 16'S THIRD ATTEMPT.
OKAY.
ドクン
TH-THIS IS MY LAST CHANCE. IF I MISS THIS ONE, IT ALL ENDS HERE. NO CHANCE AT THE FINALS. NO NEW RECORDS.
THUMP THUMP
ドクン
THUMP THUMP
WHAT SHOULD I DO?
THUMP THUMP
ドクン
THAT'S WHY YOU'LL NEVER MAKE IT.
I KNOW!
BUT... I'VE GOT TO DO SOME-THING.
HEY, SUZUKAZE!
SHIVER
?

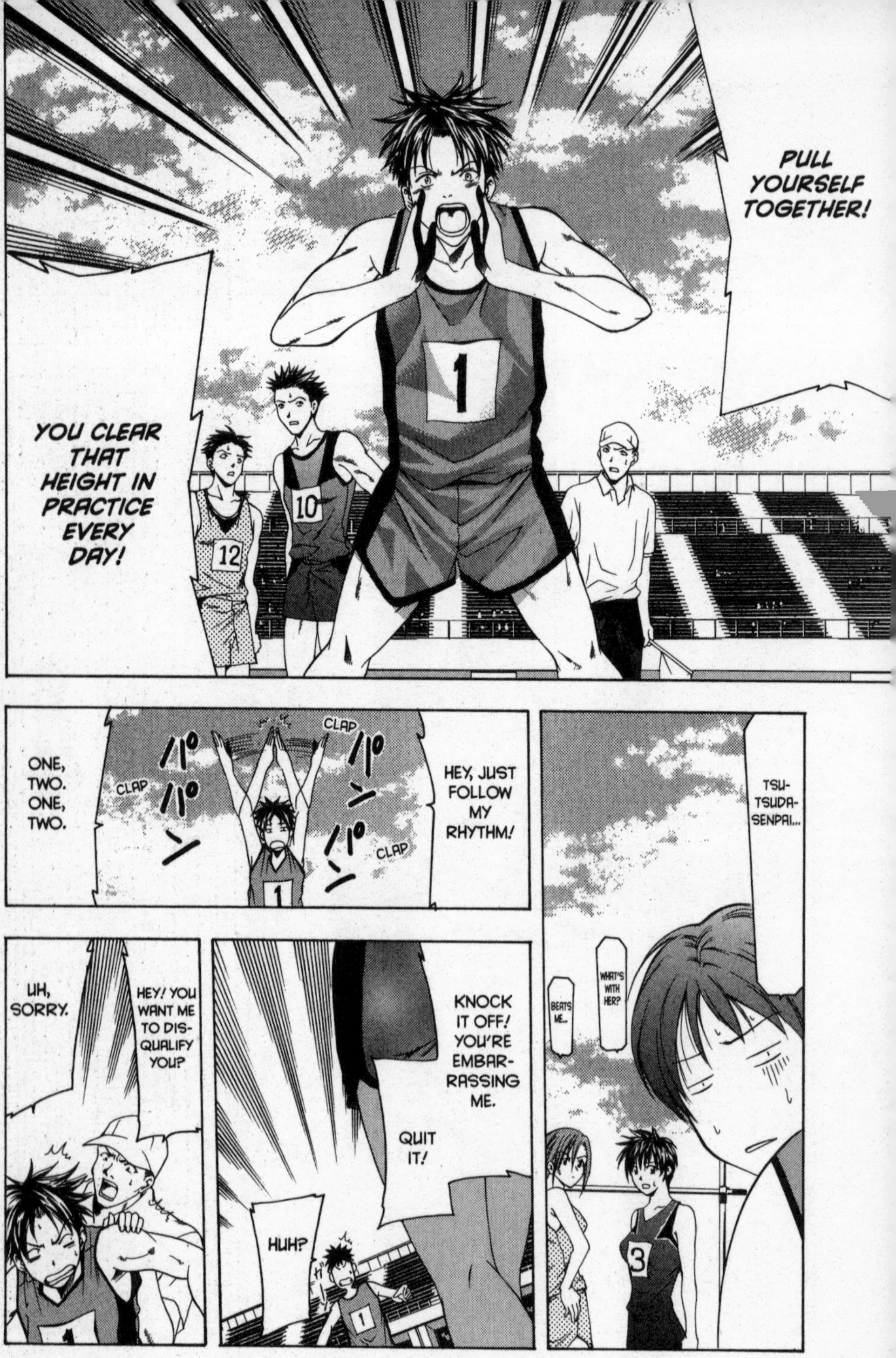
PULL YOURSELF TOGETHER!
YOU CLEAR THAT HEIGHT IN PRACTICE EVERY DAY!
TSU-TSUDA-SENPAI...
WHAT'S WITH HER?
BEATS ME...
HEY, JUST FOLLOW MY RHYTHM!
CLAP
パンパン
CLAP
CLAP
パパン
CLAP
ONE, TWO. ONE, TWO.
KNOCK IT OFF! YOU'RE EMBAR-RASSING ME.
QUIT IT!
HUH?
HEY! YOU WANT ME TO DIS-QUALIFY YOU?
UH, SORRY.

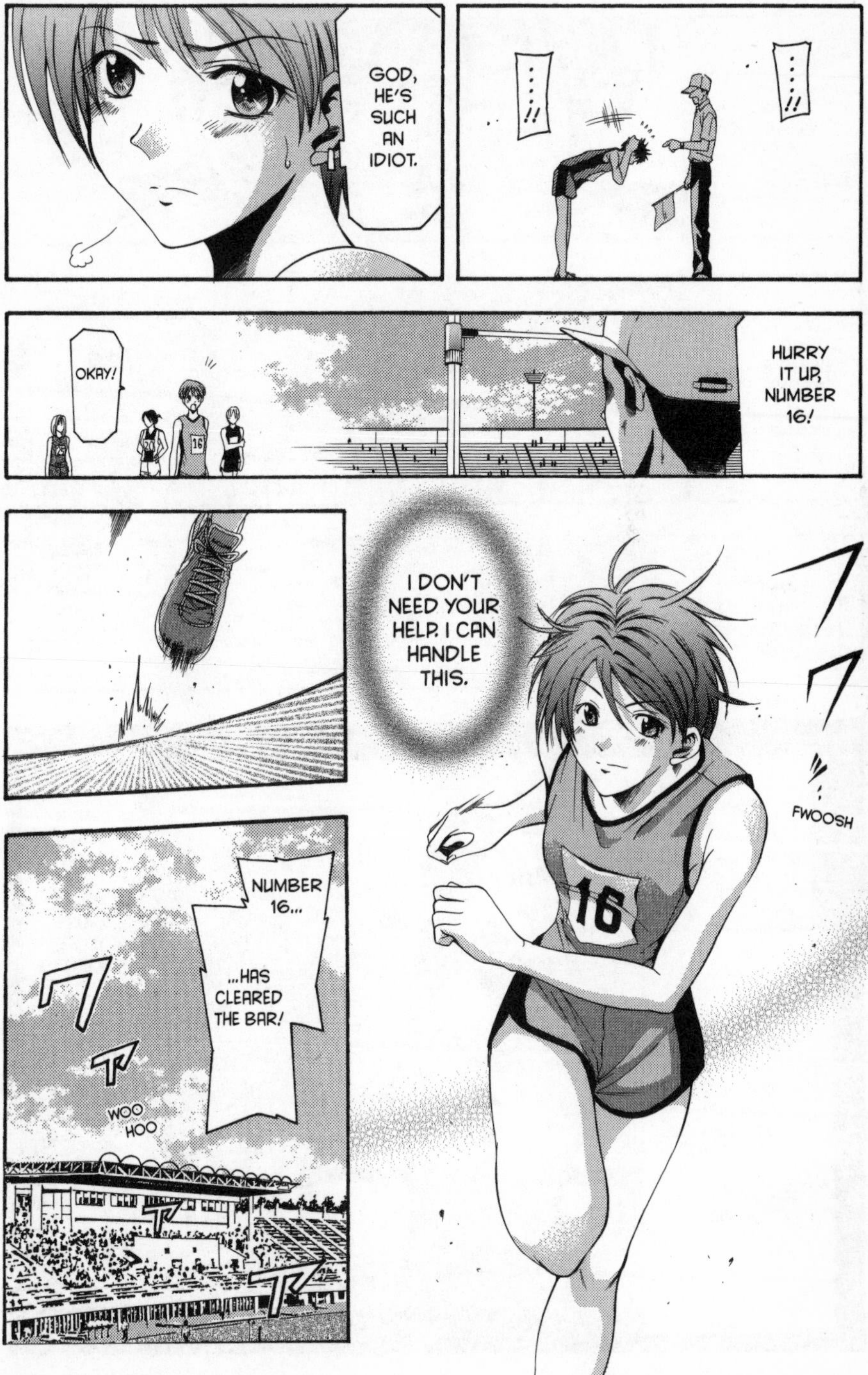
....!!
....!!
GOD, HE'S SUCH AN IDIOT.
HURRY IT UP, NUMBER 16!
OKAY!
I DON'T NEED YOUR HELP. I CAN HANDLE THIS.
FWOOSH
NUMBER 16...
...HAS CLEARED THE BAR!
WOO HOO

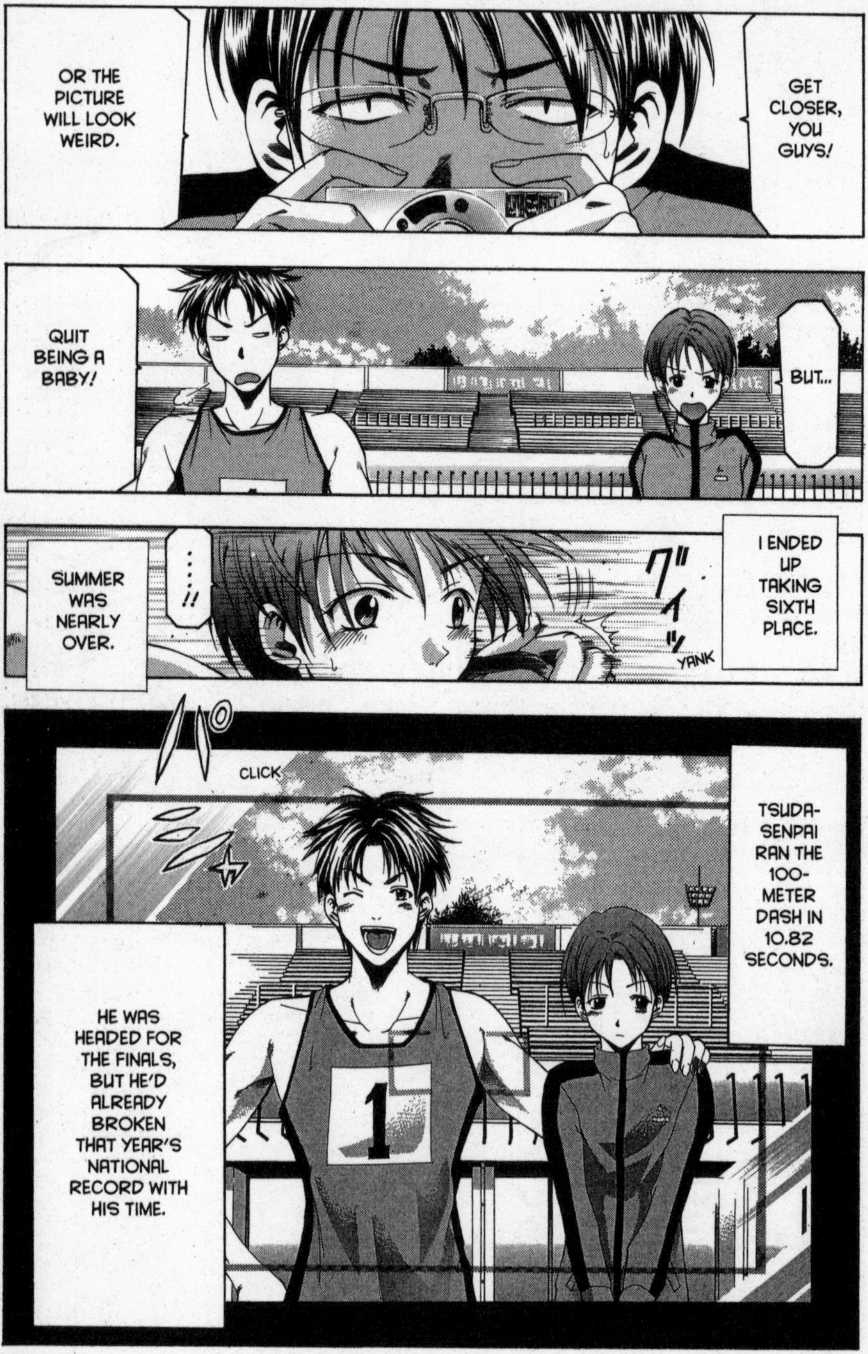
GET CLOSER, YOU GUYS!
OR THE PICTURE WILL LOOK WEIRD.
BUT...
QUIT BEING A BABY!
I ENDED UP TAKING SIXTH PLACE.
グイッ
YANK
...!!
SUMMER WAS NEARLY OVER.
パ
CLICK
TSUDA-SENPAI RAN THE 100-METER DASH IN 10.82 SECONDS.
HE WAS HEADED FOR THE FINALS, BUT HE'D ALREADY BROKEN THAT YEAR'S NATIONAL RECORD WITH HIS TIME.

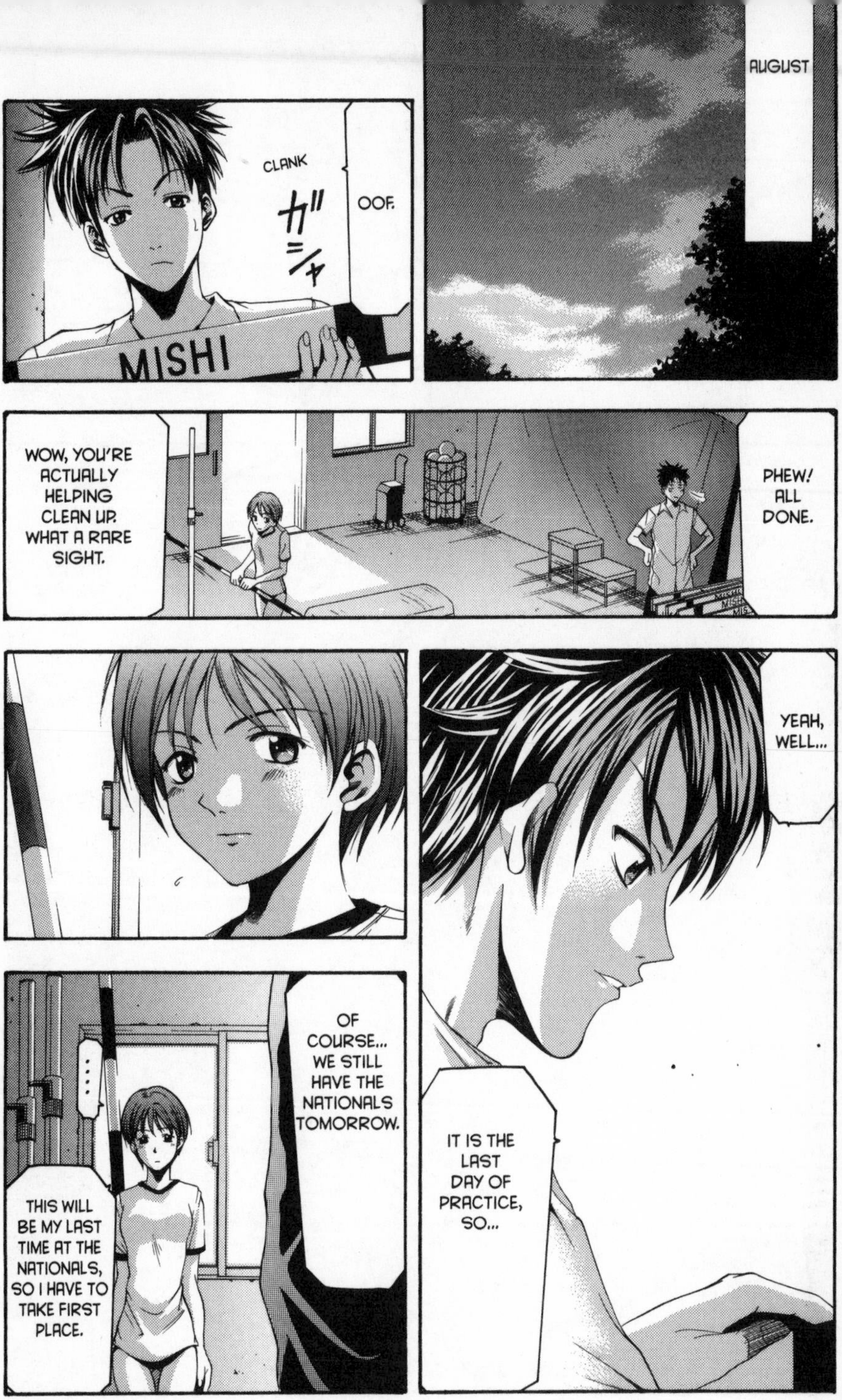
AUGUST
OOF.
CLANK
ガシャ
PHEW! ALL DONE.
WOW, YOU'RE ACTUALLY HELPING CLEAN UP. WHAT A RARE SIGHT.
MISHI
YEAH, WELL...
IT IS THE LAST DAY OF PRACTICE, SO...
OF COURSE... WE STILL HAVE THE NATIONALS TOMORROW.
.....
THIS WILL BE MY LAST TIME AT THE NATIONALS, SO I HAVE TO TAKE FIRST PLACE.

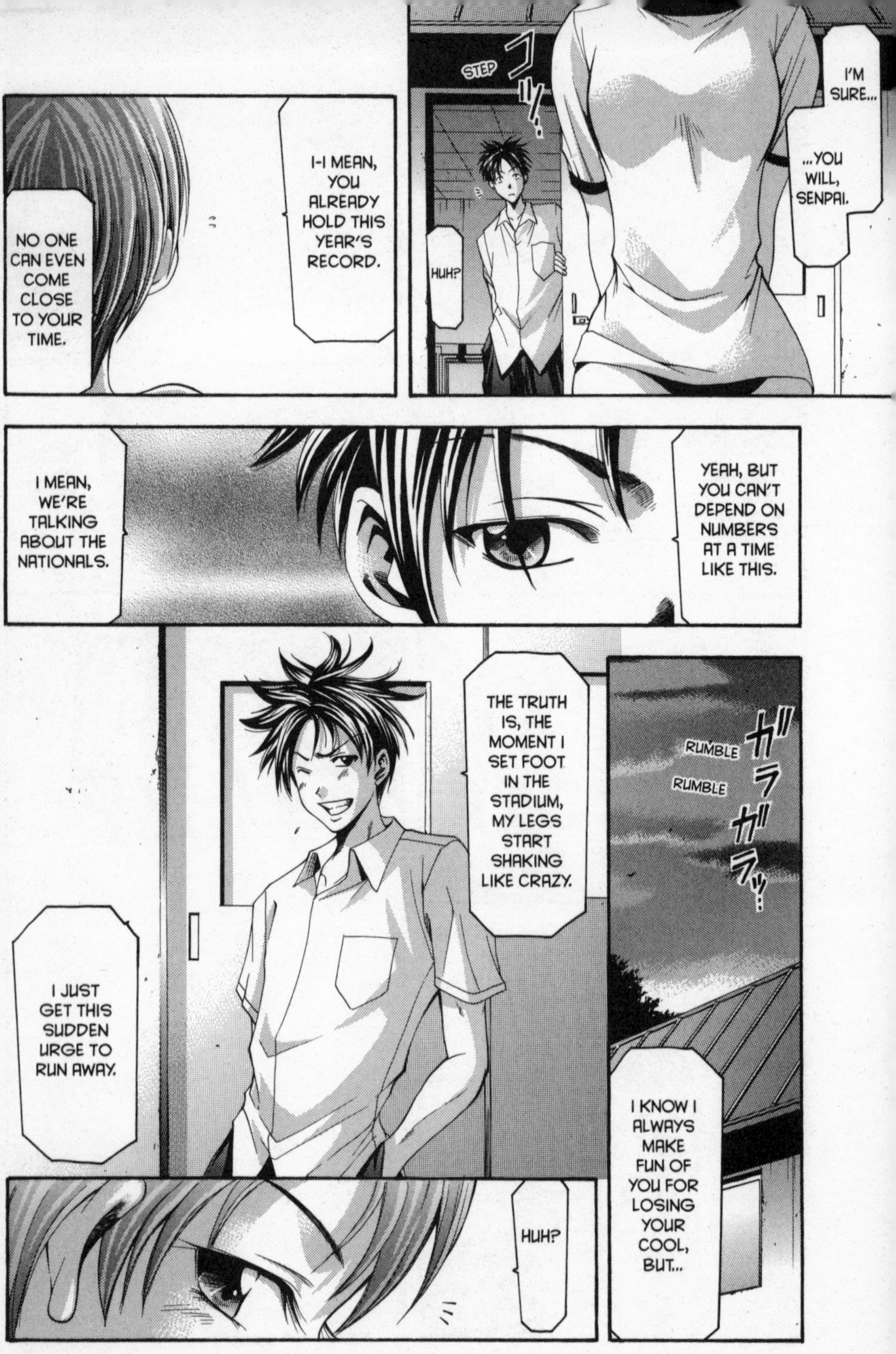
I'M SURE...
...YOU WILL, SENPAI.
STEP
HUH?
I-I MEAN, YOU ALREADY HOLD THIS YEAR'S RECORD.
NO ONE CAN EVEN COME CLOSE TO YOUR TIME.
YEAH, BUT YOU CAN'T DEPEND ON NUMBERS AT A TIME LIKE THIS.
I MEAN, WE'RE TALKING ABOUT THE NATIONALS.
RUMBLE
RUMBLE
I KNOW I ALWAYS MAKE FUN OF YOU FOR LOSING YOUR COOL, BUT...
THE TRUTH IS, THE MOMENT I SET FOOT IN THE STADIUM, MY LEGS START SHAKING LIKE CRAZY.
I JUST GET THIS SUDDEN URGE TO RUN AWAY.
HUH?

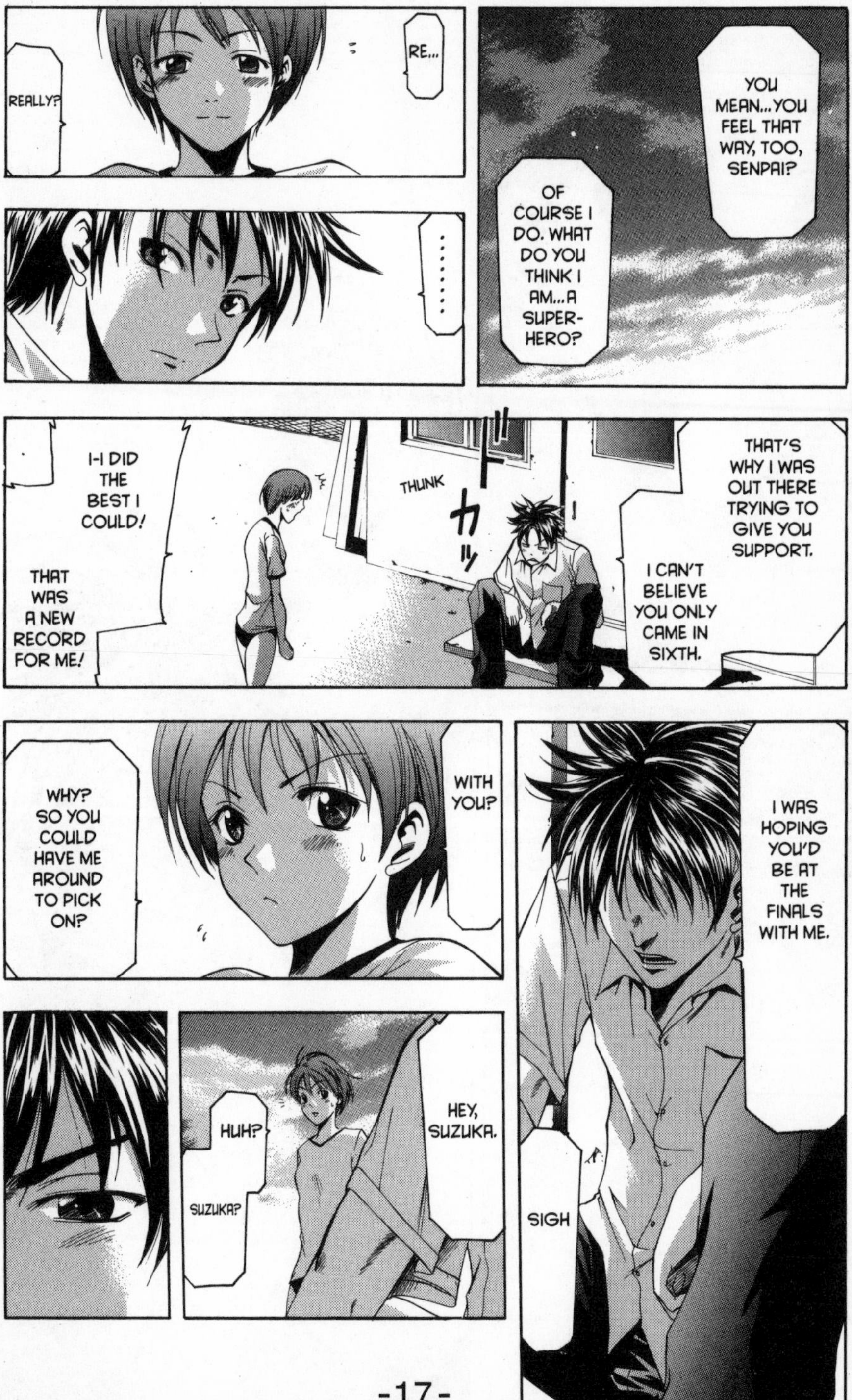
YOU MEAN...YOU FEEL THAT WAY, TOO, SENPAI?
OF COURSE I DO. WHAT DO YOU THINK I AM...A SUPER-HERO?
RE...
REALLY?
....
THAT'S WHY I WAS OUT THERE TRYING TO GIVE YOU SUPPORT.
I CAN'T BELIEVE YOU ONLY CAME IN SIXTH.
THUNK
I-I DID THE BEST I COULD!
THAT WAS A NEW RECORD FOR ME!
I WAS HOPING YOU'D BE AT THE FINALS WITH ME.
SIGH
WITH YOU?
WHY? SO YOU COULD HAVE ME AROUND TO PICK ON?
HEY, SUZUKA.
HUH?
SUZUKA?

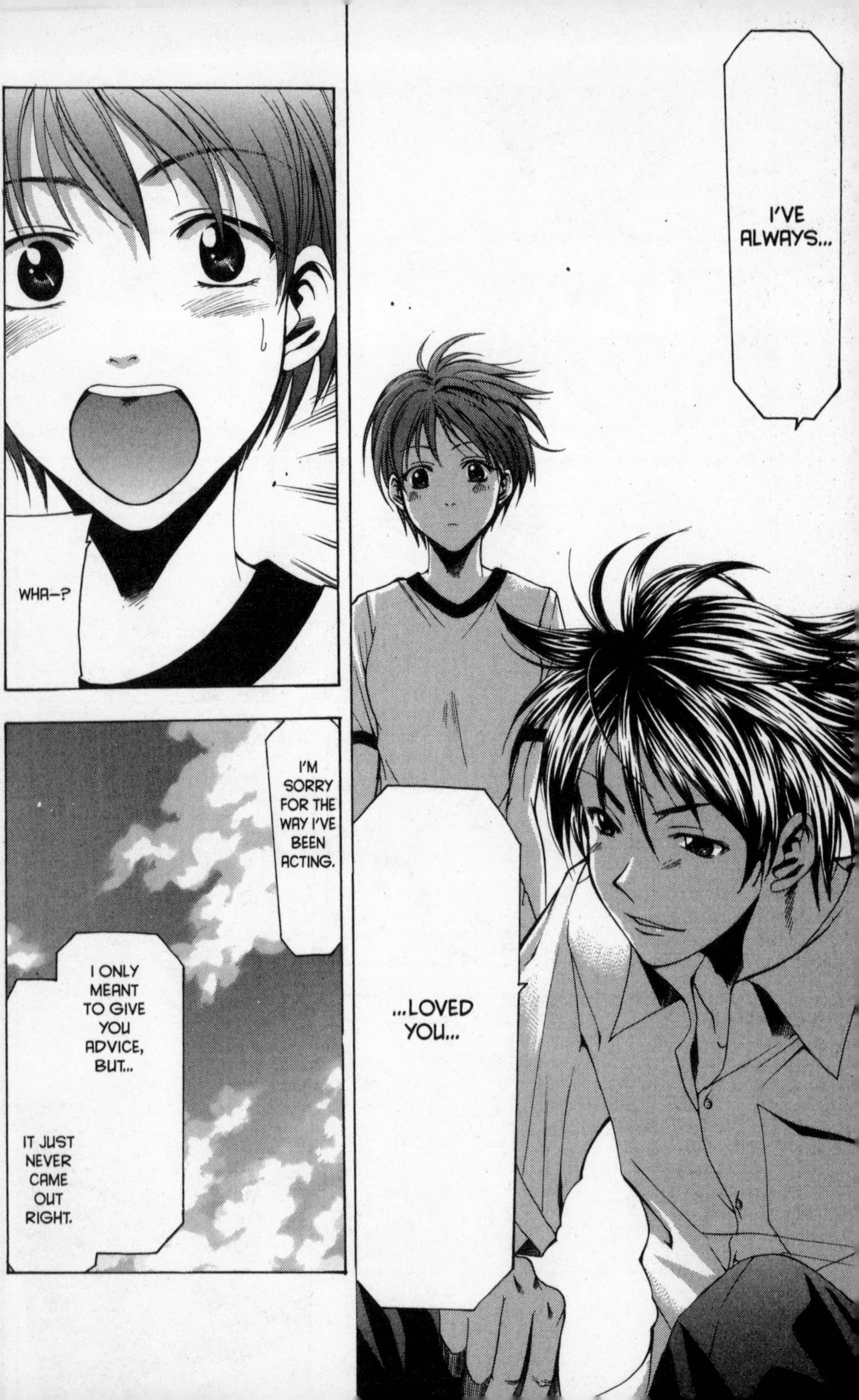
I'VE ALWAYS...
...LOVED YOU...
WHA-?
I'M SORRY FOR THE WAY I'VE BEEN ACTING.
I ONLY MEANT TO GIVE YOU ADVICE, BUT...
IT JUST NEVER CAME OUT RIGHT.

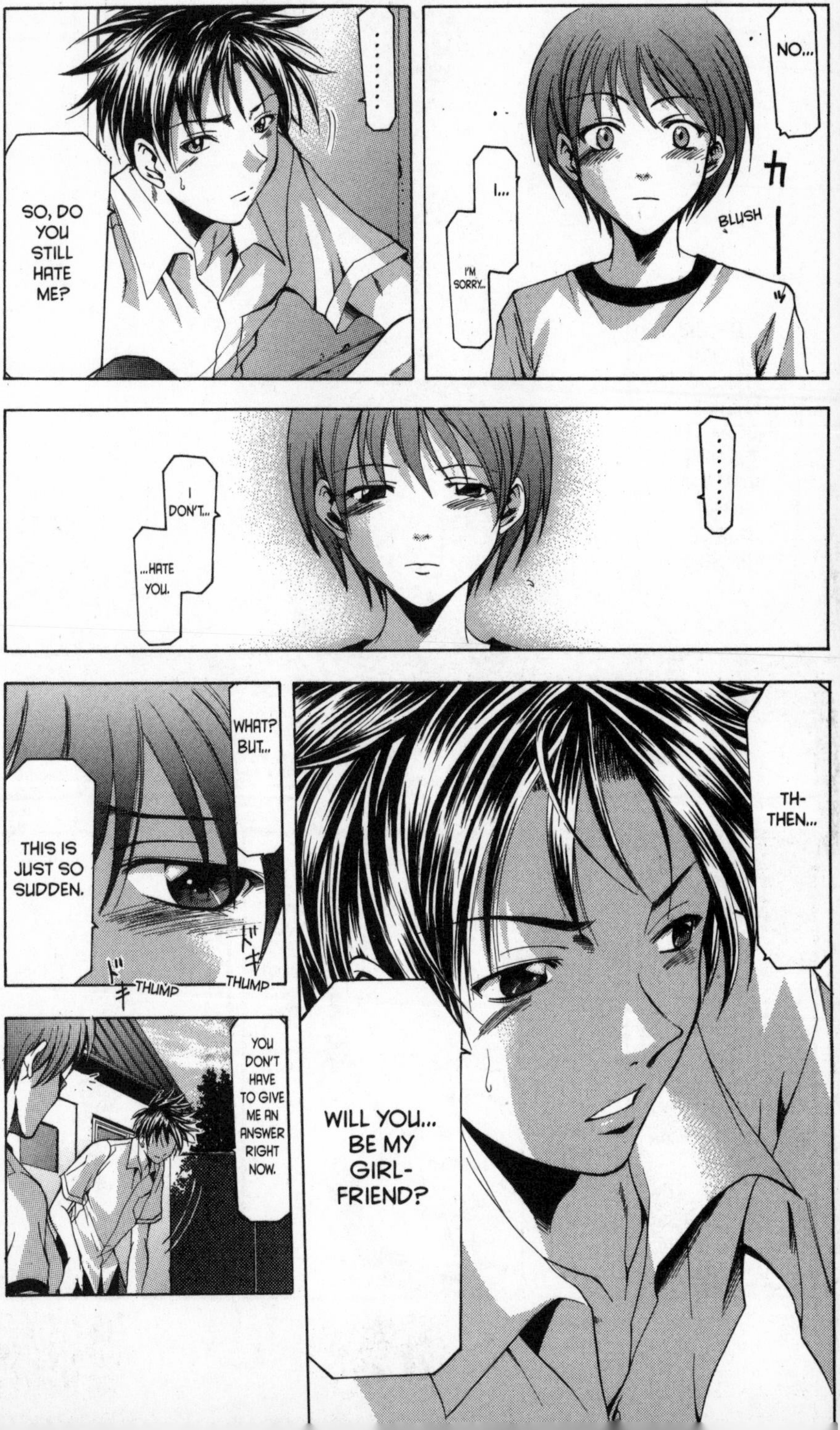
NO...
I...
I'M SORRY...
カーッ
BLUSH
......
SO, DO YOU STILL HATE ME?
......
I DON'T...
...HATE YOU.
TH-THEN...
WILL YOU... BE MY GIRL-FRIEND?
WHAT? BUT...
THIS IS JUST SO SUDDEN.
ドキ
THUMP
ドキ
THUMP
YOU DON'T HAVE TO GIVE ME AN ANSWER RIGHT NOW.

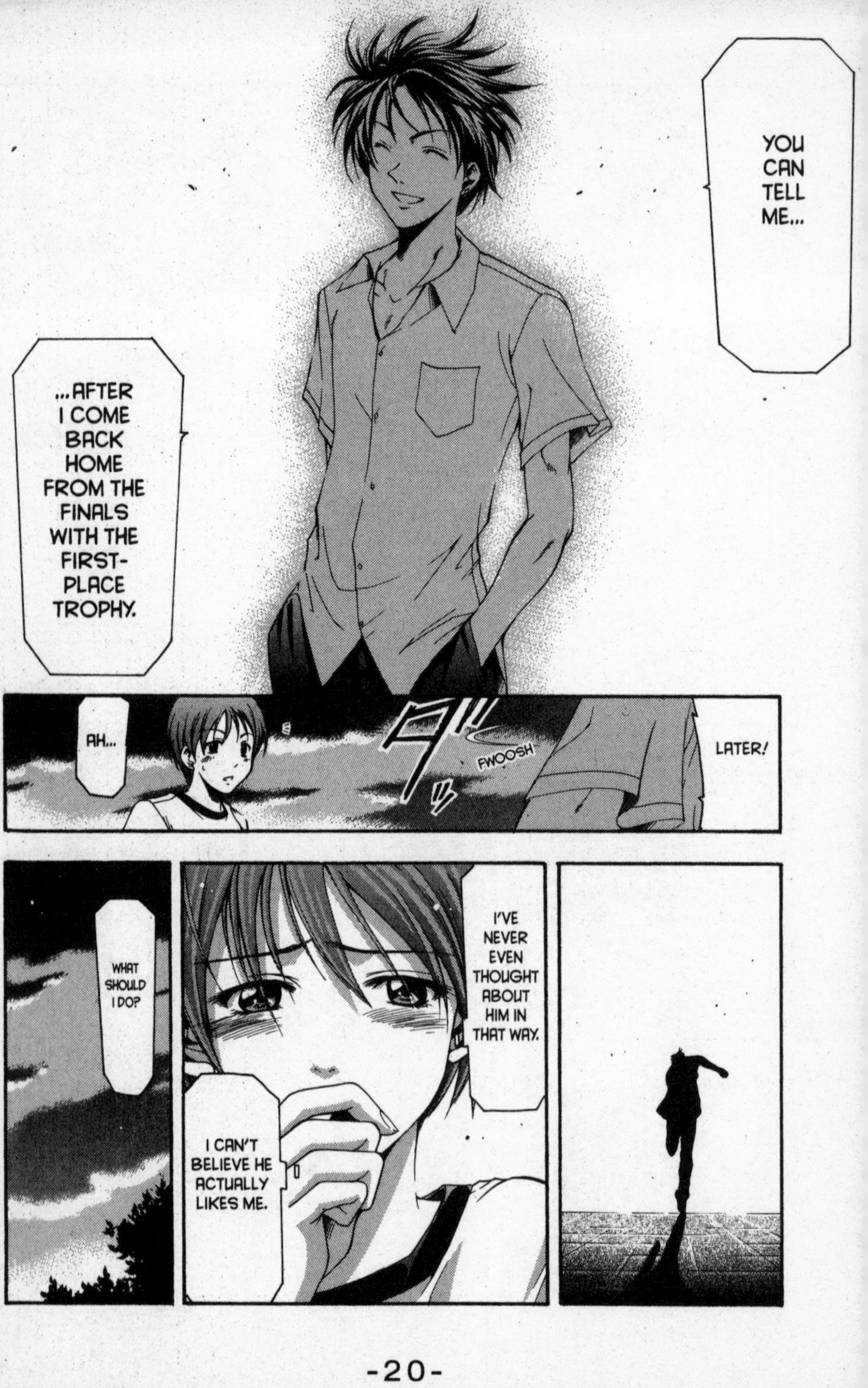
YOU CAN TELL ME...
...AFTER I COME BACK HOME FROM THE FINALS WITH THE FIRST-PLACE TROPHY.
LATER!
FWOOSH
AH...
I'VE NEVER EVEN THOUGHT ABOUT HIM IN THAT WAY.
I CAN'T BELIEVE HE ACTUALLY LIKES ME.
WHAT SHOULD I DO?

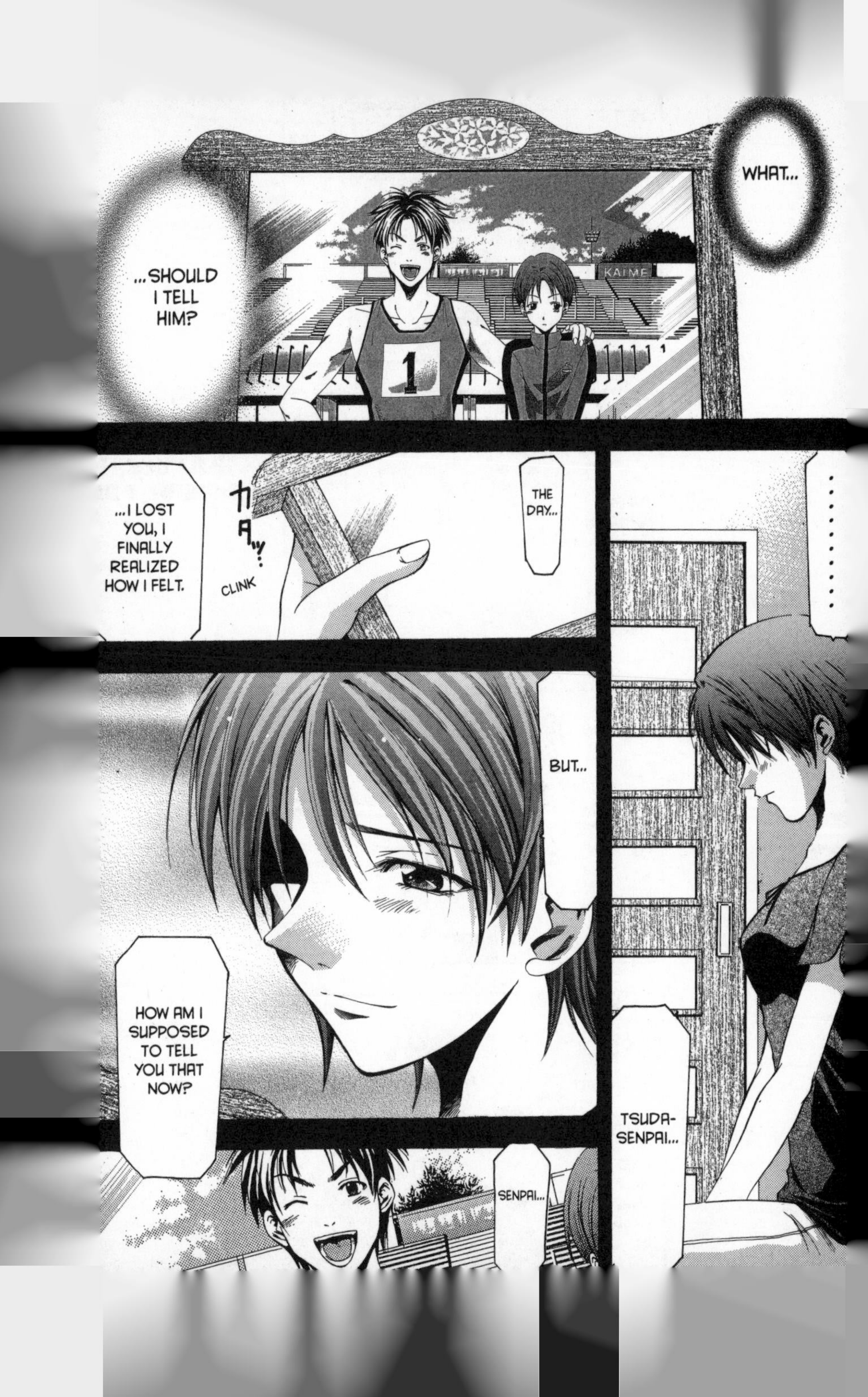
WHAT...
...SHOULD I TELL HIM?
KAIME
1
......
TSUDA-SENPAI...
THE DAY...
カタッ
CLINK
...I LOST YOU, I FINALLY REALIZED HOW I FELT.
BUT...
HOW AM I SUPPOSED TO TELL YOU THAT NOW?
SENPAI...

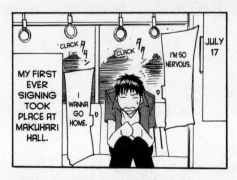

SUZUKA FOUR-PANEL THEATER NUMBER THIRTEEN

SEO GOES TO A SIGNING - PART 1

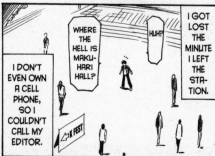

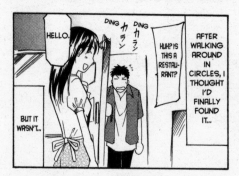

JULY 17
I'M SO NERVOUS.
CLACK
CLACK
I WANNA GO HOME.
MY FIRST EVER SIGNING TOOK PLACE AT MAKUHARI HALL.
I GOT LOST THE MINUTE I LEFT THE STATION.
HUH?
WHERE THE HELL IS MAKUHARI HALL?
I DON'T EVEN OWN A CELL PHONE, SO I COULDN'T CALL MY EDITOR.
K FEST
AFTER WALKING AROUND IN CIRCLES, I THOUGHT I'D FINALLY FOUND IT...
DING カラン
HUH? IS THIS A RESTAURANT?
DING カラン
HELLO.
BUT IT WASN'T...
...THE K FEST...
UM...IS THIS THE K FEST?
NO, THIS IS SHOU-XXX-KAN.
IT WAS SOME KIND OF DINO-SAUR EXHIBIT.

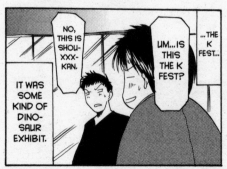

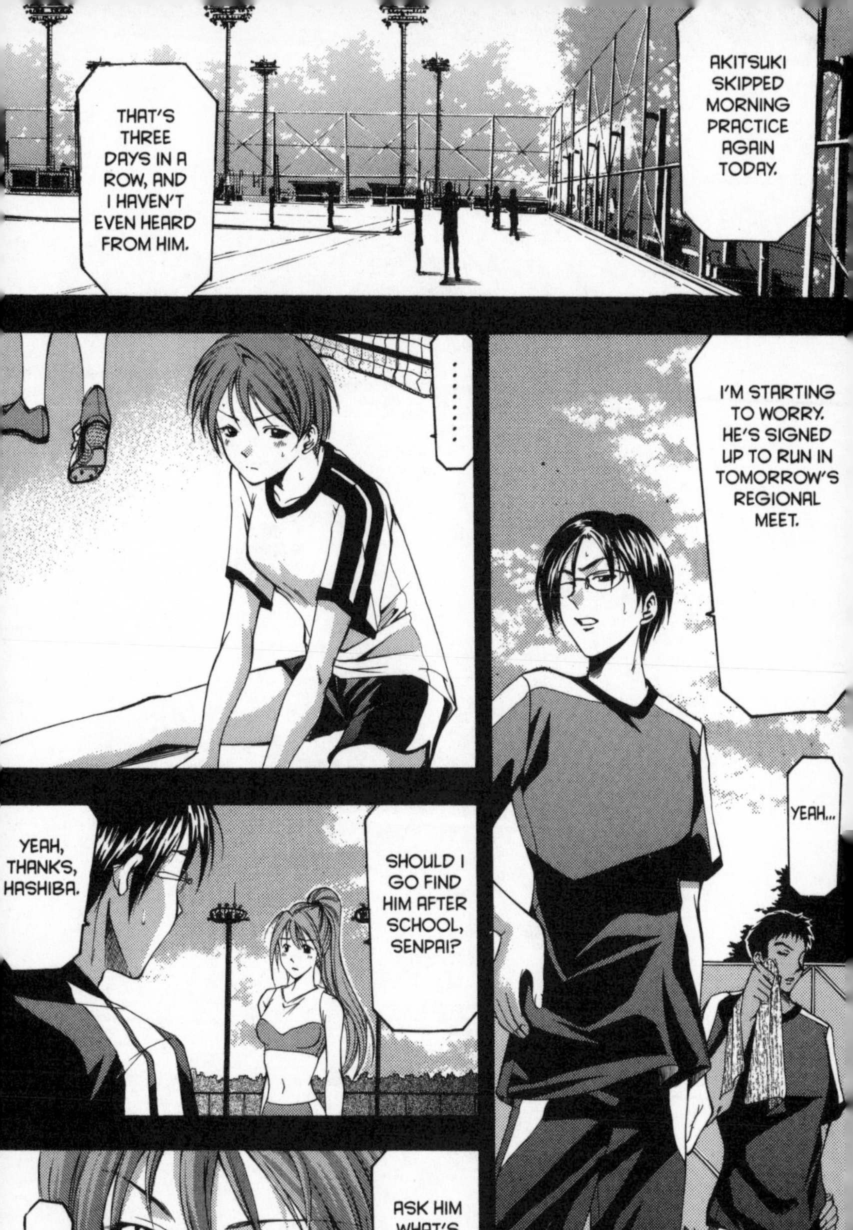
AKITSUKI SKIPPED MORNING PRACTICE AGAIN TODAY.
THAT'S THREE DAYS IN A ROW, AND I HAVEN'T EVEN HEARD FROM HIM.
I'M STARTING TO WORRY. HE'S SIGNED UP TO RUN IN TOMORROW'S REGIONAL MEET.
YEAH...
......
SHOULD I GO FIND HIM AFTER SCHOOL, SENPAI?
YEAH, THANKS, HASHIBA.
ASK HIM WHAT'S GOING ON.
OKAY.

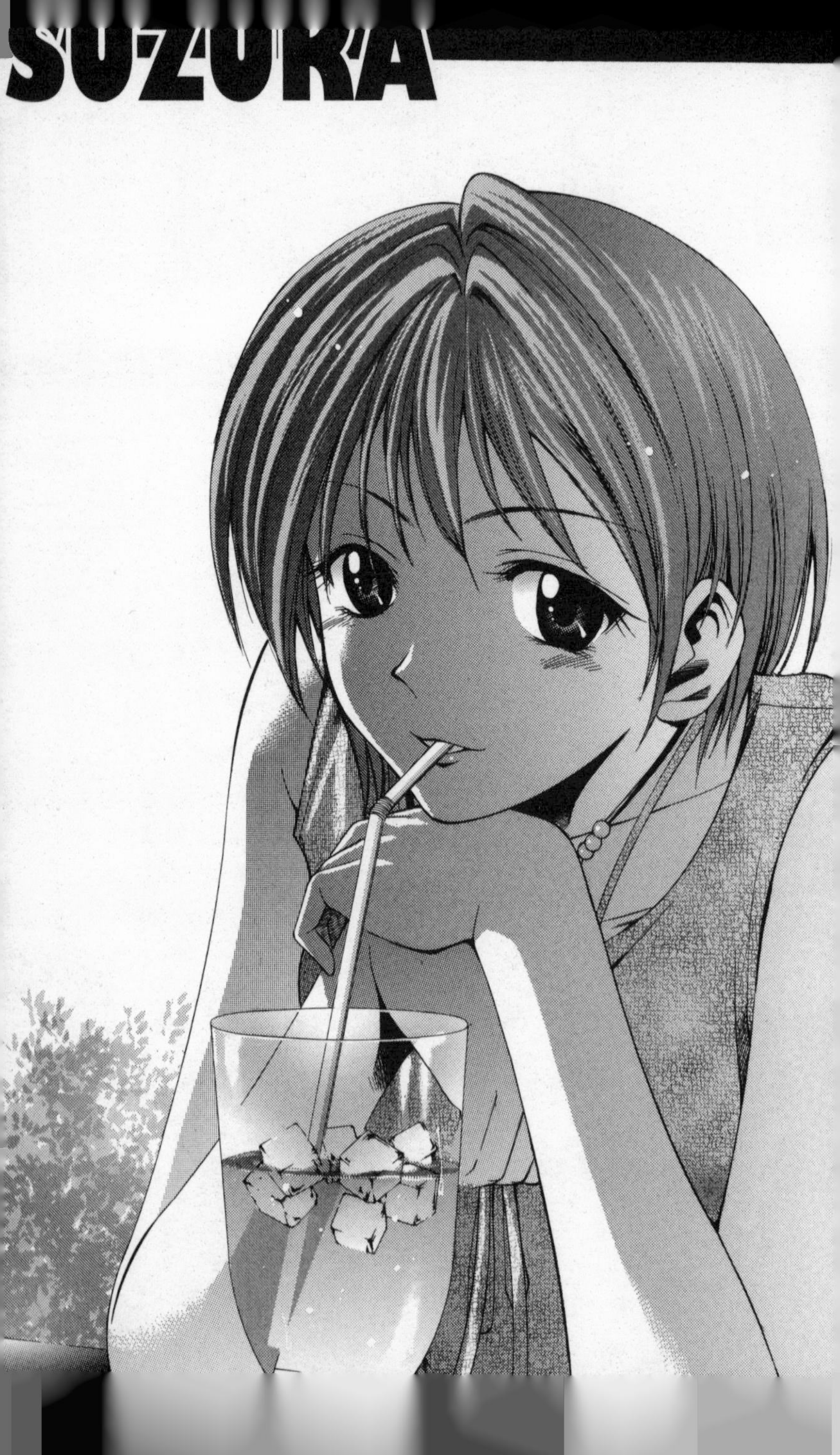
SUZUKA

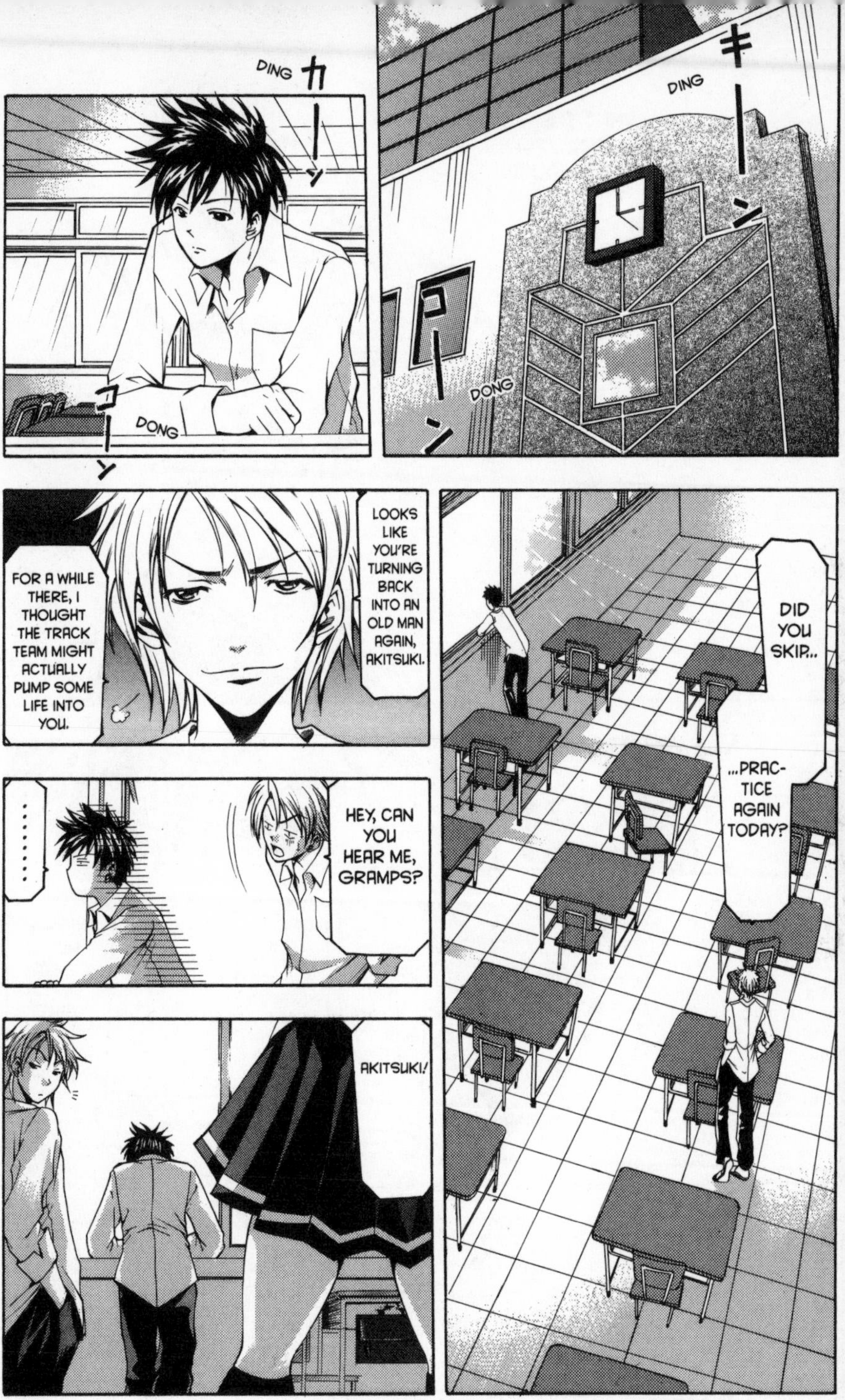
キーン
DING
DONG
カーン
DING
コーン
DONG
DID YOU SKIP...
...PRAC-TICE AGAIN TODAY?
LOOKS LIKE YOU'RE TURNING BACK INTO AN OLD MAN AGAIN, AKITSUKI.
FOR A WHILE THERE, I THOUGHT THE TRACK TEAM MIGHT ACTUALLY PUMP SOME LIFE INTO YOU.
HEY, CAN YOU HEAR ME, GRAMPS?
....
AKITSUKI!

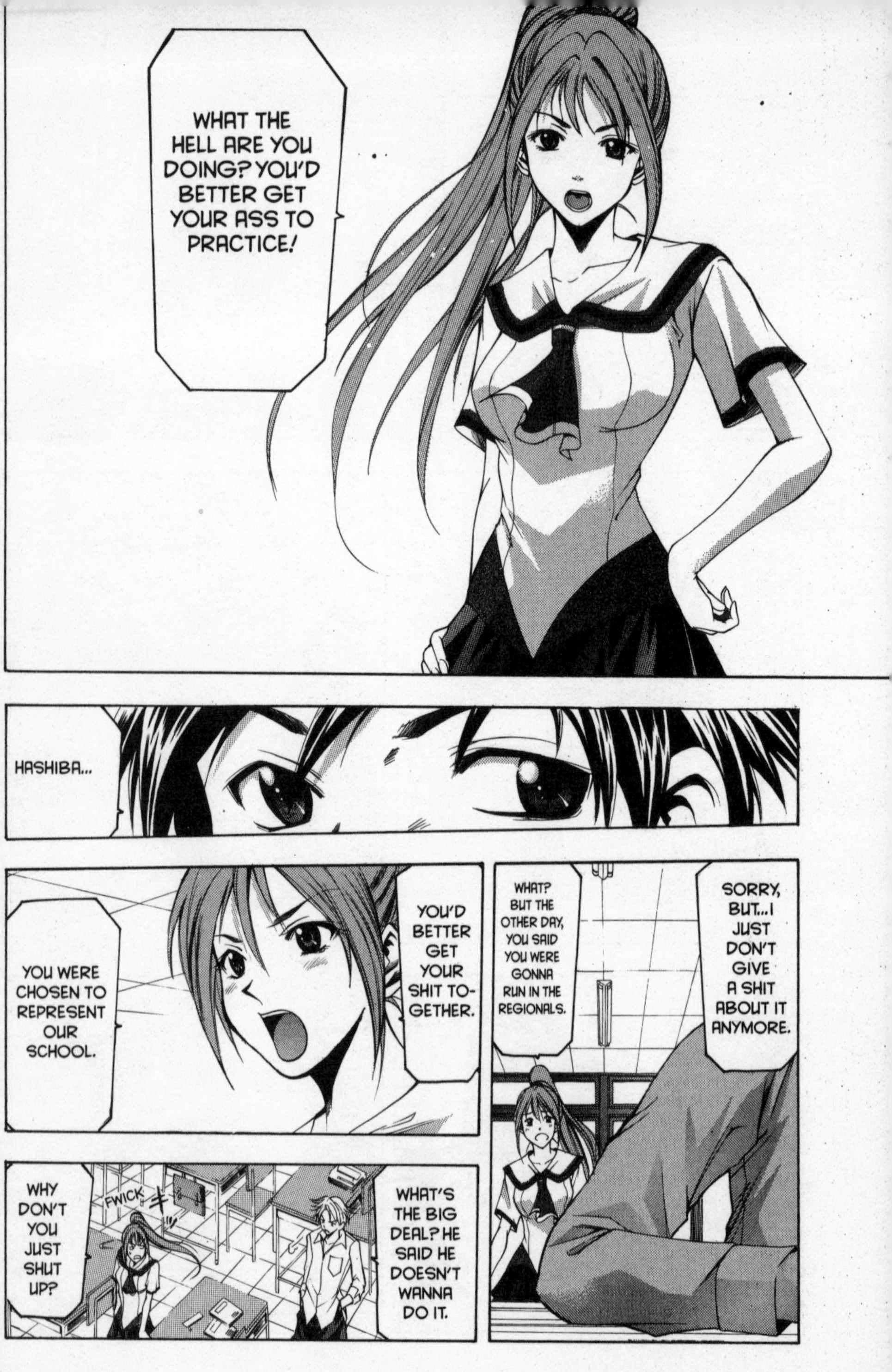
WHAT THE HELL ARE YOU DOING? YOU'D BETTER GET YOUR ASS TO PRACTICE!
HASHIBA...
SORRY, BUT...I JUST DON'T GIVE A SHIT ABOUT IT ANYMORE.
WHAT? BUT THE OTHER DAY, YOU SAID YOU WERE GONNA RUN IN THE REGIONALS.
YOU'D BETTER GET YOUR SHIT TO-GETHER.
YOU WERE CHOSEN TO REPRESENT OUR SCHOOL.
WHAT'S THE BIG DEAL? HE SAID HE DOESN'T WANNA DO IT.
FWICK
WHY DON'T YOU JUST SHUT UP?

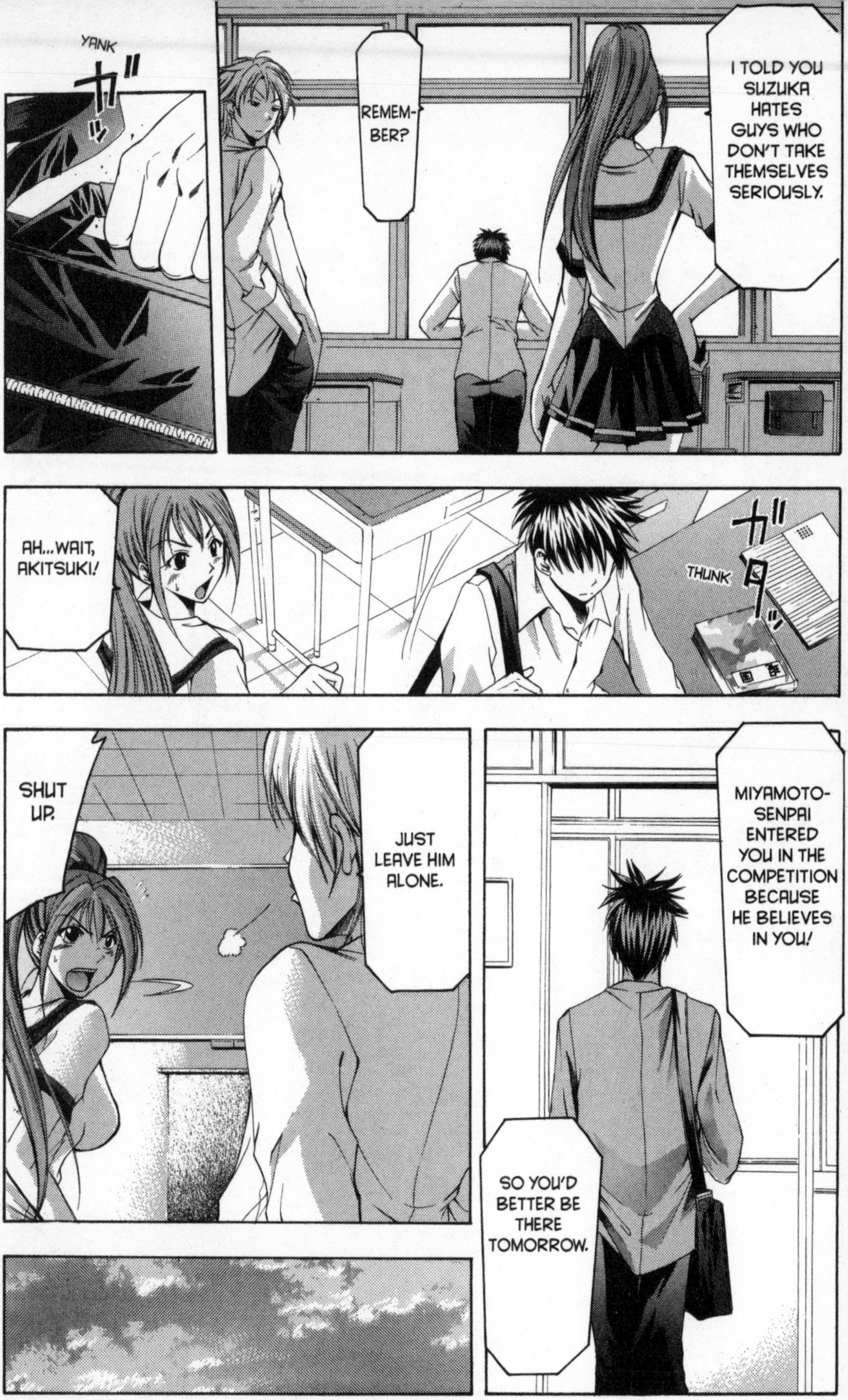
I TOLD YOU SUZUKA HATES GUYS WHO DON'T TAKE THEMSELVES SERIOUSLY.
REMEM-BER?
YANK
THUNK
AH...WAIT, AKITSUKI!
MIYAMOTO-SENPAI ENTERED YOU IN THE COMPETITION BECAUSE HE BELIEVES IN YOU!
SO YOU'D BETTER BE THERE TOMORROW.
JUST LEAVE HIM ALONE.
SHUT UP.

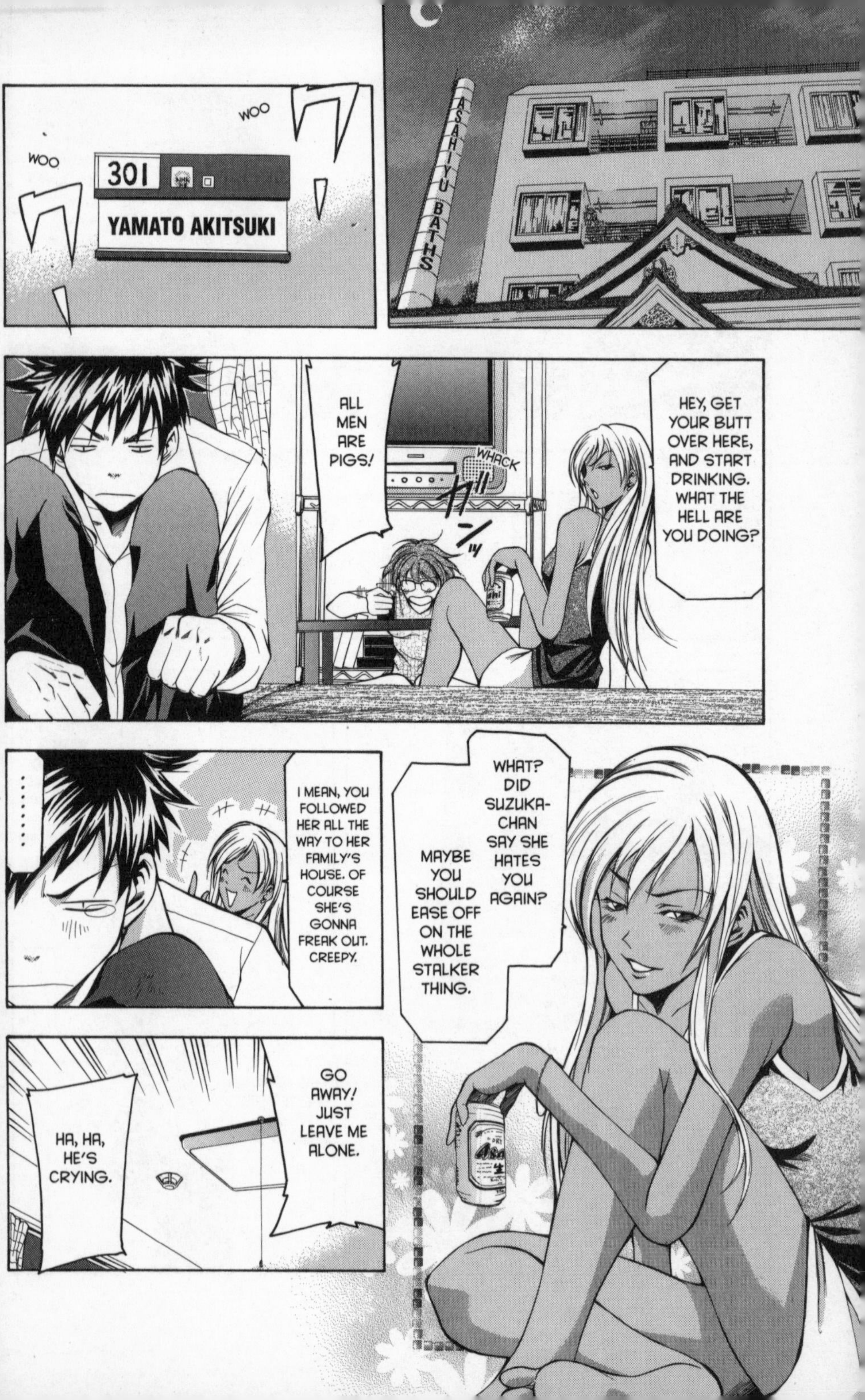
ASAHIYU BATHS
WOO
WOO
301
YAMATO AKITSUKI
HEY, GET YOUR BUTT OVER HERE, AND START DRINKING. WHAT THE HELL ARE YOU DOING?
WHACK
ALL MEN ARE PIGS!
WHAT? DID SUZUKA-CHAN SAY SHE HATES YOU AGAIN?
MAYBE YOU SHOULD EASE OFF ON THE WHOLE STALKER THING.
I MEAN, YOU FOLLOWED HER ALL THE WAY TO HER FAMILY'S HOUSE. OF COURSE SHE'S GONNA FREAK OUT. CREEPY.
......
GO AWAY! JUST LEAVE ME ALONE.
HA, HA, HE'S CRYING.

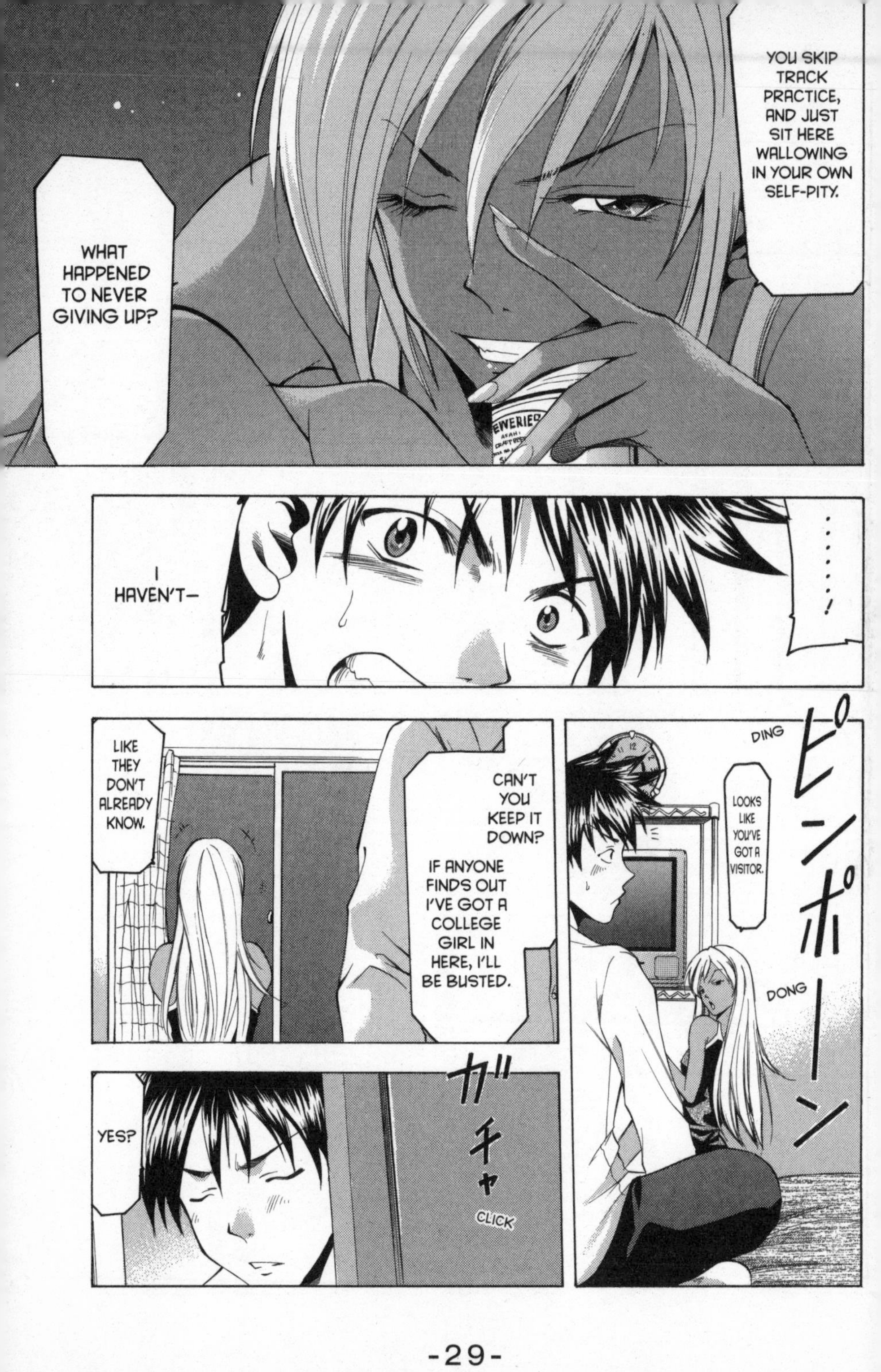
YOU SKIP TRACK PRACTICE, AND JUST SIT HERE WALLOWING IN YOUR OWN SELF-PITY.
WHAT HAPPENED TO NEVER GIVING UP?
......!
I HAVEN'T—
ピンポーン
DING
DONG
LOOKS LIKE YOU'VE GOT A VISITOR.
CAN'T YOU KEEP IT DOWN?
IF ANYONE FINDS OUT I'VE GOT A COLLEGE GIRL IN HERE, I'LL BE BUSTED.
LIKE THEY DON'T ALREADY KNOW.
ガチャ
CLICK
YES?

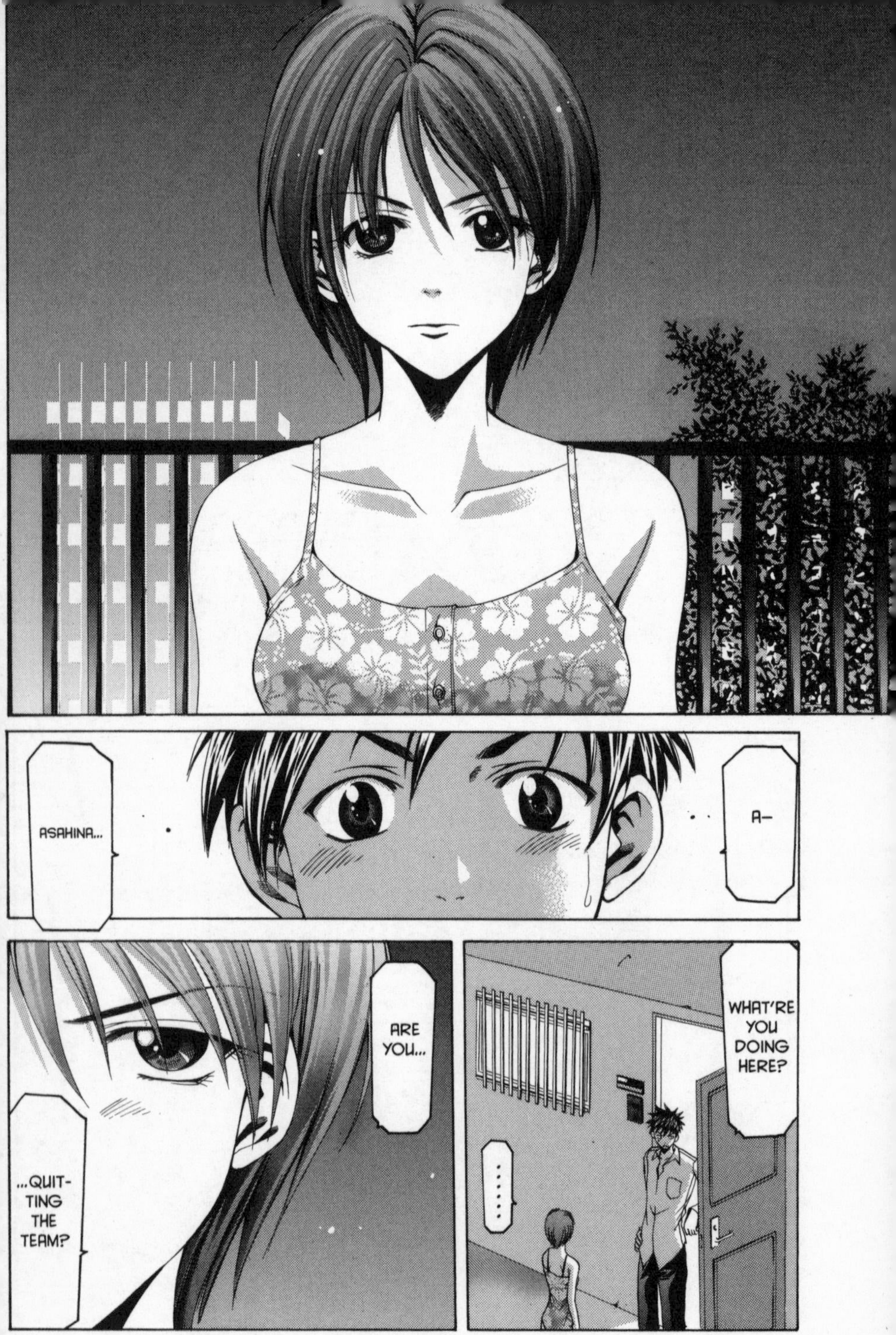
A—
ASAHINA...
WHAT'RE YOU DOING HERE?
......
ARE YOU...
...QUIT-TING THE TEAM?

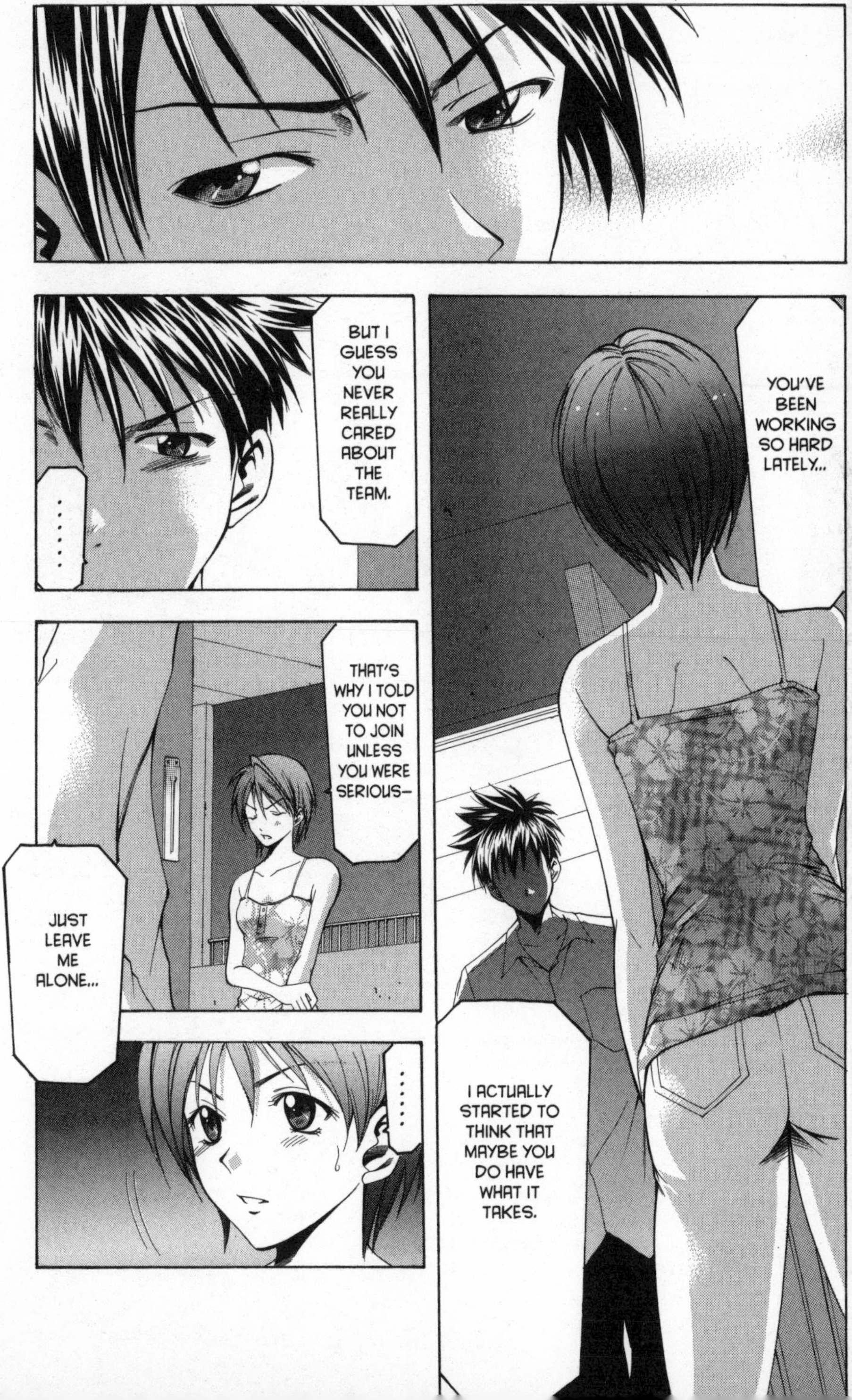
YOU'VE BEEN WORKING SO HARD LATELY...
I ACTUALLY STARTED TO THINK THAT MAYBE YOU DO HAVE WHAT IT TAKES.
BUT I GUESS YOU NEVER REALLY CARED ABOUT THE TEAM.
......
THAT'S WHY I TOLD YOU NOT TO JOIN UNLESS YOU WERE SERIOUS—
JUST LEAVE ME ALONE...
......

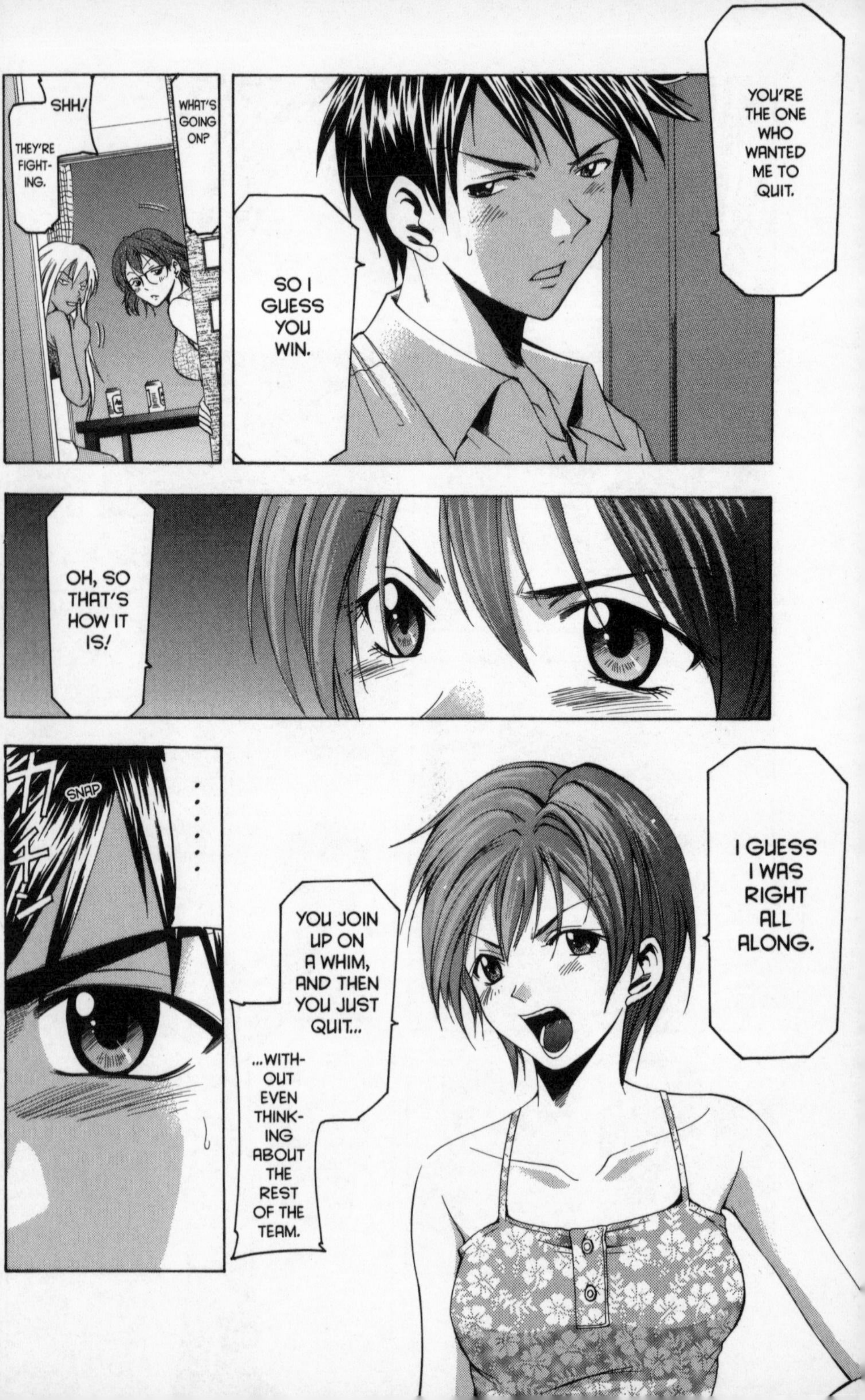
YOU'RE THE ONE WHO WANTED ME TO QUIT.
SO I GUESS YOU WIN.
WHAT'S GOING ON?
SHH!
THEY'RE FIGHTING.
OH, SO THAT'S HOW IT IS!
I GUESS I WAS RIGHT ALL ALONG.
YOU JOIN UP ON A WHIM, AND THEN YOU JUST QUIT...
...WITHOUT EVEN THINKING ABOUT THE REST OF THE TEAM.
SNAP
......

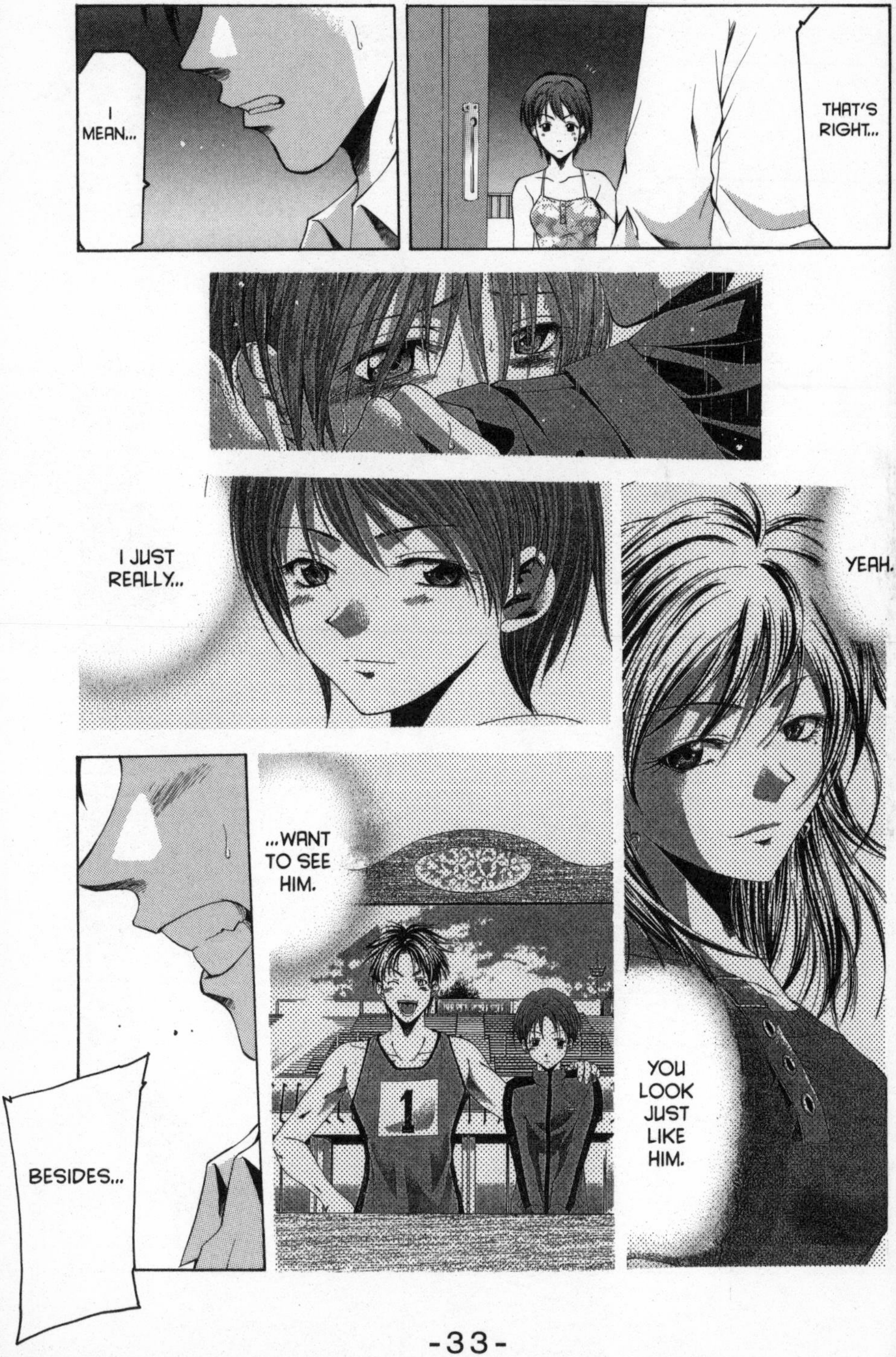
THAT'S RIGHT...
I MEAN...
YEAH.
YOU LOOK JUST LIKE HIM.
I JUST REALLY...
...WANT TO SEE HIM.
1
BESIDES...

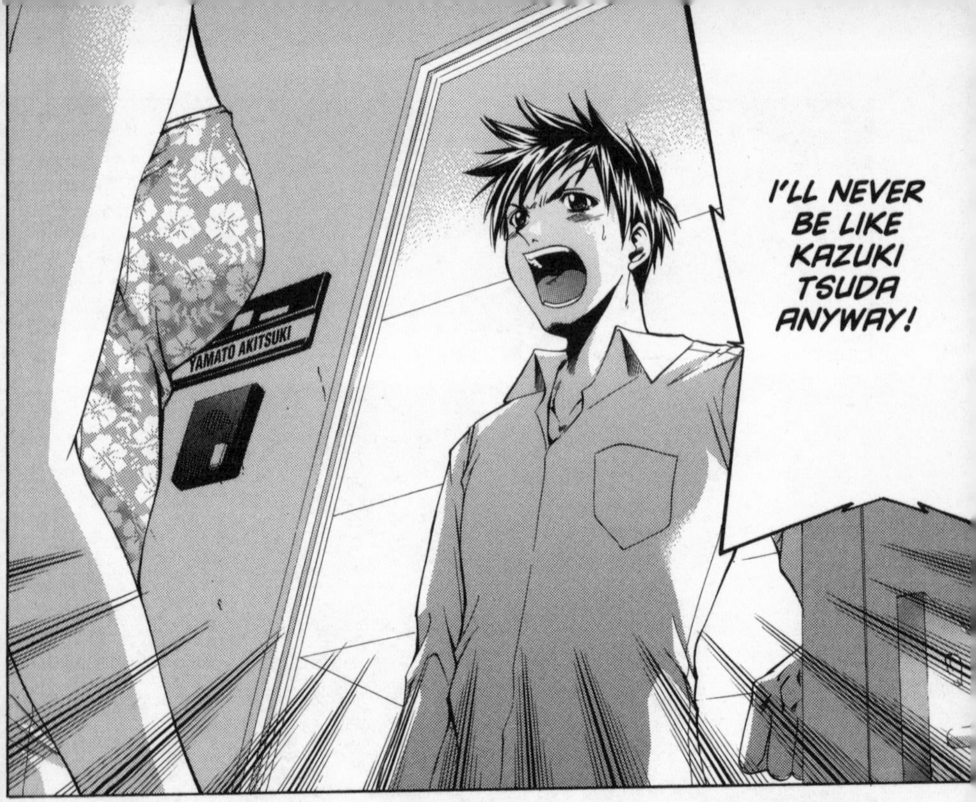
YAMATO AKITSUKI
I'LL NEVER BE LIKE KAZUKI TSUDA ANYWAY!
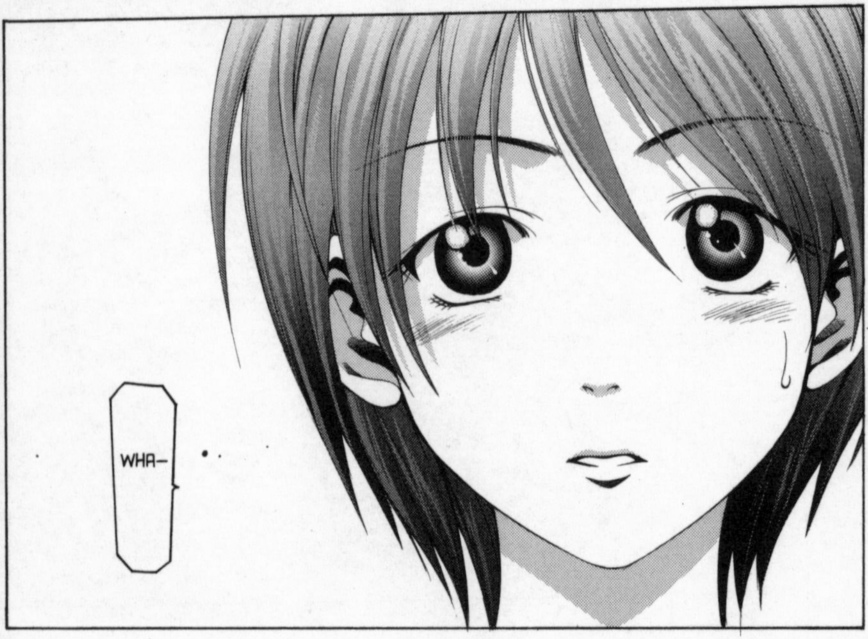
WHA—

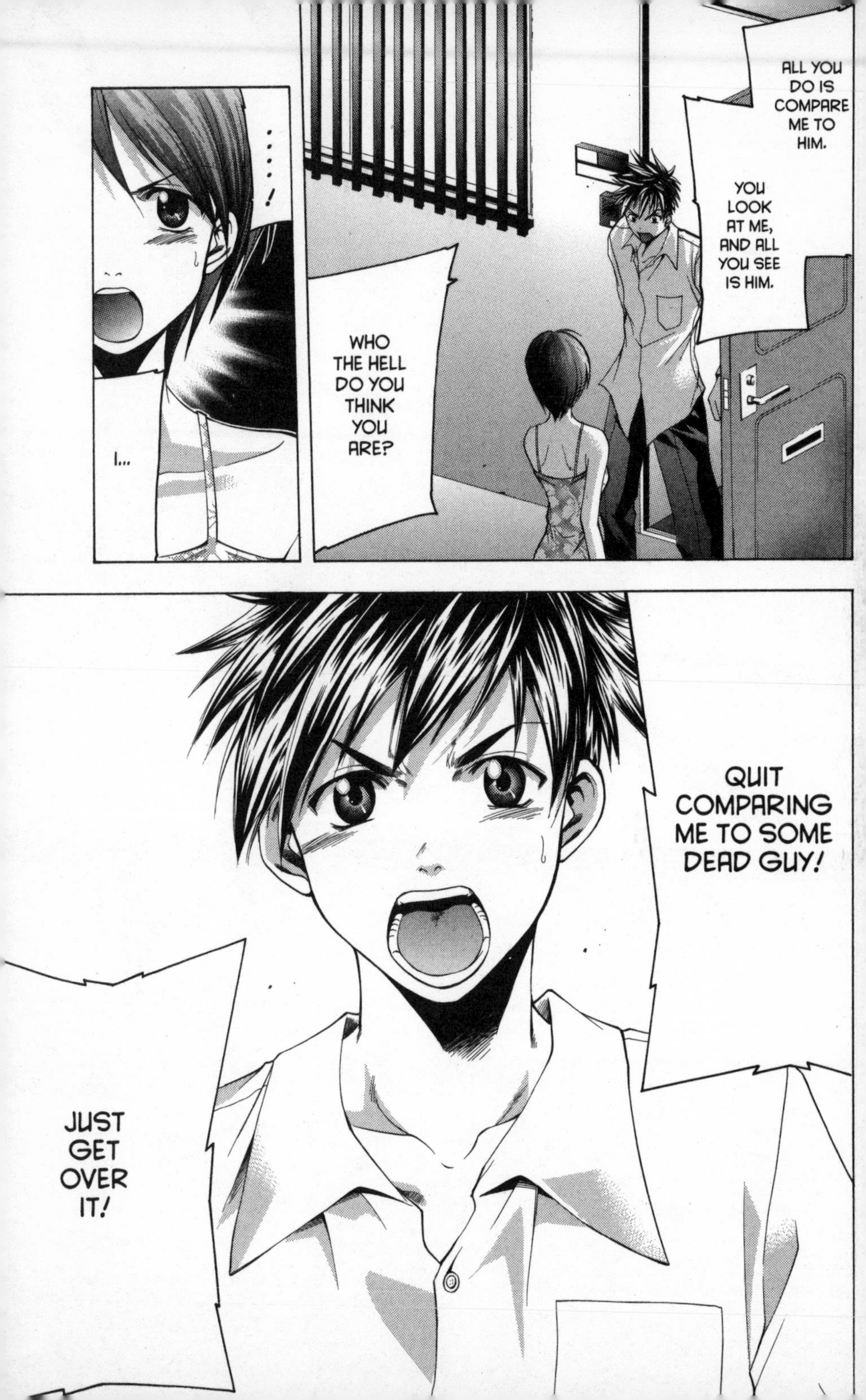
ALL YOU DO IS COMPARE ME TO HIM.
YOU LOOK AT ME, AND ALL YOU SEE IS HIM.
WHO THE HELL DO YOU THINK YOU ARE?
......!
I...
QUIT COMPARING ME TO SOME DEAD GUY!
JUST GET OVER IT!

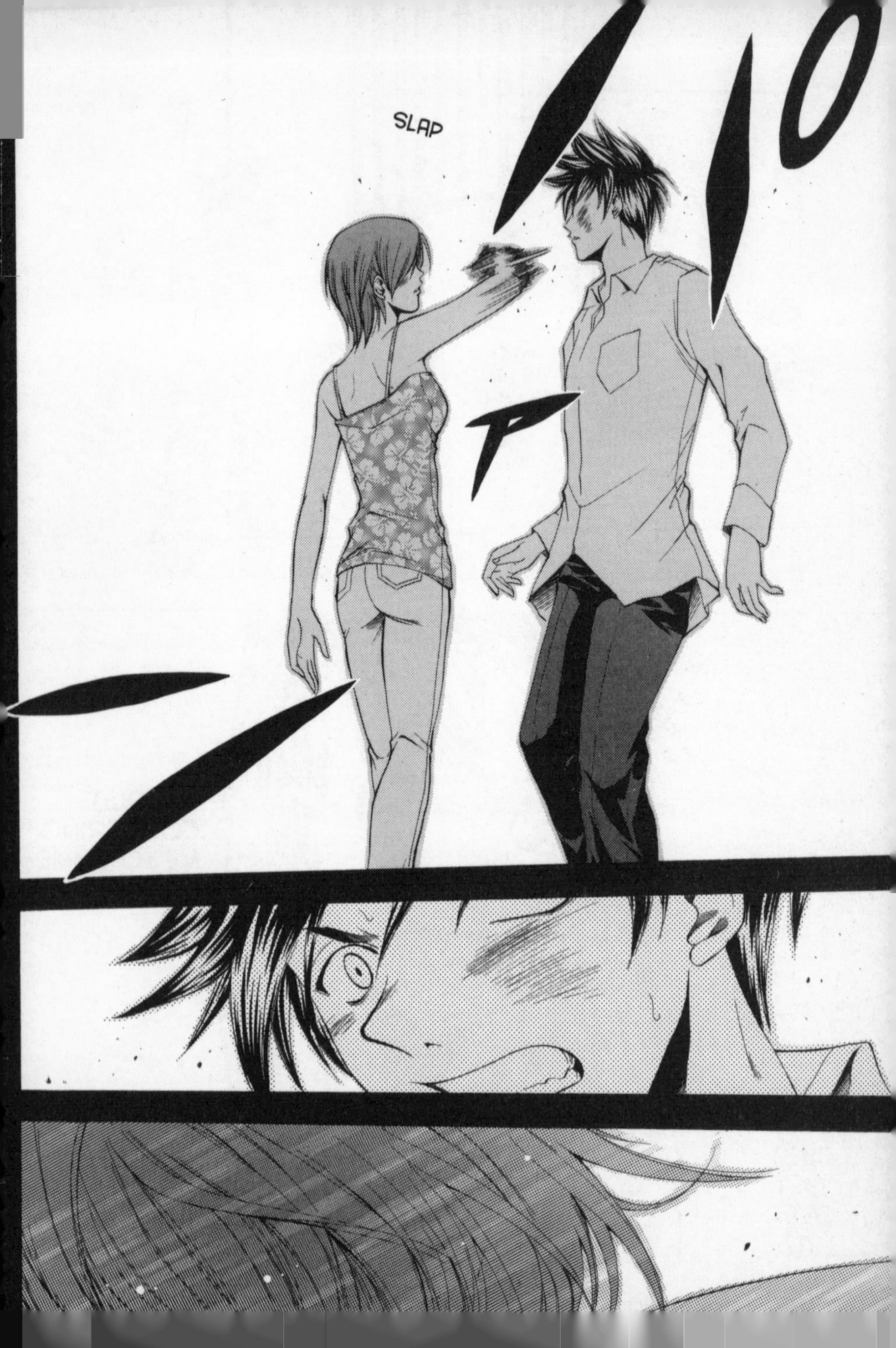
SLAP

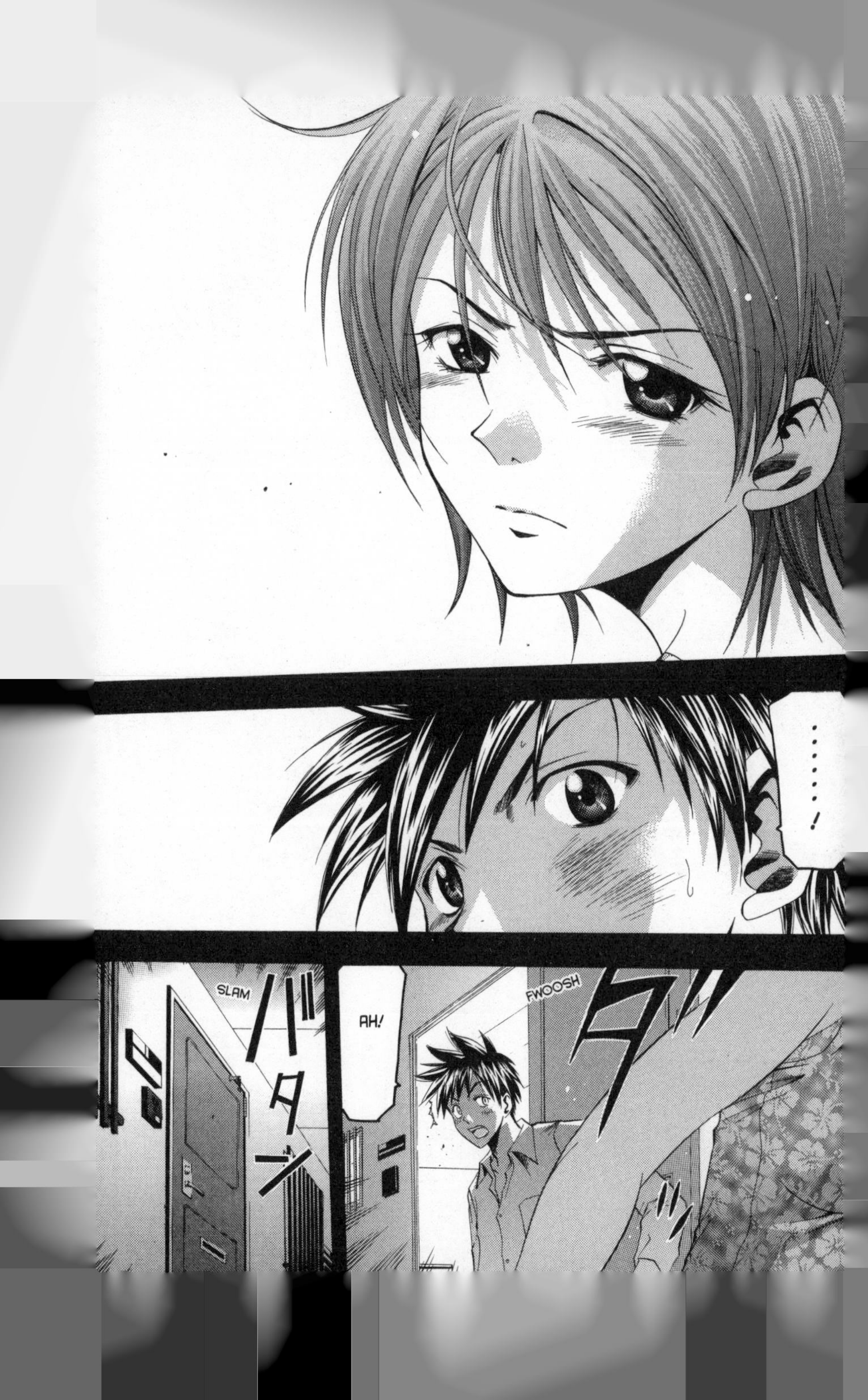
......!
FWOOSH
タッ
AH!
SLAM
バタン

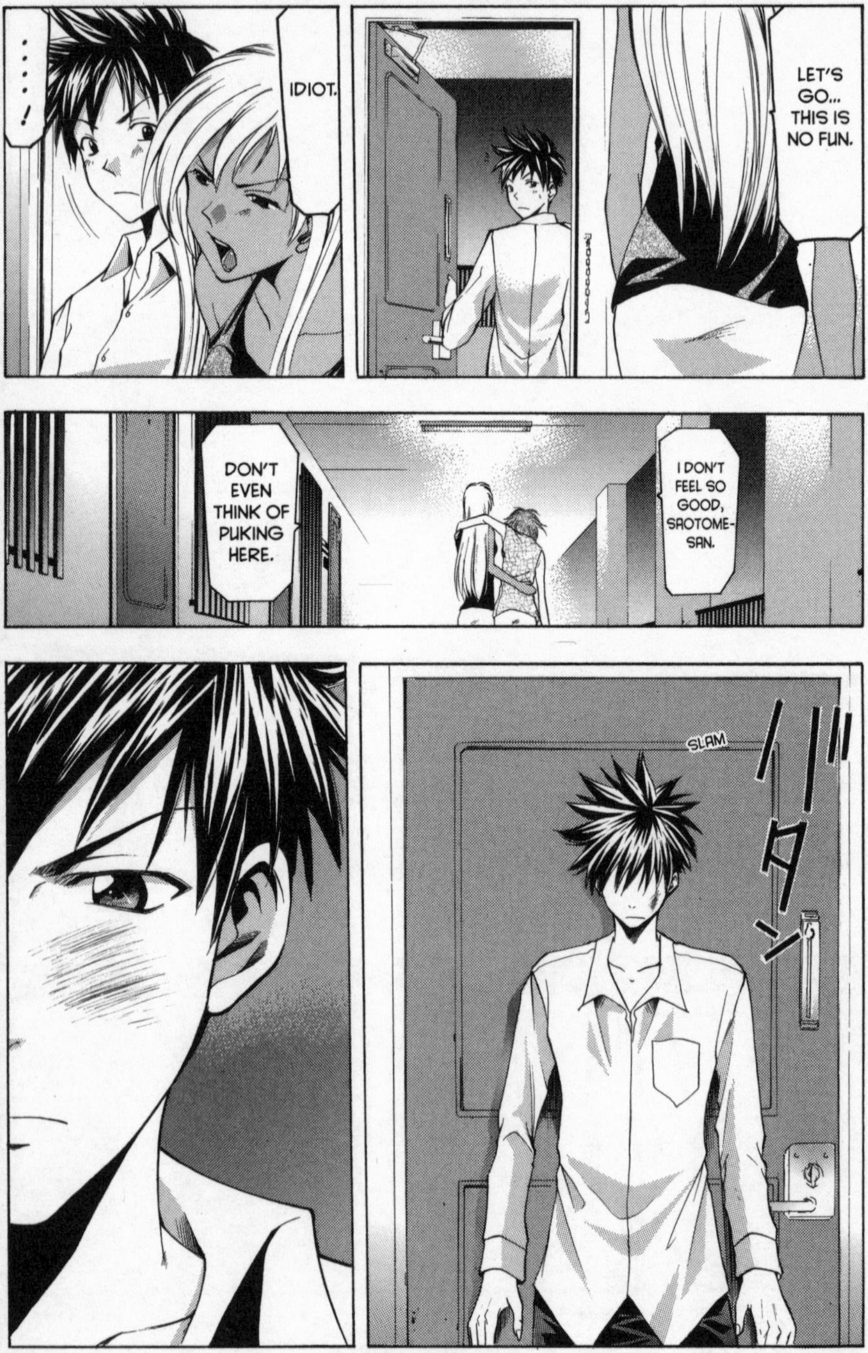
LET'S GO... THIS IS NO FUN.
IDIOT.
....!
I DON'T FEEL SO GOOD, SAOTOME-SAN.
DON'T EVEN THINK OF PUKING HERE.
SLAM
バタン

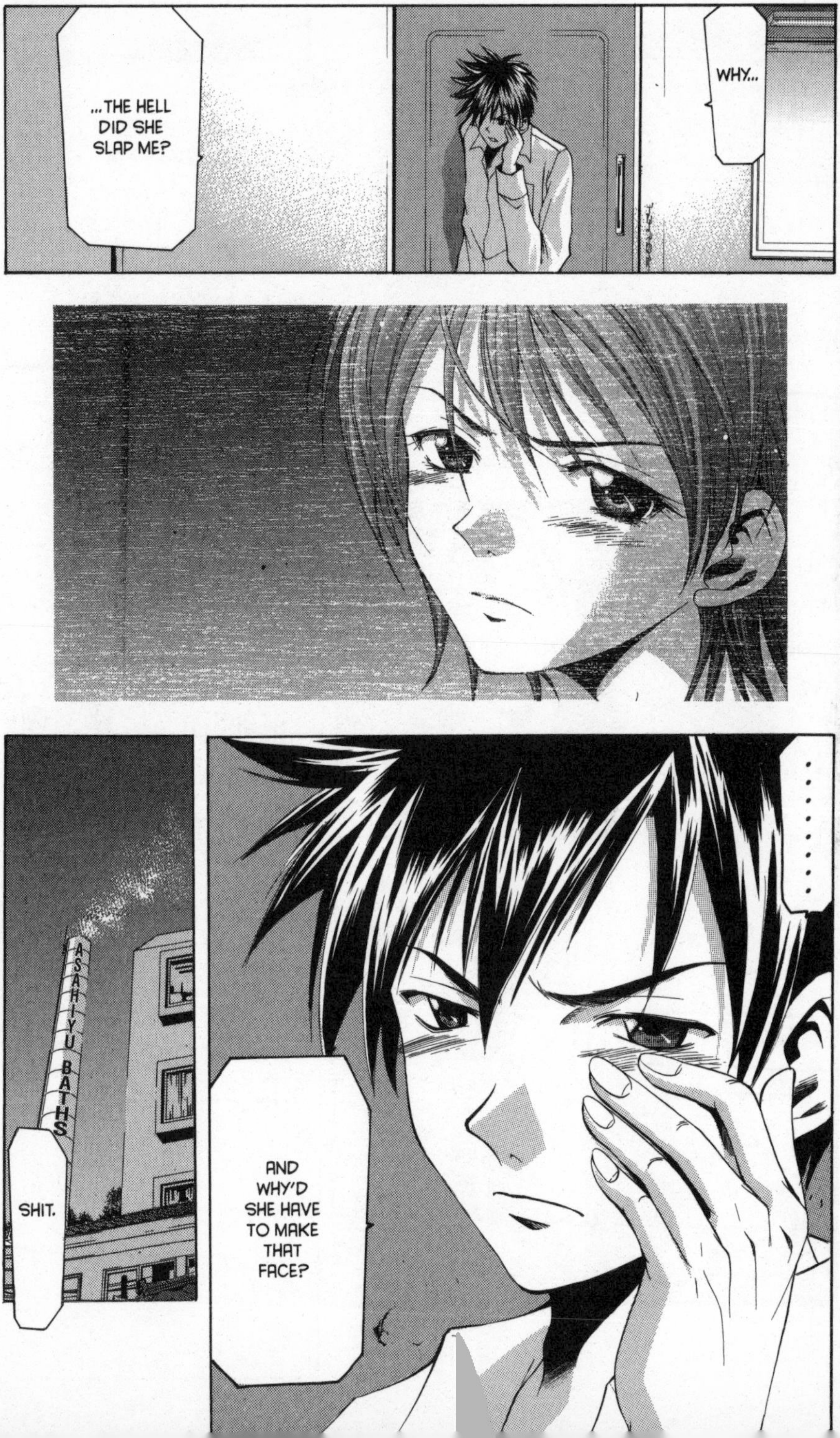
WHY...
...THE HELL DID SHE SLAP ME?
....
AND WHY'D SHE HAVE TO MAKE THAT FACE?
SHIT.

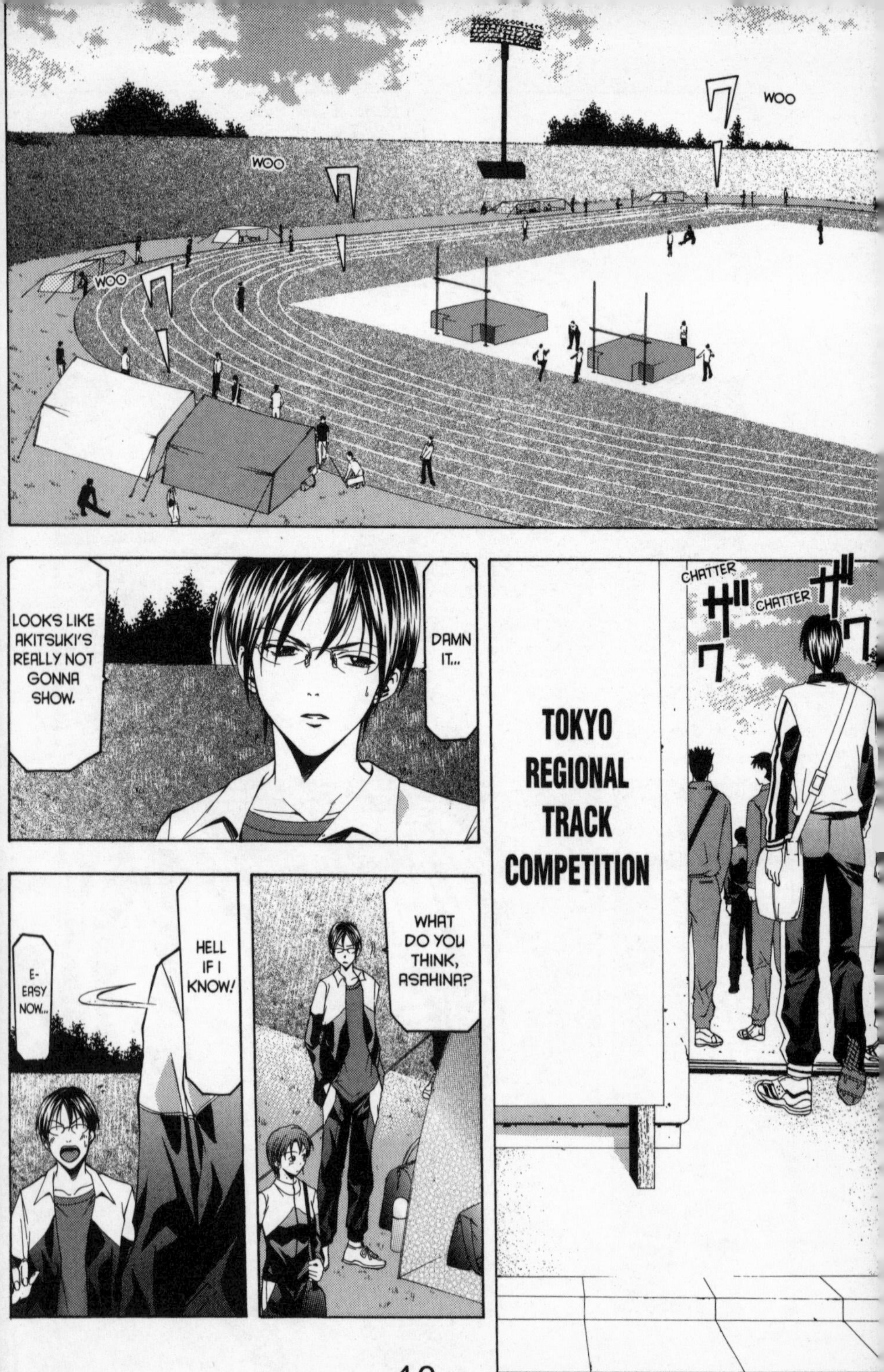
WOO
WOO
WOO
TOKYO REGIONAL TRACK COMPETITION
CHATTER
CHATTER
DAMN IT...
LOOKS LIKE AKITSUKI'S REALLY NOT GONNA SHOW.
WHAT DO YOU THINK, ASAHINA?
HELL IF I KNOW!
E- EASY NOW...

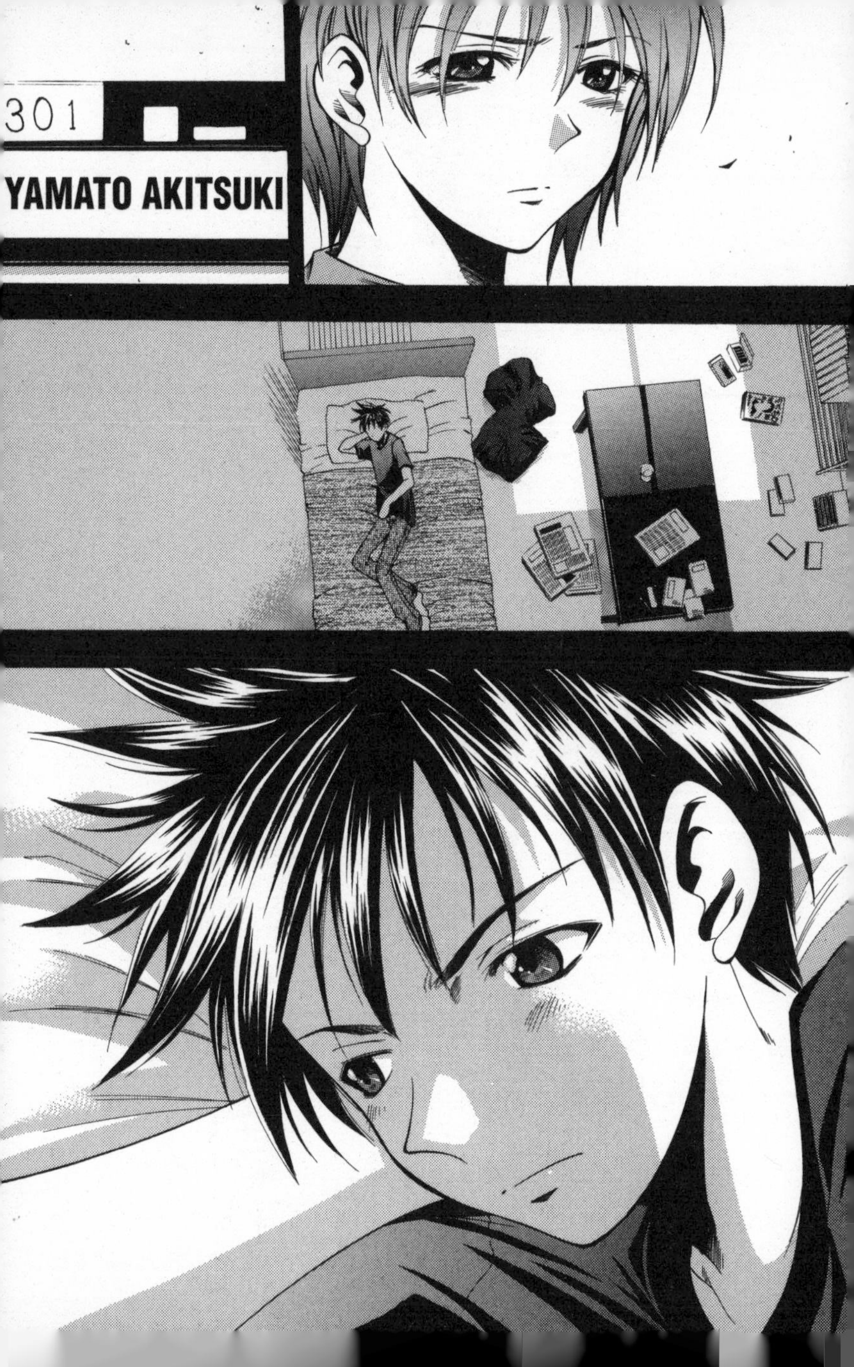
301
YAMATO AKITSUKI

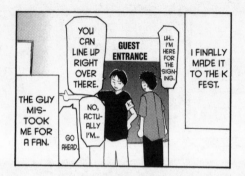

SUZUKA FOUR-PANEL THEATER NUMBER FOURTEEN

SEO GOES TO A SIGNING - PART 2

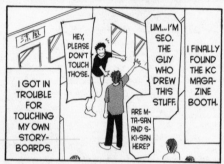

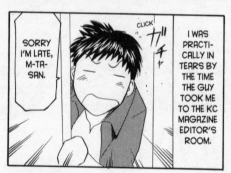

I FINALLY MADE IT TO THE K FEST.
UH... I'M HERE FOR THE SIGN-ING.
GUEST ENTRANCE
YOU CAN LINE UP RIGHT OVER THERE.
NO, ACTU-ALLY I'M...
GO AHEAD.
THE GUY MIS-TOOK ME FOR A FAN.
I FINALLY FOUND THE KC MAGA-ZINE BOOTH.
UM...I'M SEO. THE GUY WHO DREW THIS STUFF.
ARE M-TA-SAN AND S-KI-SAN HERE?
HEY, PLEASE DON'T TOUCH THOSE.
涼風
I GOT IN TROUBLE FOR TOUCHING MY OWN STORY-BOARDS.
I WAS PRACTI-CALLY IN TEARS BY THE TIME THE GUY TOOK ME TO THE KC MAGAZINE EDITOR'S ROOM.
CLICK
ガチャ
SORRY I'M LATE, M-TA-SAN.
OH, M-TA'S NOT HERE YET. HE GOT ON THE WRONG TRAIN.
HUH?
EVEN MY EDITOR WAS LATE.

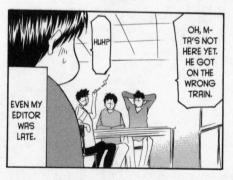

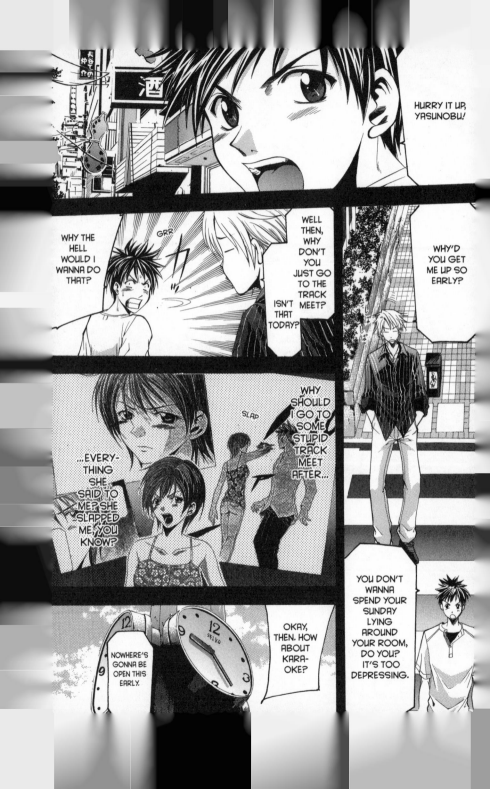

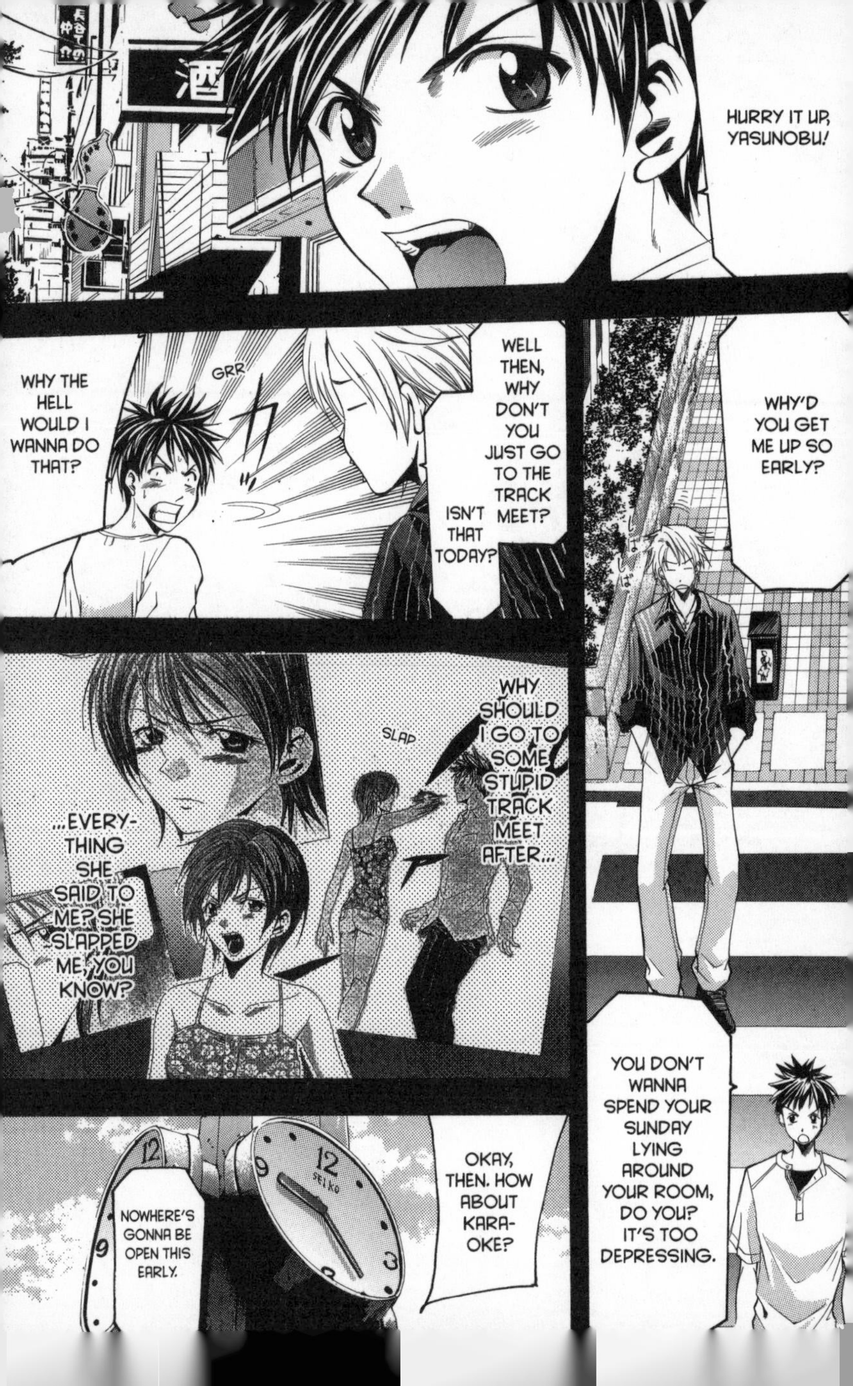
HURRY IT UP, YASUNOBU!
WHY'D YOU GET ME UP SO EARLY?
YOU DON'T WANNA SPEND YOUR SUNDAY LYING AROUND YOUR ROOM, DO YOU? IT'S TOO DEPRESSING.
WELL THEN, WHY DON'T YOU JUST GO TO THE TRACK MEET?
ISN'T THAT TODAY?
GRR
WHY THE HELL WOULD I WANNA DO THAT?
WHY SHOULD I GO TO SOME STUPID TRACK MEET AFTER...
SLAP
...EVERYTHING SHE SAID TO ME? SHE SLAPPED ME, YOU KNOW?
OKAY, THEN. HOW ABOUT KARAOKE?
NOWHERE'S GONNA BE OPEN THIS EARLY.

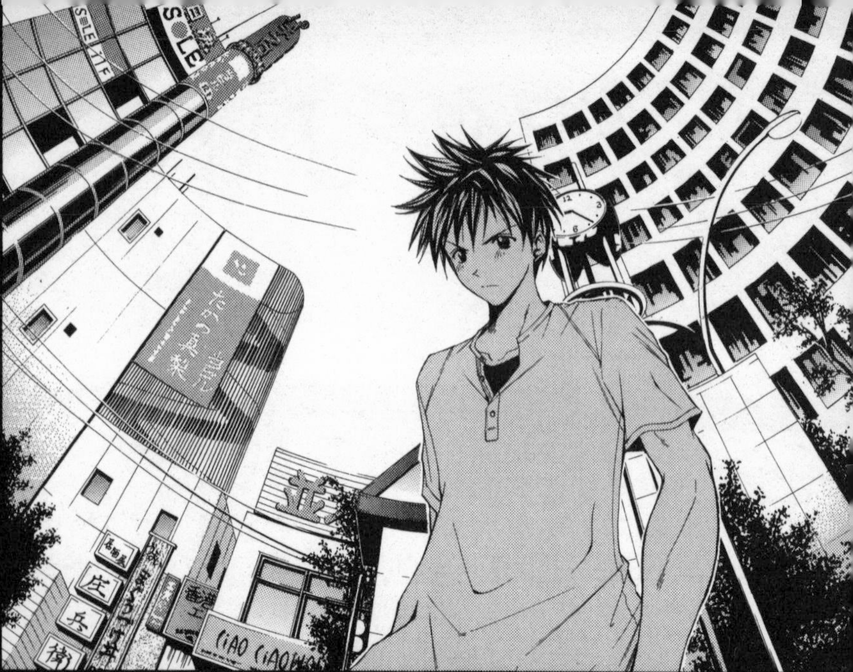

SUZUKA

#25 PROVOCATION

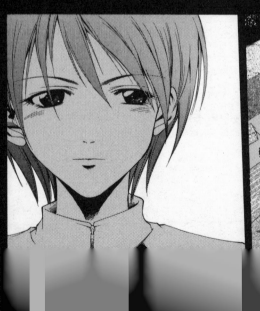

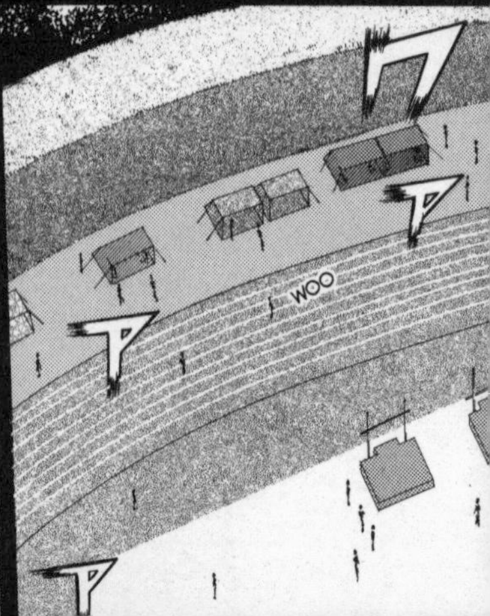
WOO

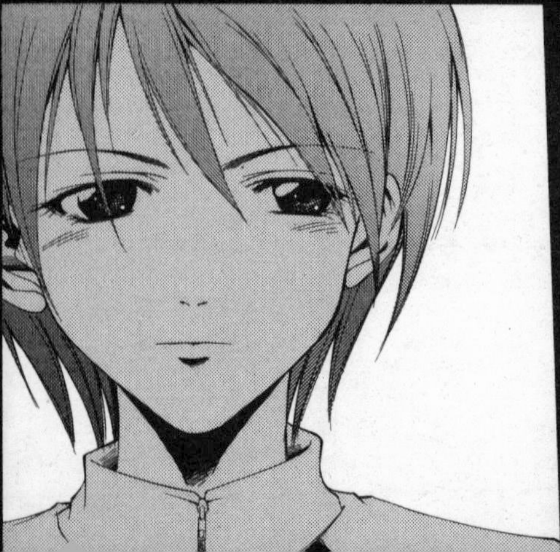

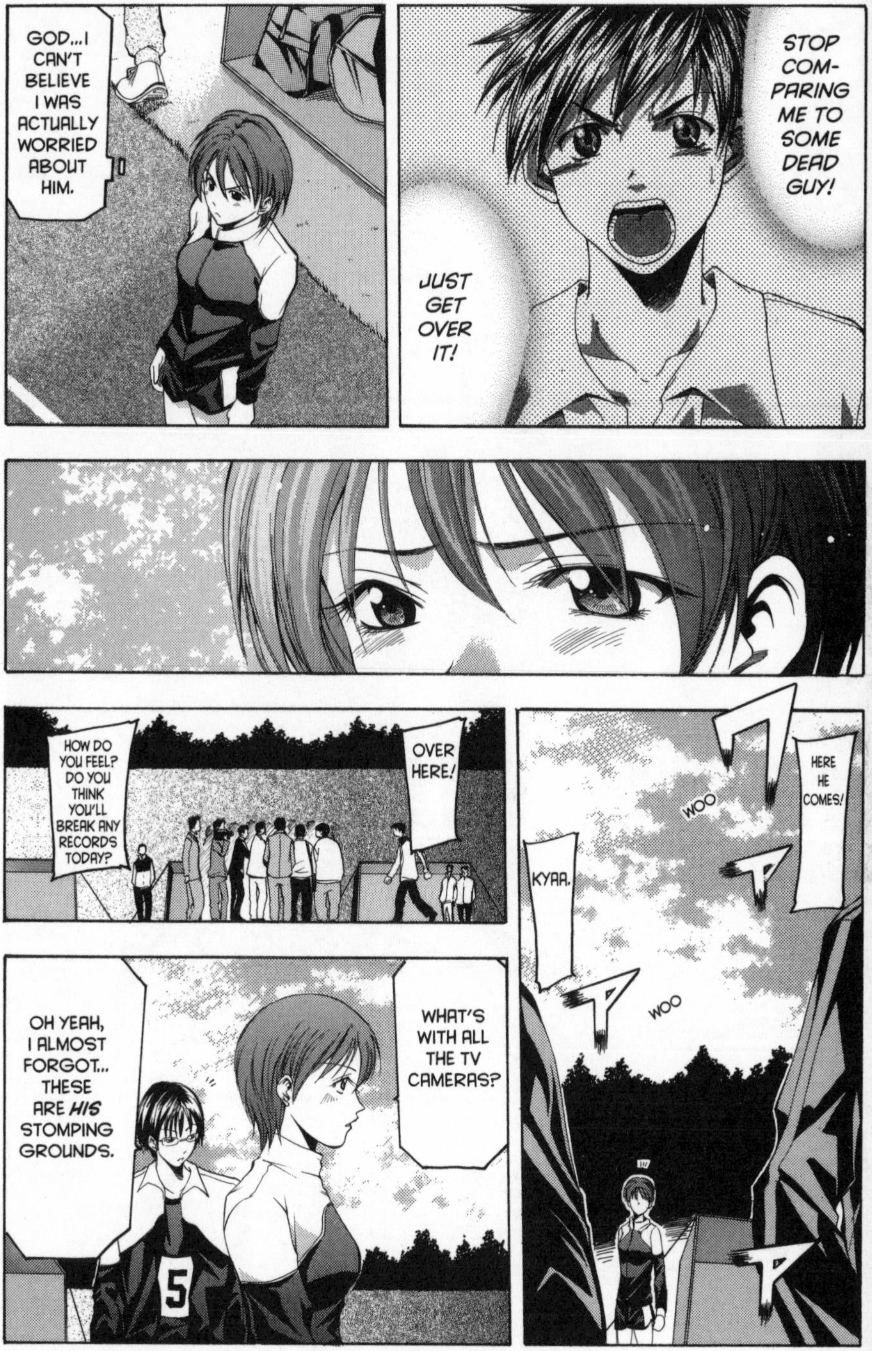
STOP COMPARING ME TO SOME DEAD GUY!
JUST GET OVER IT!
GOD...I CAN'T BELIEVE I WAS ACTUALLY WORRIED ABOUT HIM.
HERE HE COMES!
WOO
KYAA.
WOO
OVER HERE!
HOW DO YOU FEEL? DO YOU THINK YOU'LL BREAK ANY RECORDS TODAY?
WHAT'S WITH ALL THE TV CAMERAS?
OH YEAH, I ALMOST FORGOT... THESE ARE *HIS* STOMPING GROUNDS.

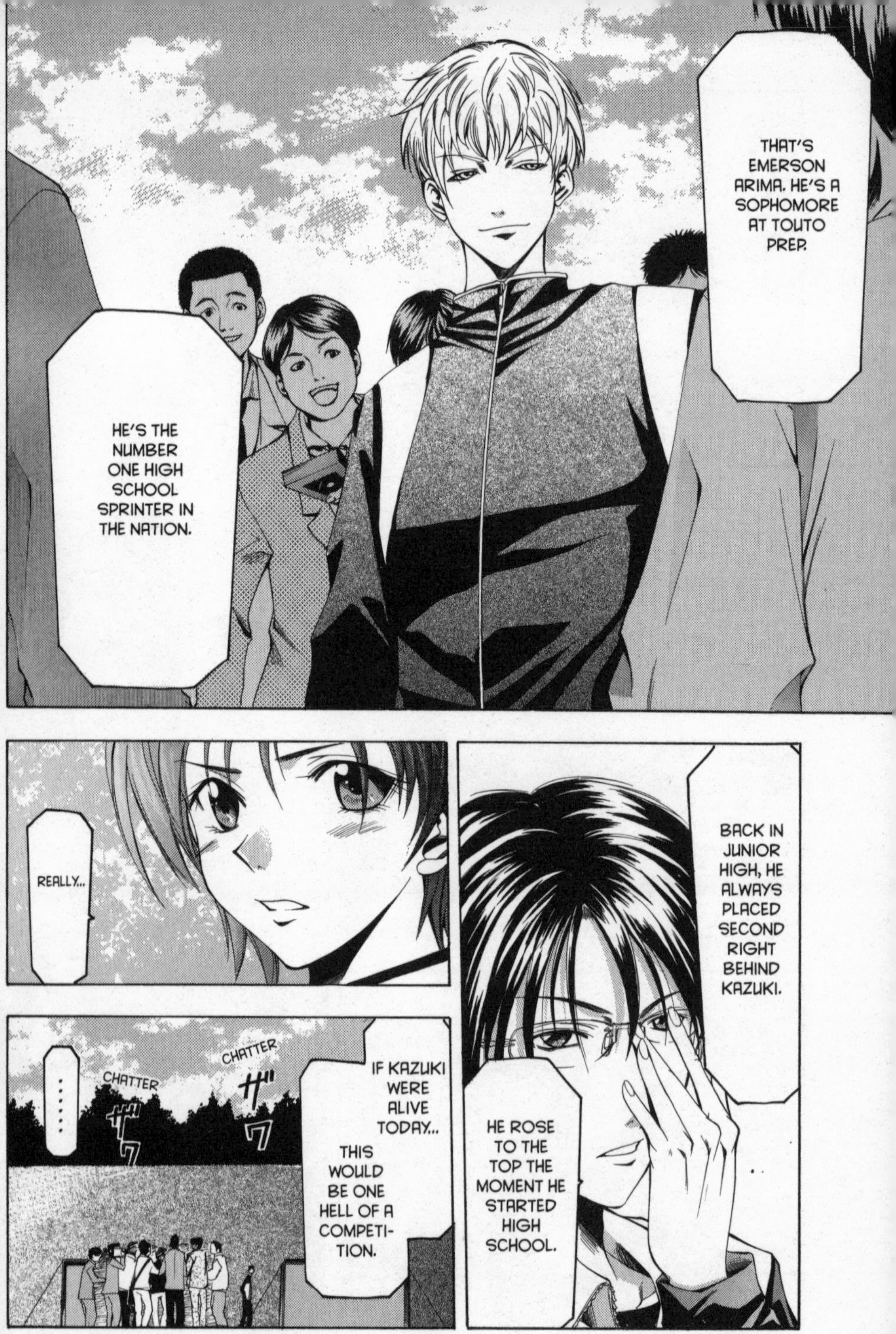
THAT'S EMERSON ARIMA. HE'S A SOPHOMORE AT TOUTO PREP.
HE'S THE NUMBER ONE HIGH SCHOOL SPRINTER IN THE NATION.
BACK IN JUNIOR HIGH, HE ALWAYS PLACED SECOND RIGHT BEHIND KAZUKI.
HE ROSE TO THE TOP THE MOMENT HE STARTED HIGH SCHOOL.
REALLY...
IF KAZUKI WERE ALIVE TODAY...
THIS WOULD BE ONE HELL OF A COMPETITION.
CHATTER
ザワ
CHATTER
ザワ
......

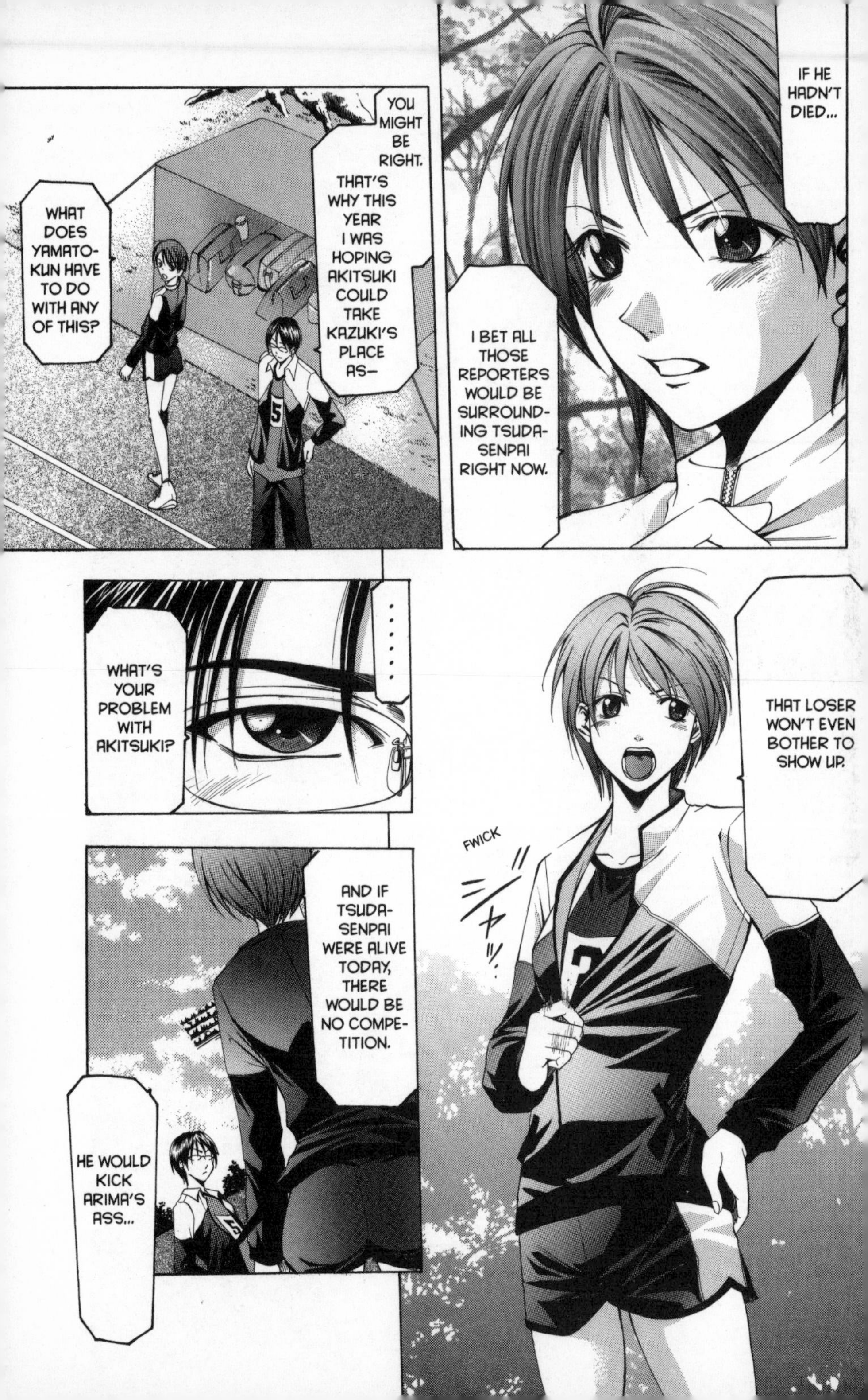
IF HE HADN'T DIED...
I BET ALL THOSE REPORTERS WOULD BE SURROUNDING TSUDA-SENPAI RIGHT NOW.
YOU MIGHT BE RIGHT.
THAT'S WHY THIS YEAR I WAS HOPING AKITSUKI COULD TAKE KAZUKI'S PLACE AS—
WHAT DOES YAMATO-KUN HAVE TO DO WITH ANY OF THIS?
THAT LOSER WON'T EVEN BOTHER TO SHOW UP.
FWICK
......
WHAT'S YOUR PROBLEM WITH AKITSUKI?
AND IF TSUDA-SENPAI WERE ALIVE TODAY, THERE WOULD BE NO COMPETITION.
HE WOULD KICK ARIMA'S ASS...

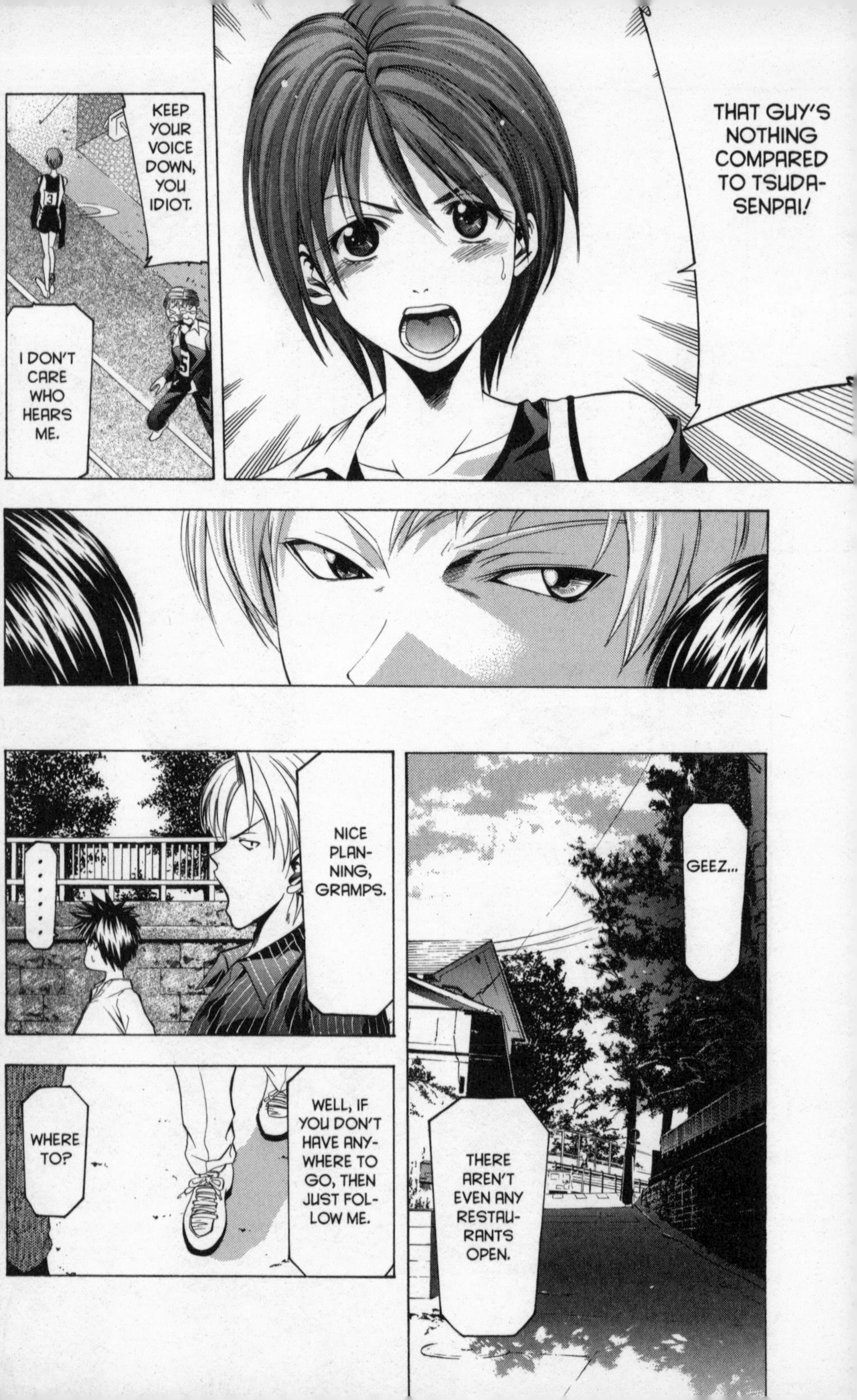
THAT GUY'S NOTHING COMPARED TO TSUDA-SENPAI!
KEEP YOUR VOICE DOWN, YOU IDIOT.
I DON'T CARE WHO HEARS ME.
GEEZ...
THERE AREN'T EVEN ANY RESTAURANTS OPEN.
NICE PLANNING, GRAMPS.
......
WELL, IF YOU DON'T HAVE ANYWHERE TO GO, THEN JUST FOLLOW ME.
WHERE TO?

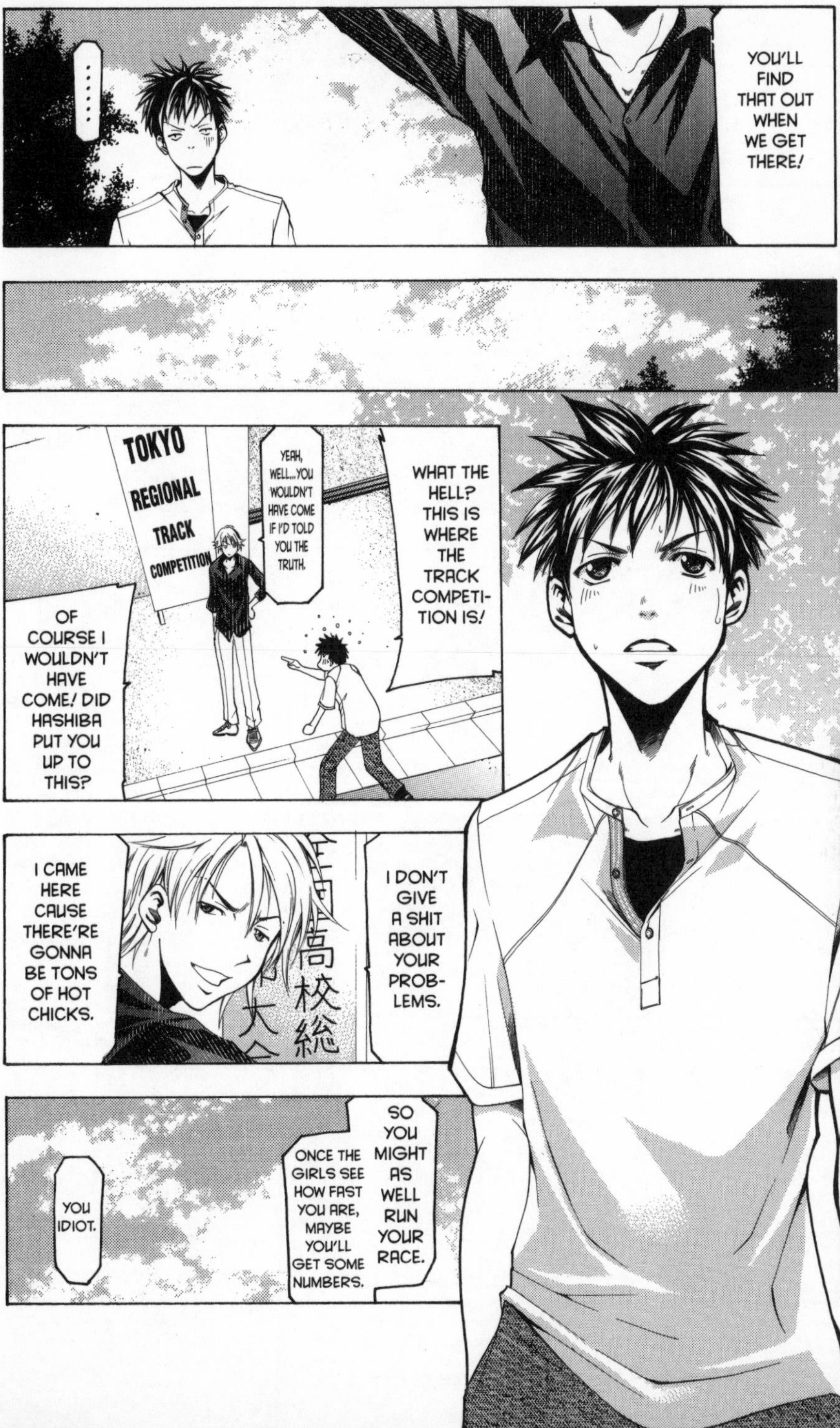
YOU'LL FIND THAT OUT WHEN WE GET THERE!
......
TOKYO REGIONAL TRACK COMPETITION
WHAT THE HELL? THIS IS WHERE THE TRACK COMPETITION IS!
YEAH, WELL...YOU WOULDN'T HAVE COME IF I'D TOLD YOU THE TRUTH.
OF COURSE I WOULDN'T HAVE COME! DID HASHIBA PUT YOU UP TO THIS?
I DON'T GIVE A SHIT ABOUT YOUR PROBLEMS.
I CAME HERE CAUSE THERE'RE GONNA BE TONS OF HOT CHICKS.
SO YOU MIGHT AS WELL RUN YOUR RACE.
ONCE THE GIRLS SEE HOW FAST YOU ARE, MAYBE YOU'LL GET SOME NUMBERS.
YOU IDIOT.

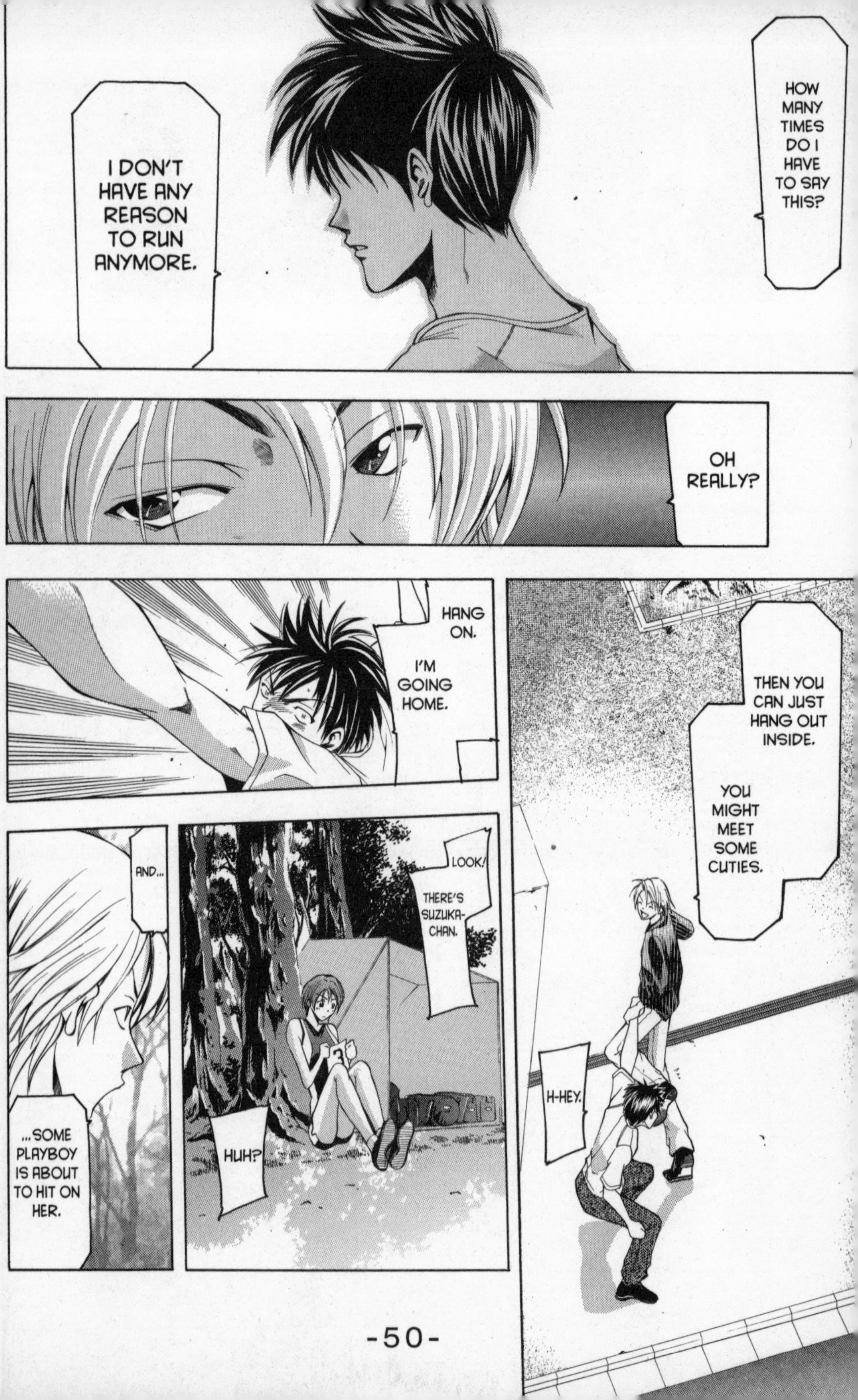
HOW MANY TIMES DO I HAVE TO SAY THIS?
I DON'T HAVE ANY REASON TO RUN ANYMORE.
OH REALLY?
THEN YOU CAN JUST HANG OUT INSIDE.
YOU MIGHT MEET SOME CUTIES.
H-HEY.
HANG ON.
I'M GOING HOME.
LOOK!
THERE'S SUZUKA-CHAN.
HUH?
AND...
...SOME PLAYBOY IS ABOUT TO HIT ON HER.

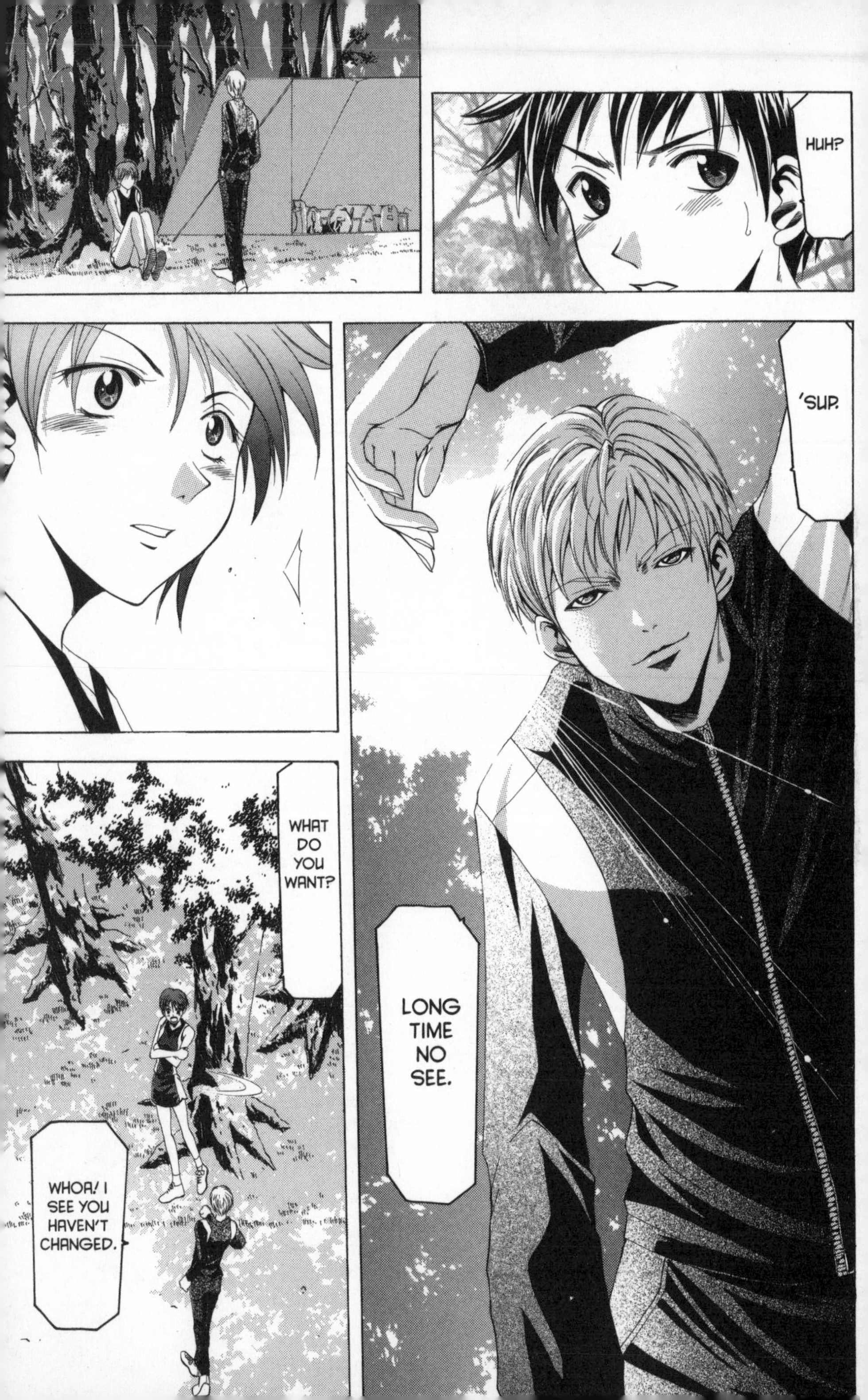
HUH?
'SUP.
LONG TIME NO SEE.
WHAT DO YOU WANT?
WHOA! I SEE YOU HAVEN'T CHANGED.

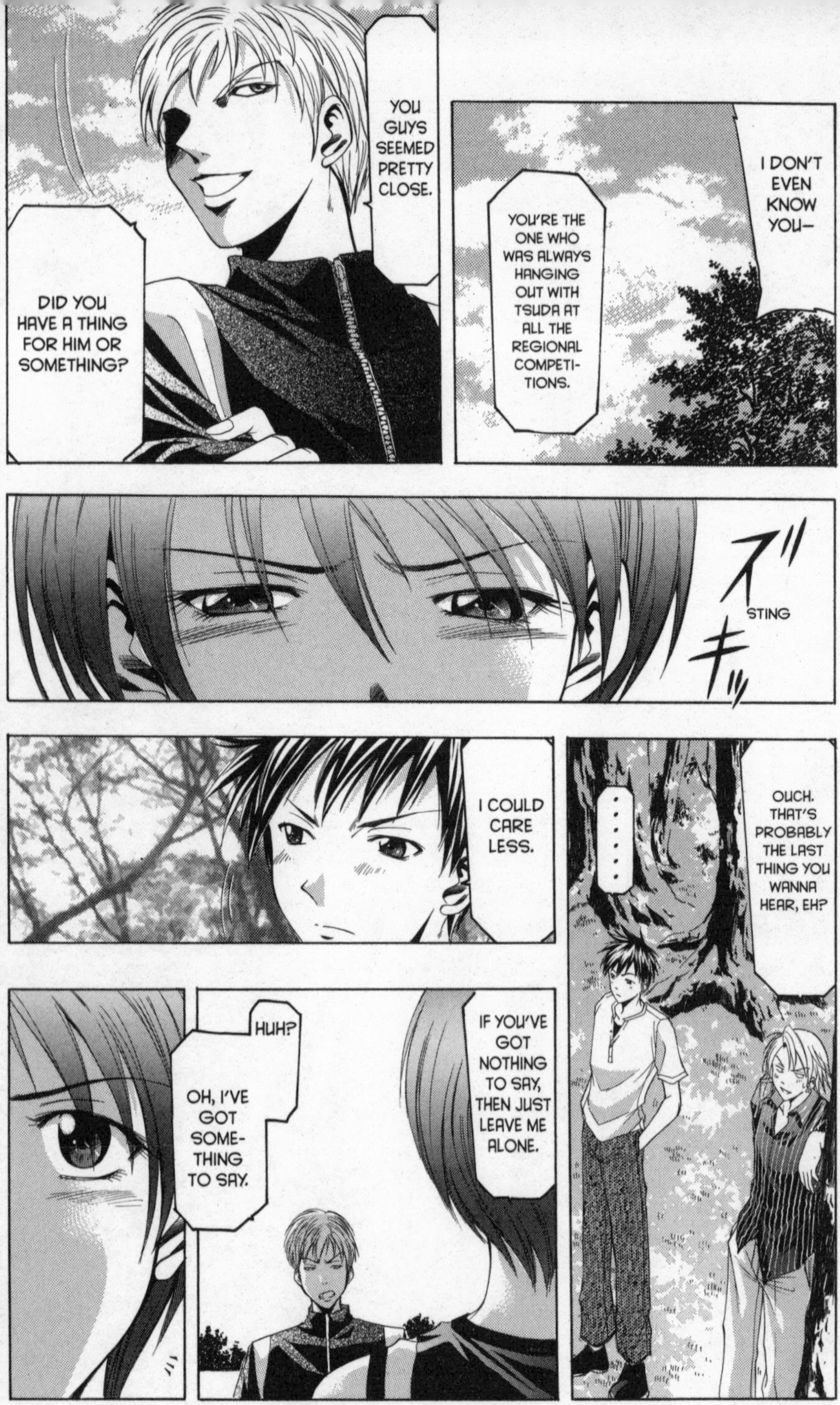
I DON'T EVEN KNOW YOU—
YOU'RE THE ONE WHO WAS ALWAYS HANGING OUT WITH TSUDA AT ALL THE REGIONAL COMPETITIONS.
YOU GUYS SEEMED PRETTY CLOSE.
DID YOU HAVE A THING FOR HIM OR SOMETHING?
ズキッ
STING
OUCH. THAT'S PROBABLY THE LAST THING YOU WANNA HEAR, EH?
......
I COULD CARE LESS.
IF YOU'VE GOT NOTHING TO SAY, THEN JUST LEAVE ME ALONE.
HUH?
OH, I'VE GOT SOME-THING TO SAY.

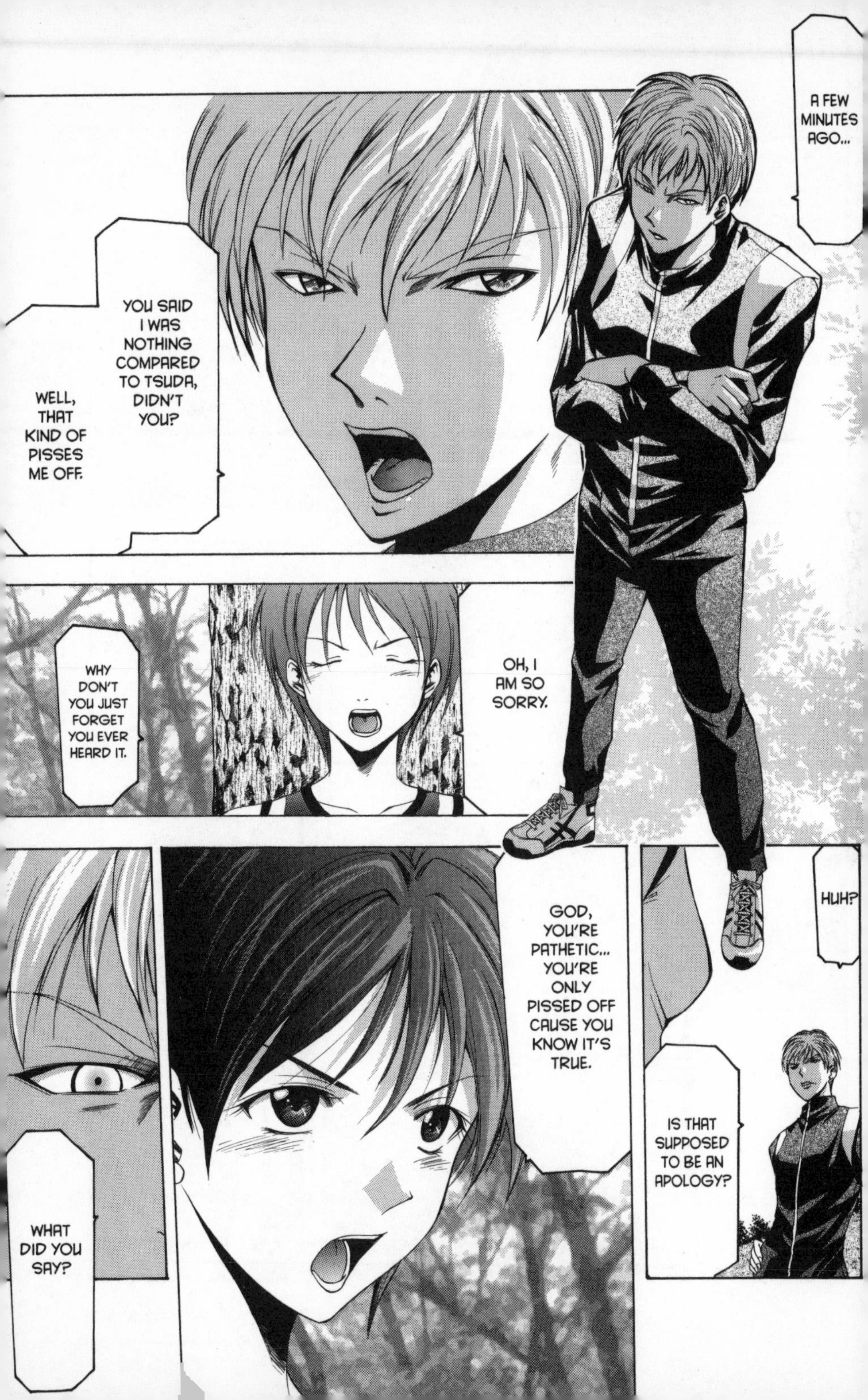
A FEW MINUTES AGO...
YOU SAID I WAS NOTHING COMPARED TO TSUDA, DIDN'T YOU?
WELL, THAT KIND OF PISSES ME OFF.
OH, I AM SO SORRY.
WHY DON'T YOU JUST FORGET YOU EVER HEARD IT.
HUH?
IS THAT SUPPOSED TO BE AN APOLOGY?
GOD, YOU'RE PATHETIC... YOU'RE ONLY PISSED OFF CAUSE YOU KNOW IT'S TRUE.
WHAT DID YOU SAY?

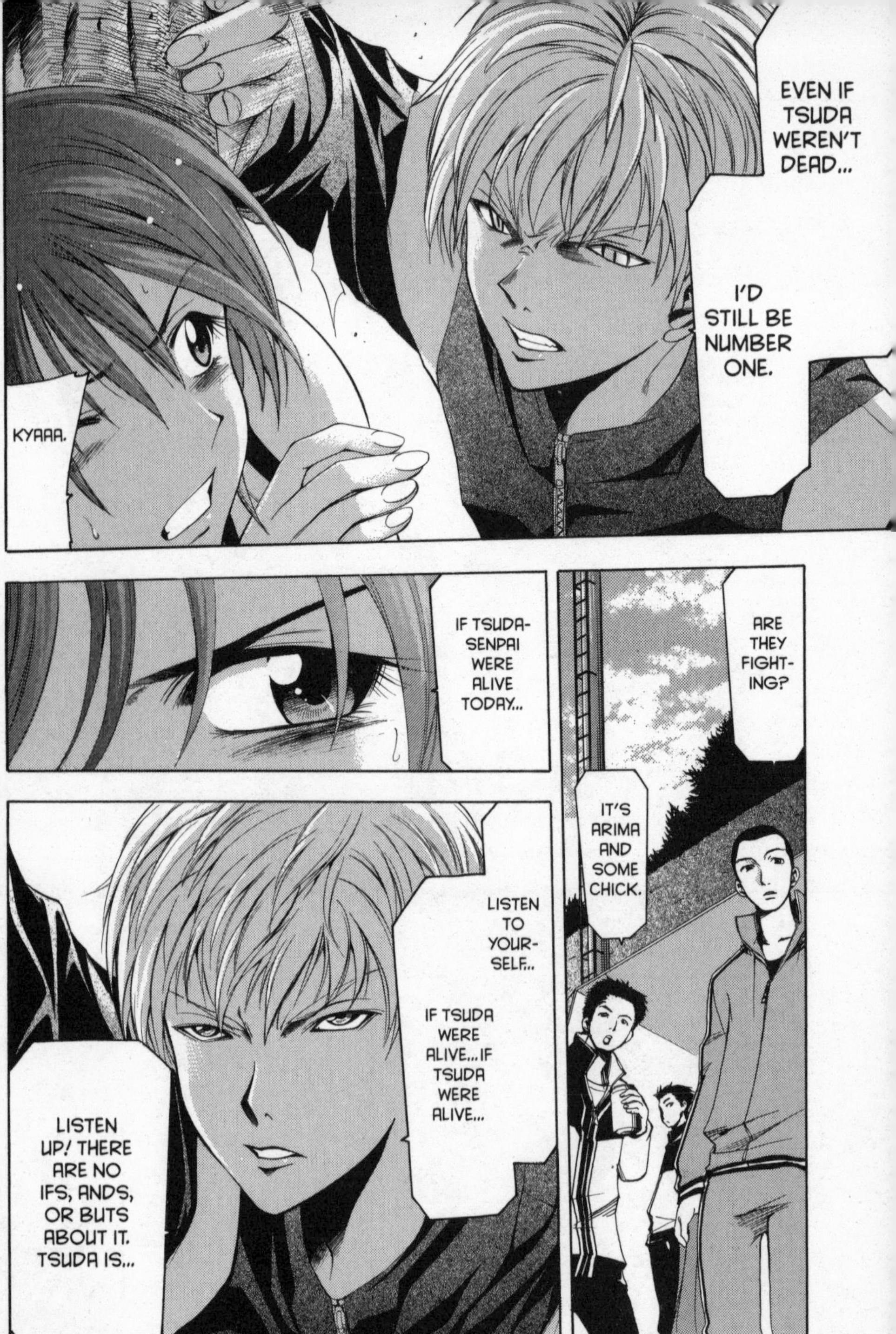
EVEN IF TSUDA WEREN'T DEAD...
I'D STILL BE NUMBER ONE.
KYAAA.
ARE THEY FIGHT-ING?
IT'S ARIMA AND SOME CHICK.
IF TSUDA-SENPAI WERE ALIVE TODAY...
LISTEN TO YOUR-SELF...
IF TSUDA WERE ALIVE...IF TSUDA WERE ALIVE...
LISTEN UP! THERE ARE NO IFS, ANDS, OR BUTS ABOUT IT. TSUDA IS...

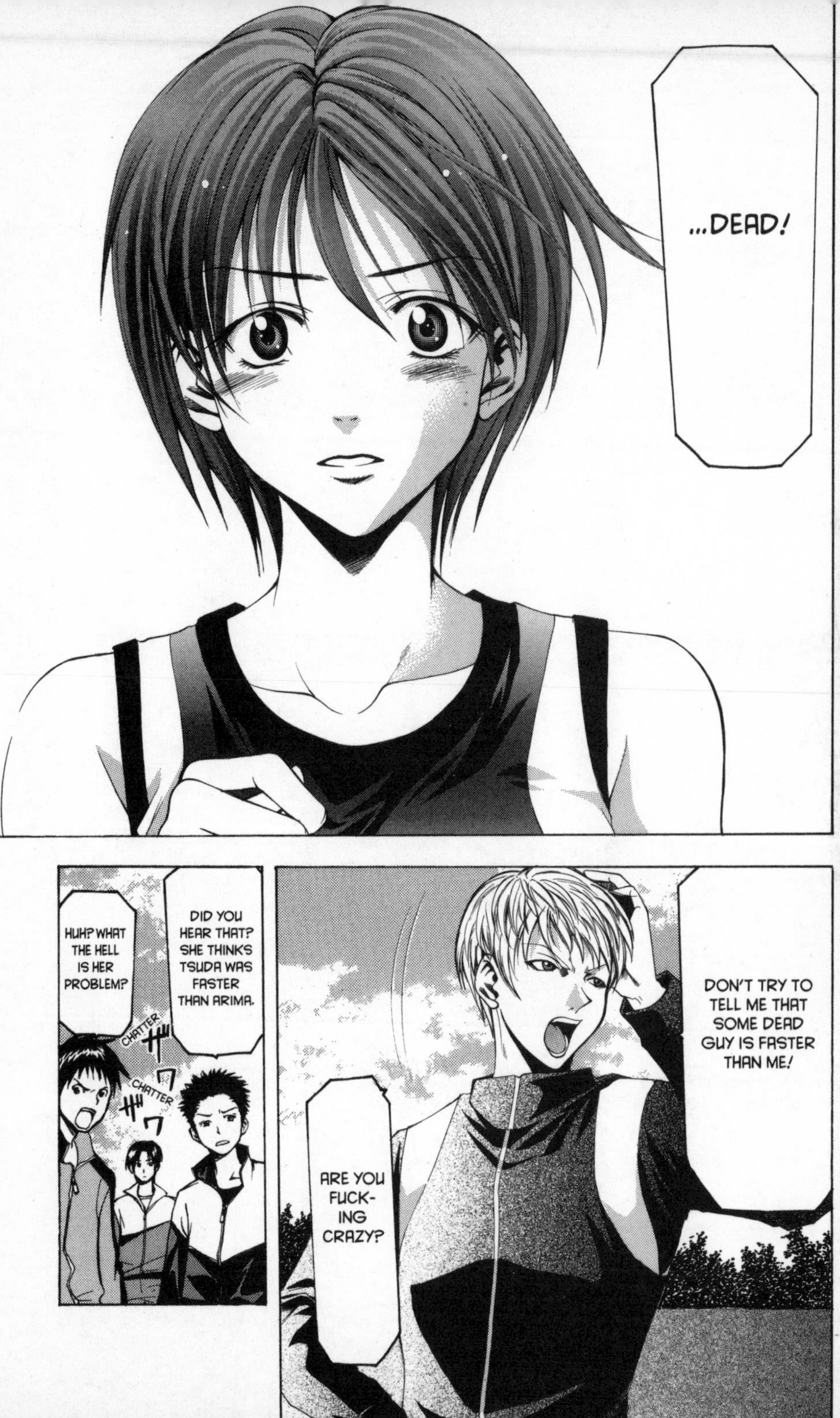
...DEAD!
DON'T TRY TO TELL ME THAT SOME DEAD GUY IS FASTER THAN ME!
ARE YOU FUCK-ING CRAZY?
DID YOU HEAR THAT? SHE THINKS TSUDA WAS FASTER THAN ARIMA.
HUH? WHAT THE HELL IS HER PROBLEM?
CHATTER
CHATTER

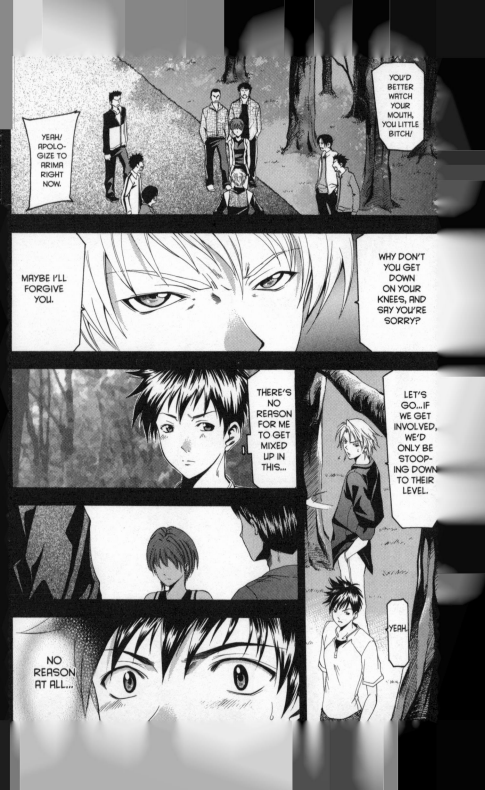

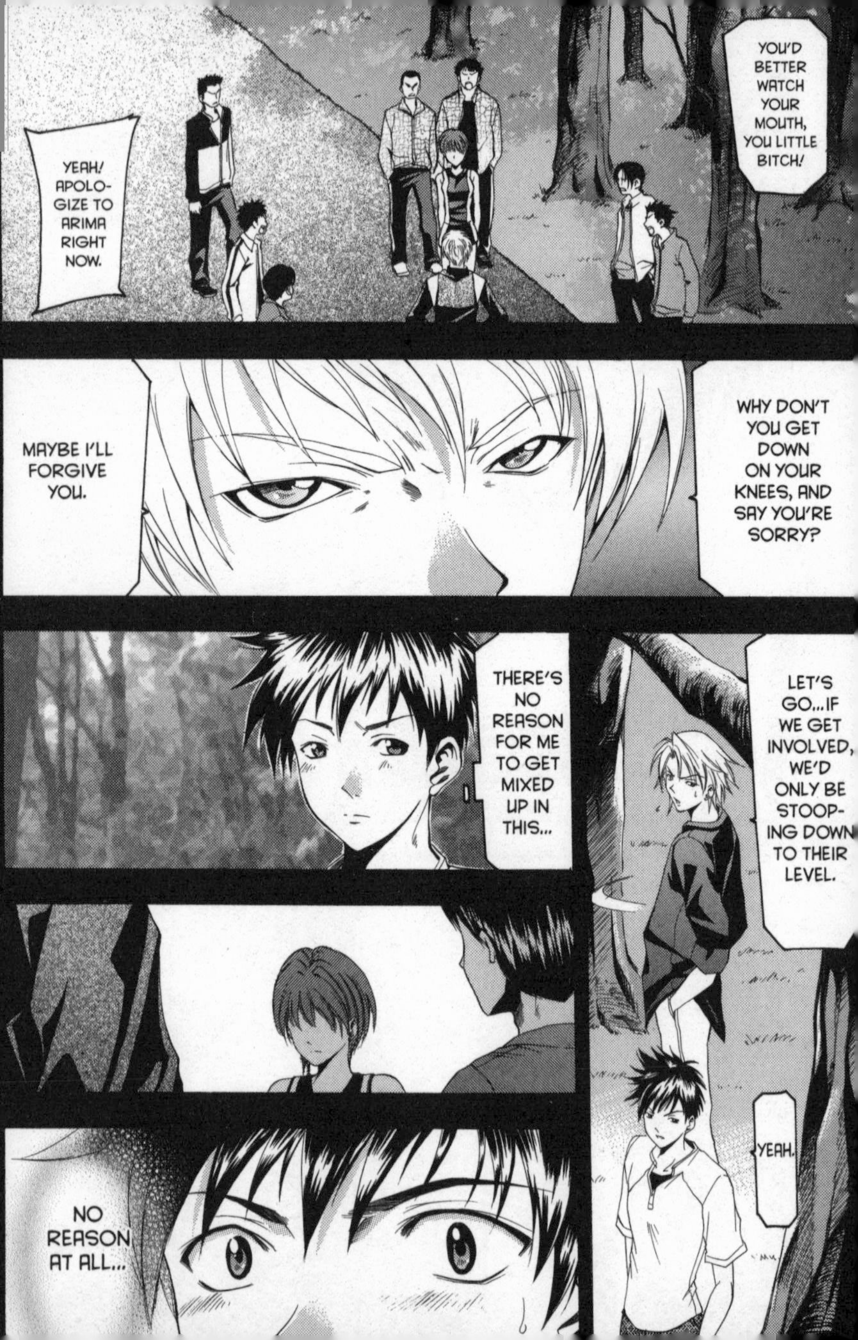
YOU'D BETTER WATCH YOUR MOUTH, YOU LITTLE BITCH!
YEAH! APOLOGIZE TO ARIMA RIGHT NOW.
WHY DON'T YOU GET DOWN ON YOUR KNEES, AND SAY YOU'RE SORRY?
MAYBE I'LL FORGIVE YOU.
LET'S GO...IF WE GET INVOLVED, WE'D ONLY BE STOOPING DOWN TO THEIR LEVEL.
YEAH.
THERE'S NO REASON FOR ME TO GET MIXED UP IN THIS...
NO REASON AT ALL...

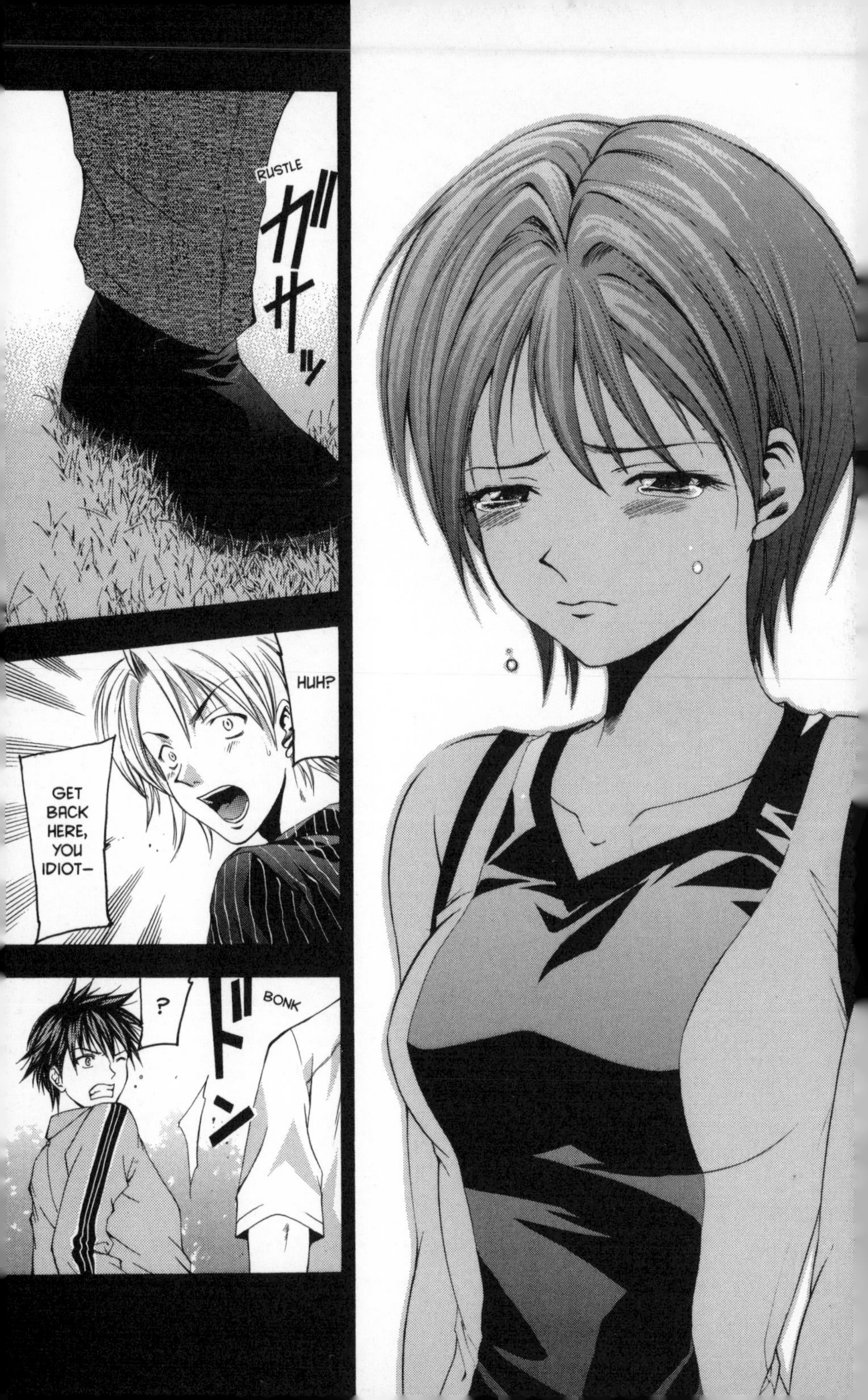
RUSTLE
ガサッ
HUH?
GET BACK HERE, YOU IDIOT—
BONK
ドン
?

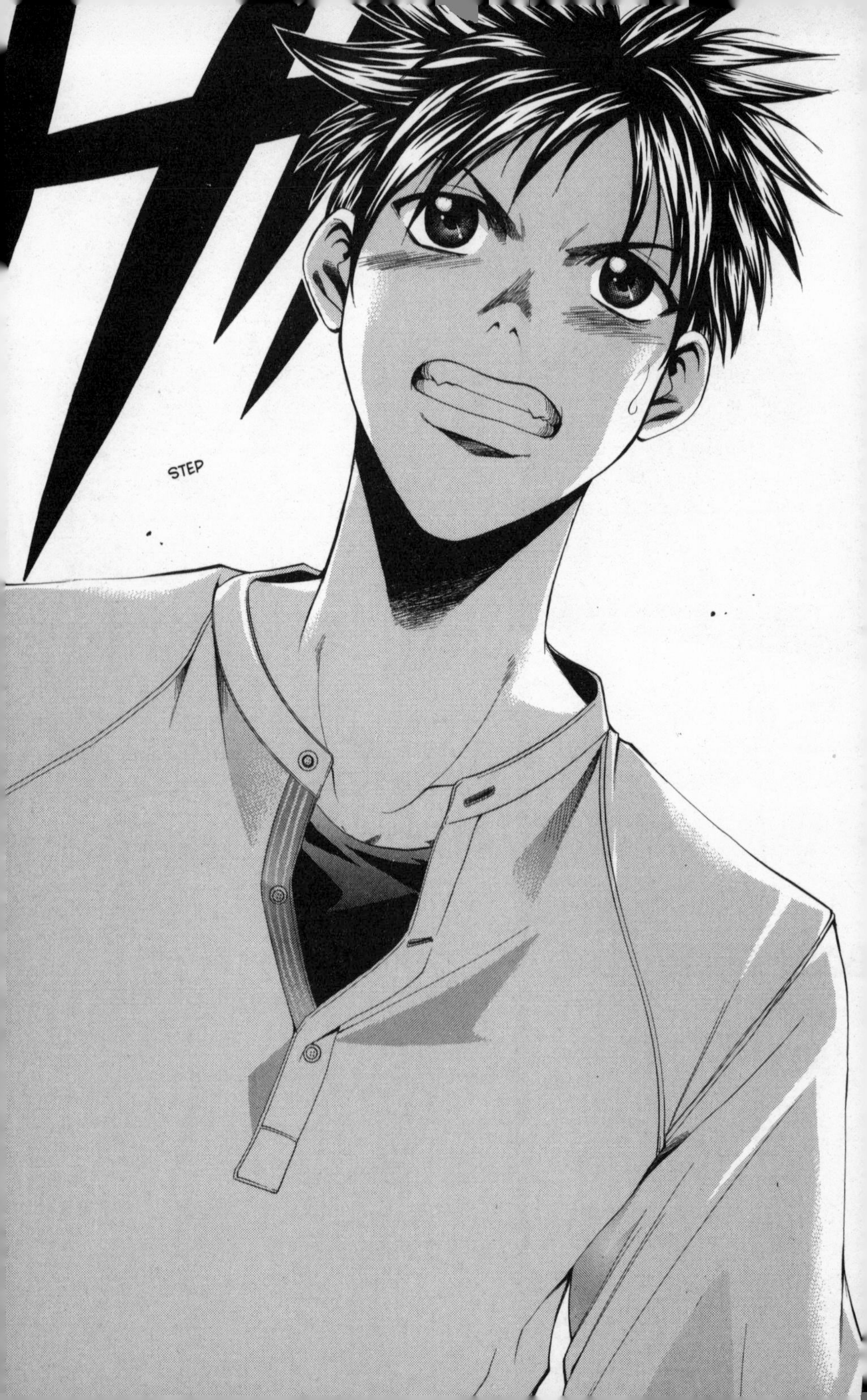
STEP

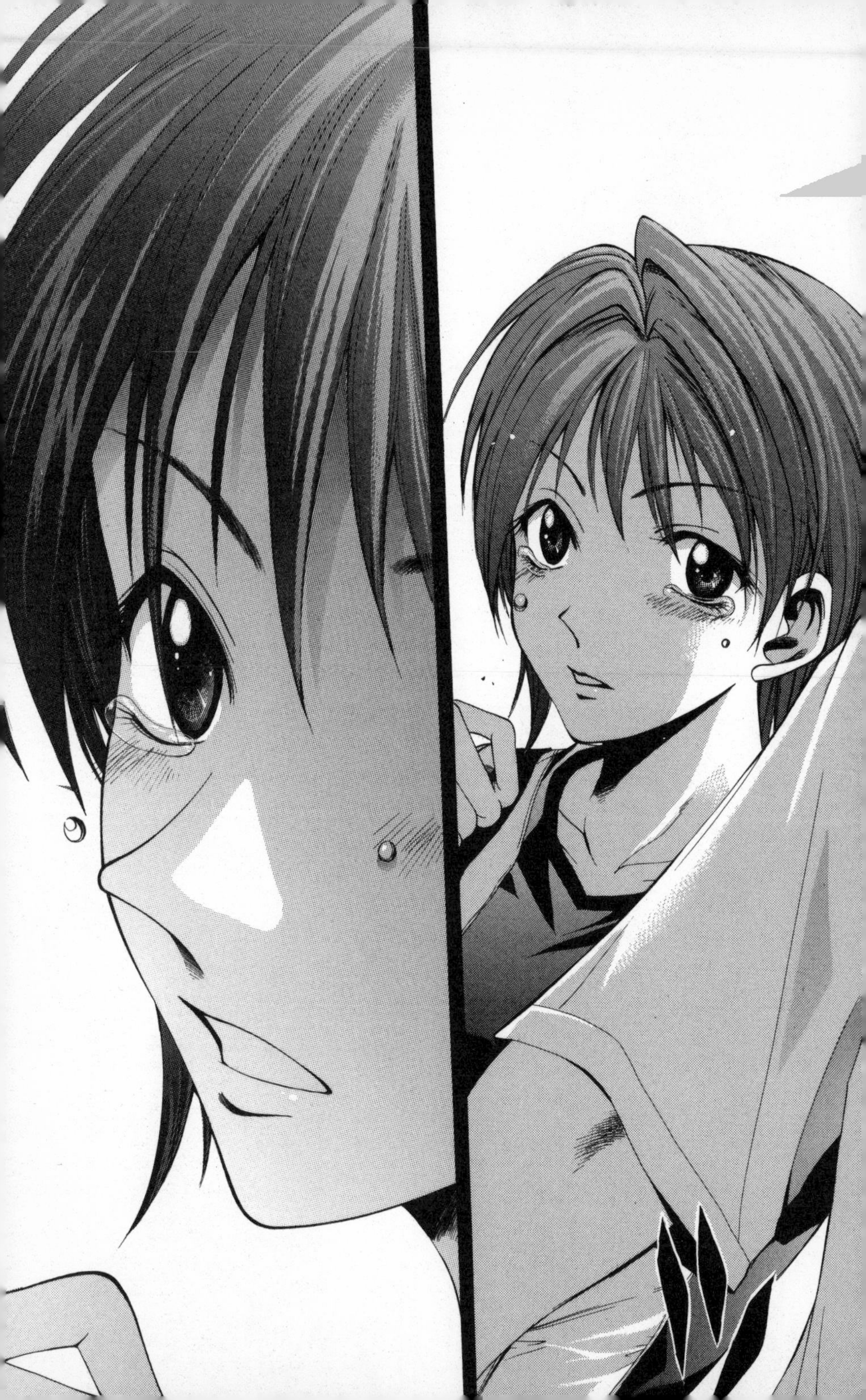

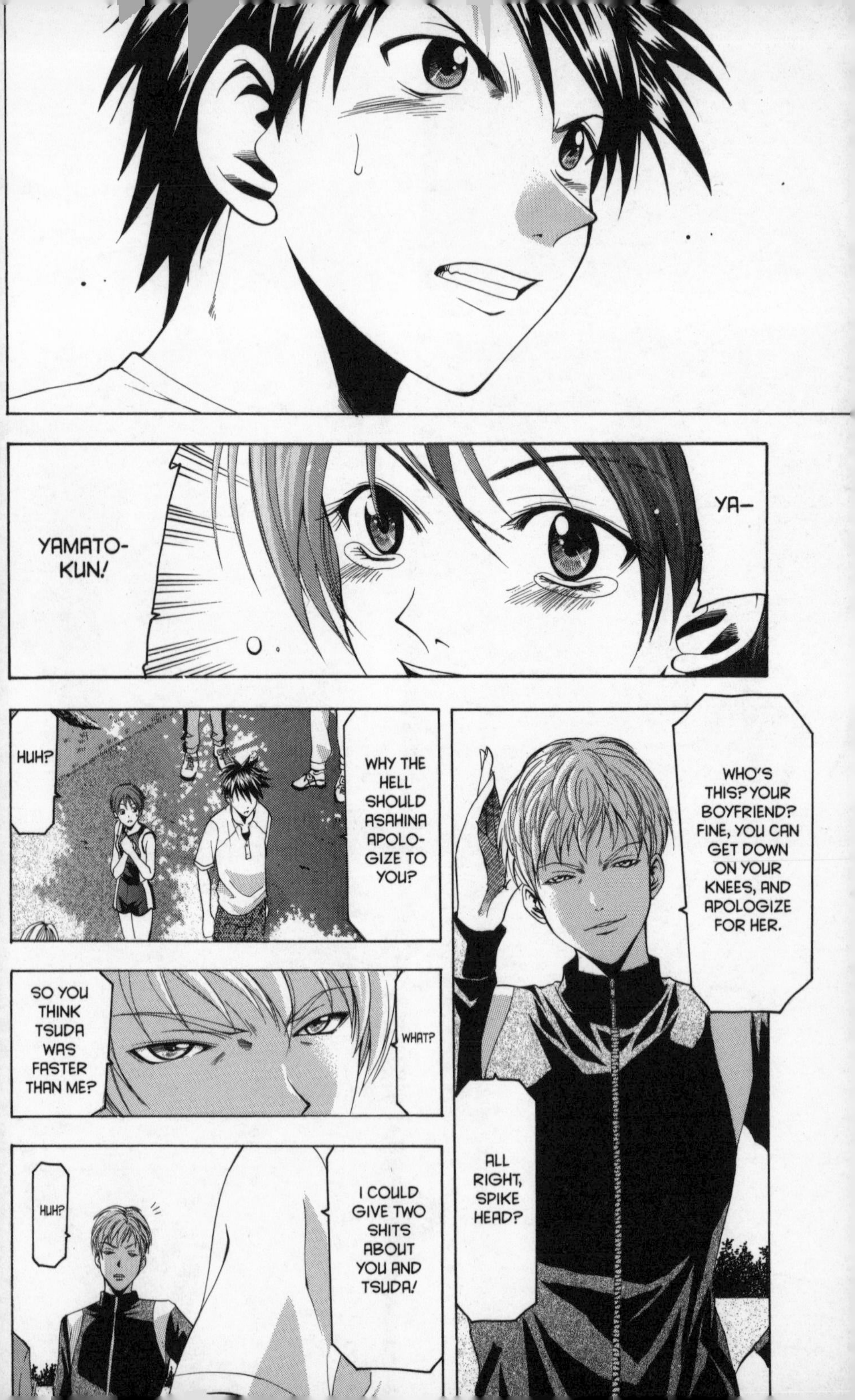
YA—
YAMATO-KUN!
WHO'S THIS? YOUR BOYFRIEND? FINE, YOU CAN GET DOWN ON YOUR KNEES, AND APOLOGIZE FOR HER.
ALL RIGHT, SPIKE HEAD?
WHY THE HELL SHOULD ASAHINA APOLOGIZE TO YOU?
HUH?
WHAT?
SO YOU THINK TSUDA WAS FASTER THAN ME?
I COULD GIVE TWO SHITS ABOUT YOU AND TSUDA!
HUH?

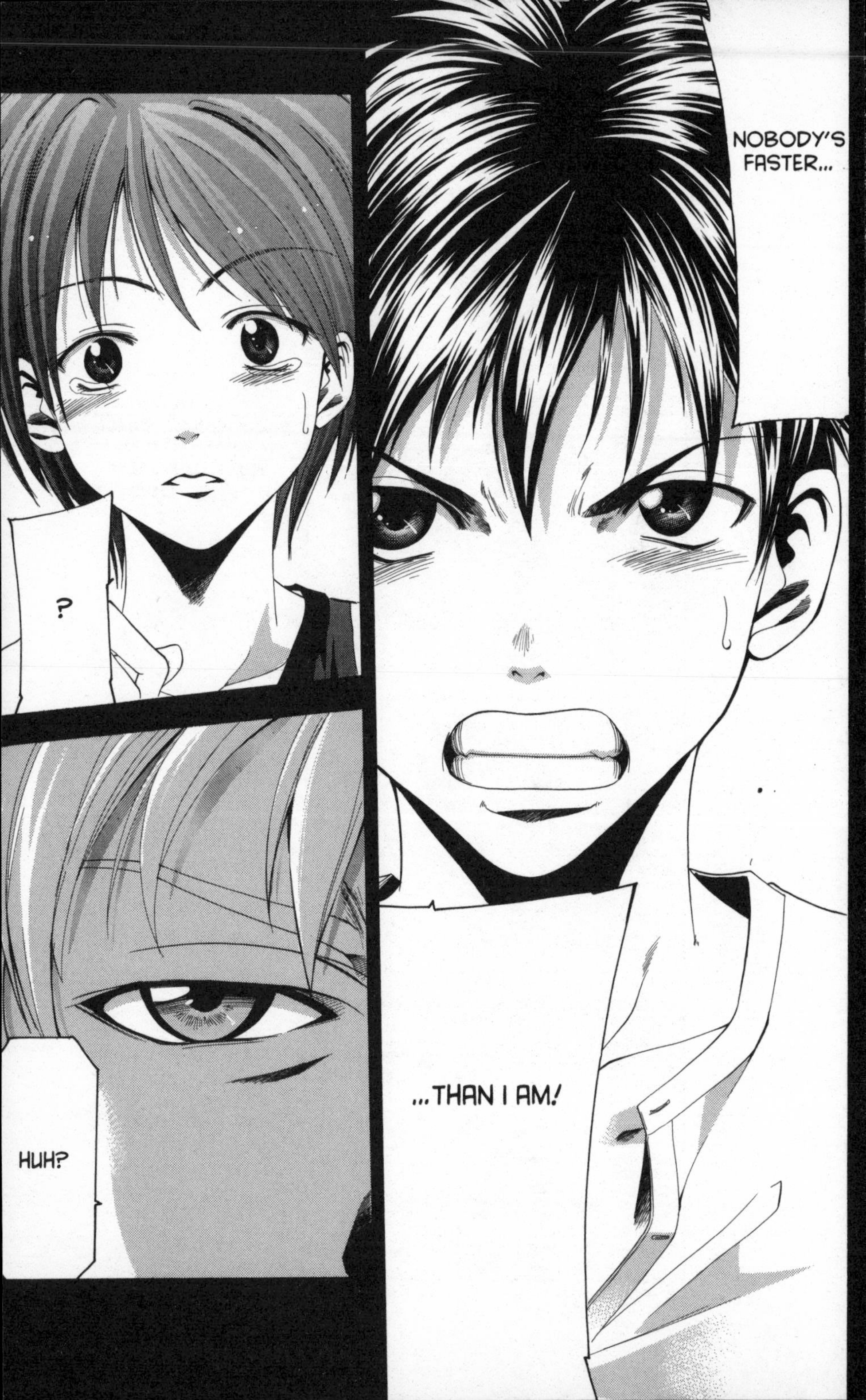
NOBODY'S FASTER...
...THAN I AM!
?
HUH?

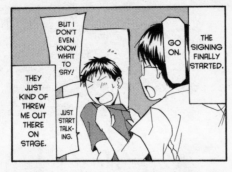

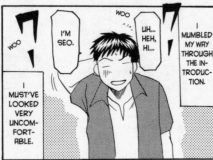

SUZUKA FOUR-PANEL THEATER NUMBER FIFTEEN

SEO GOES TO A SIGNING - PART 3

THE SIGNING FINALLY STARTED.
GO ON.
BUT I DON'T EVEN KNOW WHAT TO SAY!
JUST START TALKING.
THEY JUST KIND OF THREW ME OUT THERE ON STAGE.
I MUMBLED MY WAY THROUGH THE INTRODUCTION.
UH... HEH, HI...
WOO
I'M SEO.
WOO
I MUST'VE LOOKED VERY UNCOMFORTABLE.
THEN I JUST SAT DOWN AND...
SCRIBBLE
カタ
カタ
カタ
SCRIBBLE
...STARTED SIGNING AUTOGRAPH AFTER AUTOGRAPH LIKE SOME KIND OF MACHINE.
I GOT THROUGH A ONE HOUR SIGNING...
YOU COULD'VE AT LEAST TALKED TO THE FANS A LITTLE, SEO-SAN.
AFTER THE EVENT
NOW YOU TELL ME.
...IN JUST FIFTEEN MINUTES.

※ *SORRY IF I DIDN'T SEEM VERY INTO IT. I WAS JUST NERVOUS.

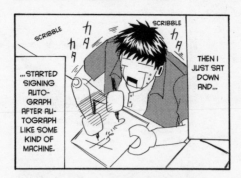

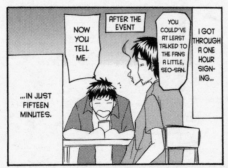

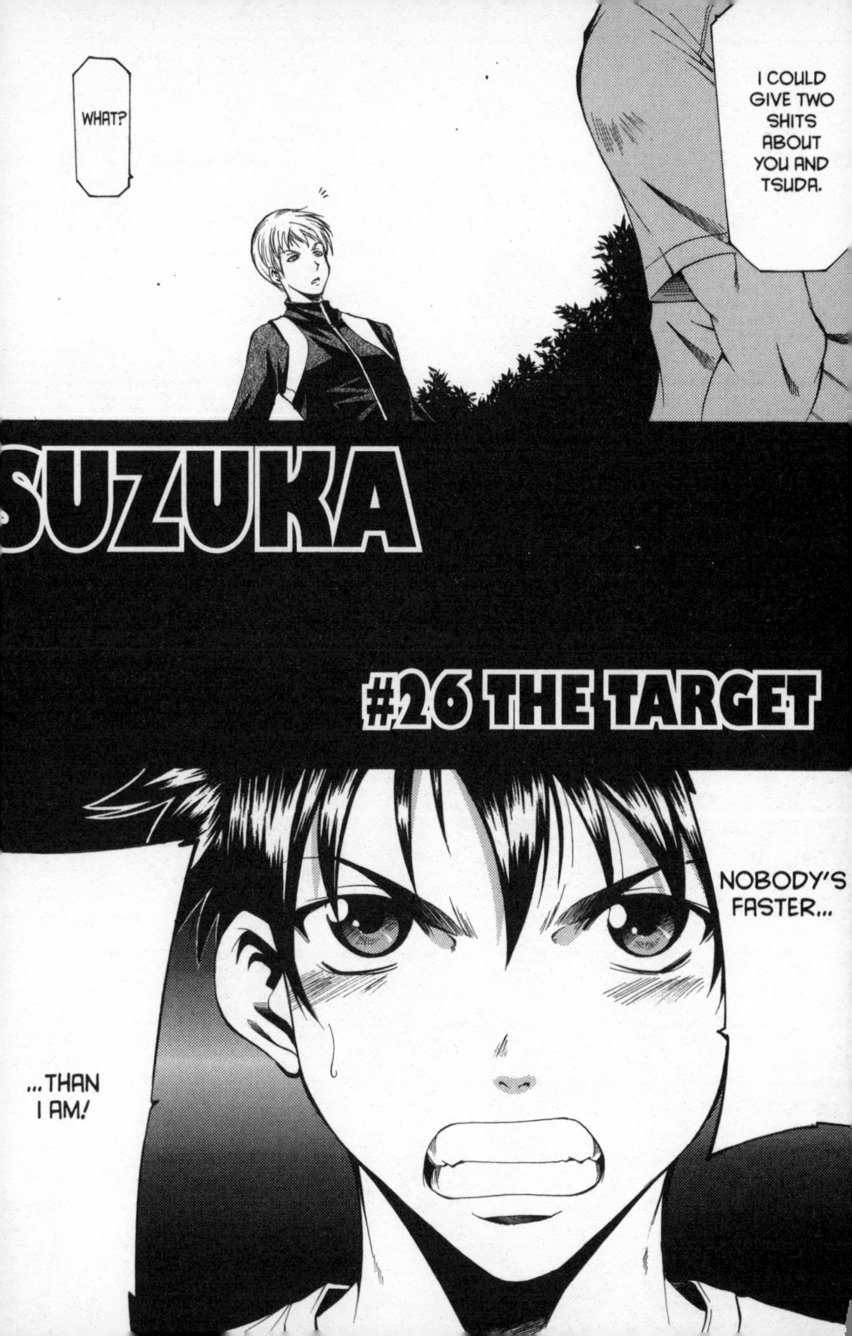
I COULD GIVE TWO SHITS ABOUT YOU AND TSUDA.
WHAT?
SUZUKA
#26 THE TARGET
NOBODY'S FASTER...
...THAN I AM!

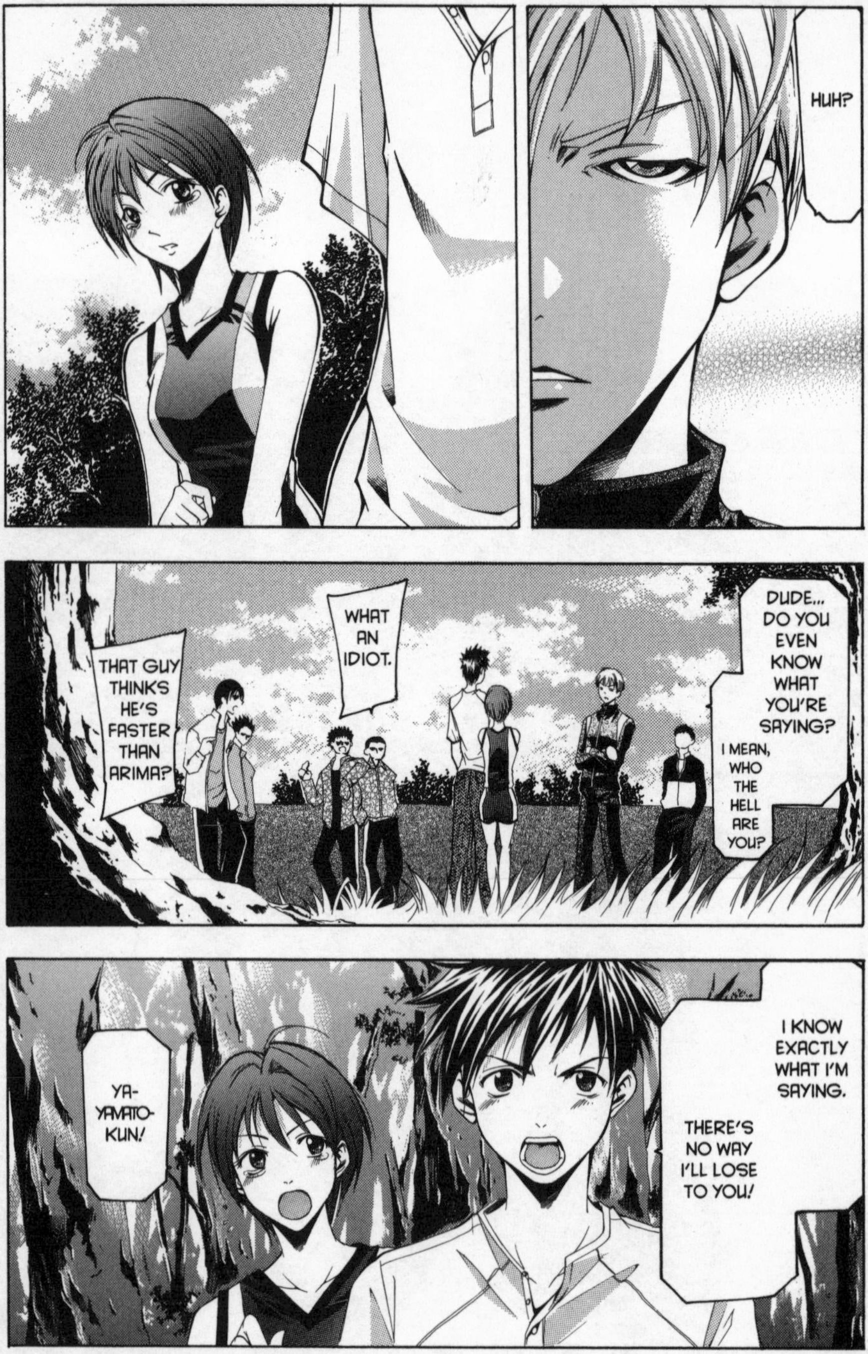
HUH?
DUDE... DO YOU EVEN KNOW WHAT YOU'RE SAYING?
I MEAN, WHO THE HELL ARE YOU?
WHAT AN IDIOT.
THAT GUY THINKS HE'S FASTER THAN ARIMA?
I KNOW EXACTLY WHAT I'M SAYING.
THERE'S NO WAY I'LL LOSE TO YOU!
YA-YAMATO-KUN!

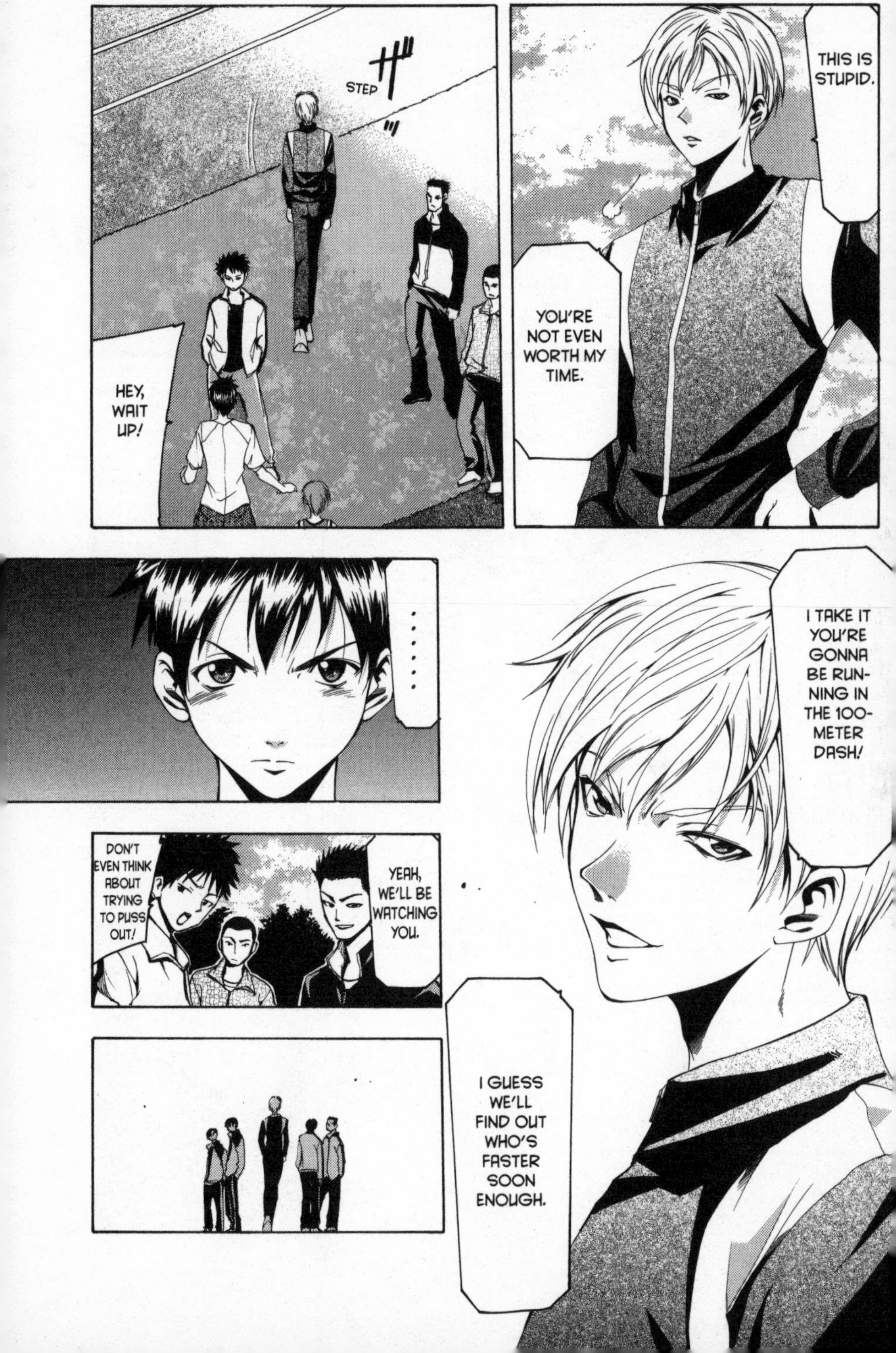
THIS IS STUPID.
YOU'RE NOT EVEN WORTH MY TIME.
STEP
HEY, WAIT UP!
I TAKE IT YOU'RE GONNA BE RUN-NING IN THE 100-METER DASH!
I GUESS WE'LL FIND OUT WHO'S FASTER SOON ENOUGH.
......
YEAH, WE'LL BE WATCHING YOU.
DON'T EVEN THINK ABOUT TRYING TO PUSS OUT!

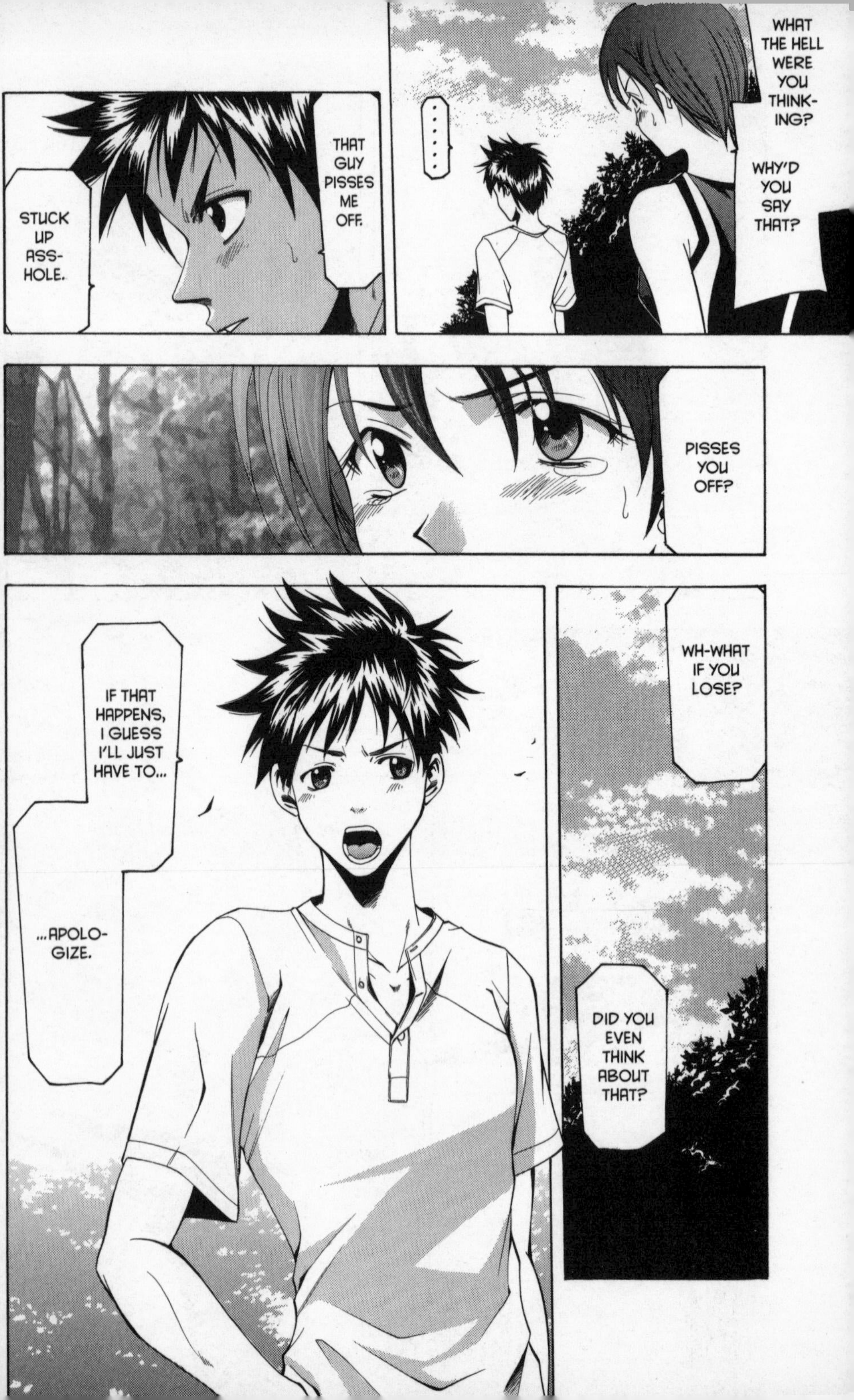
WHAT THE HELL WERE YOU THINKING?
WHY'D YOU SAY THAT?
......
THAT GUY PISSES ME OFF.
STUCK UP ASSHOLE.
PISSES YOU OFF?
WH-WHAT IF YOU LOSE?
DID YOU EVEN THINK ABOUT THAT?
IF THAT HAPPENS, I GUESS I'LL JUST HAVE TO...
...APOLOGIZE.

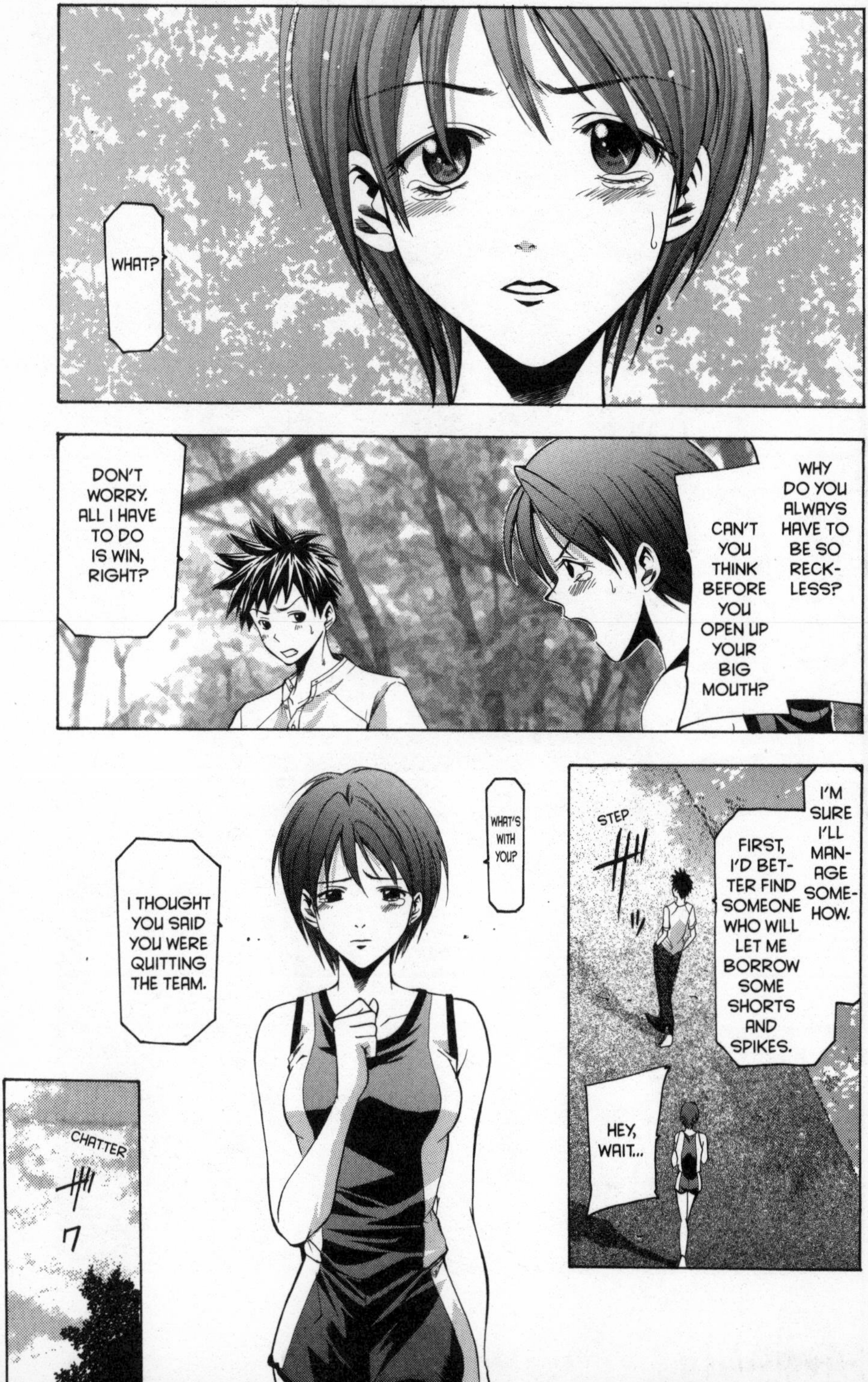
WHAT?
WHY DO YOU ALWAYS HAVE TO BE SO RECK-LESS?
CAN'T YOU THINK BEFORE YOU OPEN UP YOUR BIG MOUTH?
DON'T WORRY. ALL I HAVE TO DO IS WIN, RIGHT?
I'M SURE I'LL MAN-AGE SOME-HOW.
FIRST, I'D BET-TER FIND SOMEONE WHO WILL LET ME BORROW SOME SHORTS AND SPIKES.
STEP
HEY, WAIT...
WHAT'S WITH YOU?
I THOUGHT YOU SAID YOU WERE QUITTING THE TEAM.
CHATTER

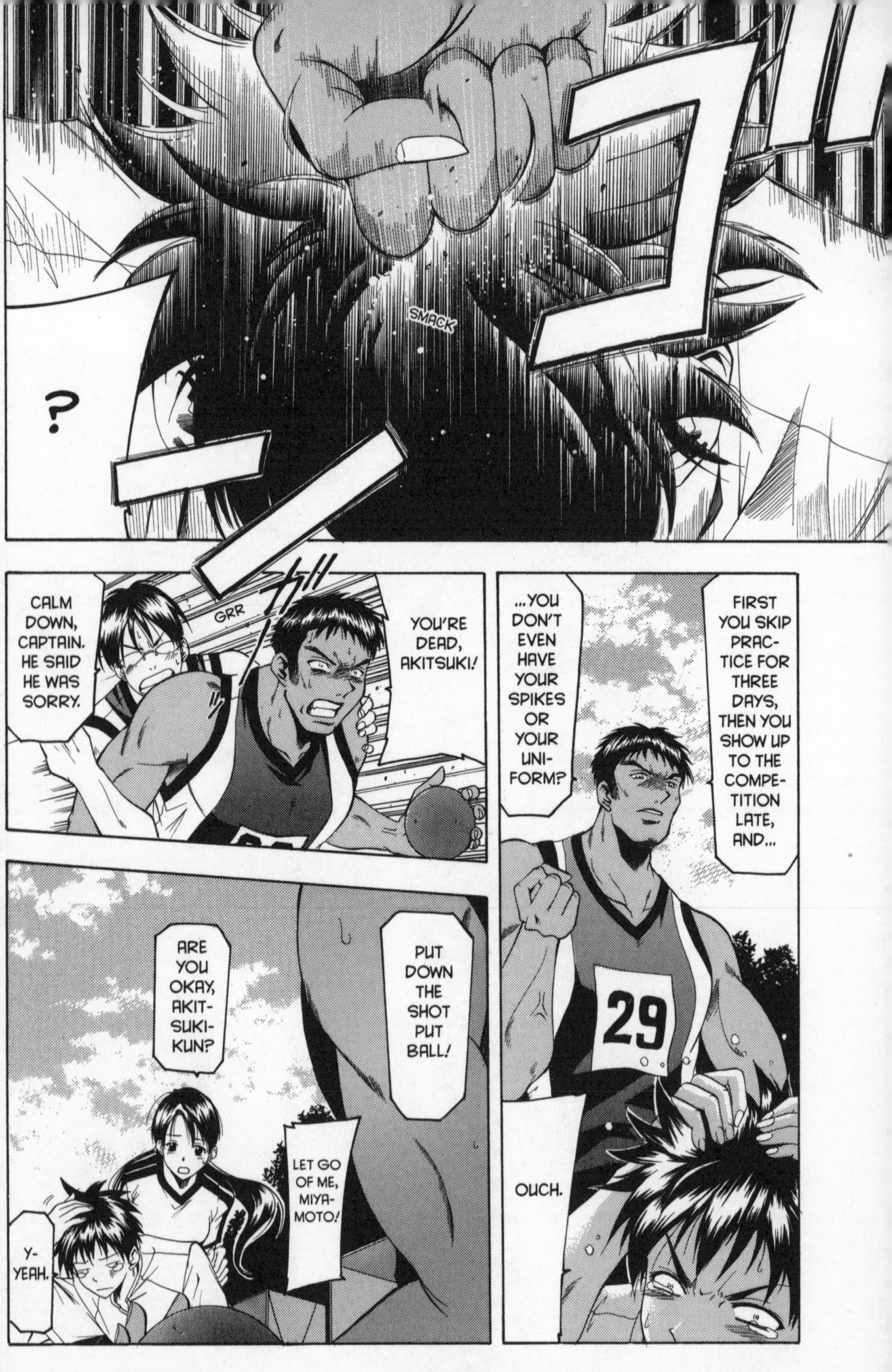
?
SMACK
FIRST YOU SKIP PRACTICE FOR THREE DAYS, THEN YOU SHOW UP TO THE COMPETITION LATE, AND...
...YOU DON'T EVEN HAVE YOUR SPIKES OR YOUR UNIFORM?
29
OUCH.
YOU'RE DEAD, AKITSUKI!
GRR
CALM DOWN, CAPTAIN. HE SAID HE WAS SORRY.
PUT DOWN THE SHOT PUT BALL!
ARE YOU OKAY, AKITSUKI-KUN?
LET GO OF ME, MIYAMOTO!
Y-YEAH.

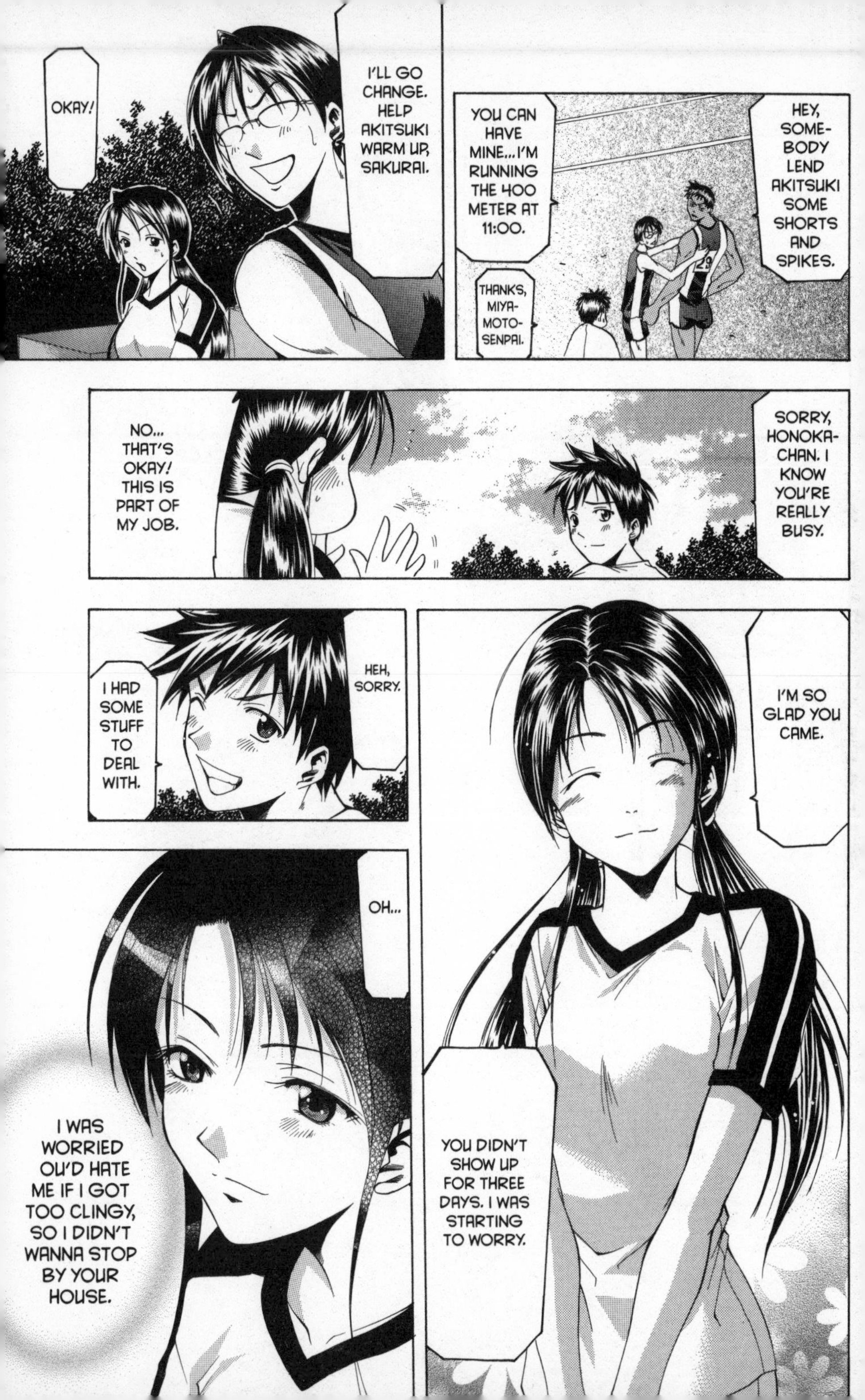
HEY, SOMEBODY LEND AKITSUKI SOME SHORTS AND SPIKES.
YOU CAN HAVE MINE...I'M RUNNING THE 400 METER AT 11:00.
THANKS, MIYA-MOTO-SENPAI.
I'LL GO CHANGE. HELP AKITSUKI WARM UP, SAKURAI.
OKAY!
SORRY, HONOKA-CHAN. I KNOW YOU'RE REALLY BUSY.
NO... THAT'S OKAY! THIS IS PART OF MY JOB.
I'M SO GLAD YOU CAME.
YOU DIDN'T SHOW UP FOR THREE DAYS. I WAS STARTING TO WORRY.
HEH, SORRY.
I HAD SOME STUFF TO DEAL WITH.
OH...
I WAS WORRIED OU'D HATE ME IF I GOT TOO CLINGY, SO I DIDN'T WANNA STOP BY YOUR HOUSE.

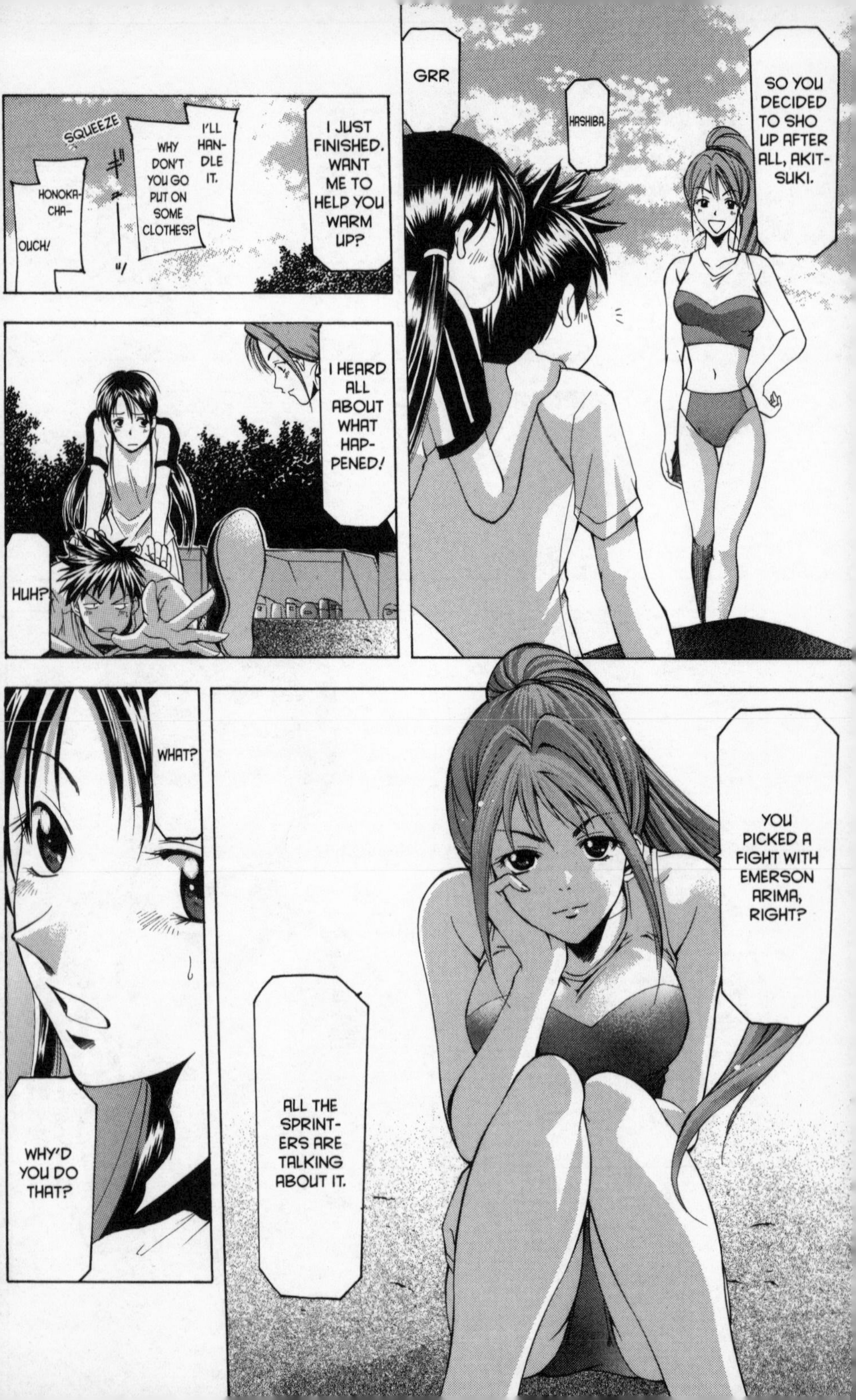
SO YOU DECIDED TO SHO UP AFTER ALL, AKIT-SUKI.
HASHIBA.
GRR
I JUST FINISHED. WANT ME TO HELP YOU WARM UP?
I'LL HAN-DLE IT.
WHY DON'T YOU GO PUT ON SOME CLOTHES?
SQUEEZE
HONOKA-CHA-
OUCH!
I HEARD ALL ABOUT WHAT HAP-PENED!
HUH?
YOU PICKED A FIGHT WITH EMERSON ARIMA, RIGHT?
ALL THE SPRINT-ERS ARE TALKING ABOUT IT.
WHAT?
WHY'D YOU DO THAT?

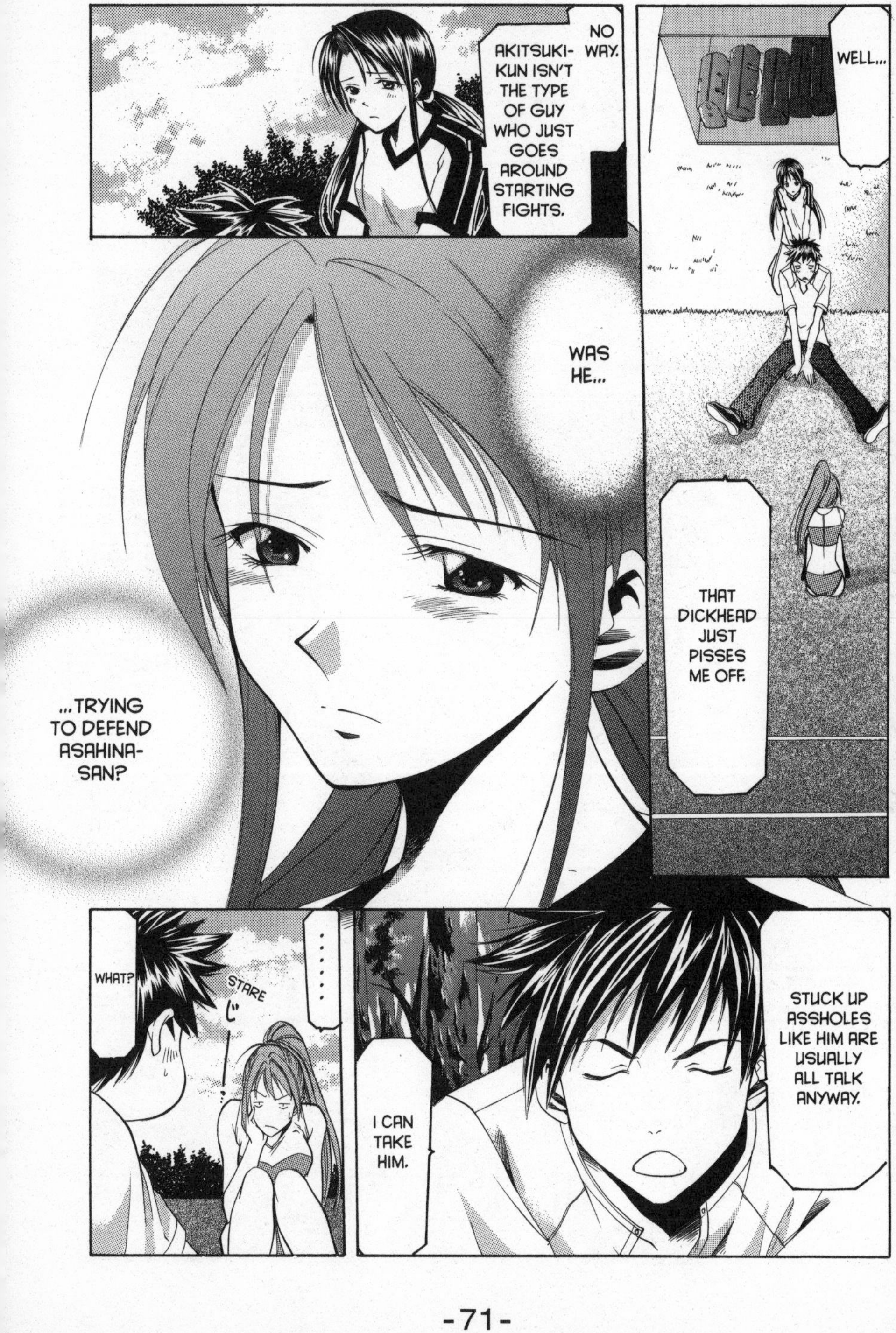
WELL...
THAT DICKHEAD JUST PISSES ME OFF.
NO WAY. AKITSUKI-KUN ISN'T THE TYPE OF GUY WHO JUST GOES AROUND STARTING FIGHTS.
WAS HE...
...TRYING TO DEFEND ASAHINA-SAN?
STUCK UP ASSHOLES LIKE HIM ARE USUALLY ALL TALK ANYWAY.
I CAN TAKE HIM.
......
STARE
WHAT?

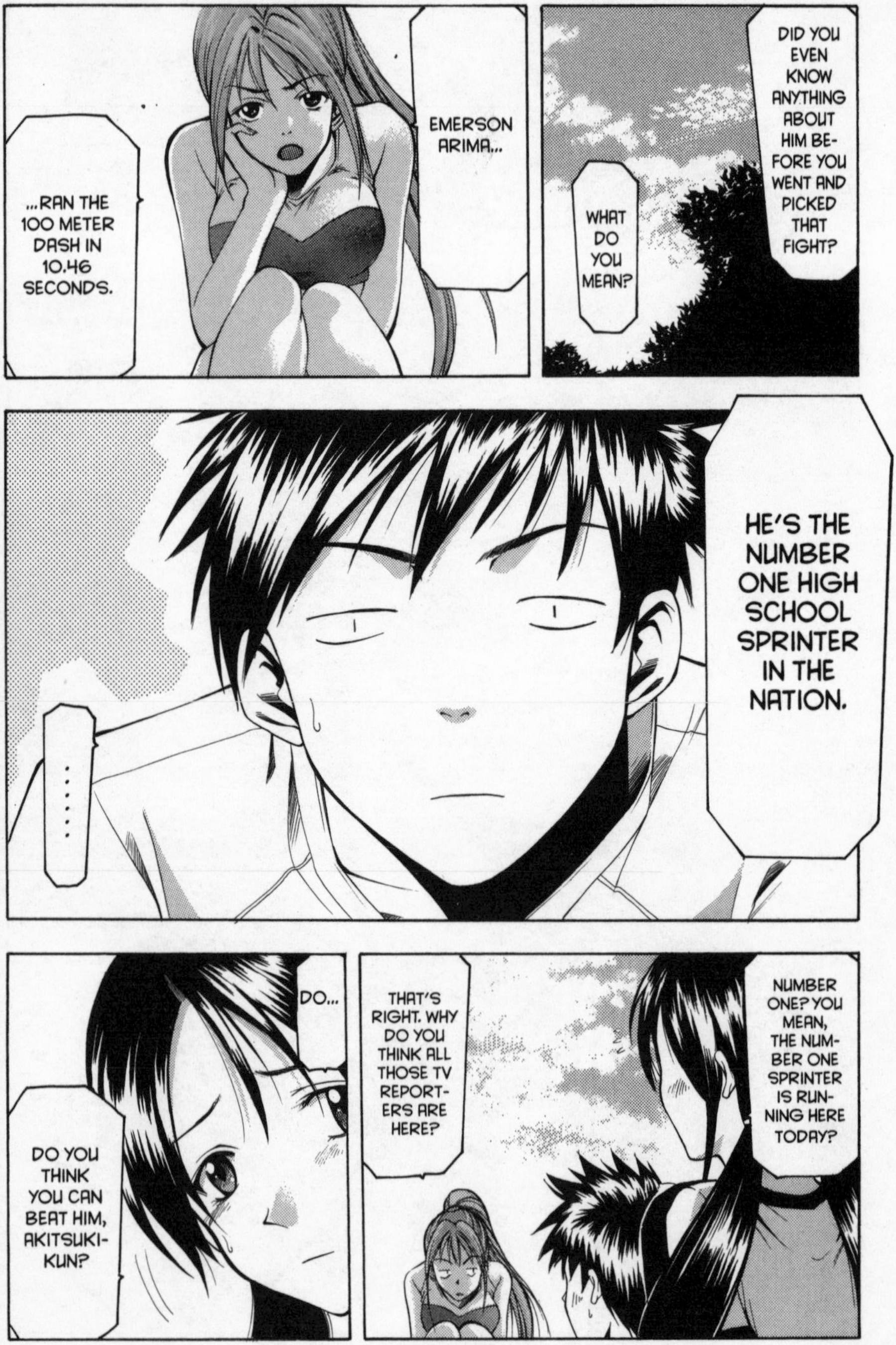
DID YOU EVEN KNOW ANYTHING ABOUT HIM BEFORE YOU WENT AND PICKED THAT FIGHT?
WHAT DO YOU MEAN?
EMERSON ARIMA...
...RAN THE 100 METER DASH IN 10.46 SECONDS.
HE'S THE NUMBER ONE HIGH SCHOOL SPRINTER IN THE NATION.
......
NUMBER ONE? YOU MEAN, THE NUMBER ONE SPRINTER IS RUNNING HERE TODAY?
THAT'S RIGHT. WHY DO YOU THINK ALL THOSE TV REPORTERS ARE HERE?
DO...
DO YOU THINK YOU CAN BEAT HIM, AKITSUKI-KUN?

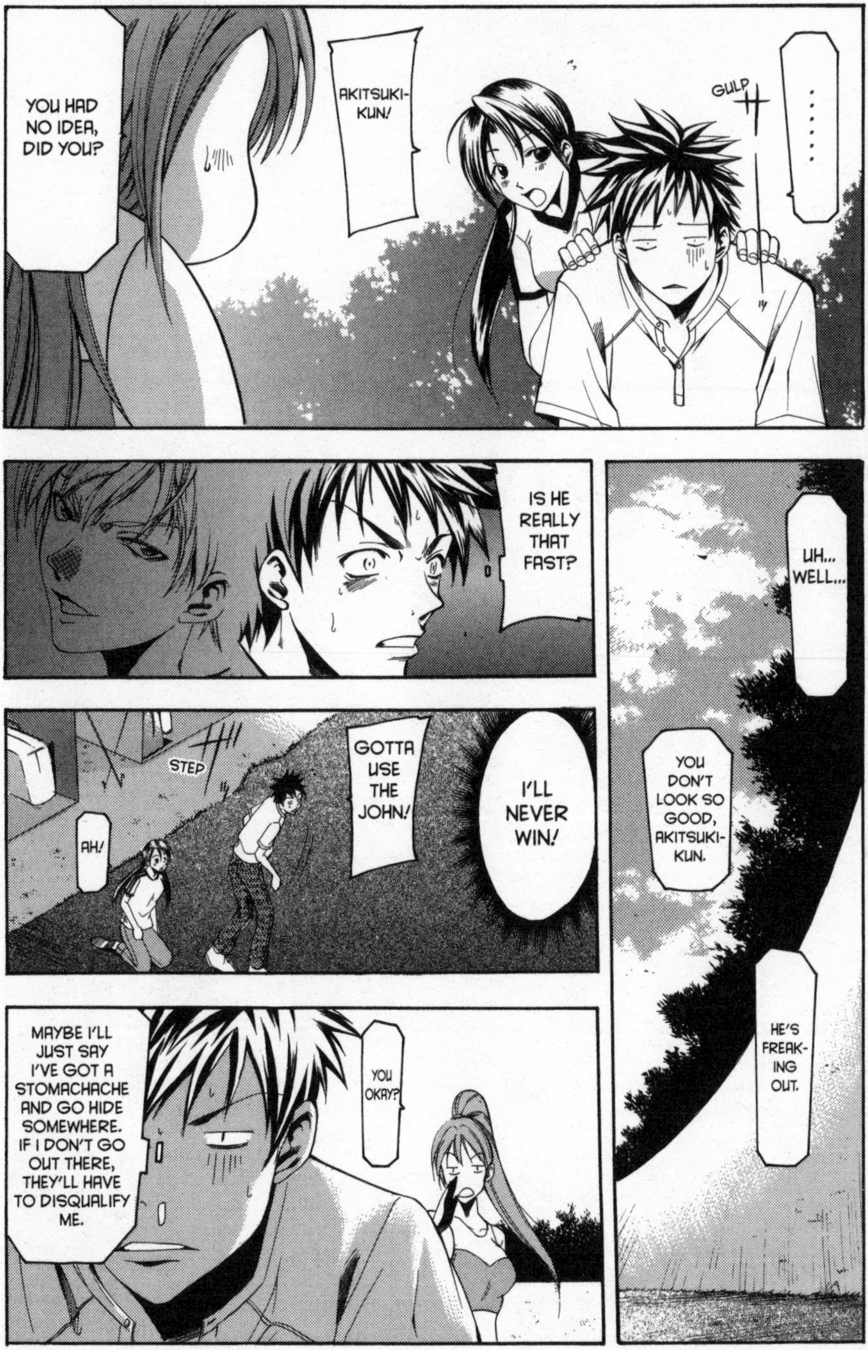
......
GULP
AKITSUKI-KUN!
YOU HAD NO IDEA, DID YOU?
UH... WELL...
YOU DON'T LOOK SO GOOD, AKITSUKI-KUN.
HE'S FREAKING OUT.
IS HE REALLY THAT FAST?
I'LL NEVER WIN!
GOTTA USE THE JOHN!
STEP
AH!
YOU OKAY?
MAYBE I'LL JUST SAY I'VE GOT A STOMACHACHE AND GO HIDE SOMEWHERE. IF I DON'T GO OUT THERE, THEY'LL HAVE TO DISQUALIFY ME.

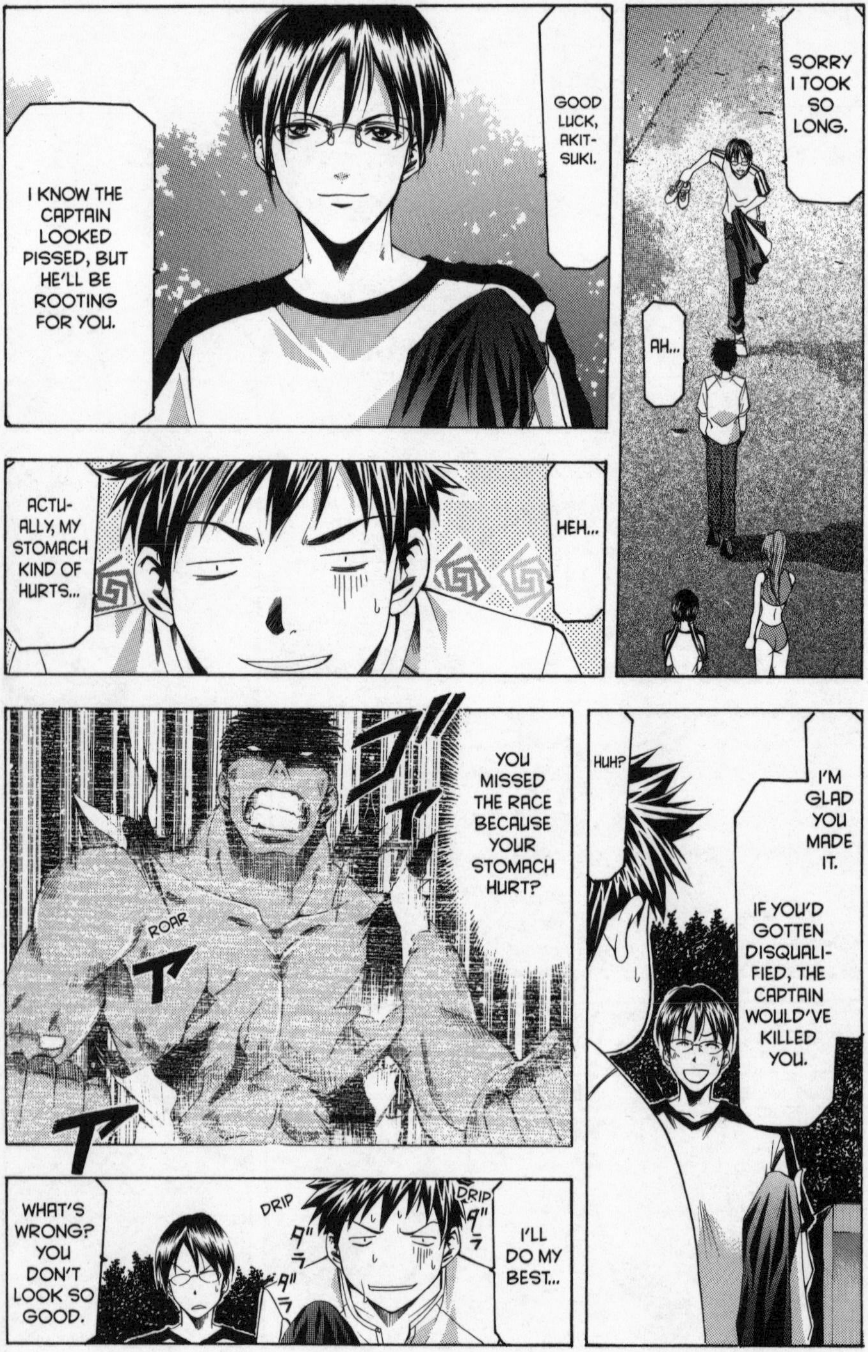
SORRY I TOOK SO LONG.
AH...
GOOD LUCK, AKIT-SUKI.
I KNOW THE CAPTAIN LOOKED PISSED, BUT HE'LL BE ROOTING FOR YOU.
HEH...
ACTU-ALLY, MY STOMACH KIND OF HURTS...
I'M GLAD YOU MADE IT.
HUH?
IF YOU'D GOTTEN DISQUALI-FIED, THE CAPTAIN WOULD'VE KILLED YOU.
YOU MISSED THE RACE BECAUSE YOUR STOMACH HURT?
ROAR
DRIP
DRIP
I'LL DO MY BEST...
WHAT'S WRONG? YOU DON'T LOOK SO GOOD.

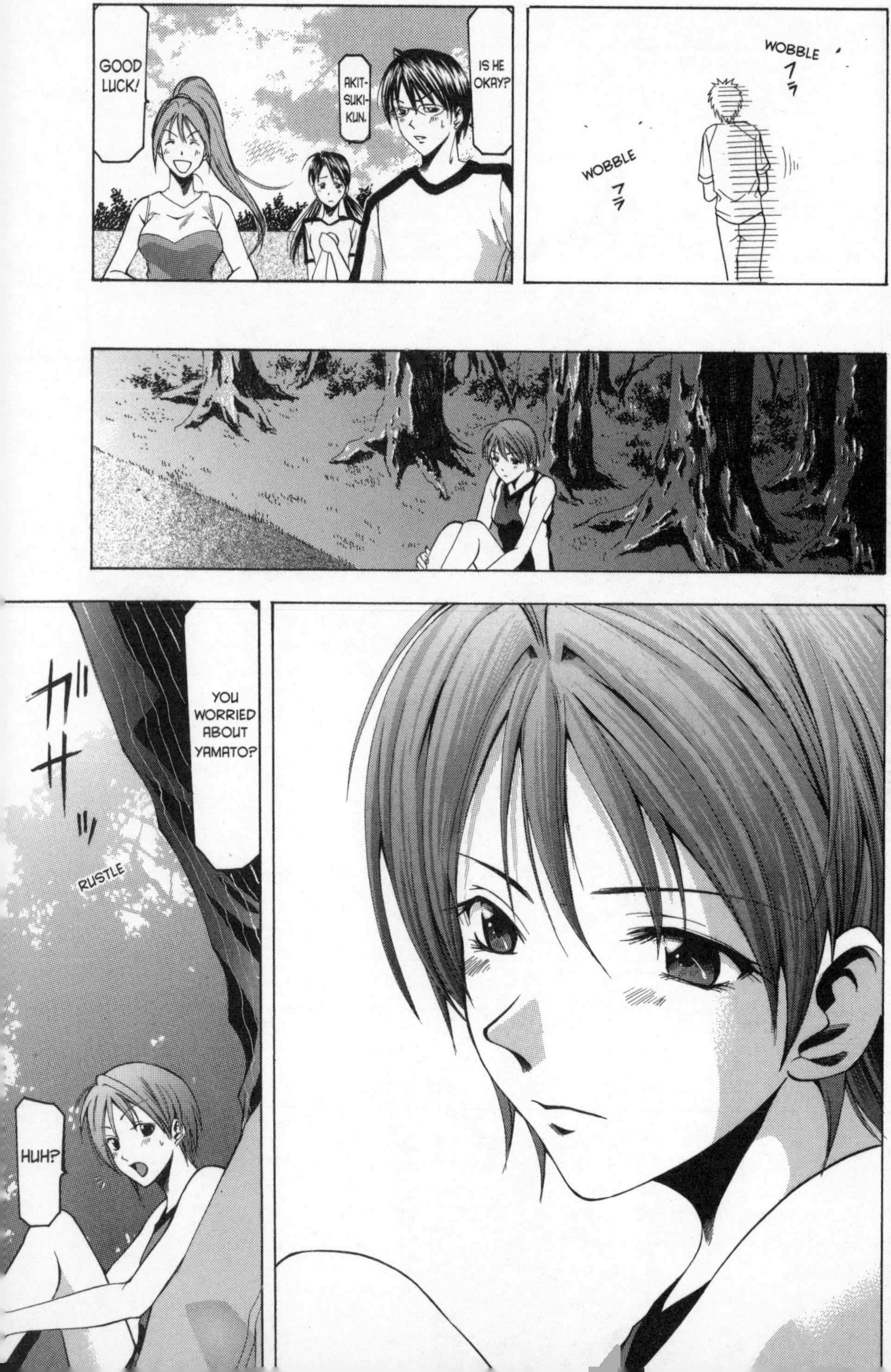
WOBBLE
WOBBLE
IS HE OKAY?
AKIT-SUKI-KUN.
GOOD LUCK!
YOU WORRIED ABOUT YAMATO?
ガサッ
RUSTLE
HUH?

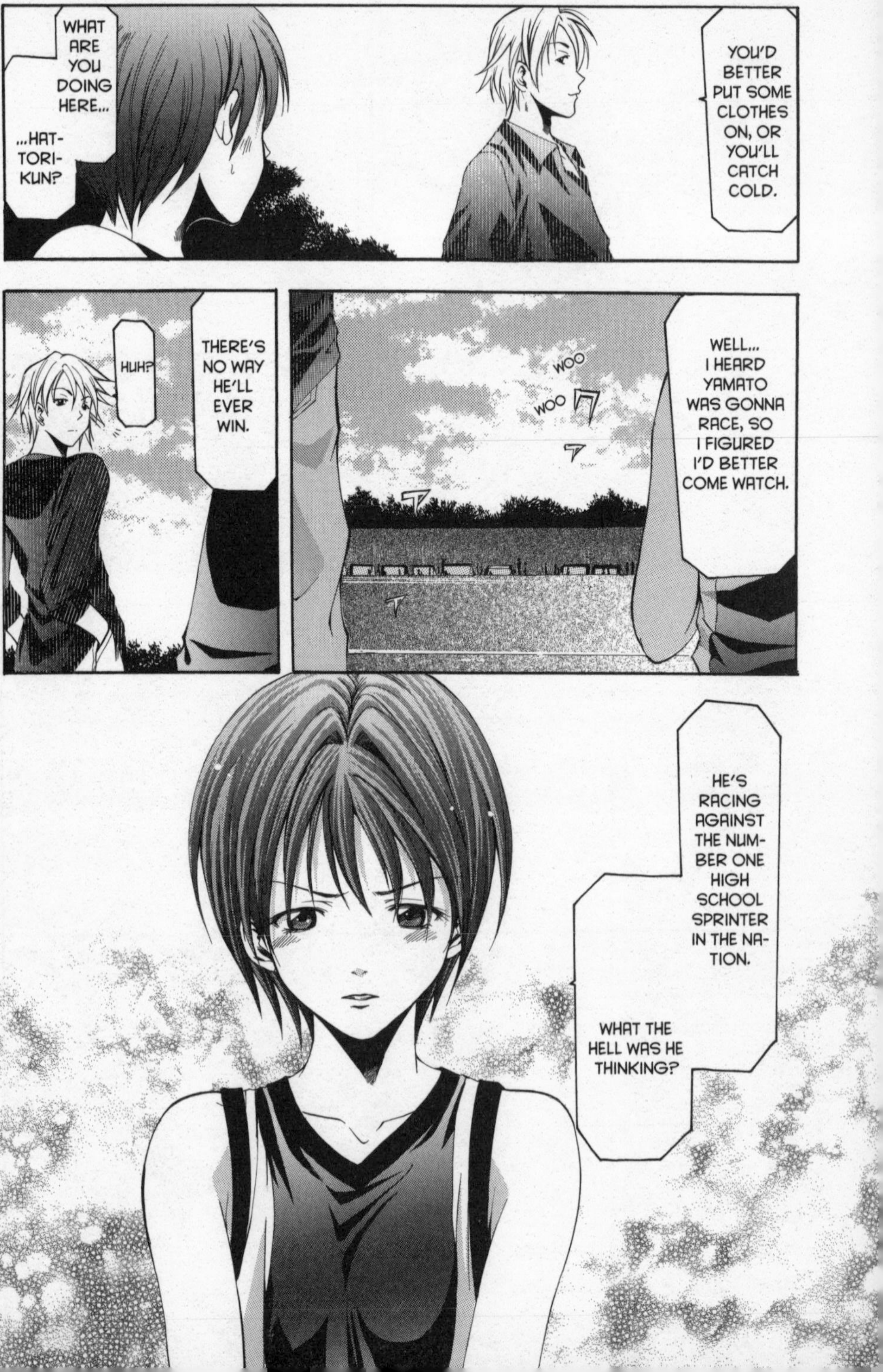

YOU'D BETTER PUT SOME CLOTHES ON, OR YOU'LL CATCH COLD.
WHAT ARE YOU DOING HERE...
...HAT-TORI-KUN?
WELL... I HEARD YAMATO WAS GONNA RACE, SO I FIGURED I'D BETTER COME WATCH.
WOO
WOO
THERE'S NO WAY HE'LL EVER WIN.
HUH?
HE'S RACING AGAINST THE NUM-BER ONE HIGH SCHOOL SPRINTER IN THE NA-TION.
WHAT THE HELL WAS HE THINKING?

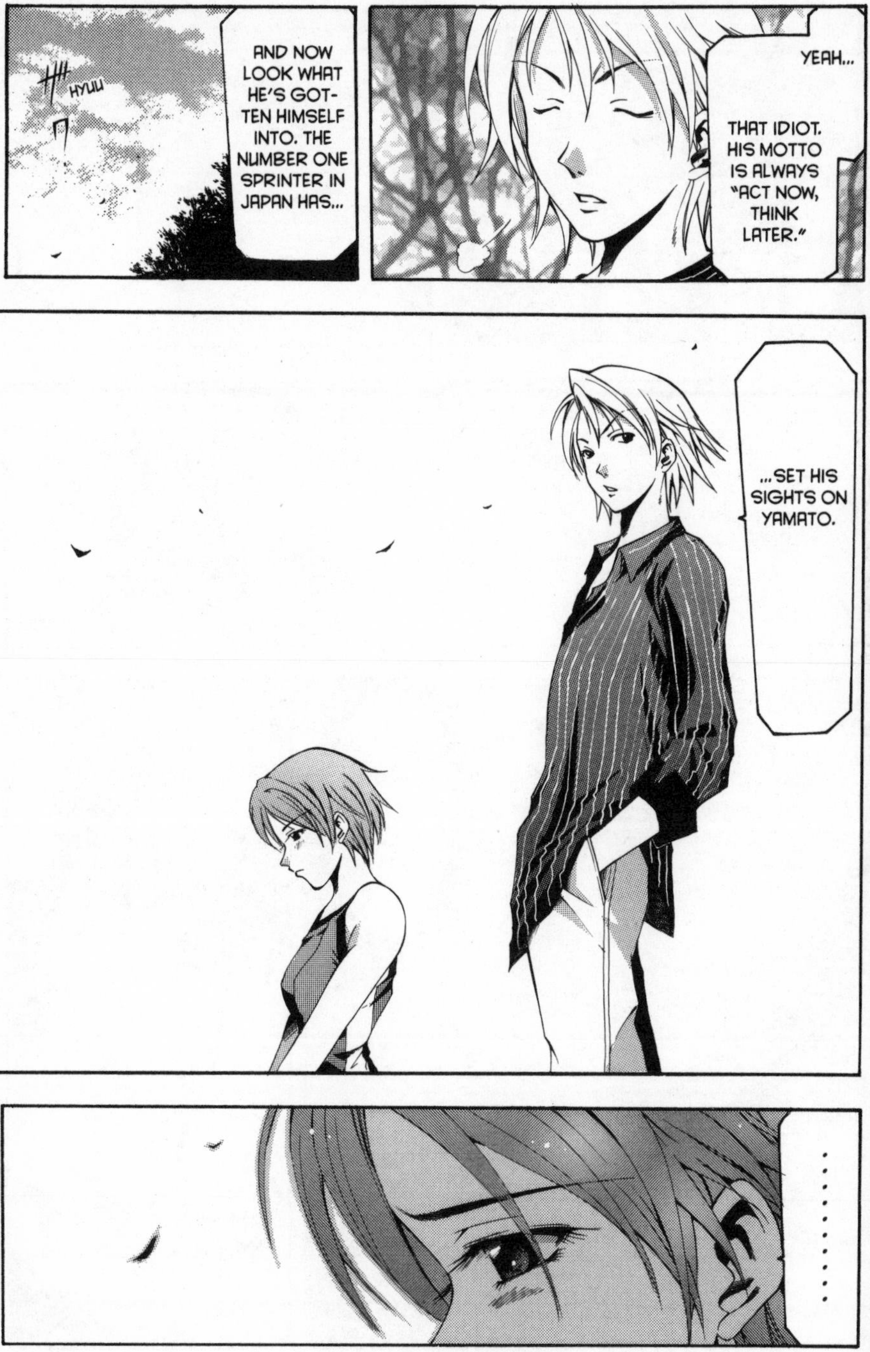
YEAH...
THAT IDIOT. HIS MOTTO IS ALWAYS "ACT NOW, THINK LATER."
AND NOW LOOK WHAT HE'S GOTTEN HIMSELF INTO. THE NUMBER ONE SPRINTER IN JAPAN HAS...
HYUU
...SET HIS SIGHTS ON YAMATO.
......

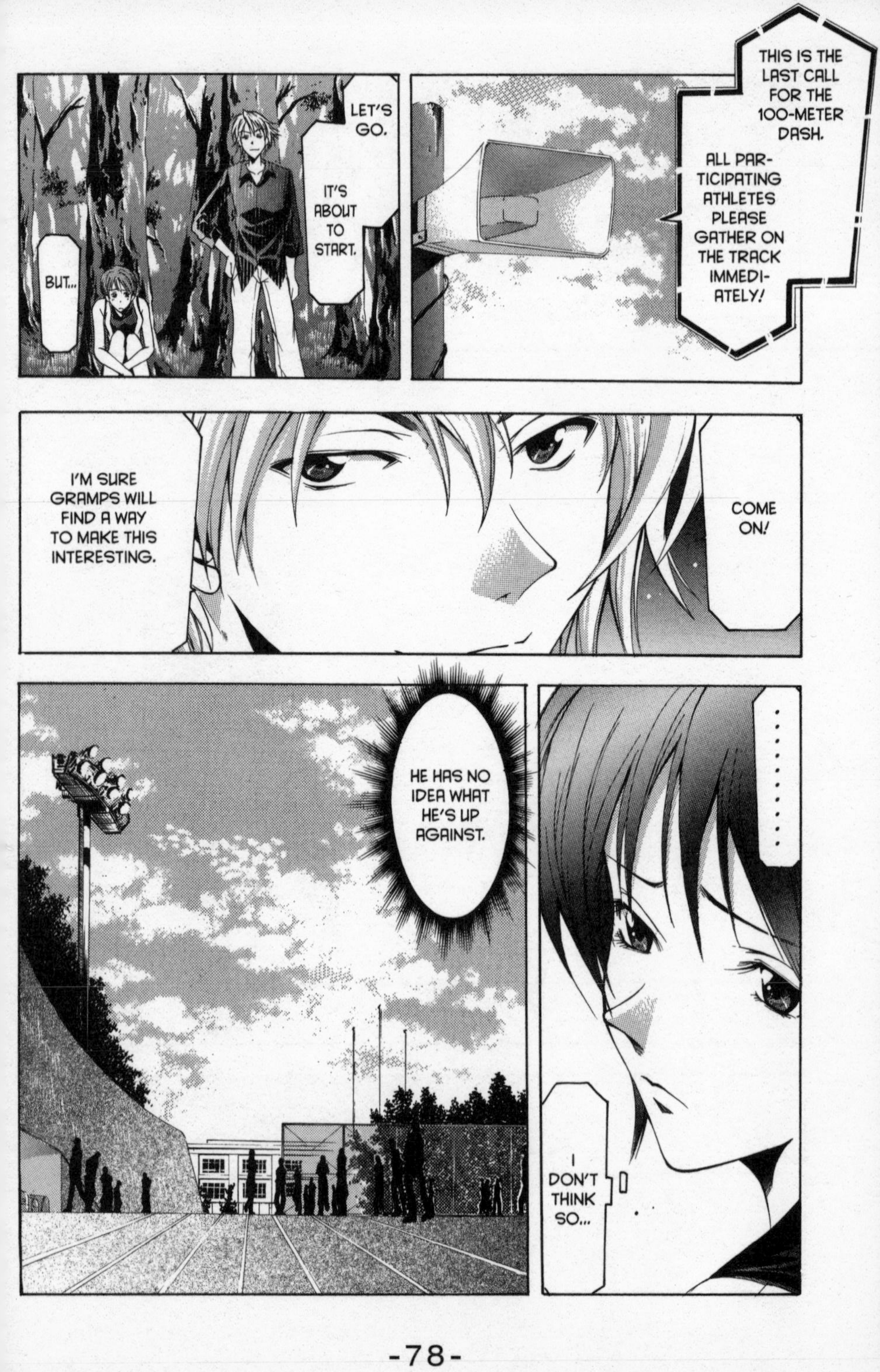
THIS IS THE LAST CALL FOR THE 100-METER DASH.
ALL PARTICIPATING ATHLETES PLEASE GATHER ON THE TRACK IMMEDIATELY!
LET'S GO.
IT'S ABOUT TO START.
BUT...
COME ON!
I'M SURE GRAMPS WILL FIND A WAY TO MAKE THIS INTERESTING.
....
I DON'T THINK SO...
HE HAS NO IDEA WHAT HE'S UP AGAINST.

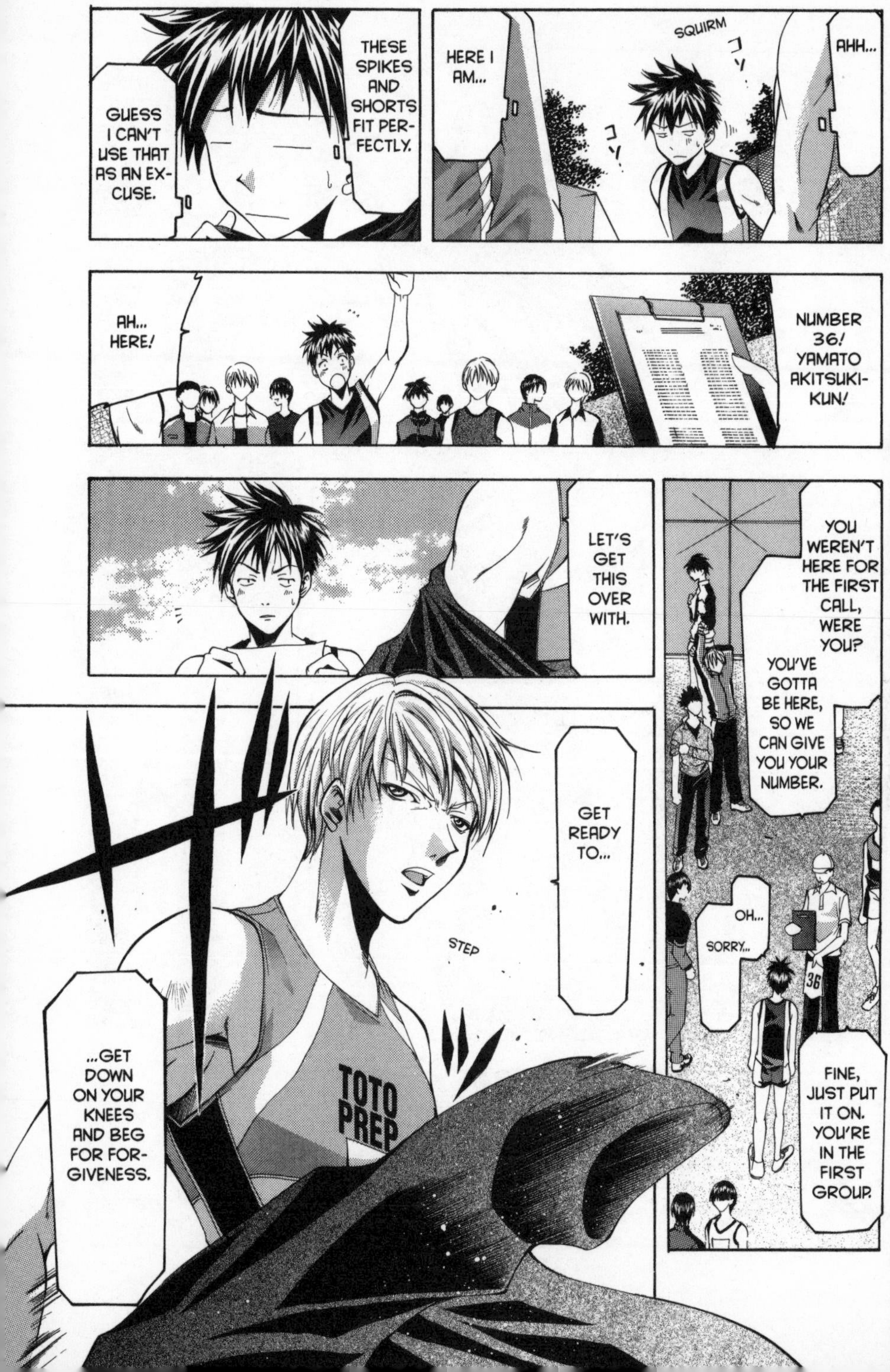
AHH...
SQUIRM
コソ
コソ
HERE I AM...
THESE SPIKES AND SHORTS FIT PER-FECTLY.
GUESS I CAN'T USE THAT AS AN EX-CUSE.
NUMBER 36! YAMATO AKITSUKI-KUN!
AH... HERE!
YOU WEREN'T HERE FOR THE FIRST CALL, WERE YOU?
YOU'VE GOTTA BE HERE, SO WE CAN GIVE YOU YOUR NUMBER.
OH...
SORRY...
FINE, JUST PUT IT ON. YOU'RE IN THE FIRST GROUP.
36
LET'S GET THIS OVER WITH.
GET READY TO...
STEP
TOTO PREP
...GET DOWN ON YOUR KNEES AND BEG FOR FOR-GIVENESS.

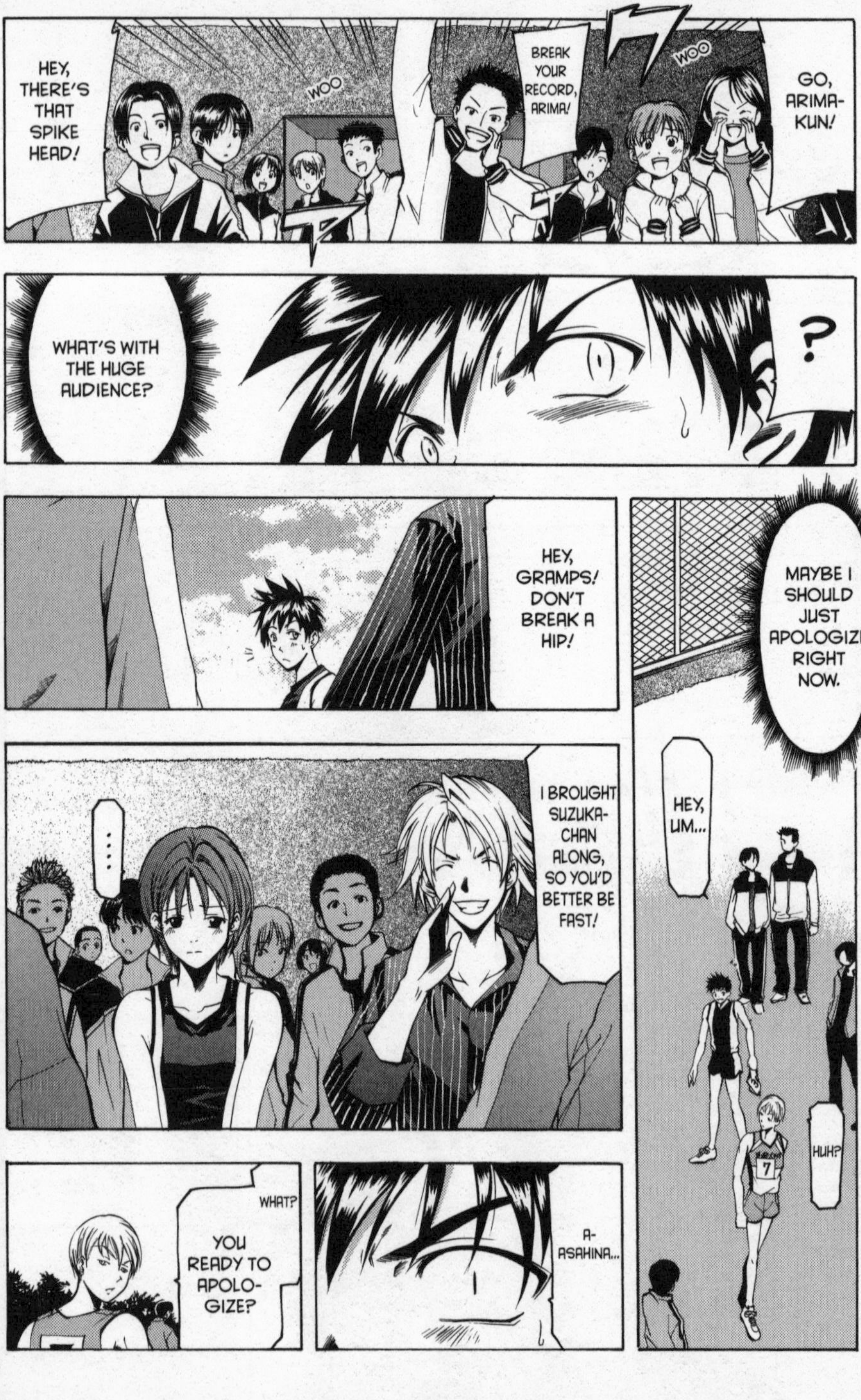
GO, ARIMA-KUN!
WOO
BREAK YOUR RECORD, ARIMA!
WOO
HEY, THERE'S THAT SPIKE HEAD!
?
WHAT'S WITH THE HUGE AUDIENCE?
MAYBE I SHOULD JUST APOLOGIZE RIGHT NOW.
HEY, UM...
HUH?
HEY, GRAMPS! DON'T BREAK A HIP!
I BROUGHT SUZUKA-CHAN ALONG, SO YOU'D BETTER BE FAST!
....
A- ASAHINA...
WHAT?
YOU READY TO APOLO-GIZE?

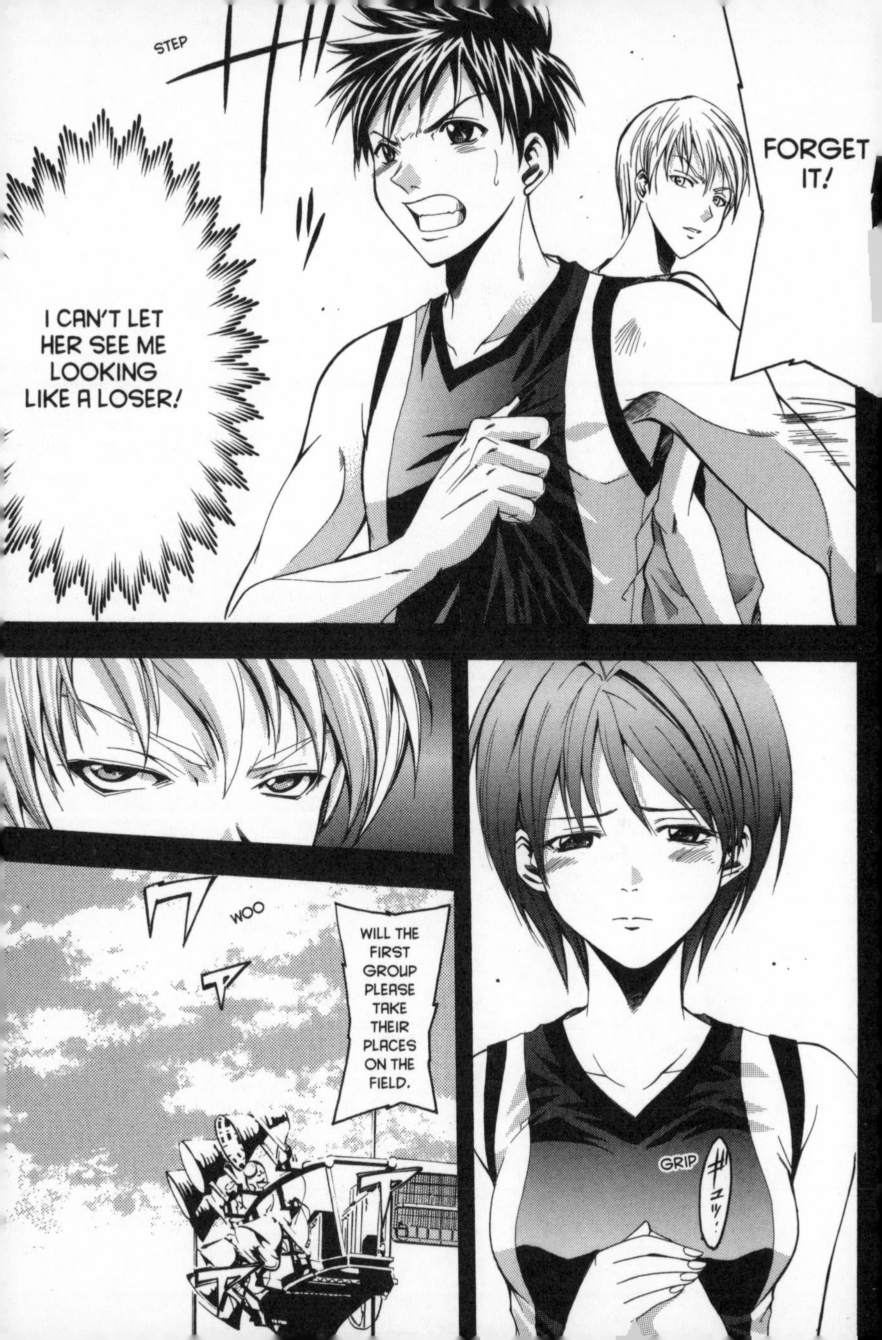
FORGET IT!
STEP
I CAN'T LET HER SEE ME LOOKING LIKE A LOSER!
GRIP
ギュッ!
WOO
WILL THE FIRST GROUP PLEASE TAKE THEIR PLACES ON THE FIELD.

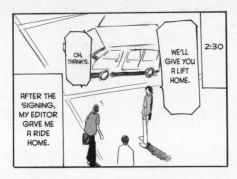

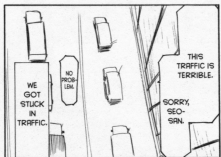

SUZUKA FOUR-PANEL THEATER NUMBER SIXTEEN

SEO GOES TO A SIGNING - PART 4

2:30
WE'LL GIVE YOU A LIFT HOME.
OH, THANKS.
AFTER THE SIGNING, MY EDITOR GAVE ME A RIDE HOME.
THIS TRAFFIC IS TERRIBLE.
SORRY, SEO-SAN.
NO PROBLEM.
WE GOT STUCK IN TRAFFIC.
HUH? WAIT, ARE WE SUPPOSED TO BE GOING THIS WAY?
CLICK CLICK
カチ カチ
ARE YOU KIDDING?
WE MISREAD THE MAP.
Z
BY THE TIME I FINALLY MADE IT HOME, IT WAS AFTER 8:00.
MAKE SURE YOU GET THE STORYBOARDS TO ME BY 10:00.
DON'T BE LATE.
IN TWO HOURS? NO WAY!

*IT TOOK ME TILL 11:00.

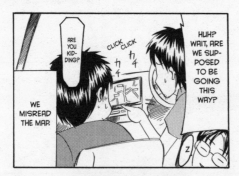

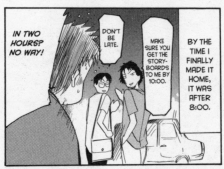

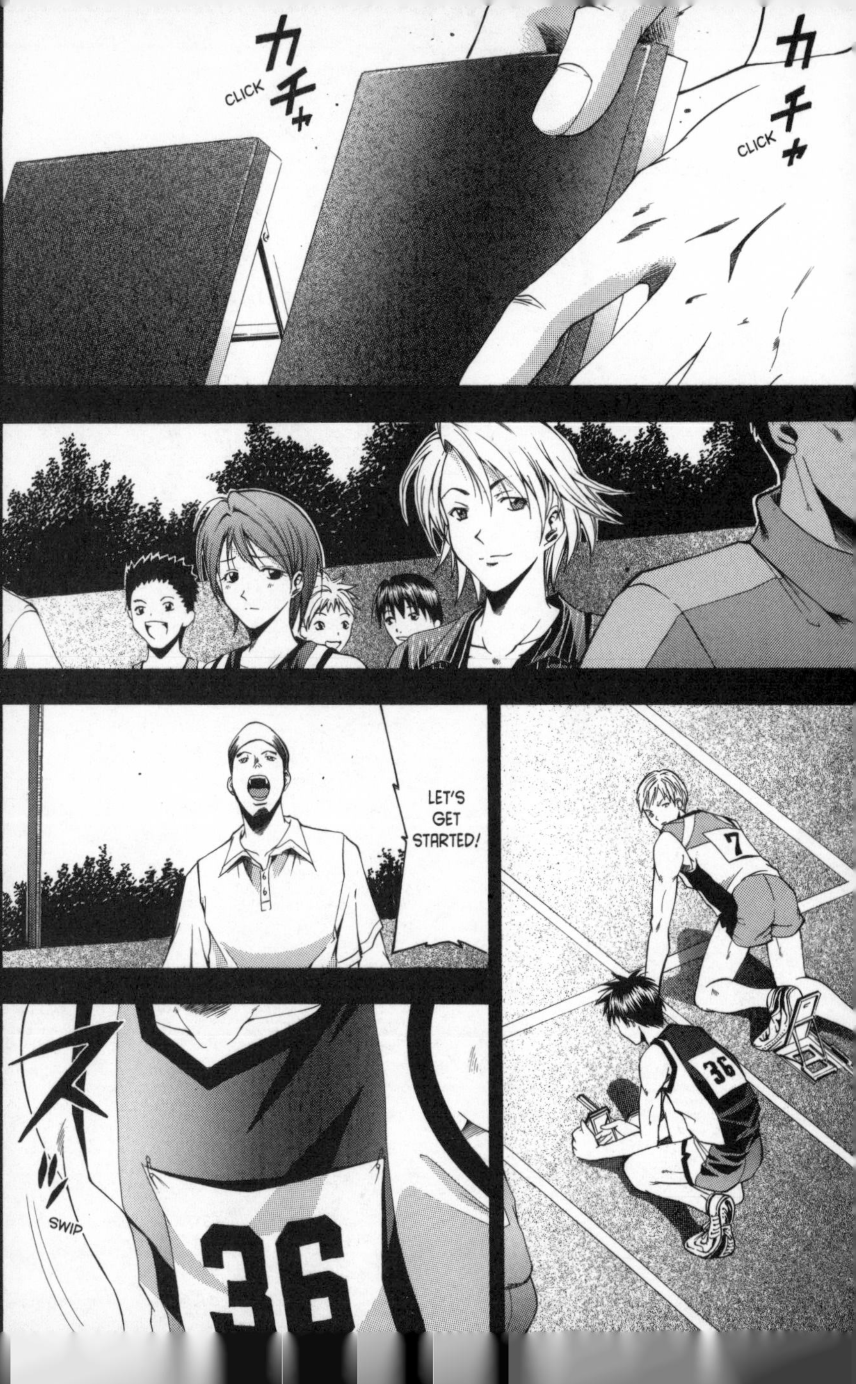
カチャ
CLICK
カチャ
CLICK
LET'S GET STARTED!
ス
SWIP

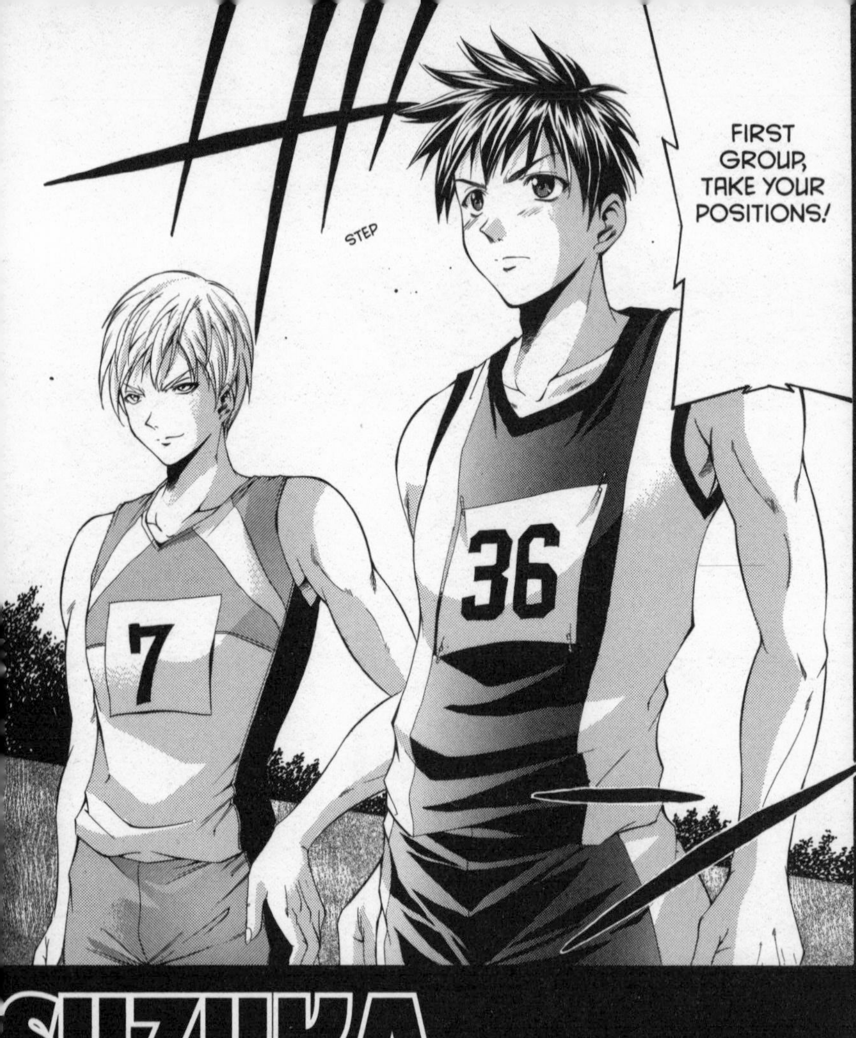
FIRST GROUP, TAKE YOUR POSITIONS!
STEP
36
7

SUZUKA

#27 THE SHOWDOWN

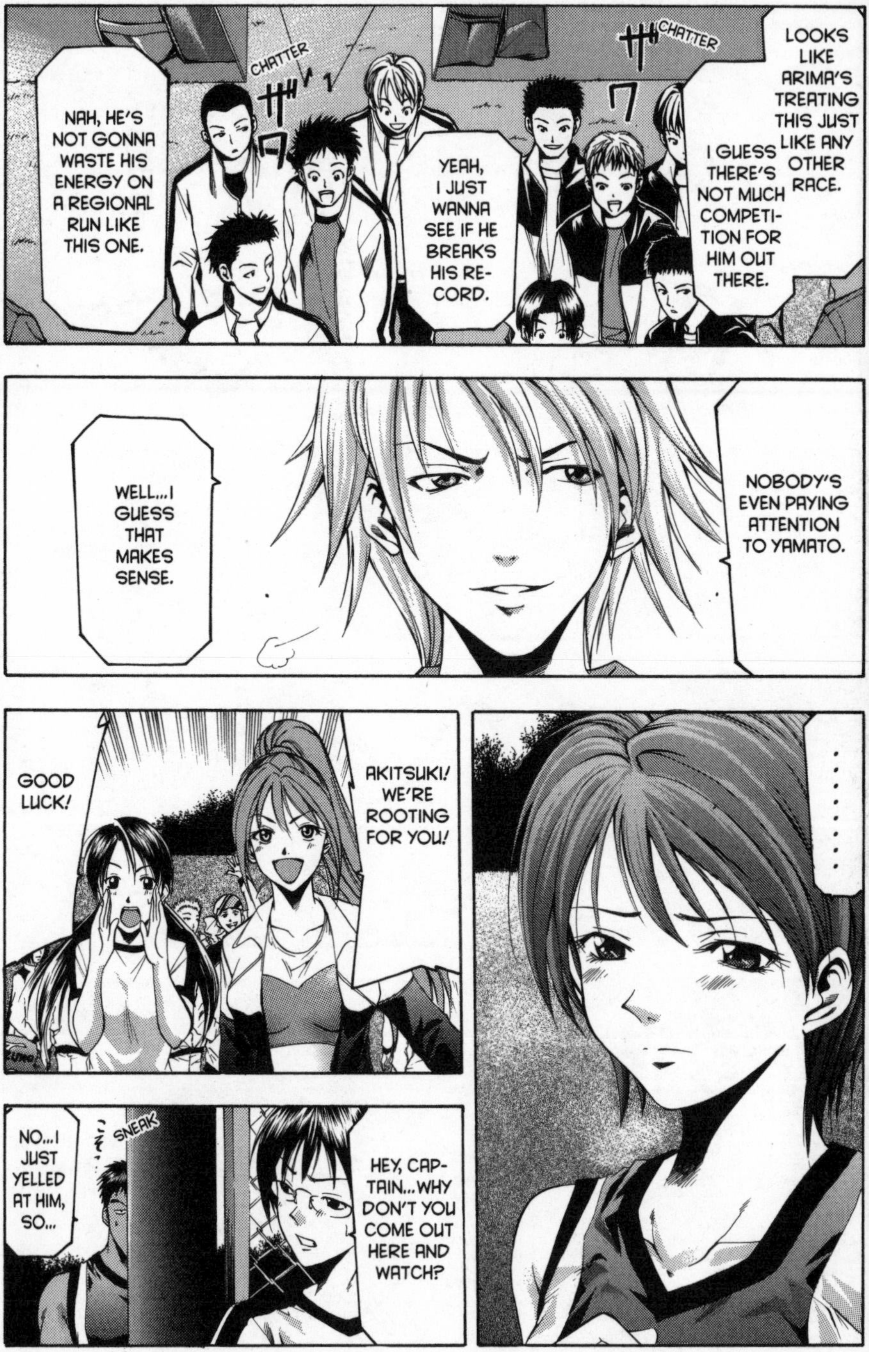
LOOKS LIKE ARIMA'S TREATING THIS JUST LIKE ANY OTHER RACE.
I GUESS THERE'S NOT MUCH COMPETITION FOR HIM OUT THERE.
CHATTER
YEAH, I JUST WANNA SEE IF HE BREAKS HIS RECORD.
CHATTER
NAH, HE'S NOT GONNA WASTE HIS ENERGY ON A REGIONAL RUN LIKE THIS ONE.
NOBODY'S EVEN PAYING ATTENTION TO YAMATO.
WELL...I GUESS THAT MAKES SENSE.
....
AKITSUKI! WE'RE ROOTING FOR YOU!
GOOD LUCK!
HEY, CAPTAIN...WHY DON'T YOU COME OUT HERE AND WATCH?
SNEAK
NO...I JUST YELLED AT HIM, SO...

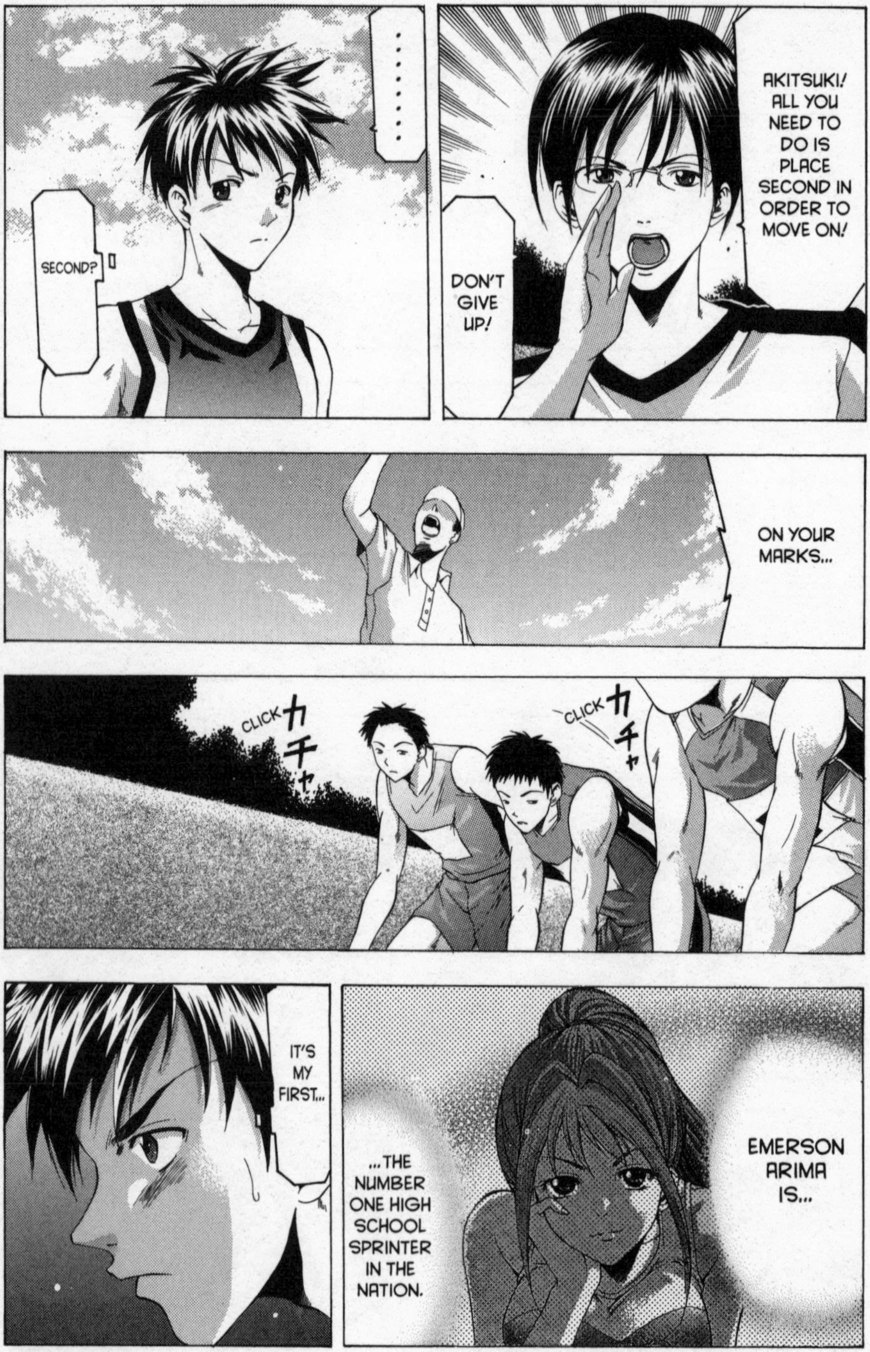
AKITSUKI! ALL YOU NEED TO DO IS PLACE SECOND IN ORDER TO MOVE ON!
DON'T GIVE UP!
....
SECOND?
ON YOUR MARKS...
CLICK カチャ
CLICK カチャ
EMERSON ARIMA IS...
...THE NUMBER ONE HIGH SCHOOL SPRINTER IN THE NATION.
IT'S MY FIRST...

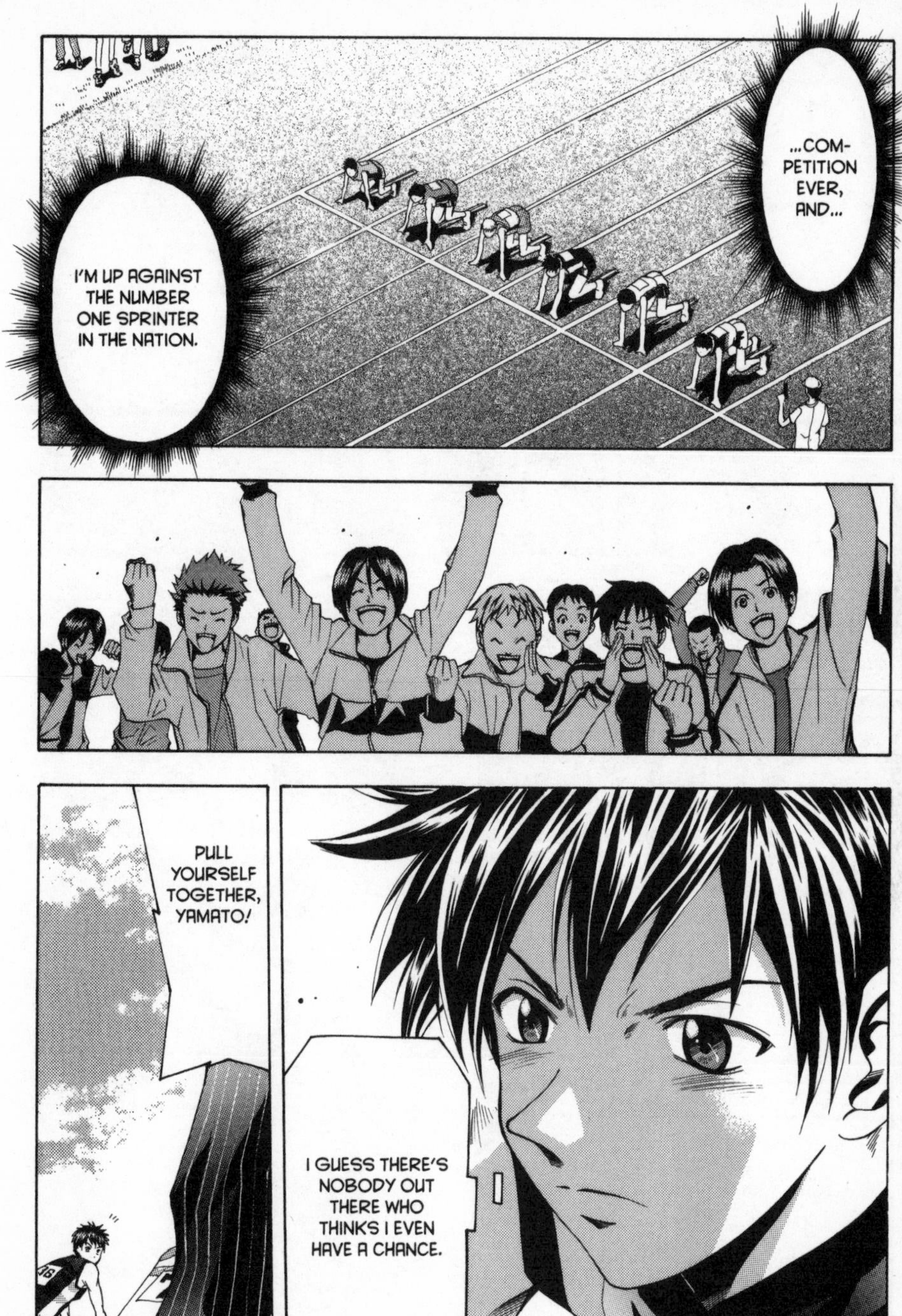
...COM-
PETITION
EVER,
AND...
I'M UP AGAINST
THE NUMBER
ONE SPRINTER
IN THE NATION.
I GUESS THERE'S
NOBODY OUT
THERE WHO
THINKS I EVEN
HAVE A CHANCE.
PULL
YOURSELF
TOGETHER,
YAMATO!

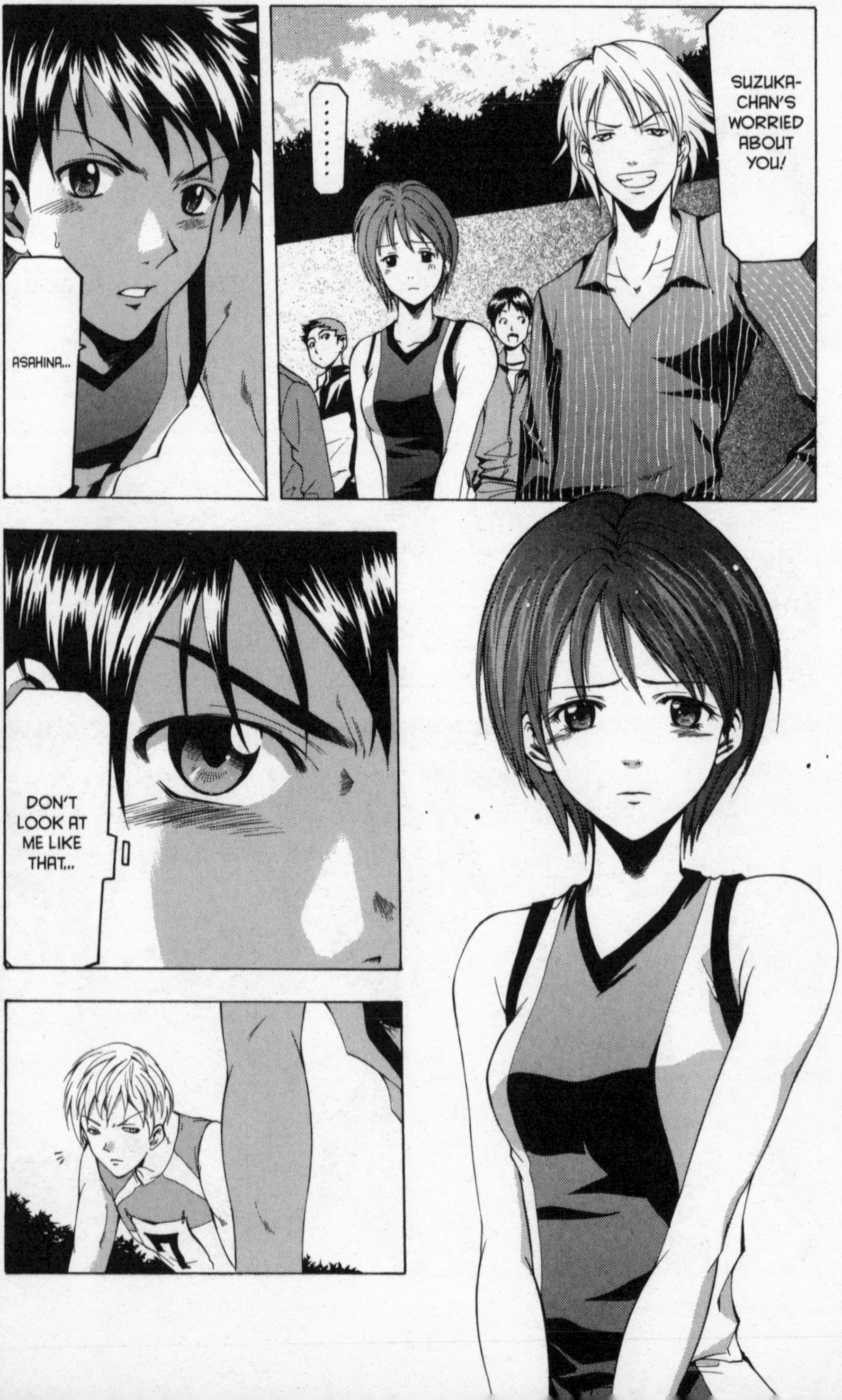
SUZUKA-CHAN'S WORRIED ABOUT YOU!
......
ASAHINA...
DON'T LOOK AT ME LIKE THAT...

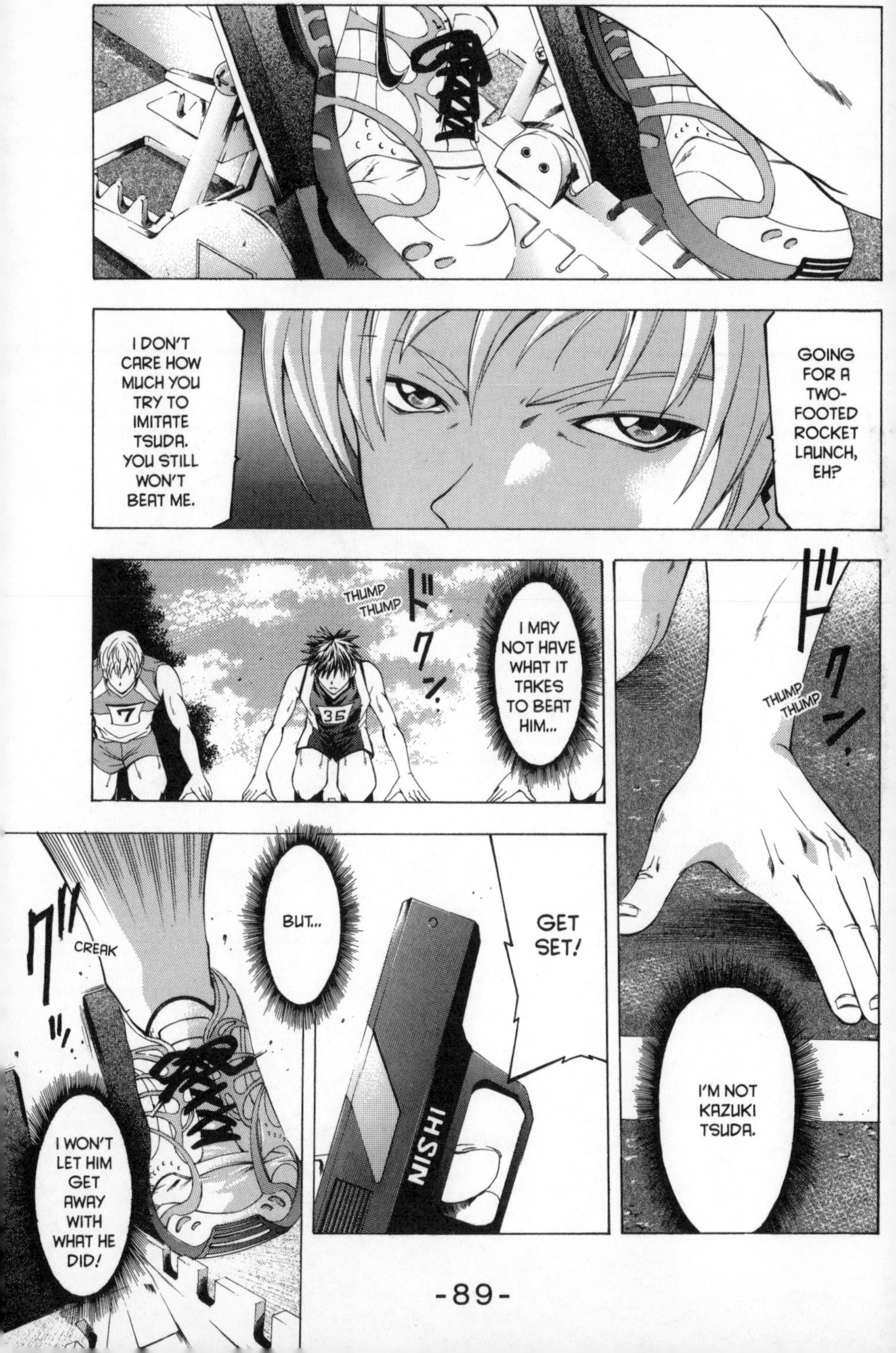
GOING FOR A TWO-FOOTED ROCKET LAUNCH, EH?
I DON'T CARE HOW MUCH YOU TRY TO IMITATE TSUDA. YOU STILL WON'T BEAT ME.
THUMP THUMP
I'M NOT KAZUKI TSUDA.
THUMP THUMP
I MAY NOT HAVE WHAT IT TAKES TO BEAT HIM...
GET SET!
NISHI
BUT...
CREAK
I WON'T LET HIM GET AWAY WITH WHAT HE DID!

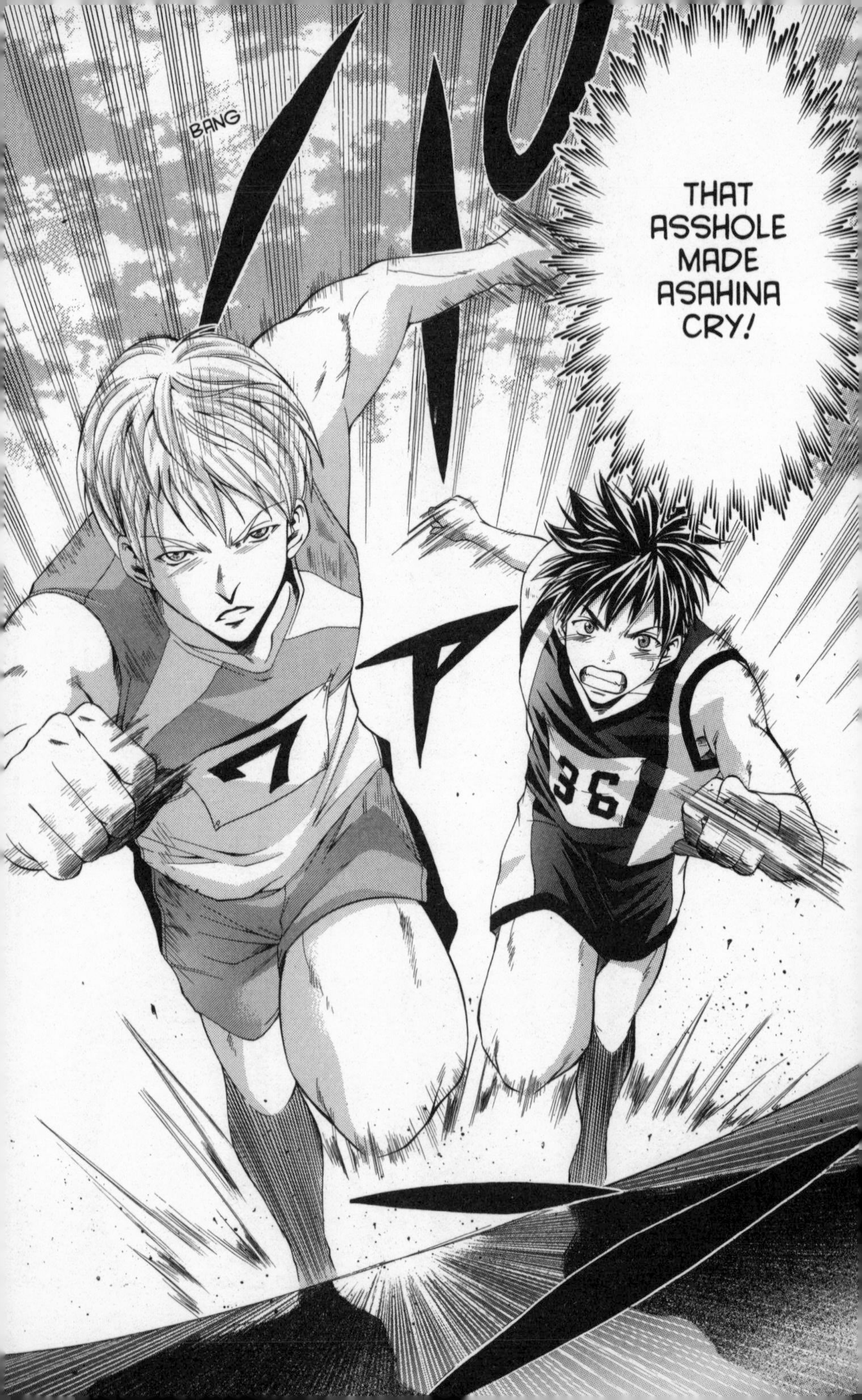
BANG
THAT ASSHOLE MADE ASAHINA CRY!

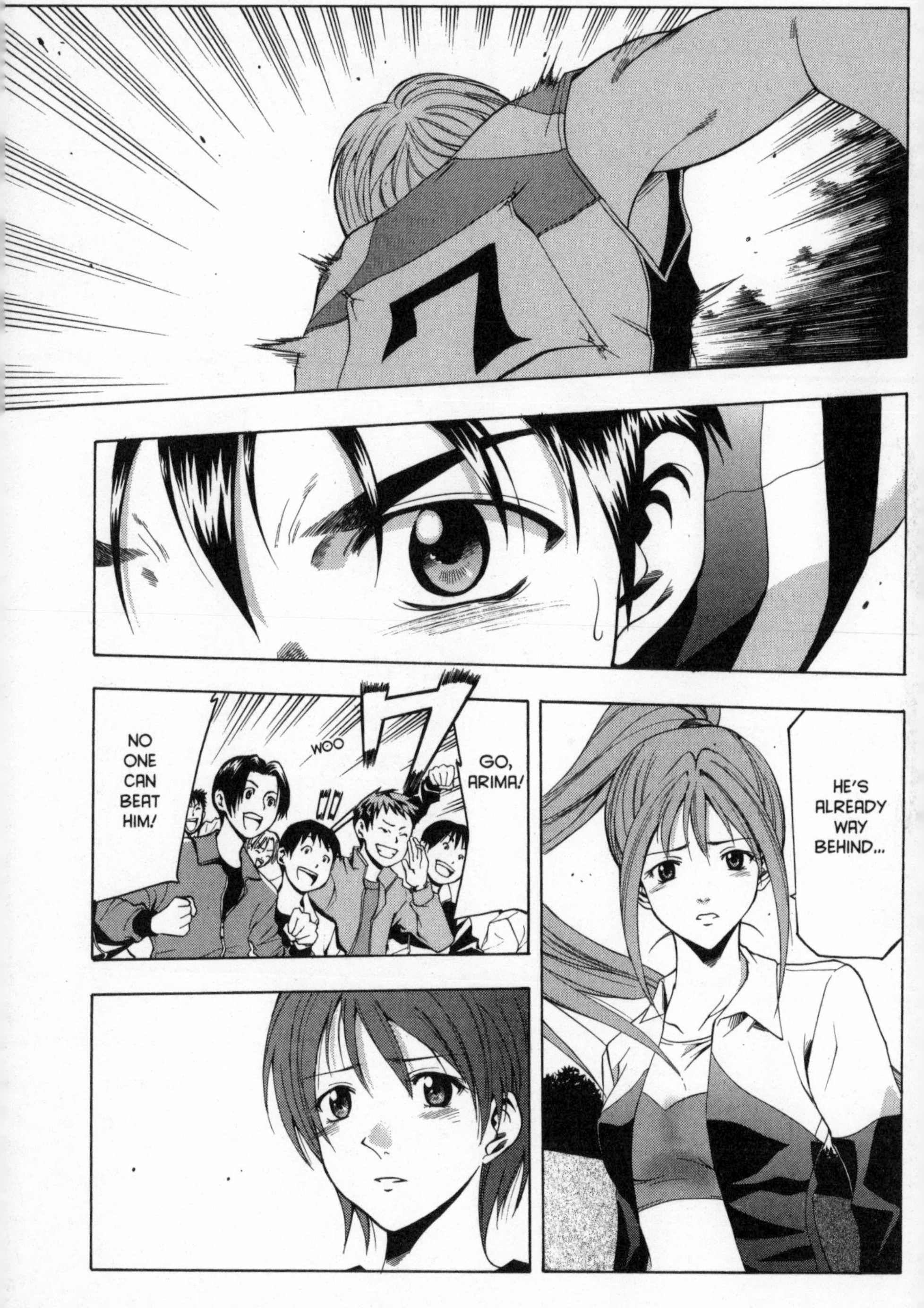
HE'S ALREADY WAY BEHIND...
GO, ARIMA!
WOO
NO ONE CAN BEAT HIM!

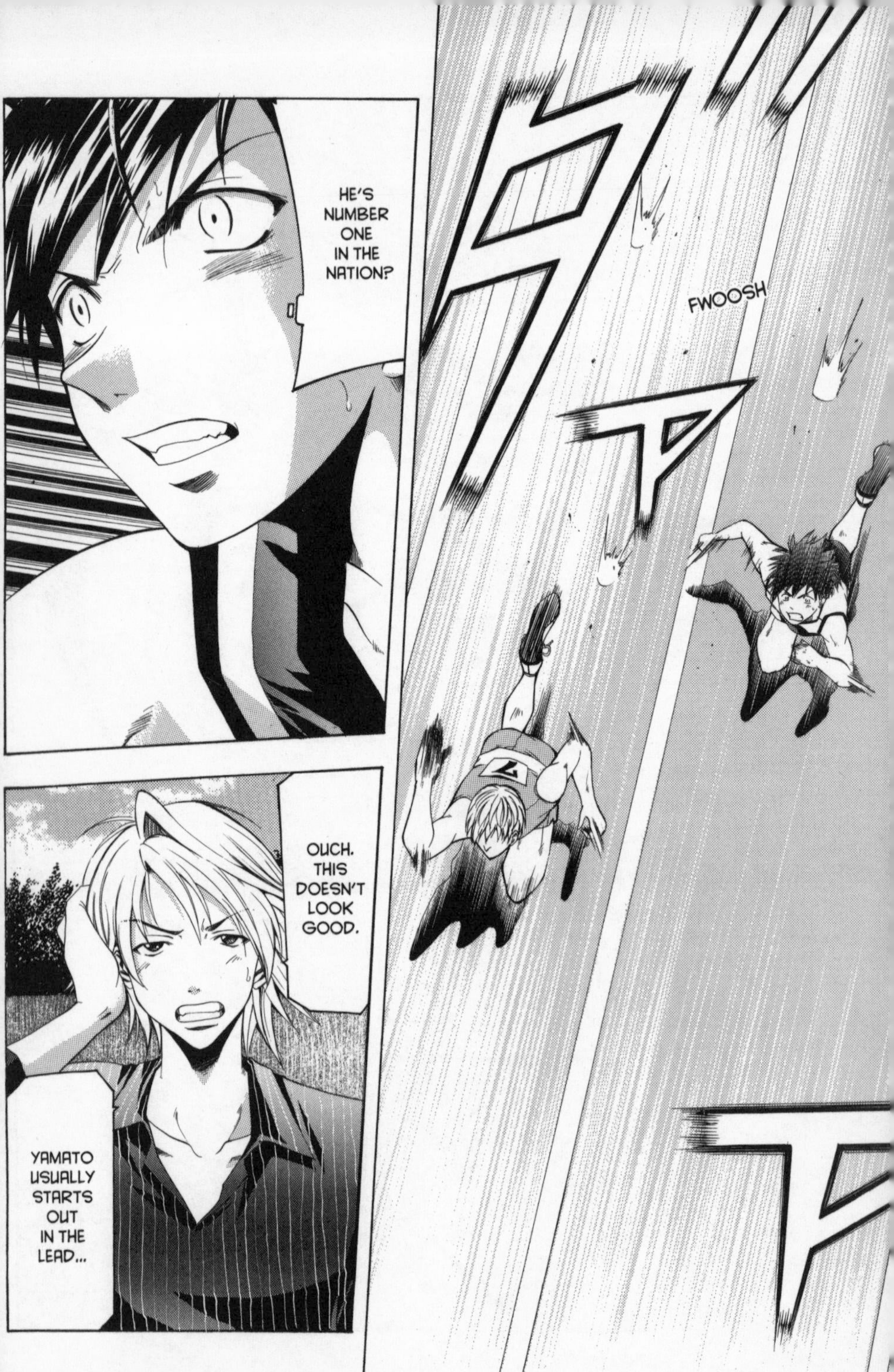
FWOOSH
HE'S NUMBER ONE IN THE NATION?
OUCH. THIS DOESN'T LOOK GOOD.
YAMATO USUALLY STARTS OUT IN THE LEAD...

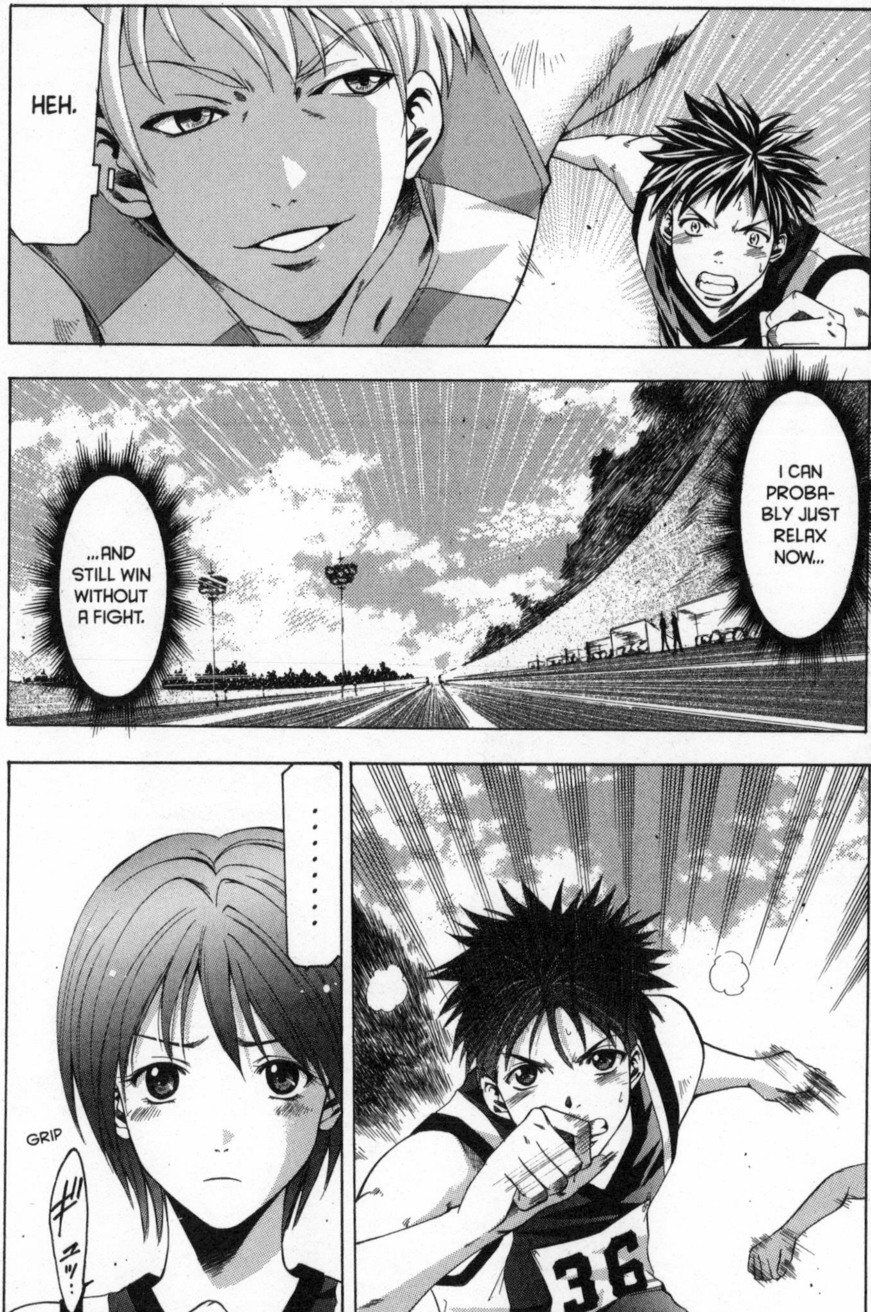
HEH.
I CAN PROBA-BLY JUST RELAX NOW...
...AND STILL WIN WITHOUT A FIGHT.
....
GRIP

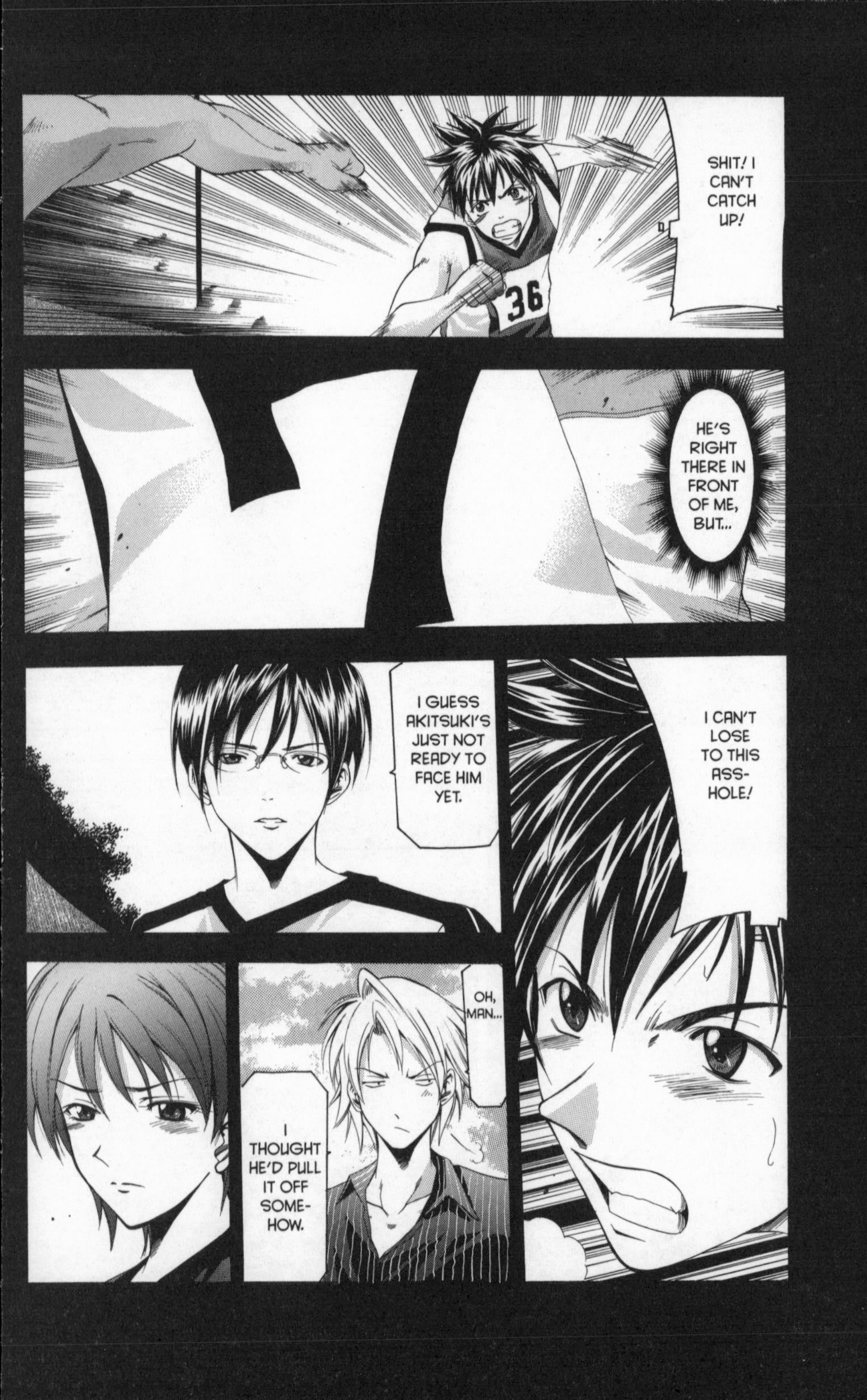
SHIT! I CAN'T CATCH UP!
HE'S RIGHT THERE IN FRONT OF ME, BUT...
I CAN'T LOSE TO THIS ASS-HOLE!
I GUESS AKITSUKI'S JUST NOT READY TO FACE HIM YET.
OH, MAN...
I THOUGHT HE'D PULL IT OFF SOME-HOW.

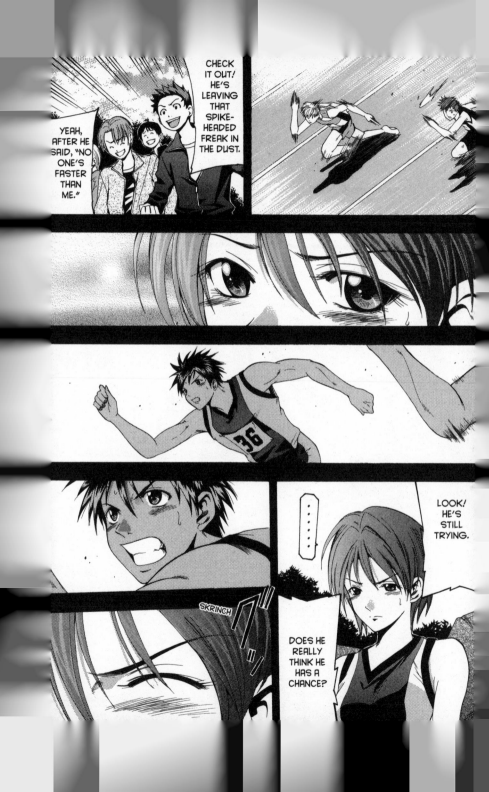

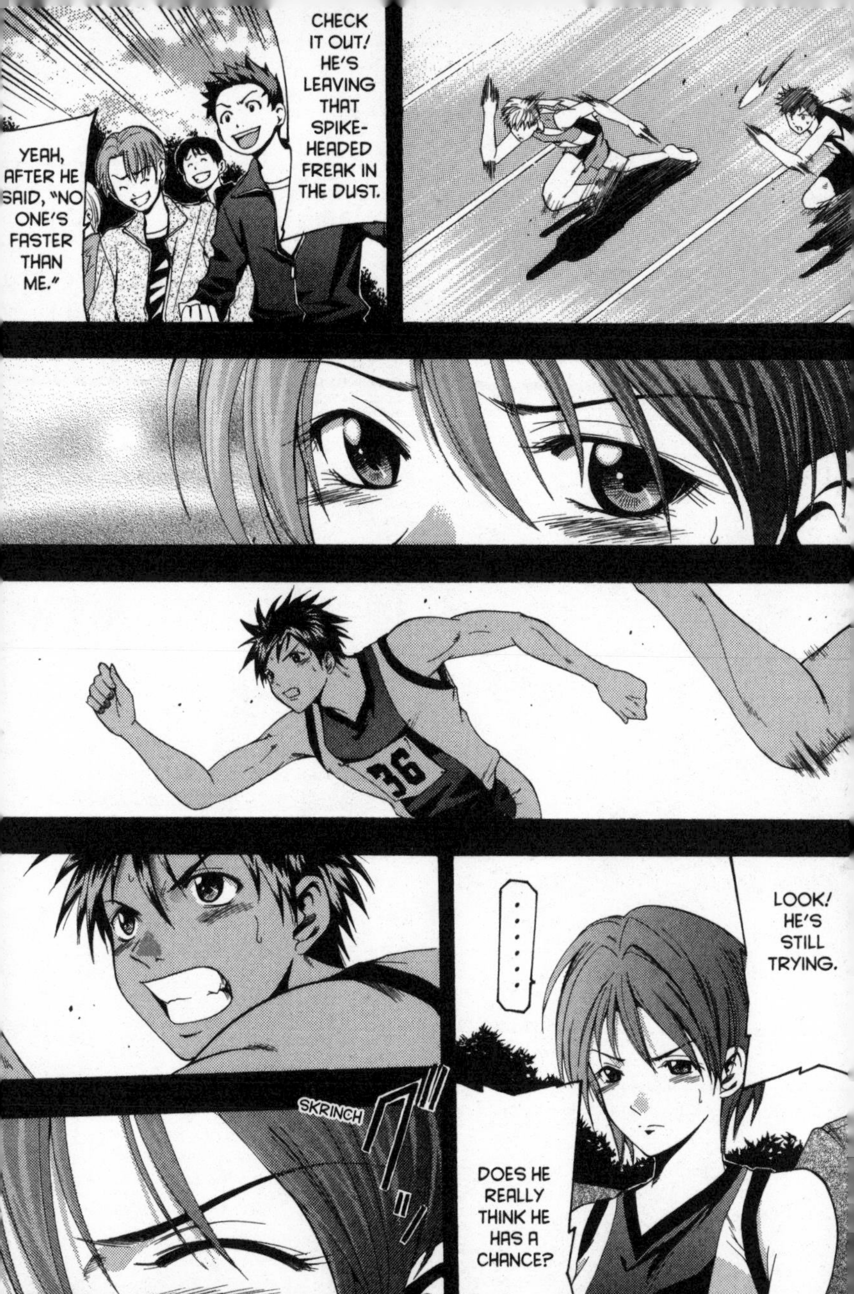
CHECK IT OUT! HE'S LEAVING THAT SPIKE-HEADED FREAK IN THE DUST.
YEAH, AFTER HE SAID, "NO ONE'S FASTER THAN ME."
LOOK! HE'S STILL TRYING.
......
DOES HE REALLY THINK HE HAS A CHANCE?
SKRINCH

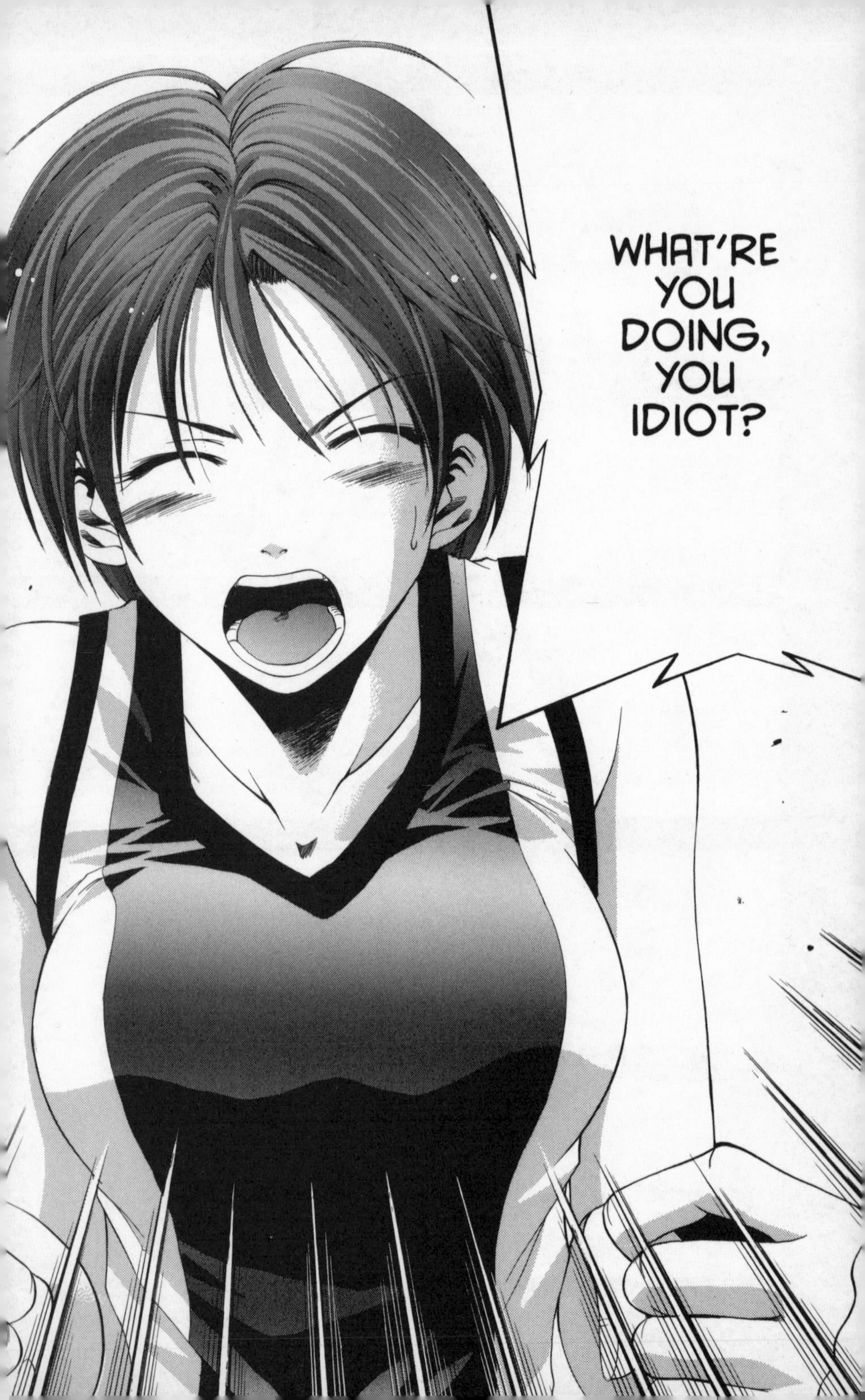
WHAT'RE YOU DOING, YOU IDIOT?

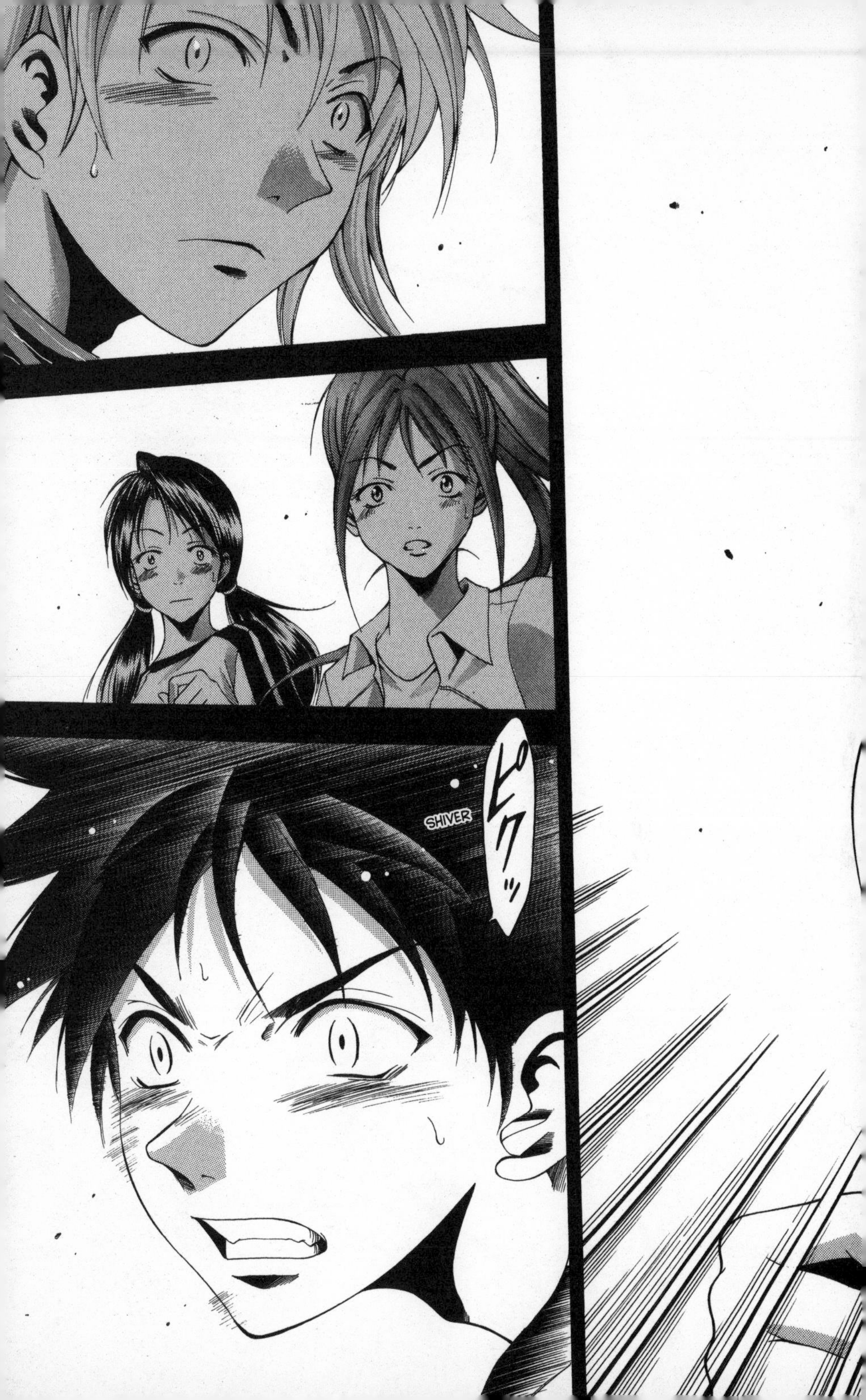
ピクッ
SHIVER

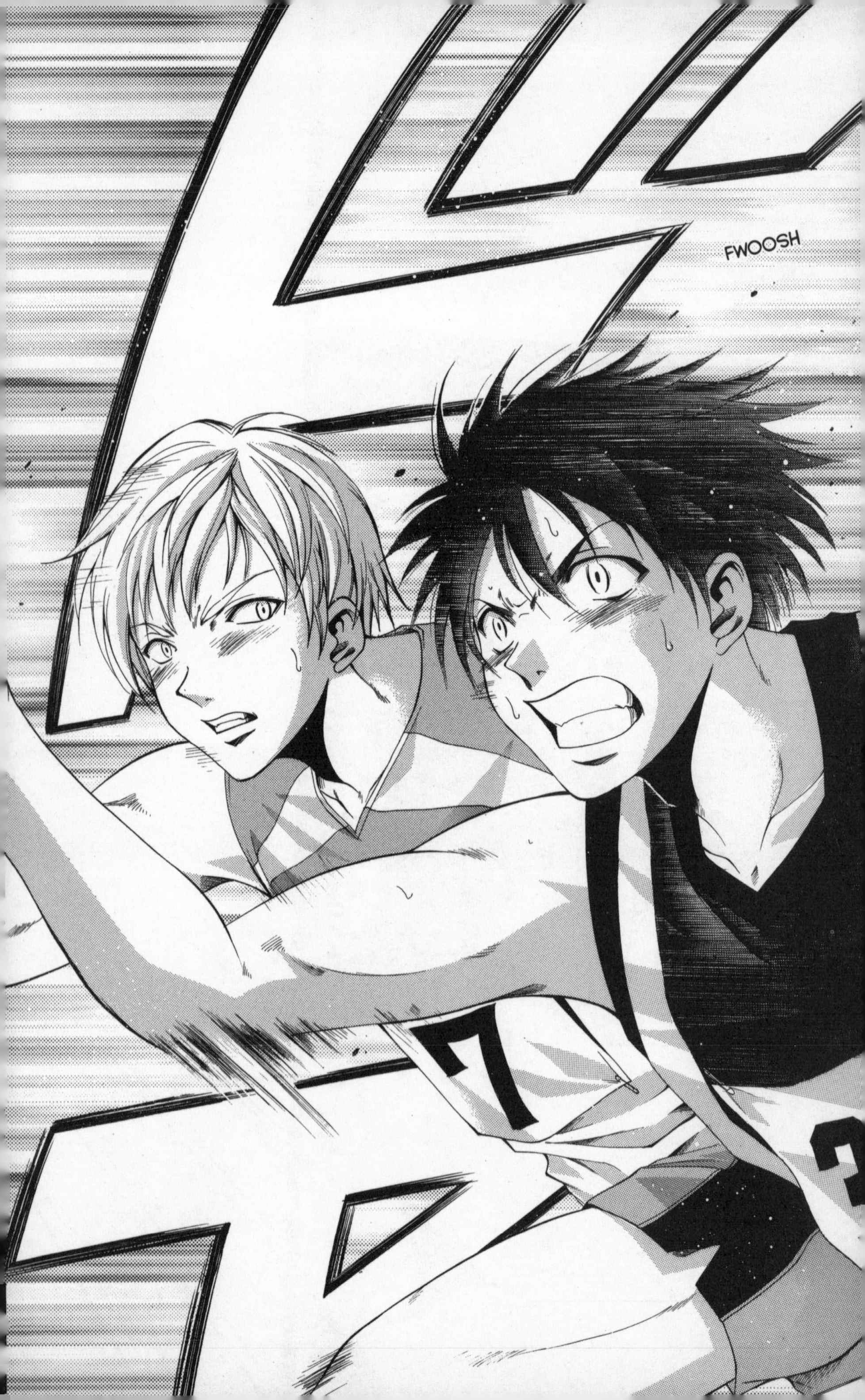
FWOOSH

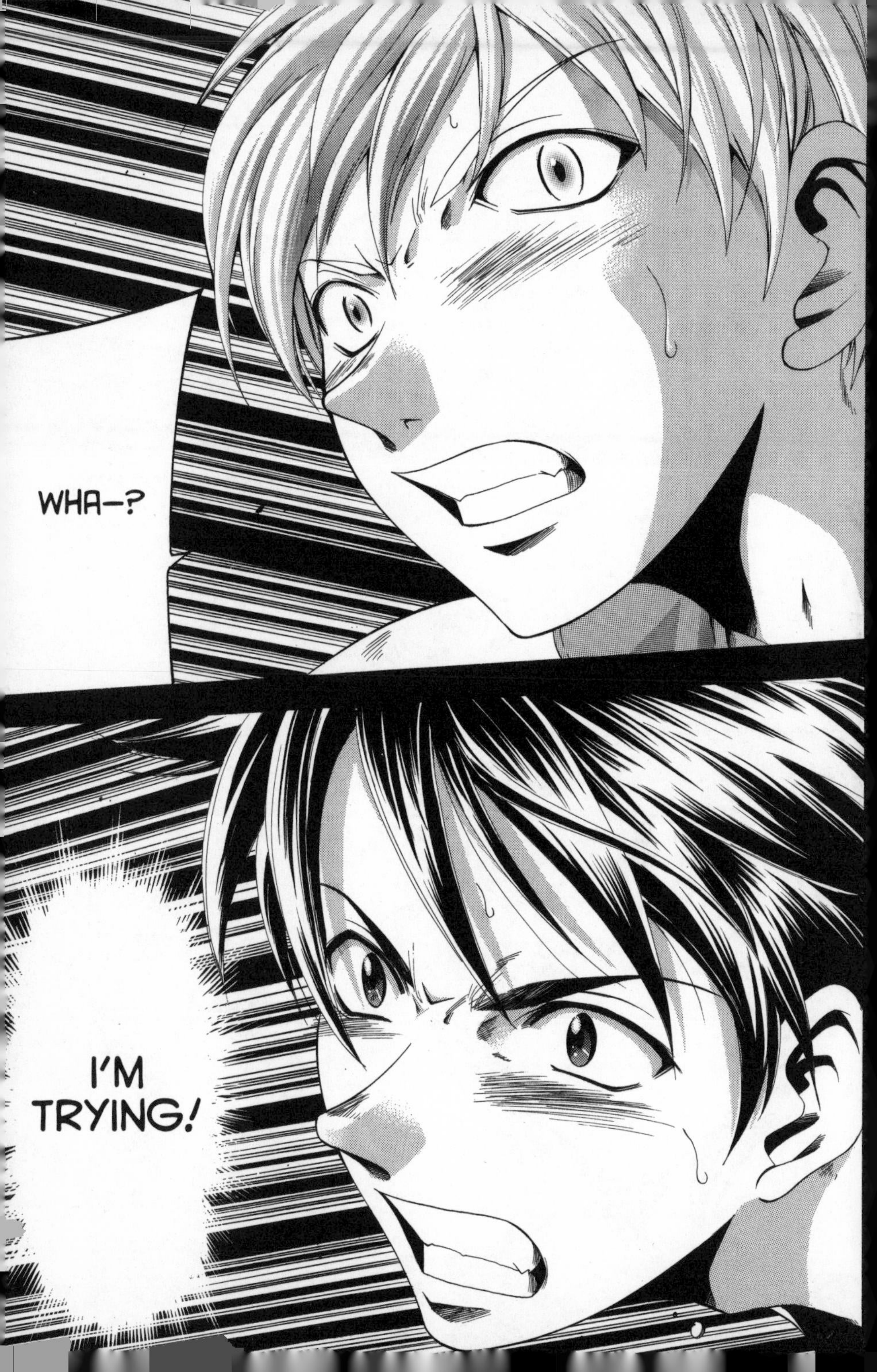
WHA-?
I'M TRYING!

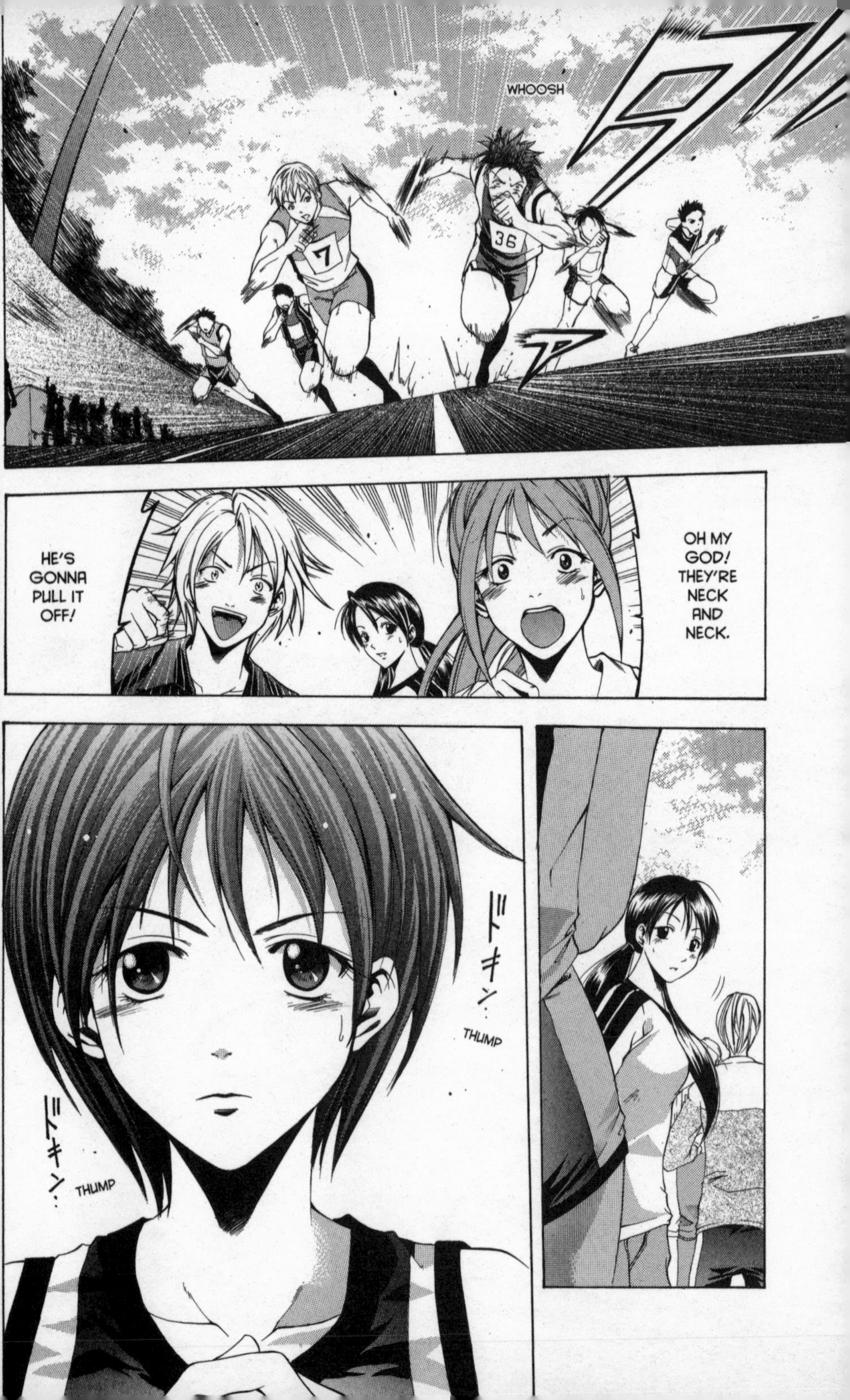
WHOOSH
OH MY GOD! THEY'RE NECK AND NECK.
HE'S GONNA PULL IT OFF!
ドキン
THUMP
ドキン
THUMP

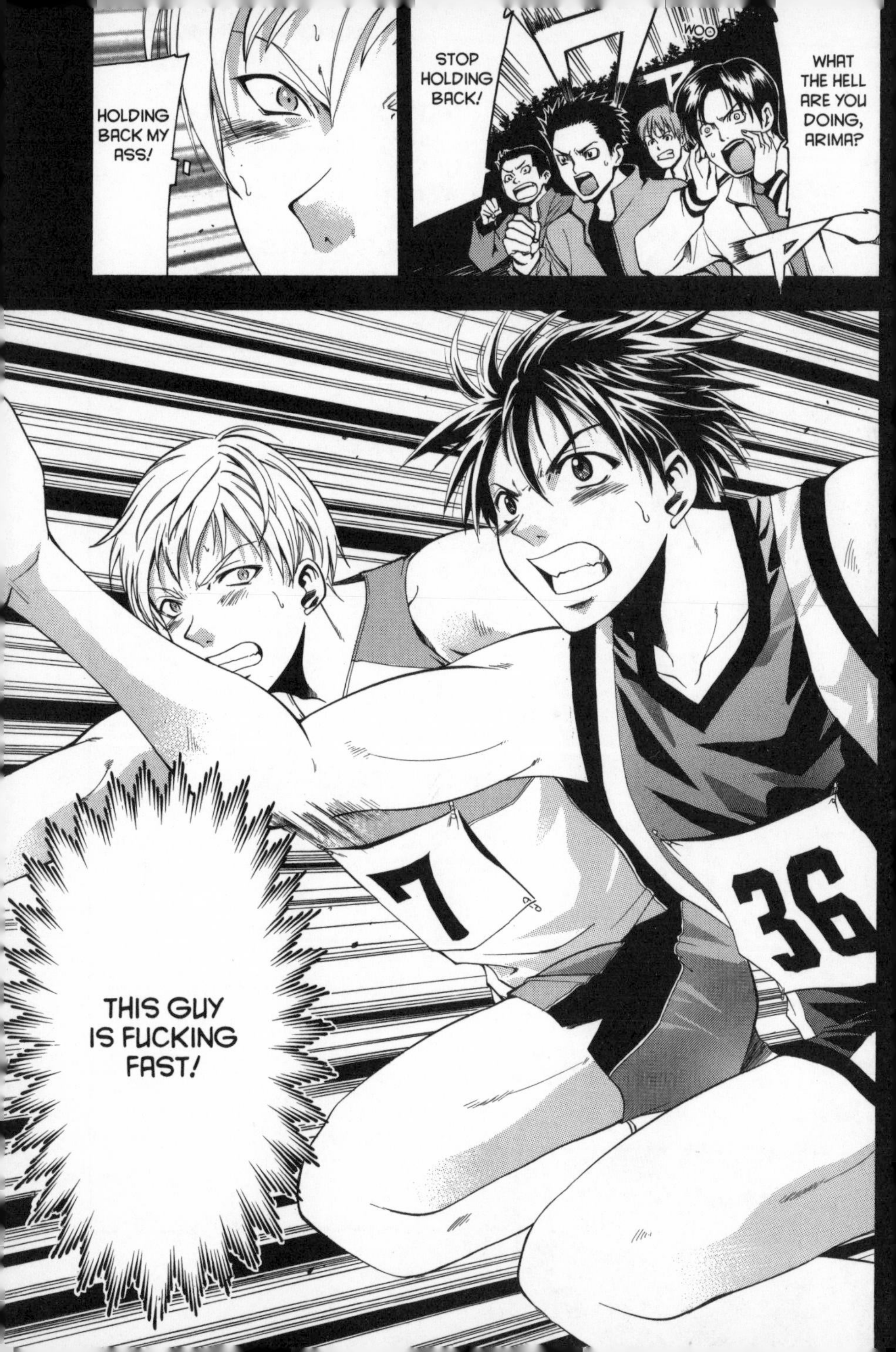
WHAT THE HELL ARE YOU DOING, ARIMA?
WOO
STOP HOLDING BACK!
HOLDING BACK MY ASS!
THIS GUY IS FUCKING FAST!

CHARACTER PROFILE NO. 9

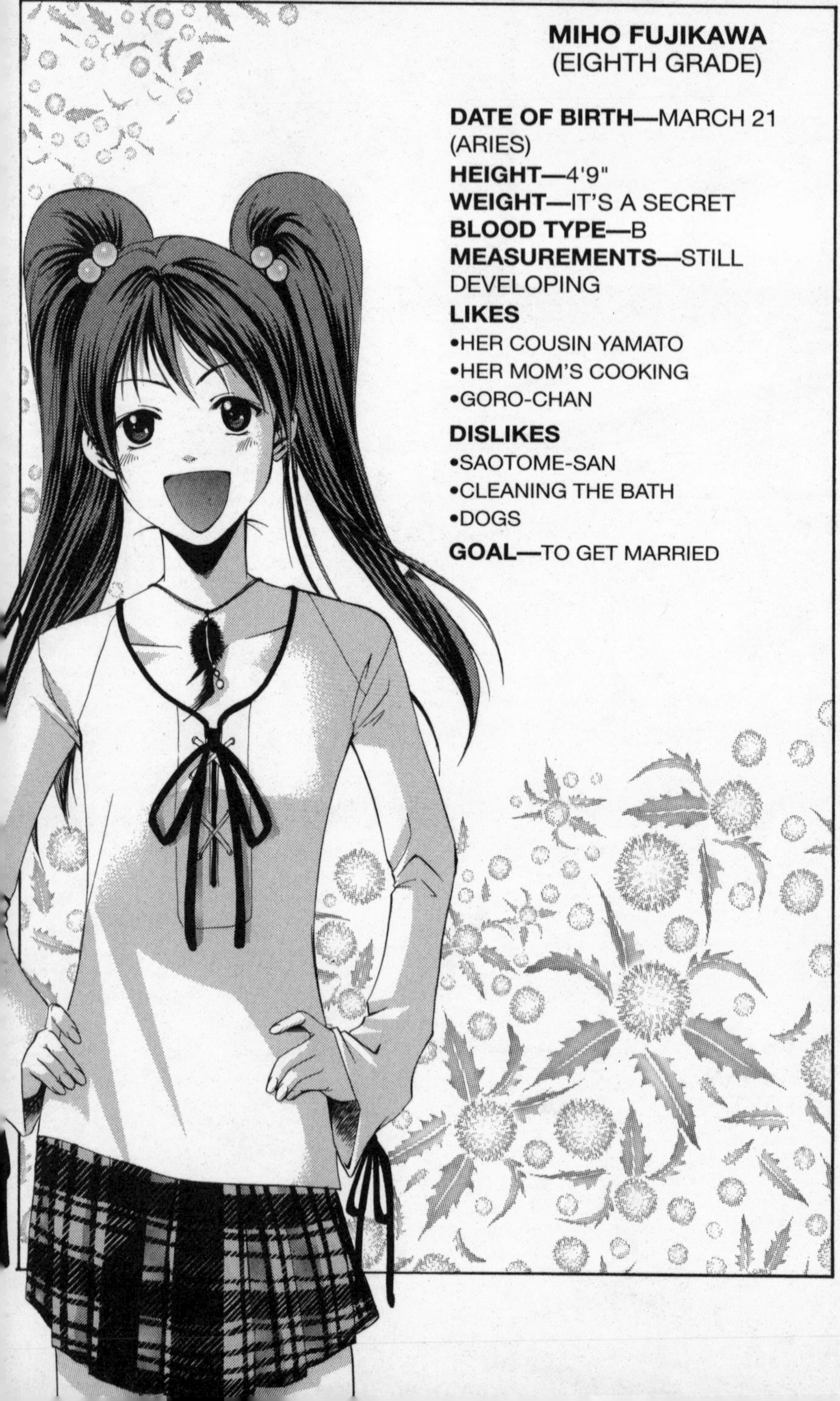

MIHO FUJIKAWA
(EIGHTH GRADE)

DATE OF BIRTH—MARCH 21 (ARIES)

HEIGHT—4'9"

WEIGHT—IT'S A SECRET

BLOOD TYPE—B

MEASUREMENTS—STILL DEVELOPING

LIKES

- HER COUSIN YAMATO
- HER MOM'S COOKING
- GORO-CHAN

DISLIKES

- SAOTOME-SAN
- CLEANING THE BATH
- DOGS

GOAL—TO GET MARRIED

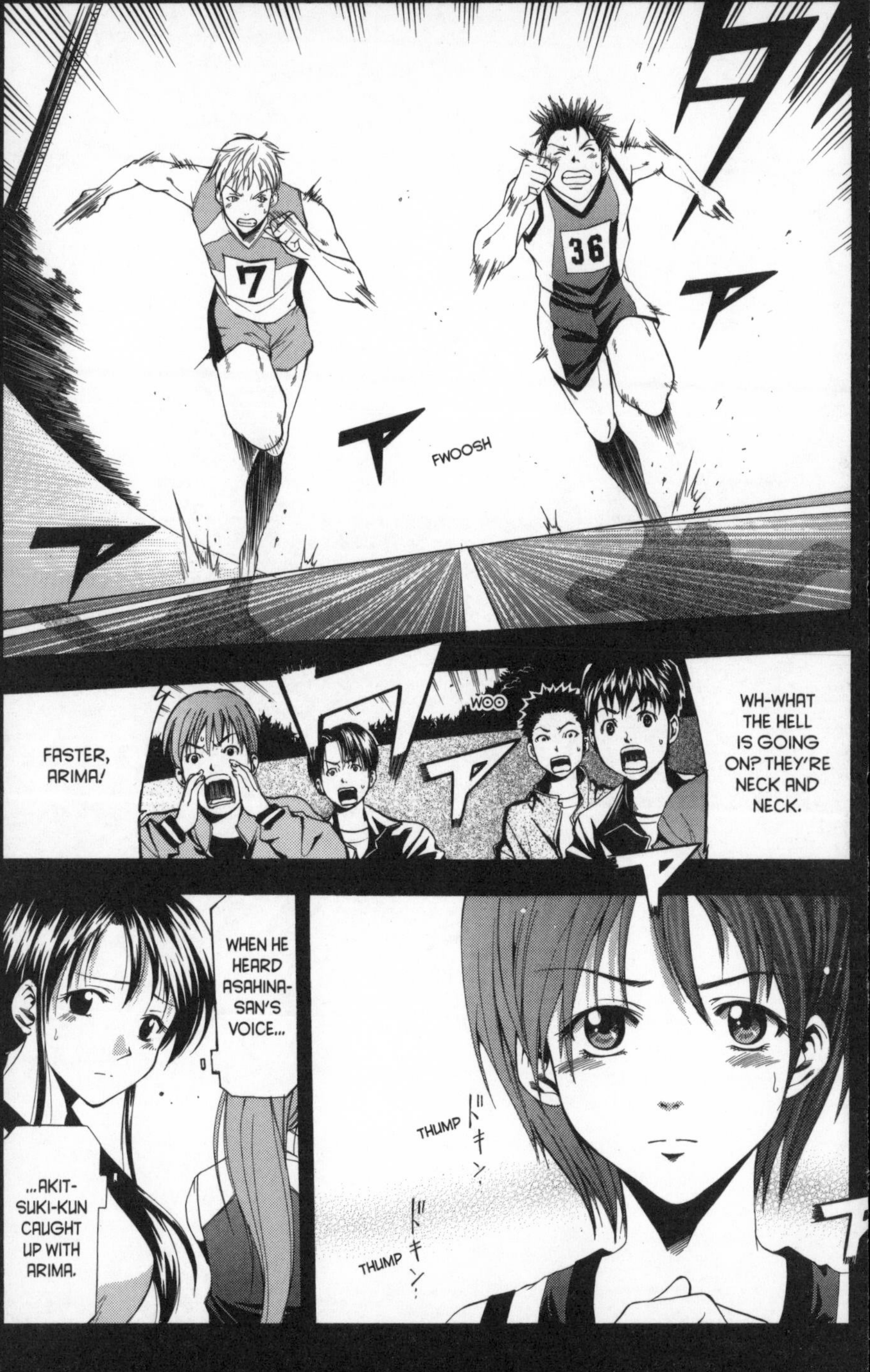
FWOOSH
WH-WHAT THE HELL IS GOING ON? THEY'RE NECK AND NECK.
WOO
FASTER, ARIMA!
THUMP
ドキン
THUMP
ドキン
WHEN HE HEARD ASAHINA-SAN'S VOICE...
...AKIT-SUKI-KUN CAUGHT UP WITH ARIMA.

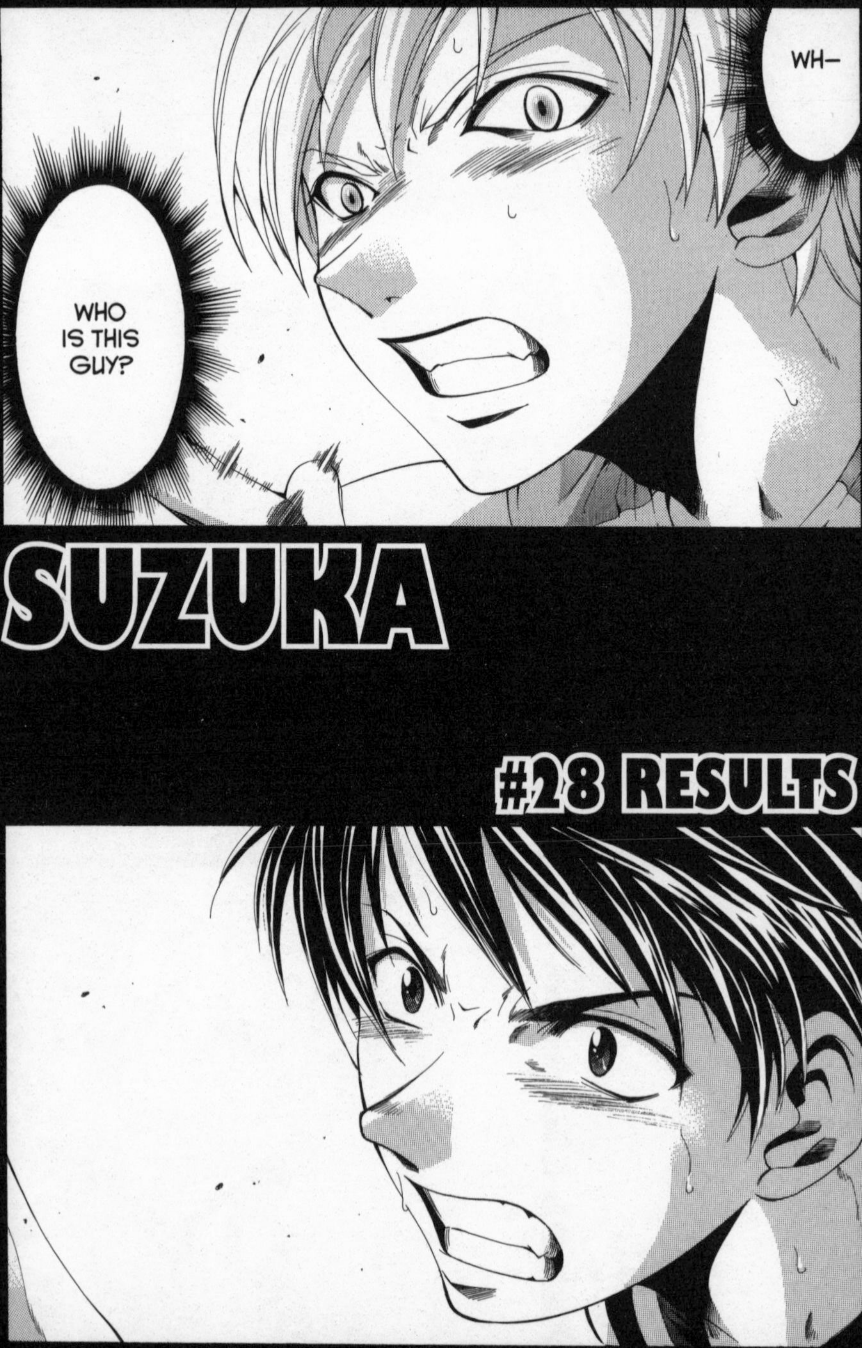
WH—
WHO IS THIS GUY?
SUZUKA
#28 RESULTS

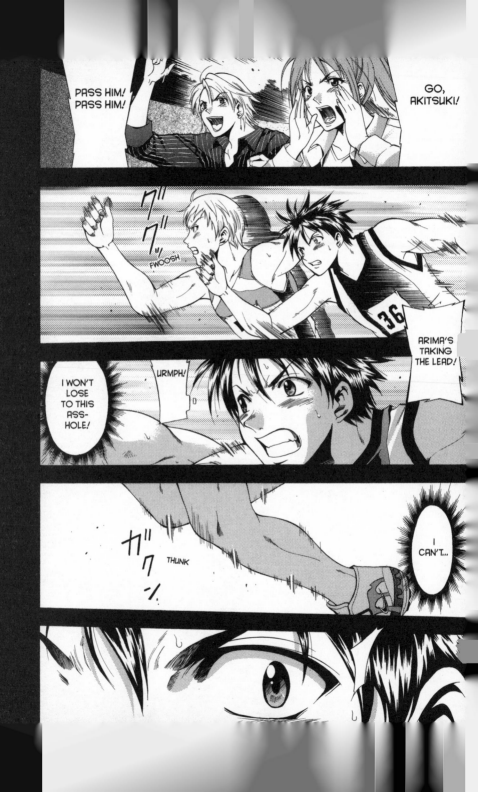

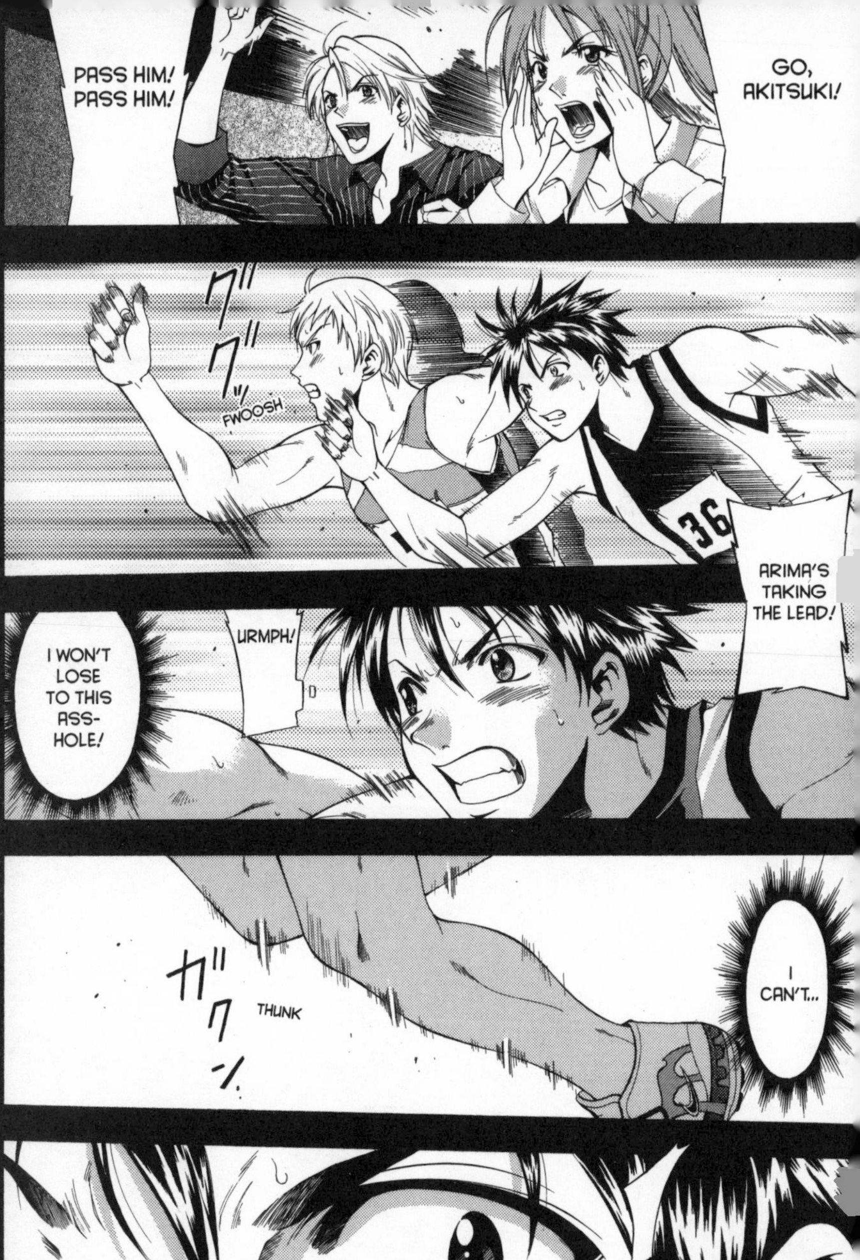
GO, AKITSUKI!
PASS HIM! PASS HIM!
FWOOSH
ARIMA'S TAKING THE LEAD!
URMPH!
I WON'T LOSE TO THIS ASS-HOLE!
I CAN'T...
THUNK

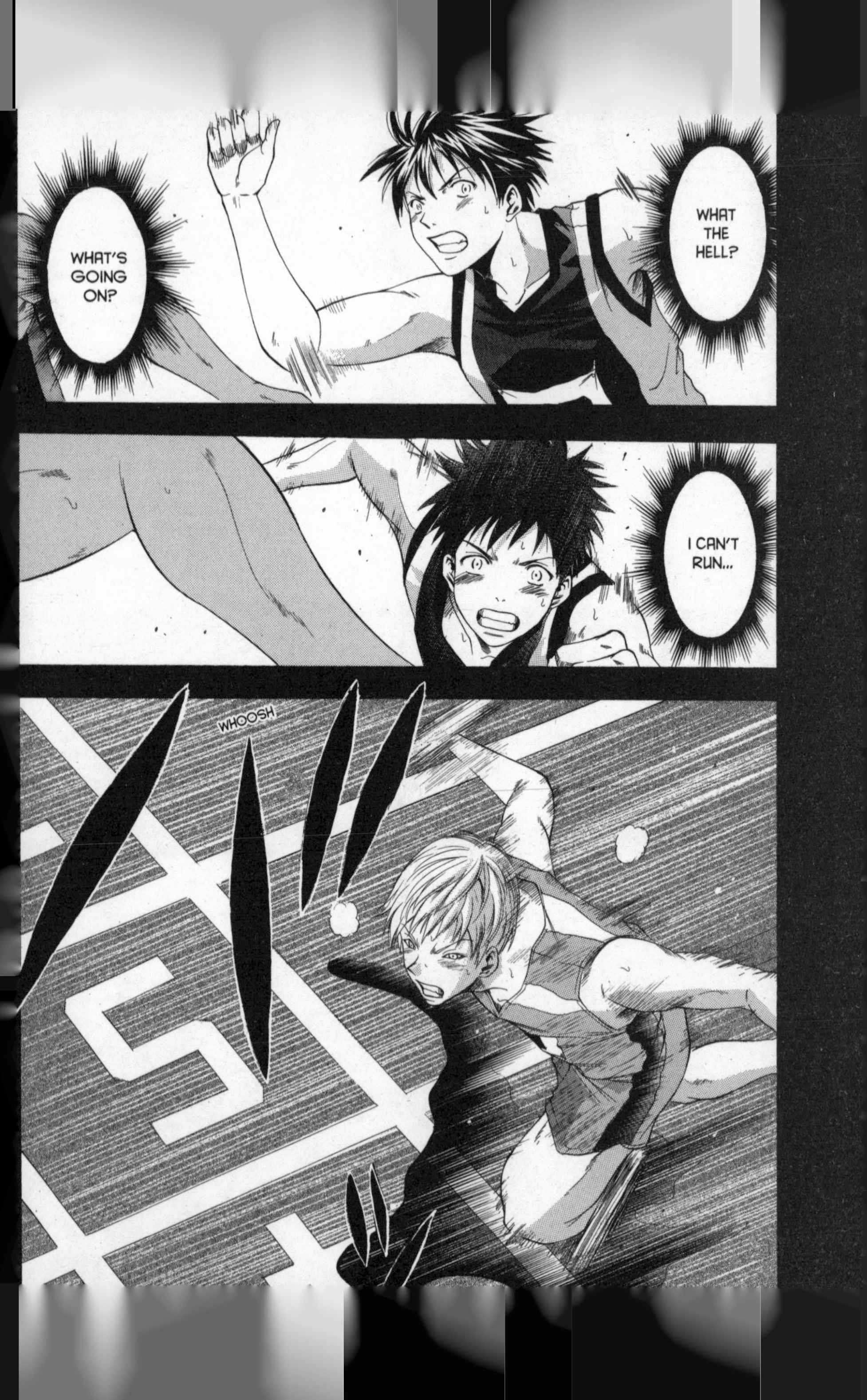
WHAT THE HELL?
WHAT'S GOING ON?
I CAN'T RUN...
WHOOSH

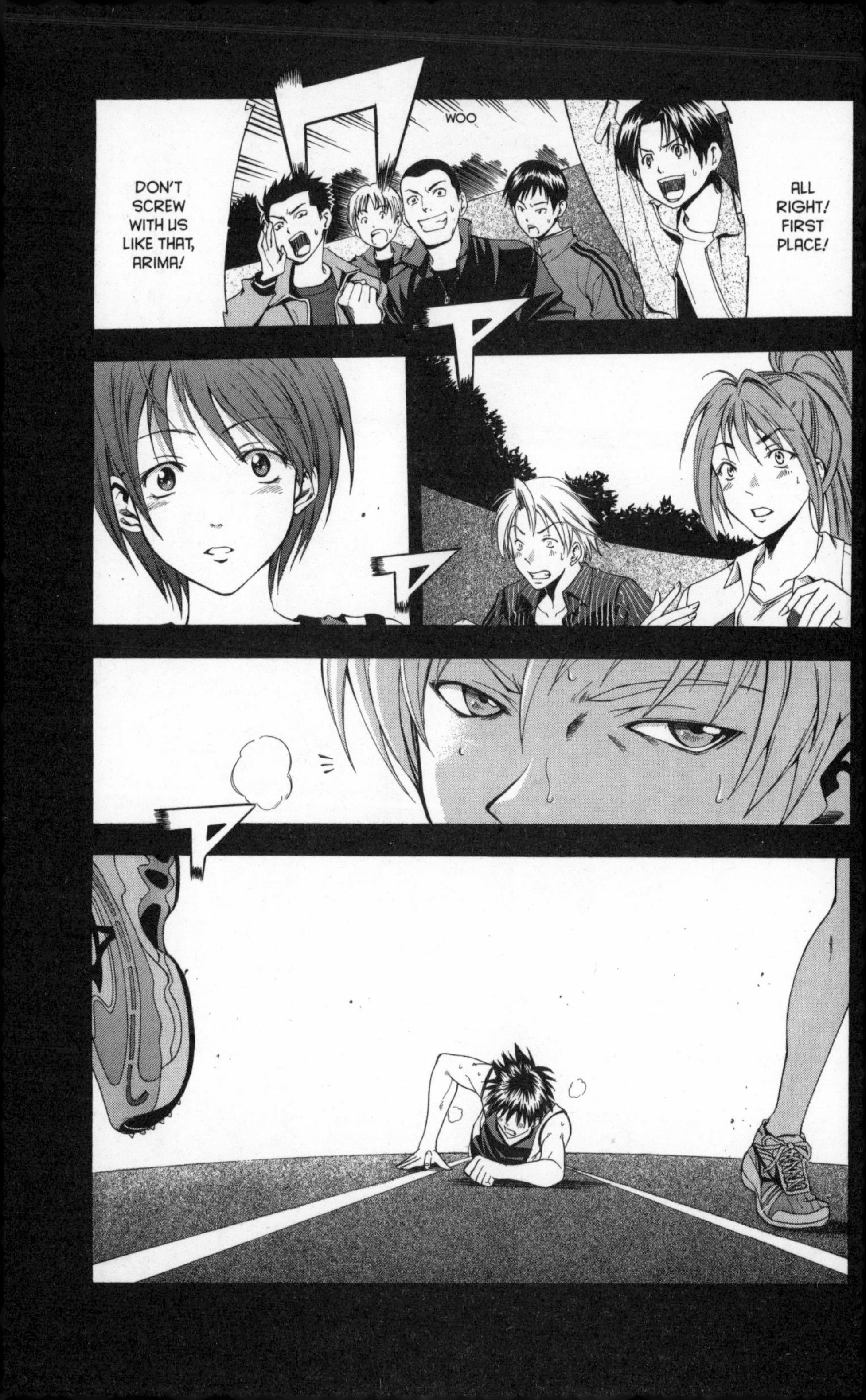
ALL RIGHT! FIRST PLACE!
WOO
DON'T SCREW WITH US LIKE THAT, ARIMA!

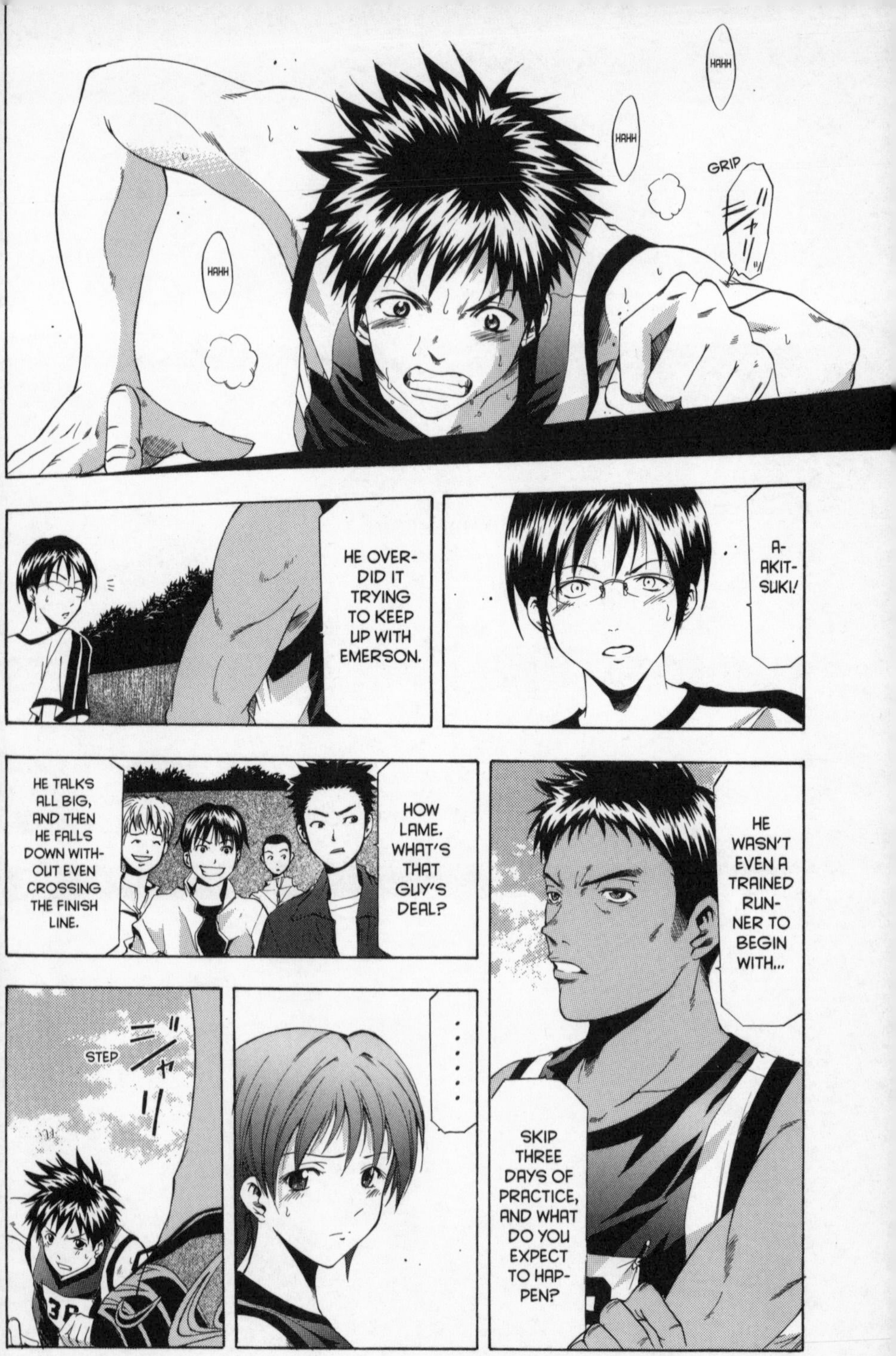
HAHH
HAHH
GRIP
HAHH
A-AKIT-SUKI!
HE OVER-DID IT TRYING TO KEEP UP WITH EMERSON.
HE WASN'T EVEN A TRAINED RUN-NER TO BEGIN WITH...
SKIP THREE DAYS OF PRACTICE, AND WHAT DO YOU EXPECT TO HAP-PEN?
HOW LAME. WHAT'S THAT GUY'S DEAL?
HE TALKS ALL BIG, AND THEN HE FALLS DOWN WITH-OUT EVEN CROSSING THE FINISH LINE.
......
STEP

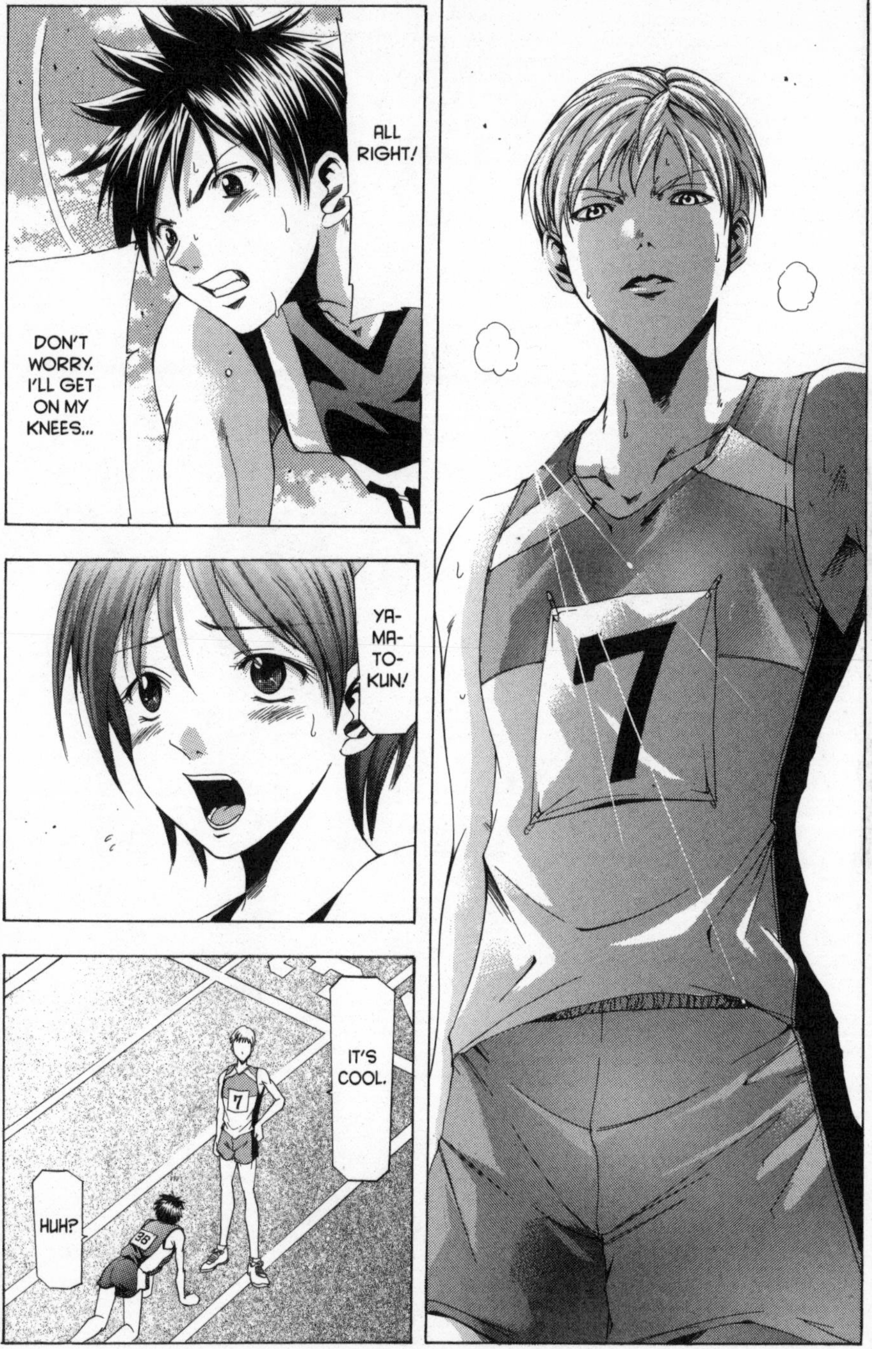
ALL RIGHT!
DON'T WORRY. I'LL GET ON MY KNEES...
YA-MA-TO-KUN!
IT'S COOL.
HUH?

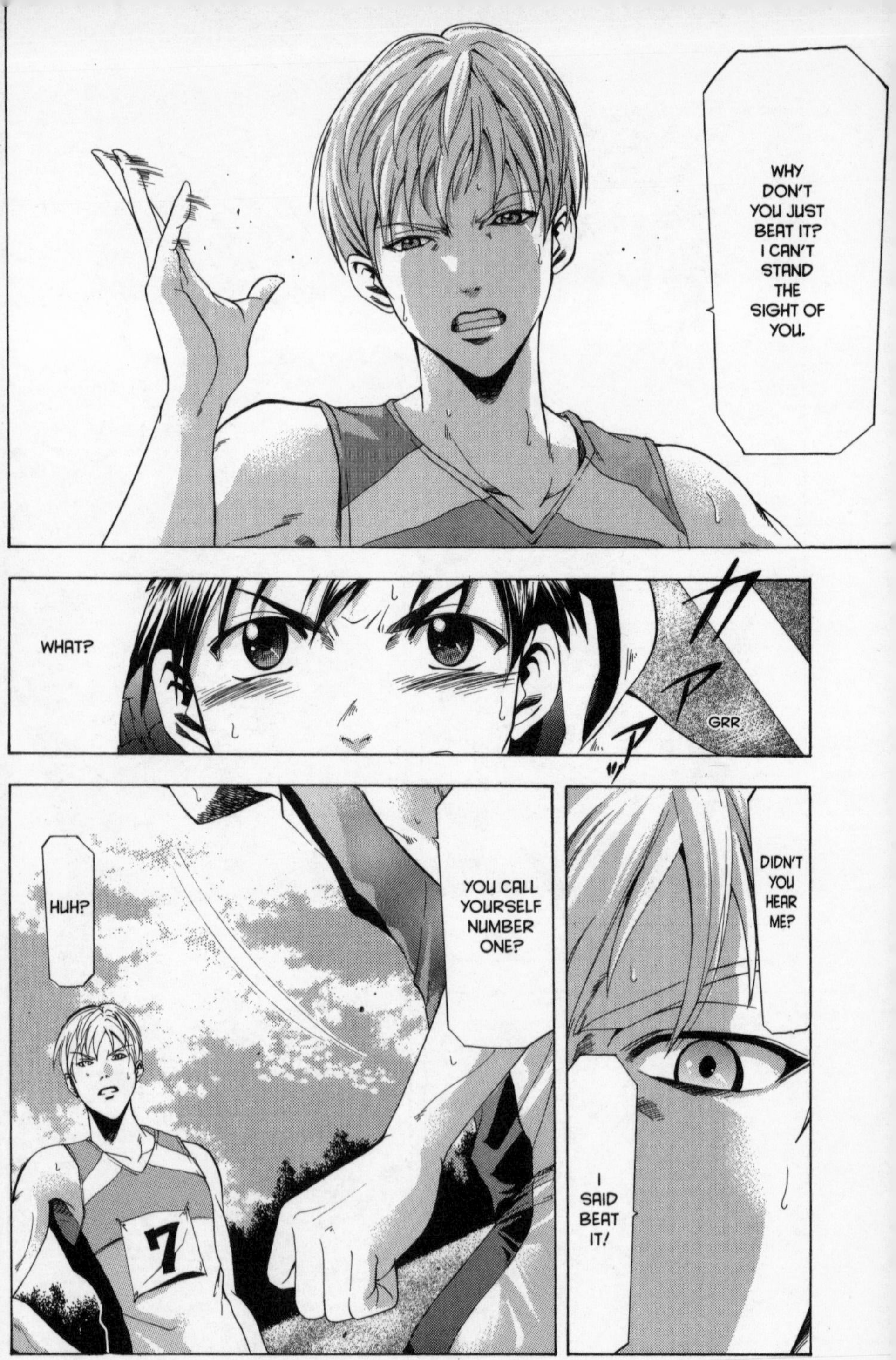
WHY DON'T YOU JUST BEAT IT? I CAN'T STAND THE SIGHT OF YOU.
GRR
WHAT?
DIDN'T YOU HEAR ME?
I SAID BEAT IT!
YOU CALL YOURSELF NUMBER ONE?
HUH?

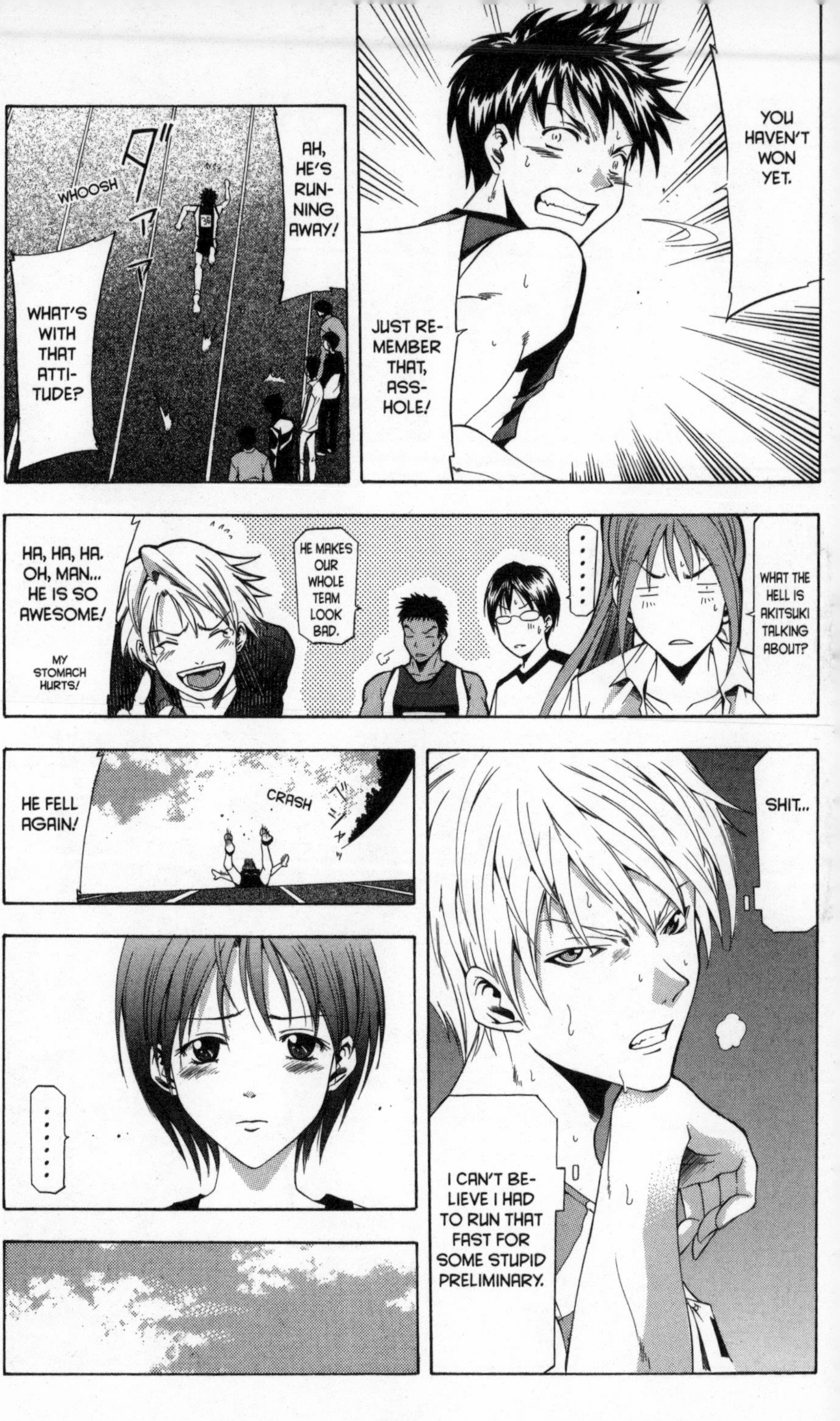
YOU HAVEN'T WON YET.
JUST RE-MEMBER THAT, ASS-HOLE!
WHOOSH
AH, HE'S RUN-NING AWAY!
WHAT'S WITH THAT ATTI-TUDE?
WHAT THE HELL IS AKITSUKI TALKING ABOUT?
......
HE MAKES OUR WHOLE TEAM LOOK BAD.
HA, HA, HA. OH, MAN... HE IS SO AWESOME!
MY STOMACH HURTS!
SHIT...
I CAN'T BE-LIEVE I HAD TO RUN THAT FAST FOR SOME STUPID PRELIMINARY.
CRASH
HE FELL AGAIN!
......

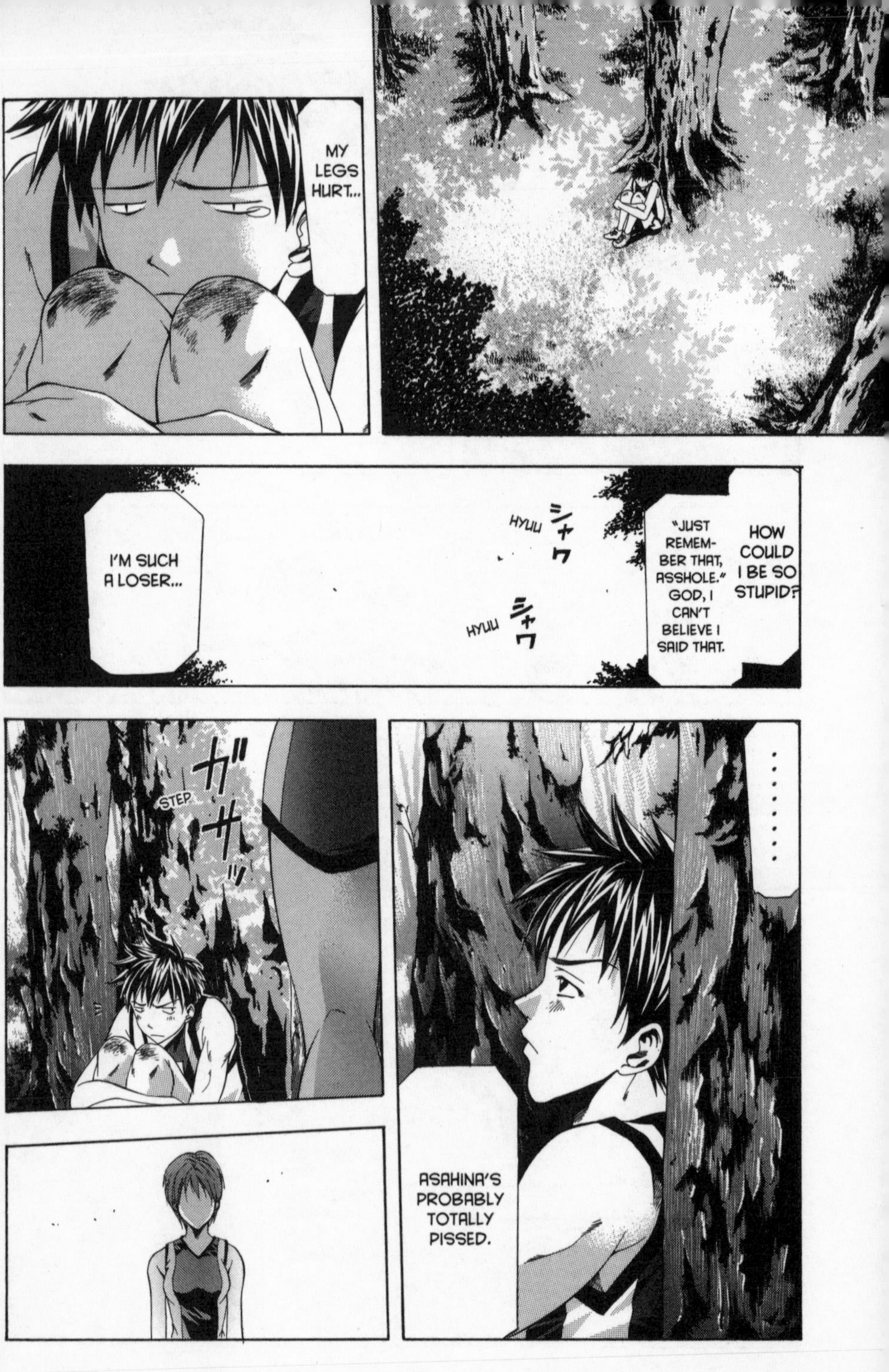
MY LEGS HURT...
HOW COULD I BE SO STUPID?
"JUST REMEMBER THAT, ASSHOLE." GOD, I CAN'T BELIEVE I SAID THAT.
シャワ
HYUU
シャワ
HYUU
I'M SUCH A LOSER...
....
ASAHINA'S PROBABLY TOTALLY PISSED.
ガサッ
STEP

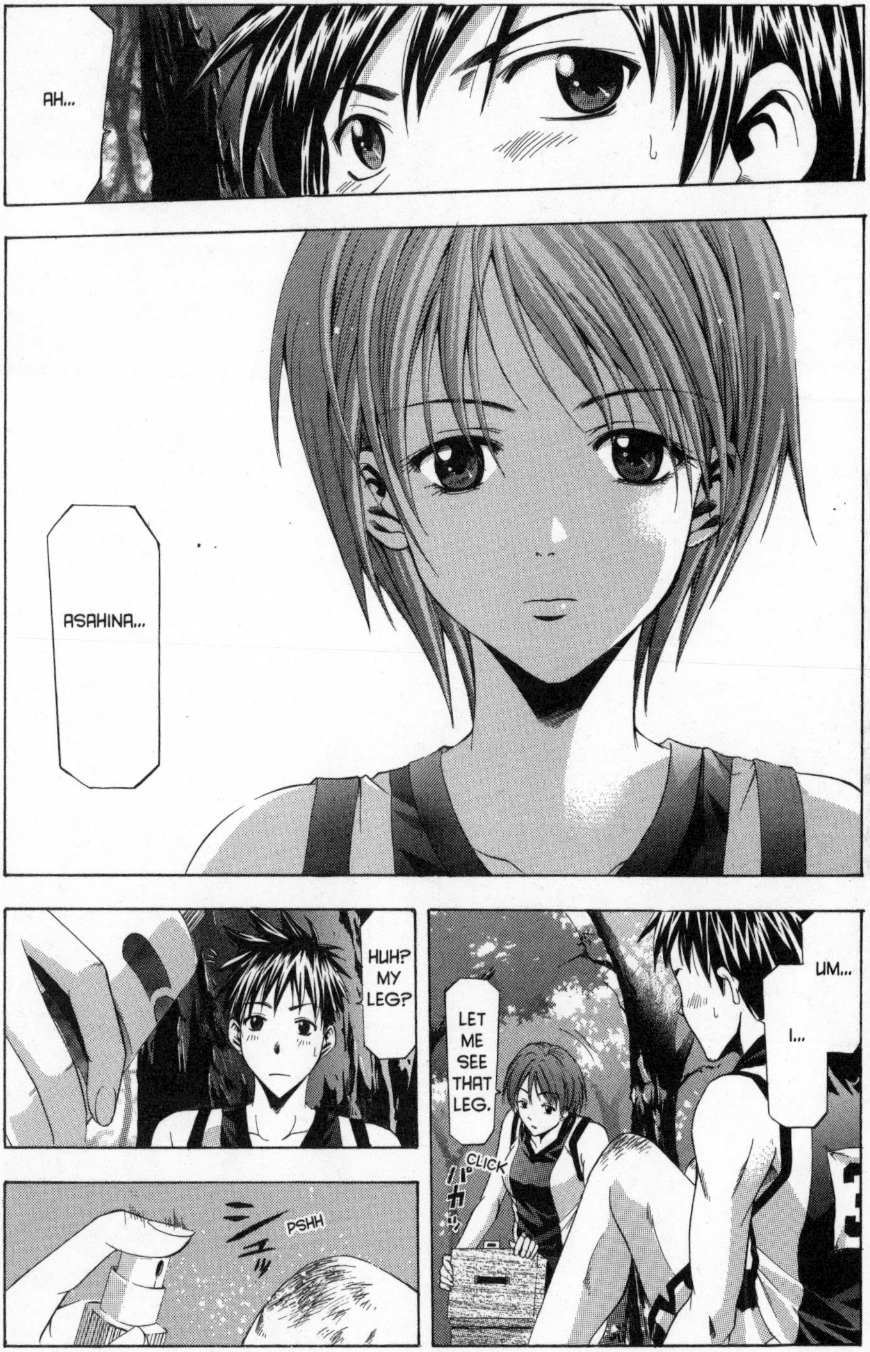
AH...
ASAHINA...
UM...
I...
LET ME SEE THAT LEG.
CLICK
パカッ
HUH? MY LEG?
シュッ
PSHH

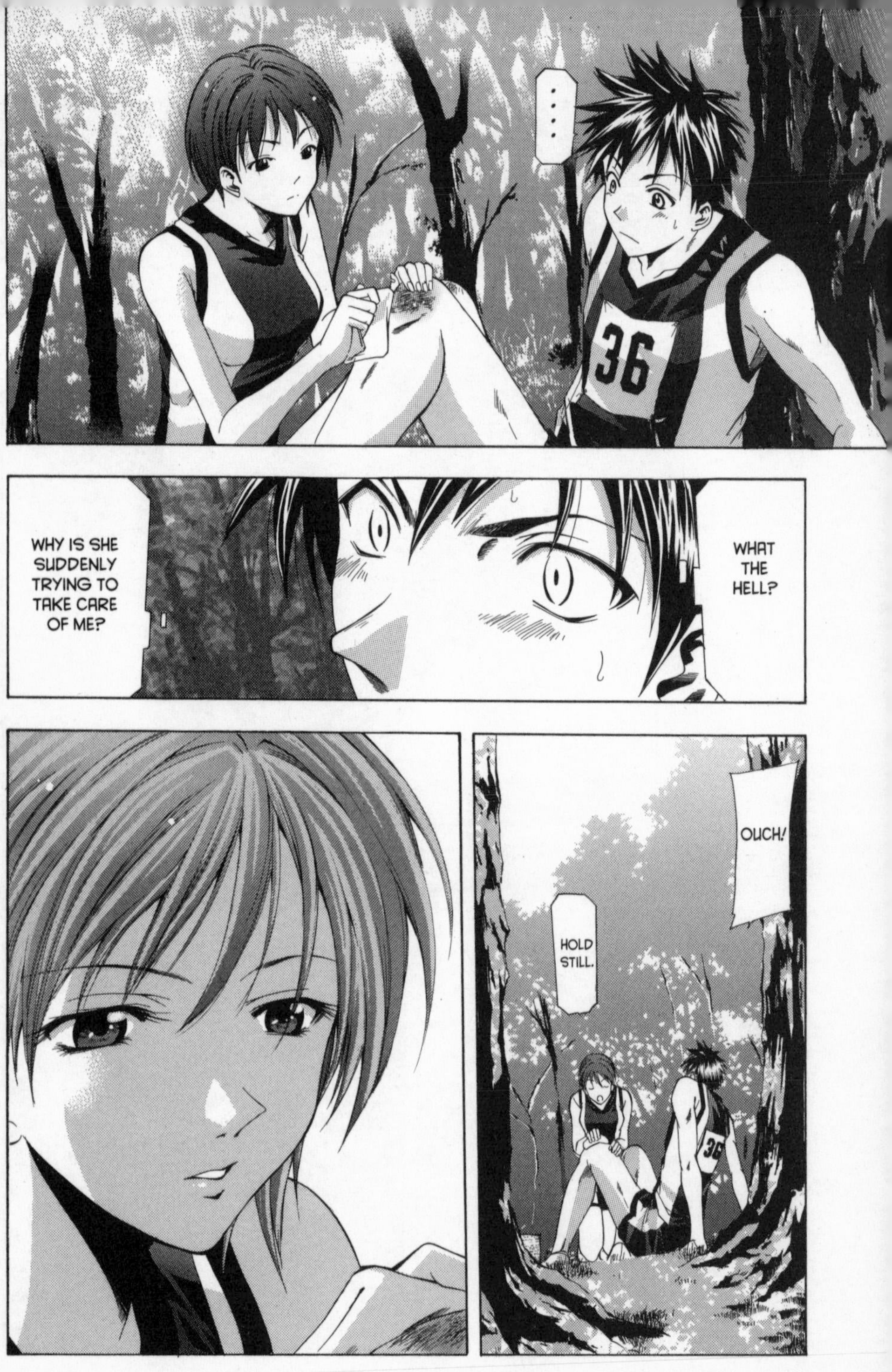
.....
WHAT THE HELL?
WHY IS SHE SUDDENLY TRYING TO TAKE CARE OF ME?
OUCH!
HOLD STILL.

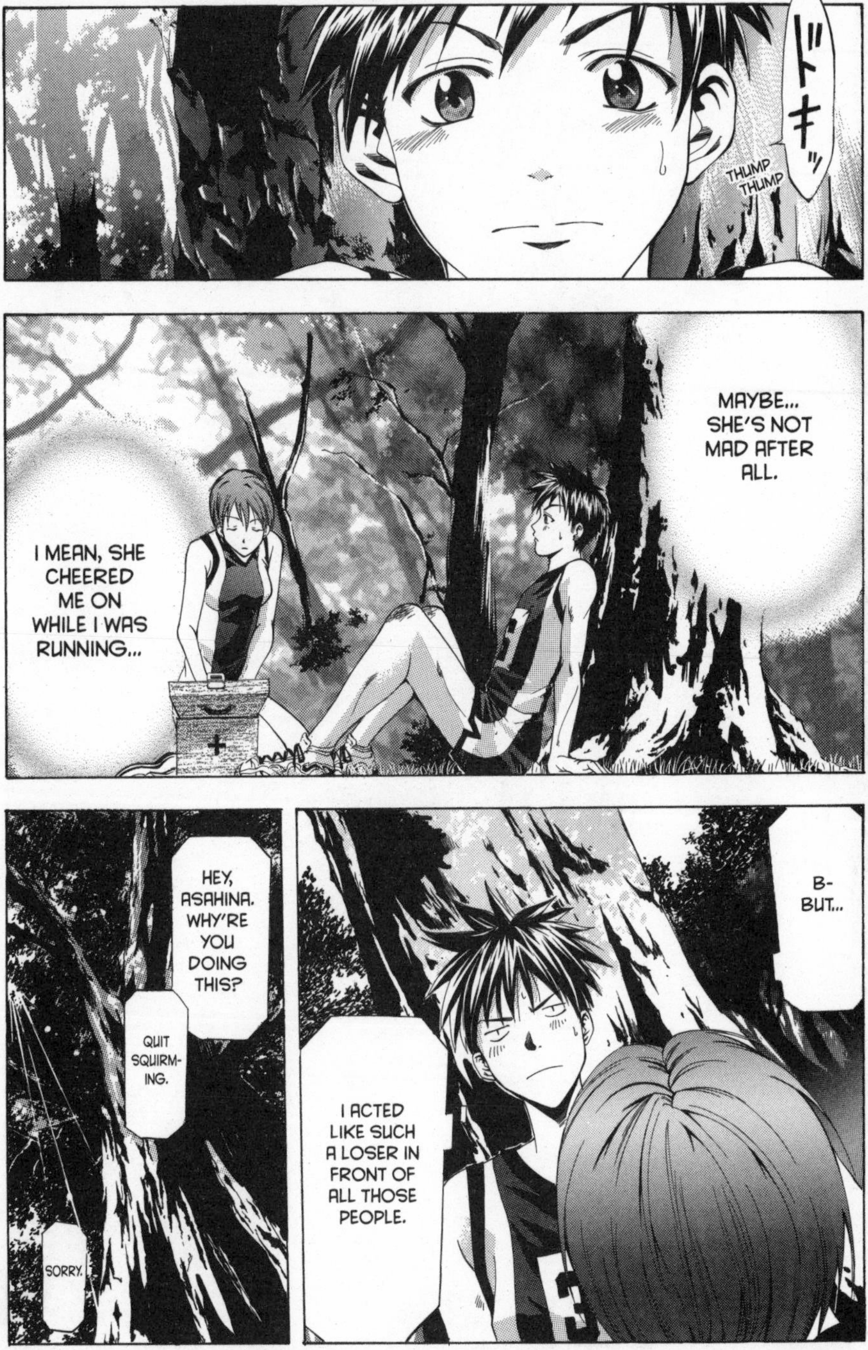
ドキッ
THUMP THUMP
MAYBE... SHE'S NOT MAD AFTER ALL.
I MEAN, SHE CHEERED ME ON WHILE I WAS RUNNING...
B- BUT...
I ACTED LIKE SUCH A LOSER IN FRONT OF ALL THOSE PEOPLE.
HEY, ASAHINA. WHY'RE YOU DOING THIS?
QUIT SQUIRM- ING.
SORRY.

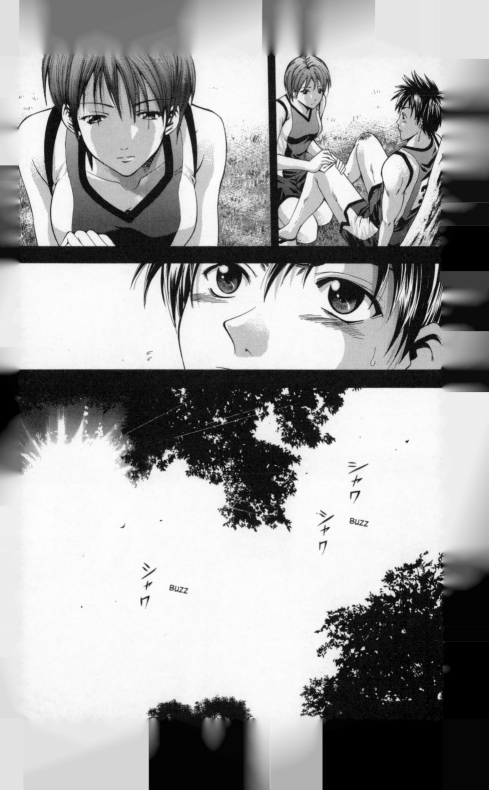

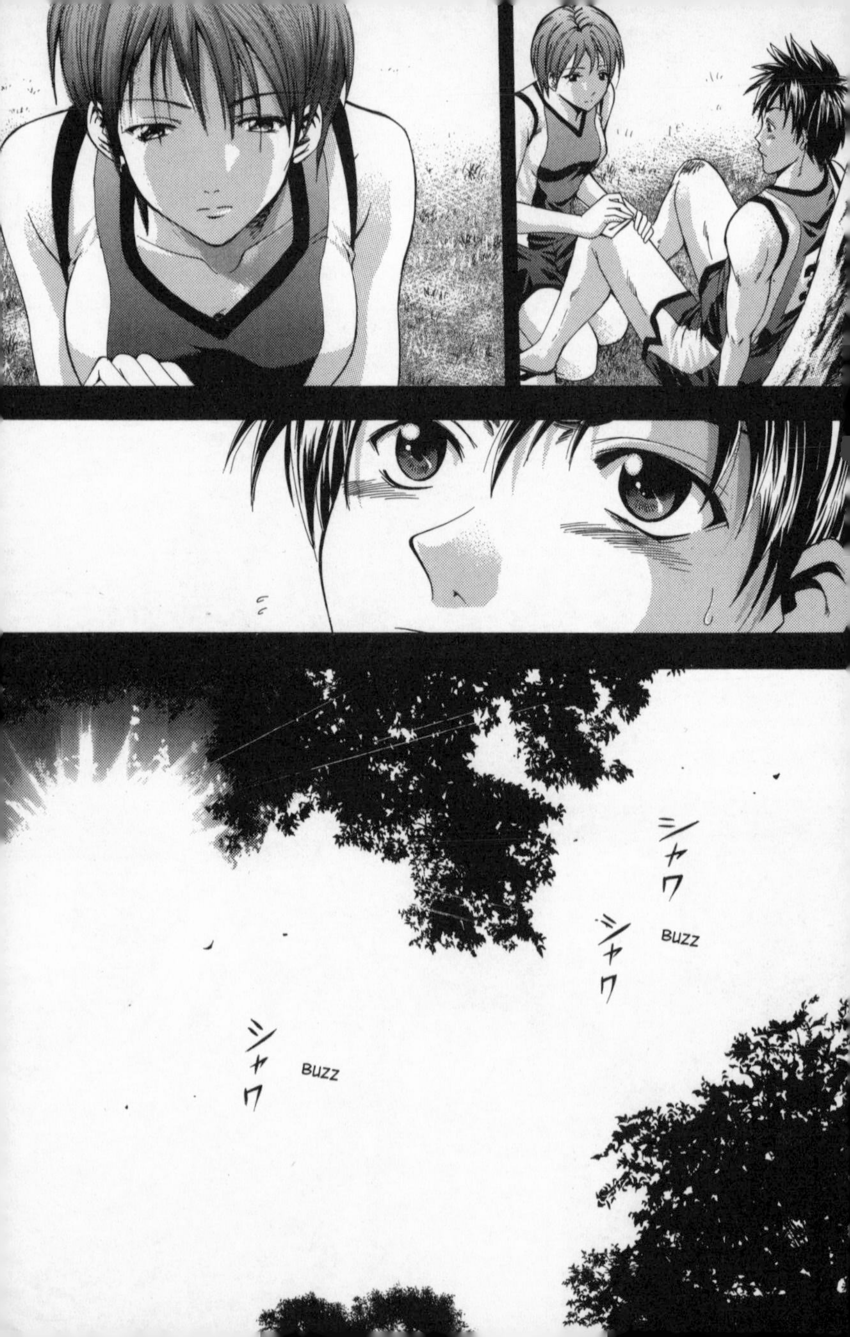
シャワ
シャワ
Buzz
シャワ
Buzz

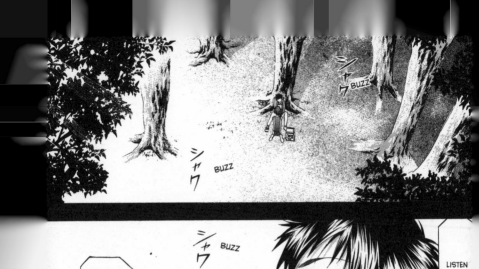

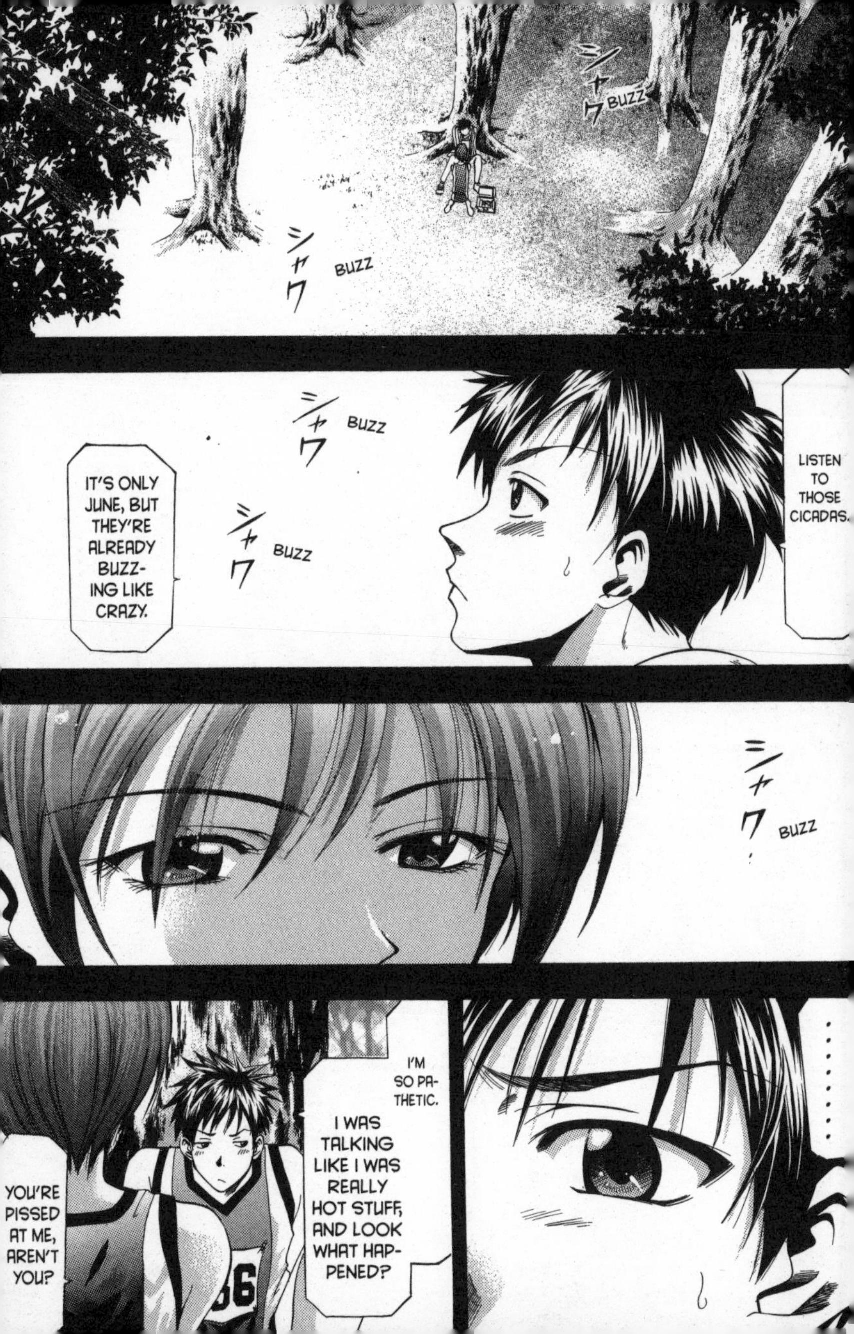
シャワ BUZZ
シャワ BUZZ
LISTEN TO THOSE CICADAS.
シャワ BUZZ
シャワ BUZZ
IT'S ONLY JUNE, BUT THEY'RE ALREADY BUZZ-ING LIKE CRAZY.
シャワ BUZZ
......
I'M SO PA-THETIC.
I WAS TALKING LIKE I WAS REALLY HOT STUFF, AND LOOK WHAT HAP-PENED?
YOU'RE PISSED AT ME, AREN'T YOU?
56

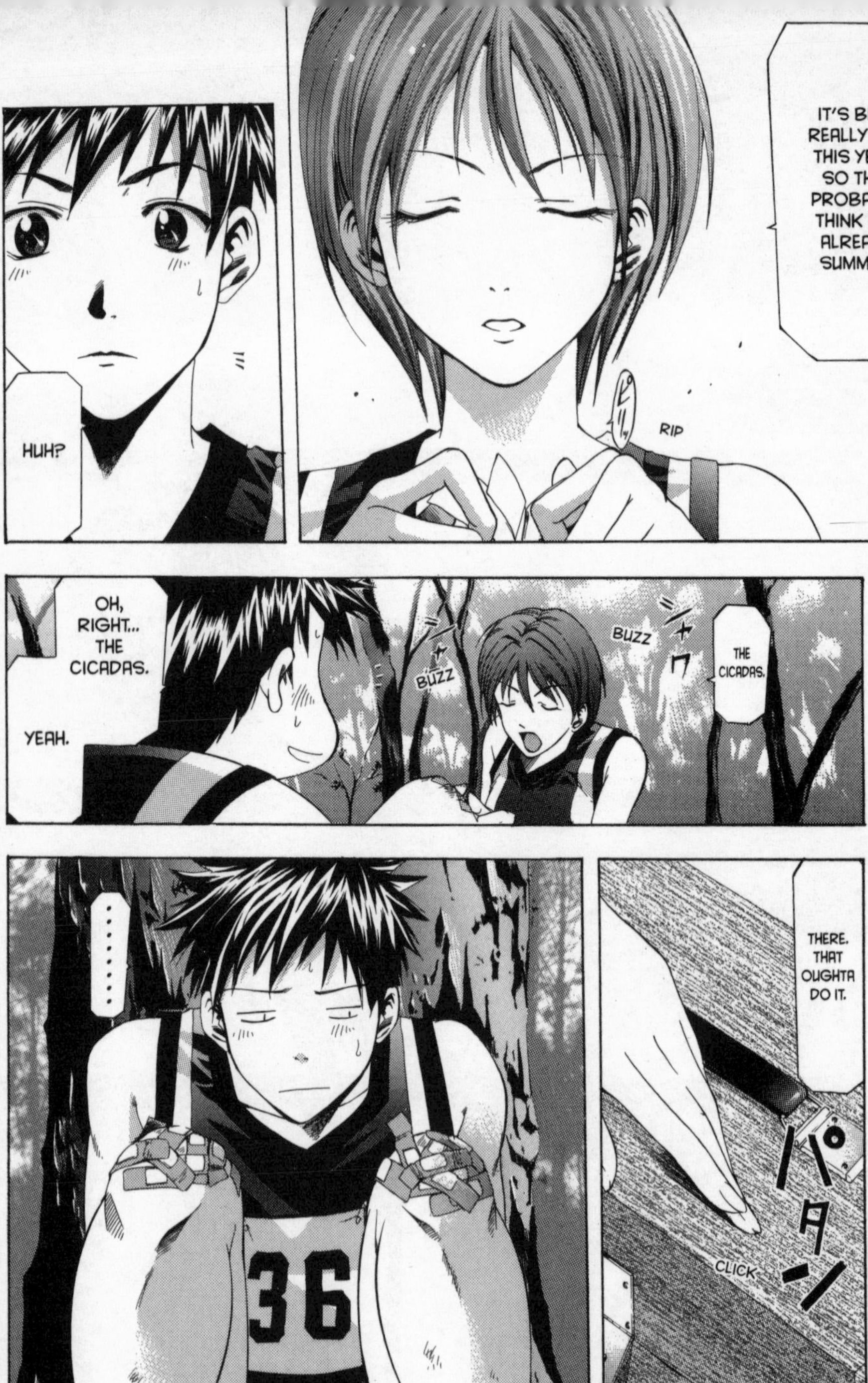
IT'S BEEN REALLY HOT THIS YEAR, SO THEY PROBABLY THINK IT'S ALREADY SUMMER.
RIP
HUH?
THE CICADAS.
BUZZ
BUZZ
OH, RIGHT... THE CICADAS.
YEAH.
THERE. THAT OUGHTA DO IT.
CLICK
......

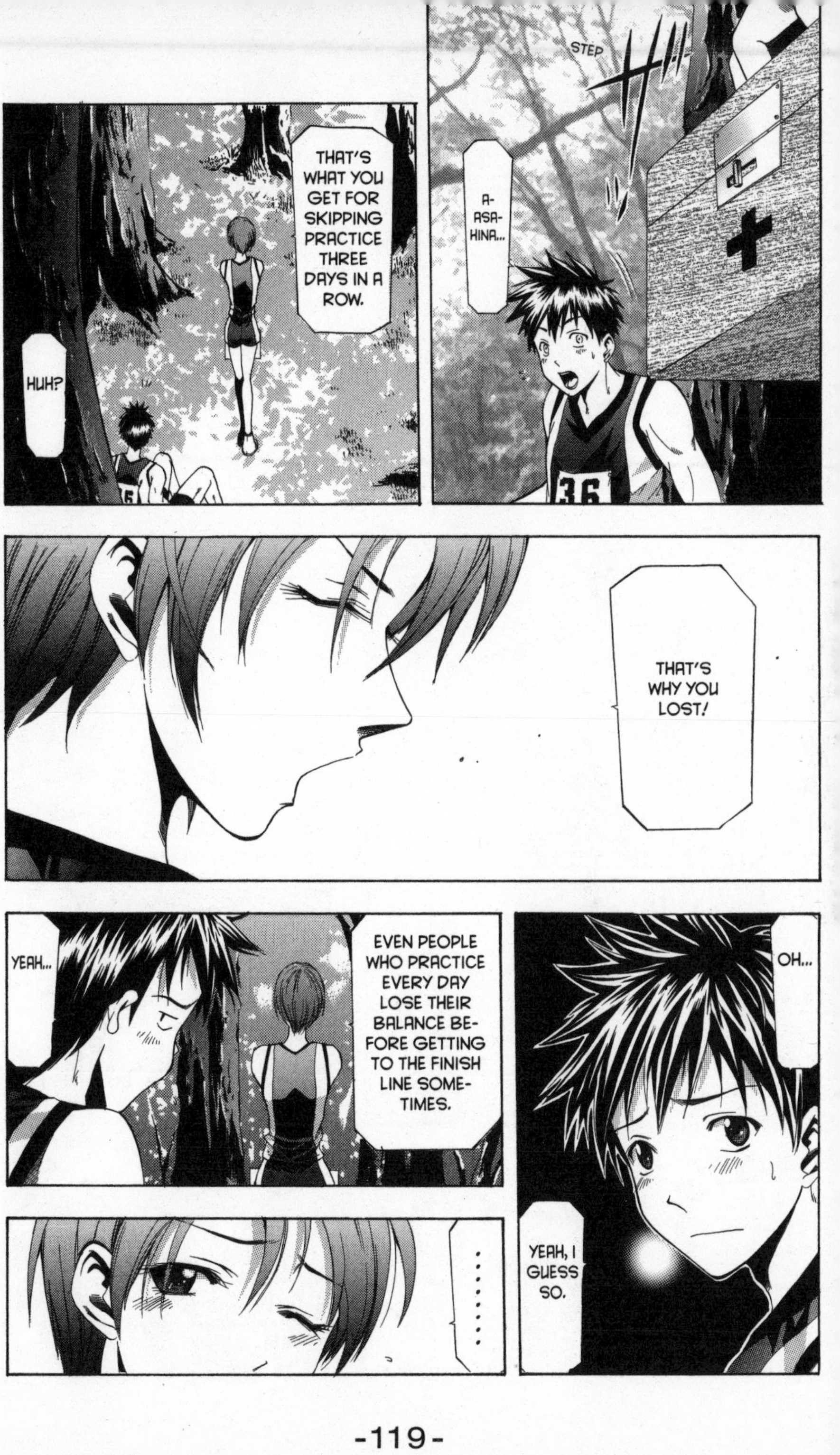
STEP
A- ASA- HINA...
THAT'S WHAT YOU GET FOR SKIPPING PRACTICE THREE DAYS IN A ROW.
HUH?
THAT'S WHY YOU LOST!
OH...
YEAH, I GUESS SO.
EVEN PEOPLE WHO PRACTICE EVERY DAY LOSE THEIR BALANCE BE- FORE GETTING TO THE FINISH LINE SOME- TIMES.
YEAH...
......

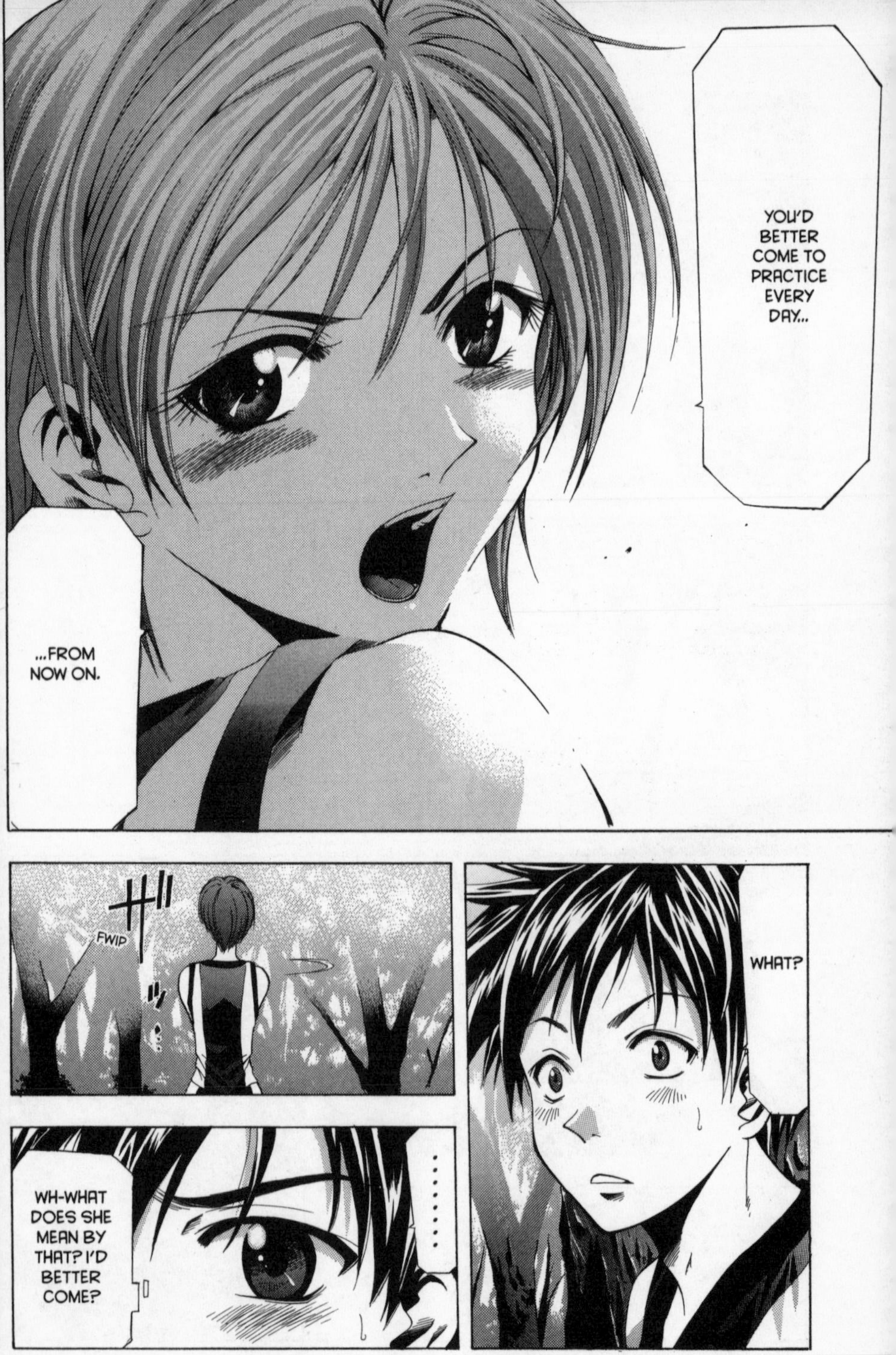
YOU'D BETTER COME TO PRACTICE EVERY DAY...
...FROM NOW ON.
WHAT?
FWIP
......
WH-WHAT DOES SHE MEAN BY THAT? I'D BETTER COME?

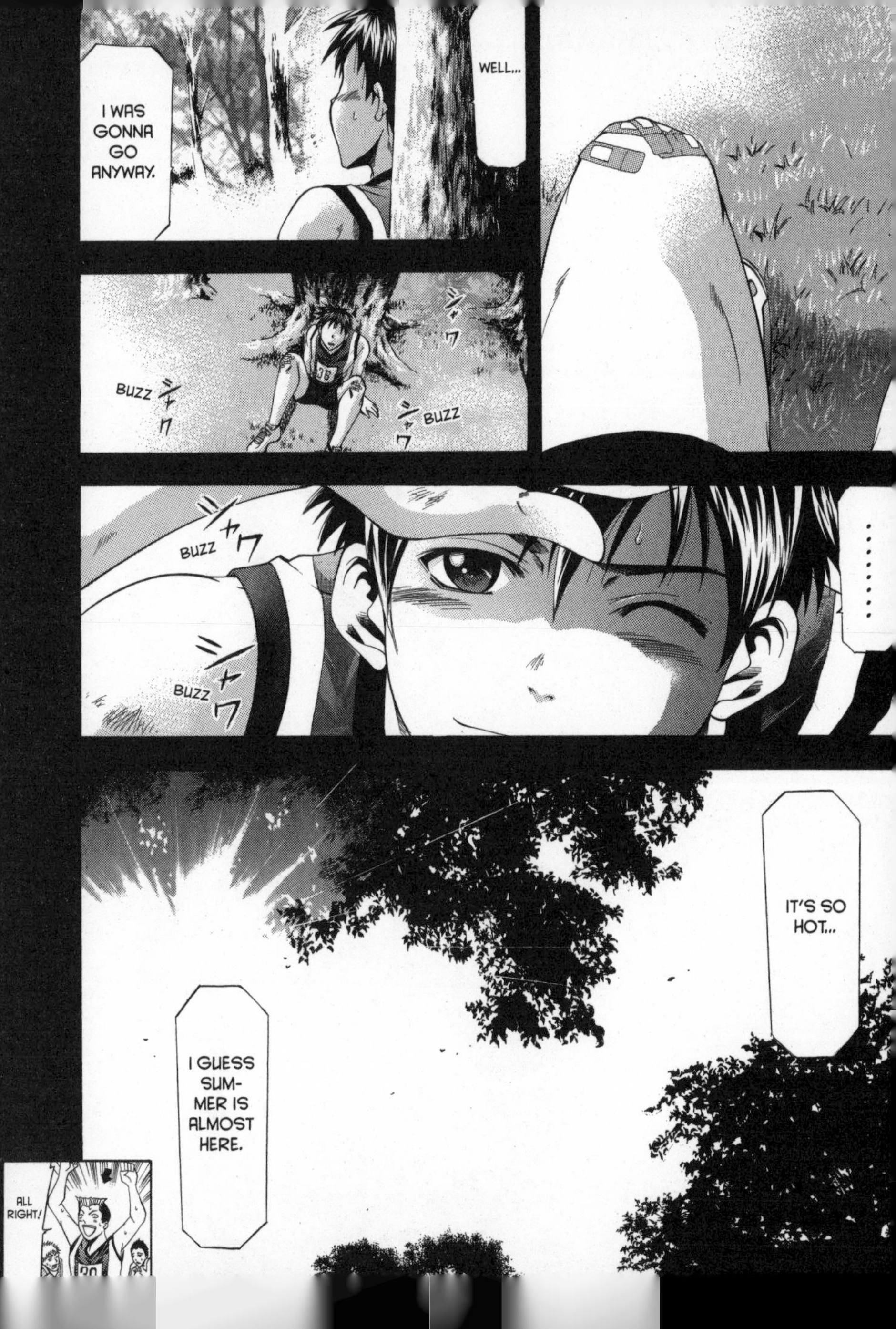
WELL...
I WAS GONNA GO ANYWAY.
BUZZ
BUZZ
......
BUZZ
BUZZ
IT'S SO HOT...
I GUESS SUM-MER IS ALMOST HERE.
ALL RIGHT!

CHARACTER PROFILE NO. 10

AYANO FUJIKAWA
(AGE 32)

DATE OF BIRTH—FEBRUARY 11 (AQUARIUS)
HEIGHT—5'3"
WEIGHT—100 LBS
MEASUREMENTS—35, 23, 36

LIKES
- MIHO, YAMATO-KUN
- HOUSEWORK
- HER DECEASED HUSBAND

DISLIKES
- BEING UNPRODUCTIVE
- PLACES WHERE YOUNG PEOPLE HANG OUT
- BEING CALLED "LADY"

GOAL—TO FIND A HUSBAND FOR MIHO

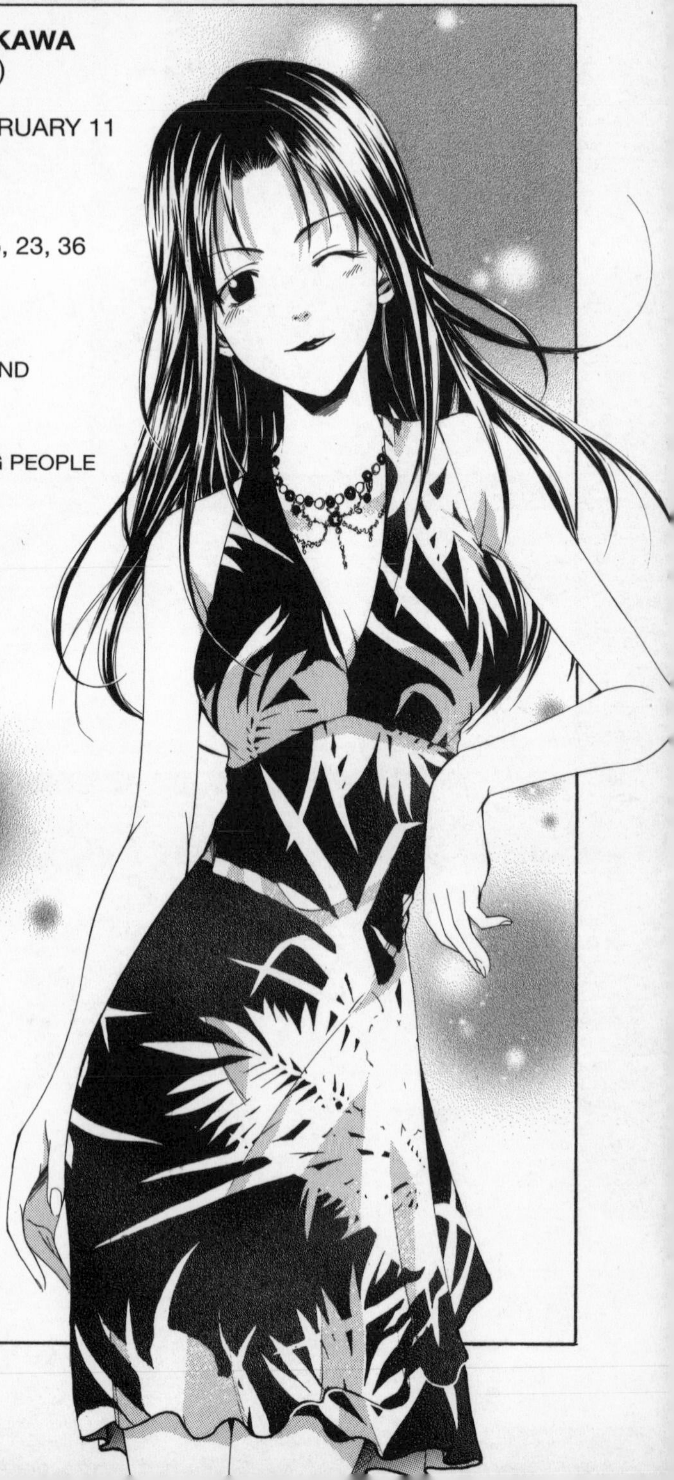

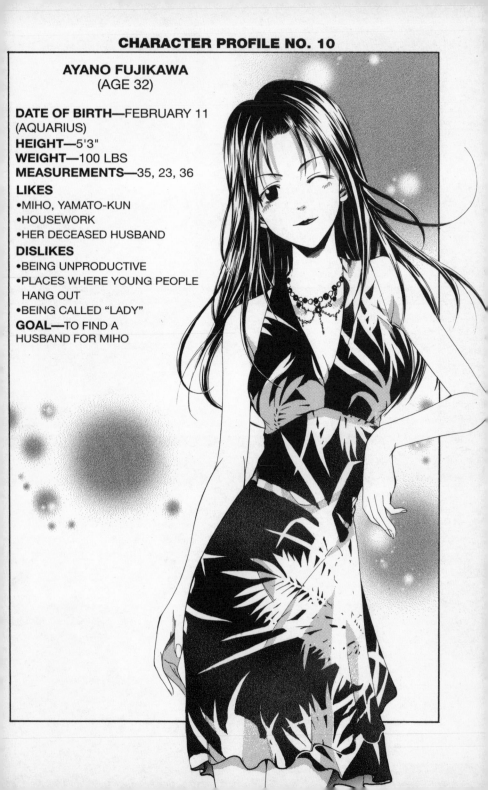

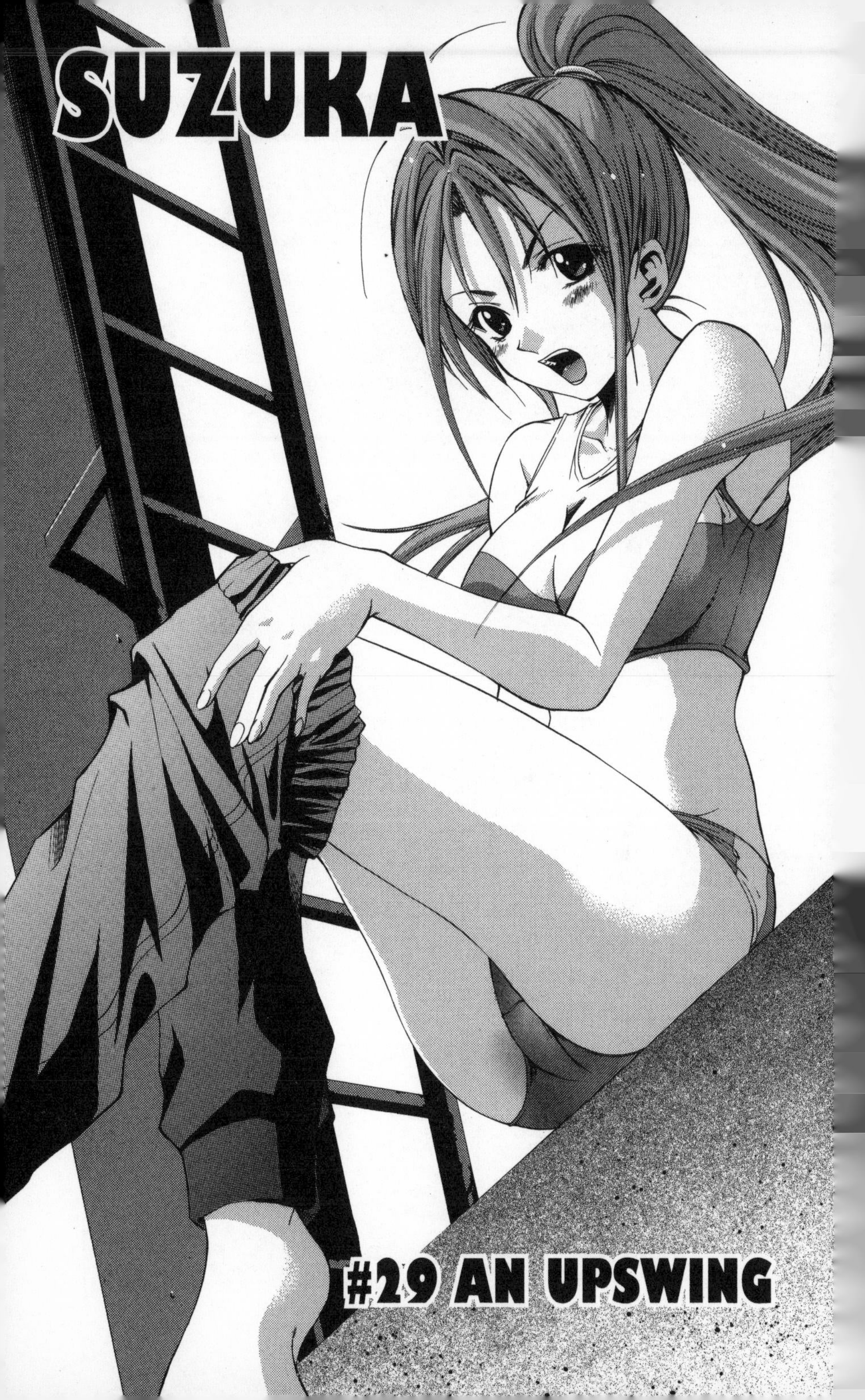
SUZUKA
#29 AN UPSWING

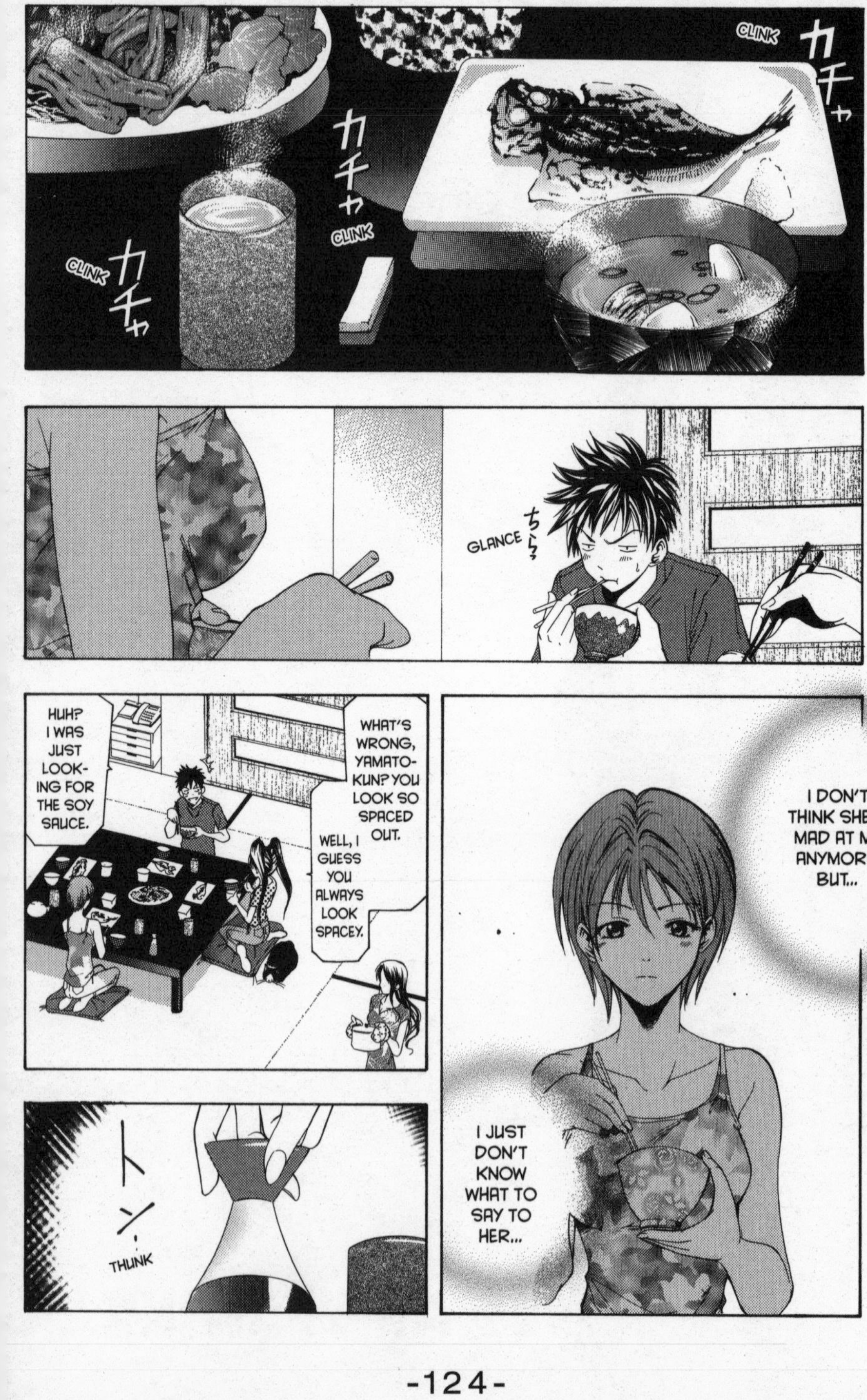
CLINK
カチャ
カチャ
CLINK
CLINK
カチャ
GLANCE
ちら
I DON'T THINK SHE'S MAD AT ME ANYMORE, BUT...
I JUST DON'T KNOW WHAT TO SAY TO HER...
WHAT'S WRONG, YAMATO-KUN? YOU LOOK SO SPACED OUT.
HUH? I WAS JUST LOOKING FOR THE SOY SAUCE.
WELL, I GUESS YOU ALWAYS LOOK SPACEY.
トン
THUNK

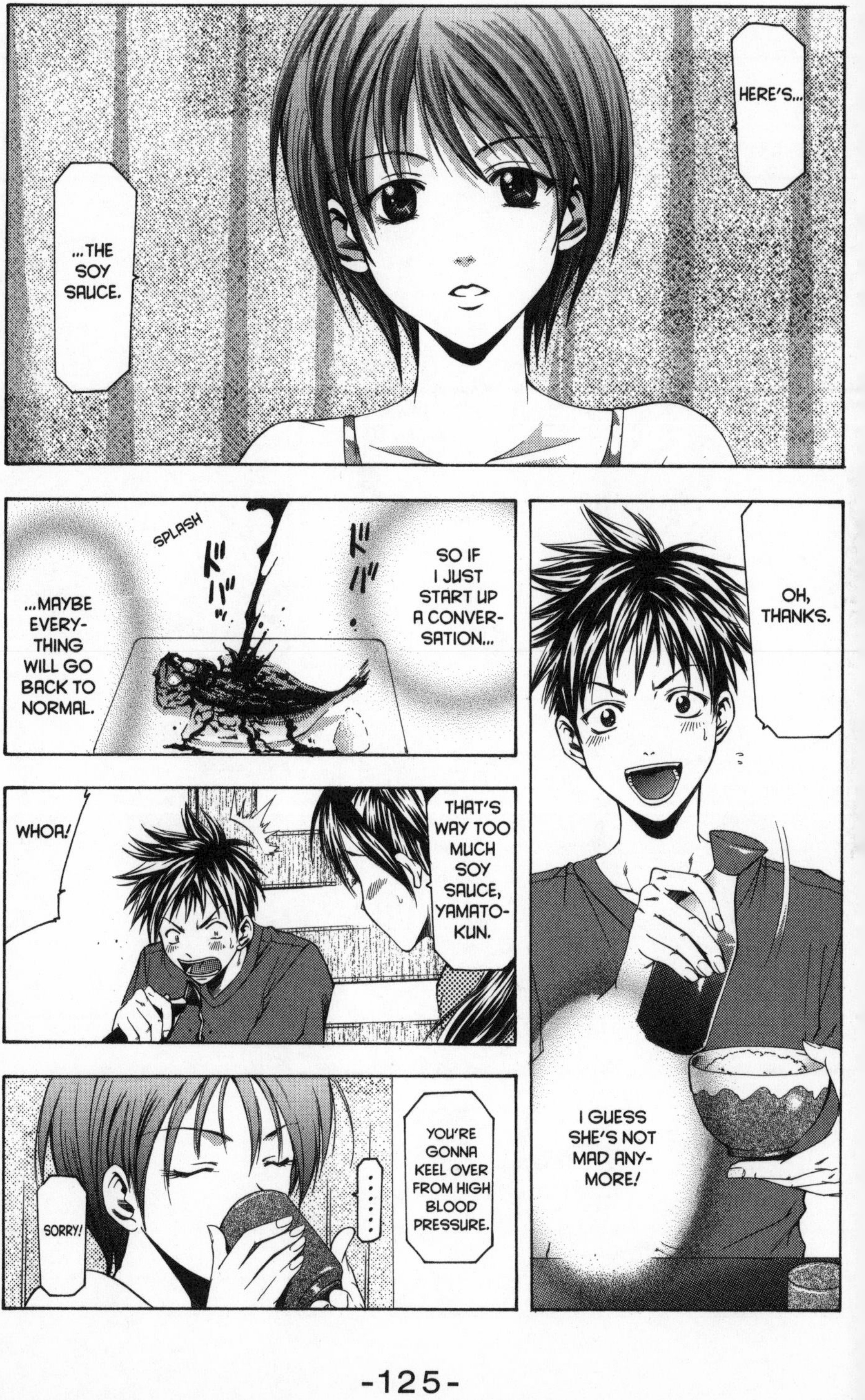
HERE'S...
...THE SOY SAUCE.
OH, THANKS.
I GUESS SHE'S NOT MAD ANYMORE!
ドバ
SO IF I JUST START UP A CONVERSATION...
SPLASH
ドバ
...MAYBE EVERYTHING WILL GO BACK TO NORMAL.
THAT'S WAY TOO MUCH SOY SAUCE, YAMATO-KUN.
WHOA!
YOU'RE GONNA KEEL OVER FROM HIGH BLOOD PRESSURE.
......
SORRY!

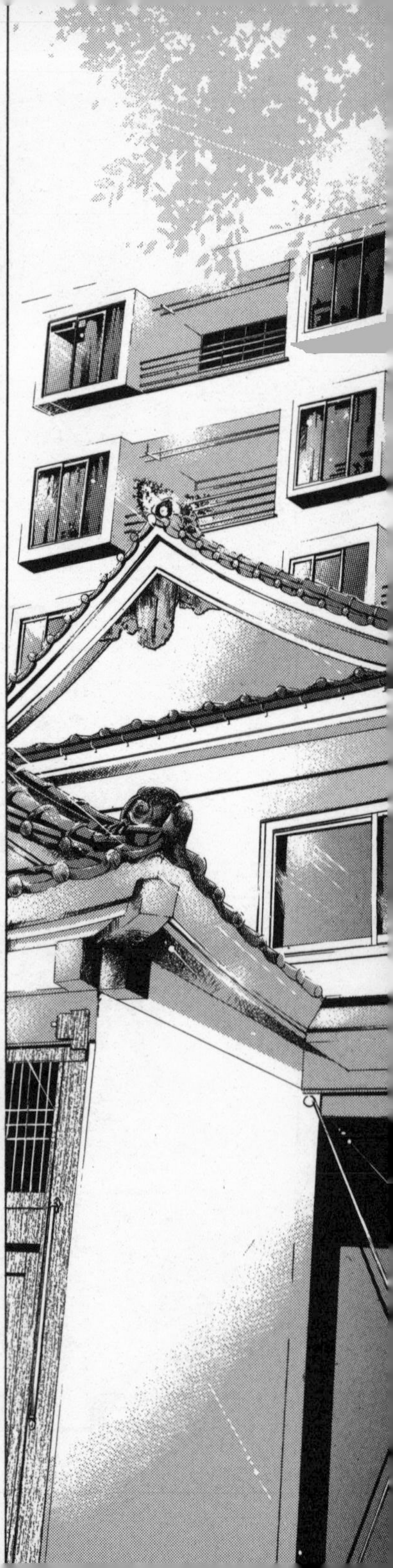

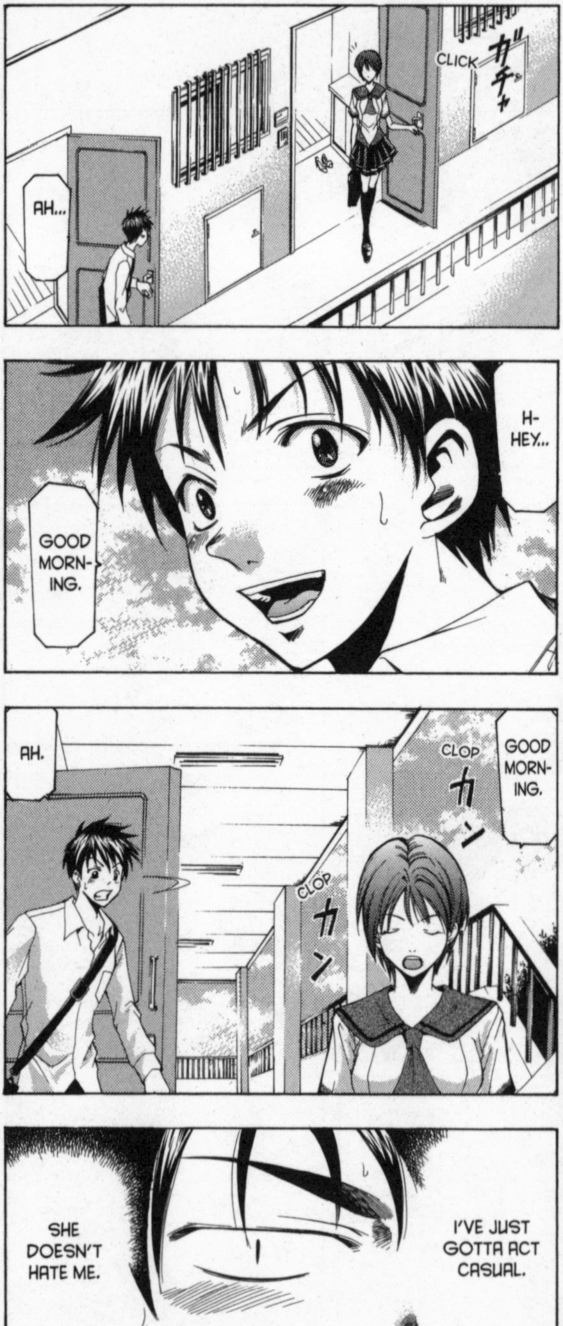
ガチャ
CLICK
AH...
H-HEY...
GOOD MORNING.
GOOD MORNING.
カン
CLOP
カン
CLOP
AH.
I'VE JUST GOTTA ACT CASUAL.
SHE DOESN'T HATE ME.

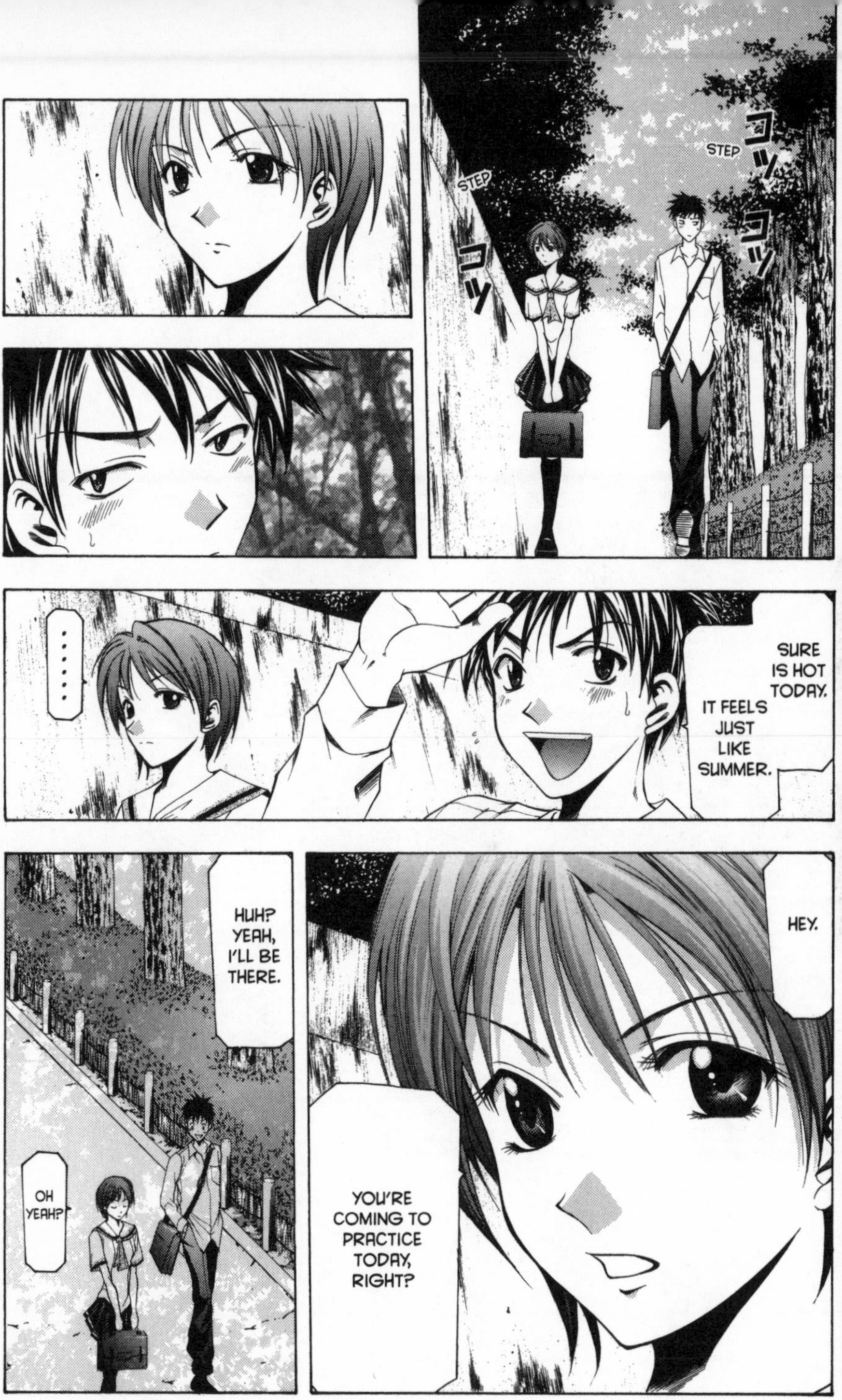
STEP
コツ コツ
STEP
コツ
SURE IS HOT TODAY.
IT FEELS JUST LIKE SUMMER.
......
HEY.
YOU'RE COMING TO PRACTICE TODAY, RIGHT?
HUH? YEAH, I'LL BE THERE.
OH YEAH?

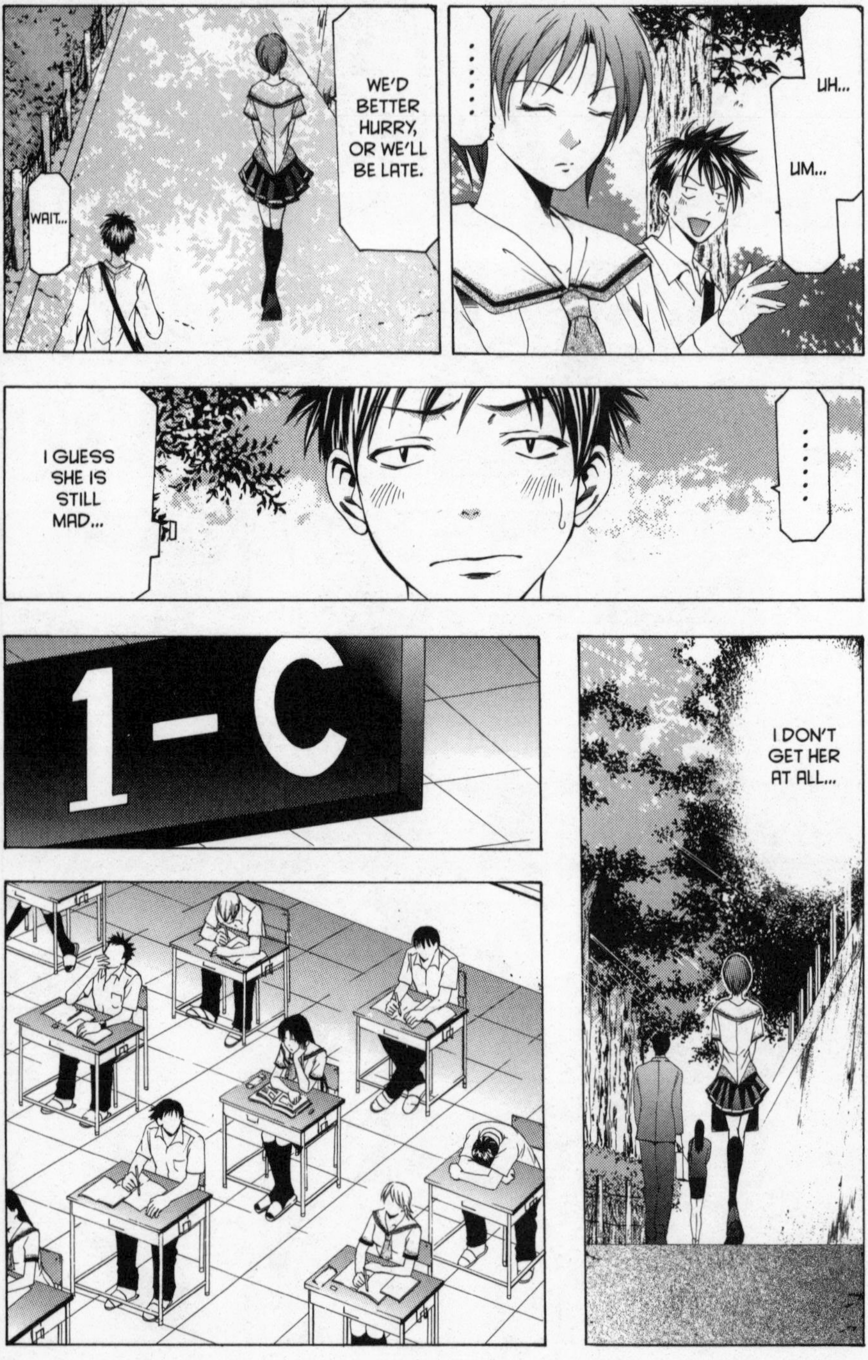
......
UH...
UM...
WE'D BETTER HURRY, OR WE'LL BE LATE.
WAIT...
......
I GUESS SHE IS STILL MAD...
I DON'T GET HER AT ALL...
1-C

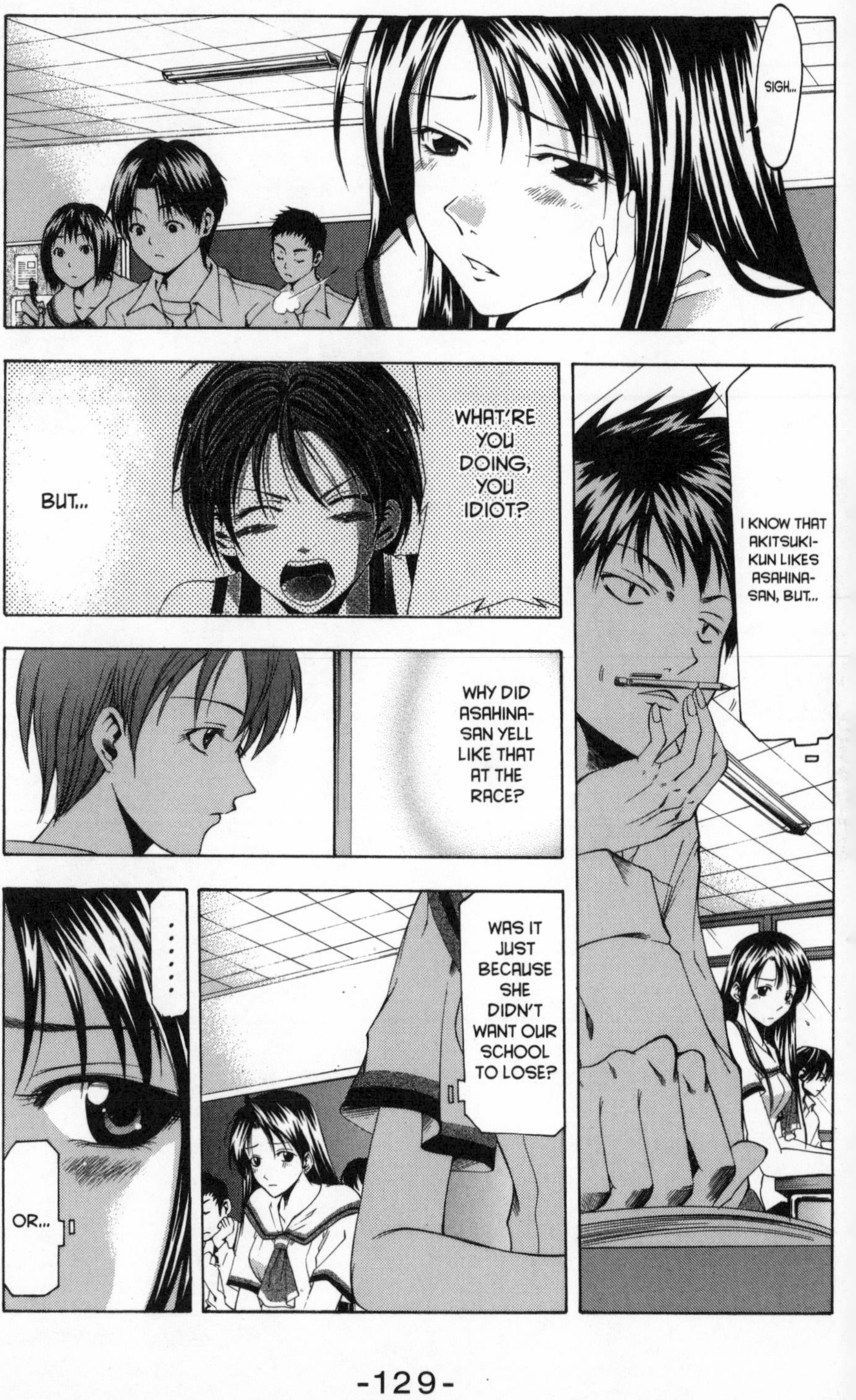
SIGH...
I KNOW THAT AKITSUKI-KUN LIKES ASAHINA-SAN, BUT...
WHAT'RE YOU DOING, YOU IDIOT?
BUT...
WHY DID ASAHINA-SAN YELL LIKE THAT AT THE RACE?
WAS IT JUST BECAUSE SHE DIDN'T WANT OUR SCHOOL TO LOSE?
......
OR...

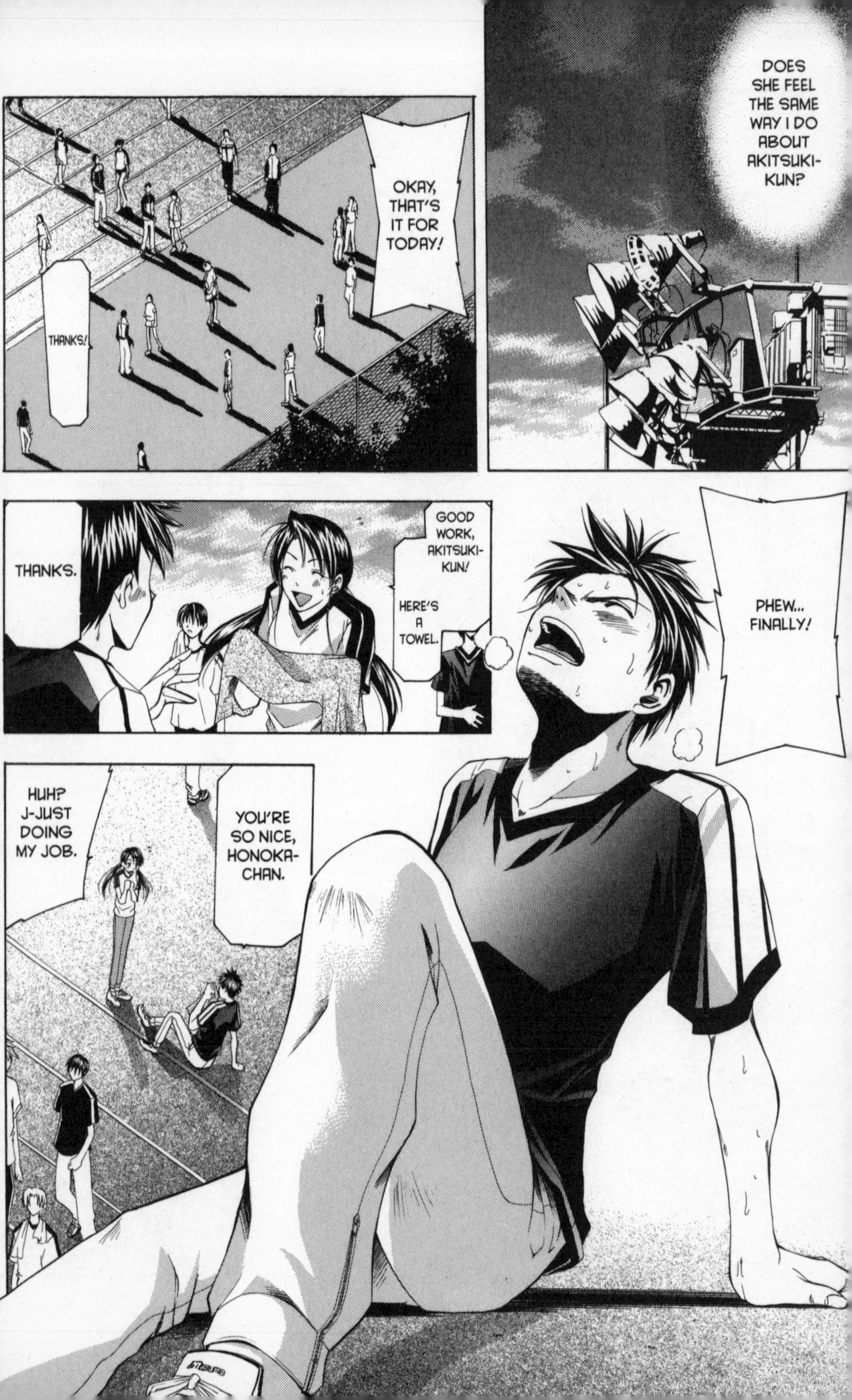
DOES SHE FEEL THE SAME WAY I DO ABOUT AKITSUKI-KUN?
OKAY, THAT'S IT FOR TODAY!
THANKS!
PHEW... FINALLY!
GOOD WORK, AKITSUKI-KUN!
HERE'S A TOWEL.
THANKS.
YOU'RE SO NICE, HONOKA-CHAN.
HUH? J-JUST DOING MY JOB.

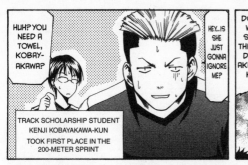

HEY, MAN-AGER. WHERE'S MY TOWEL?
DO YOU WANT SOME-THING TO DRINK, AKITSUKI-KUN?
HEY...IS SHE JUST GONNA IGNORE ME?
HUH? YOU NEED A TOWEL, KOBAY-AKAWA?
TRACK SCHOLARSHIP STUDENT KENJI KOBAYAKAWA-KUN
TOOK FIRST PLACE IN THE 200-METER SPRINT
WELL, TIME TO GO HOME.
FWIP
AH.
UM, AKITSUKI-KUN?
YEAH?
UM, IF YOU DON'T MIND...
I'D LIKE YOU TO WALK ME HOME...
FWUMP

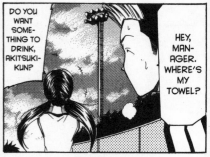

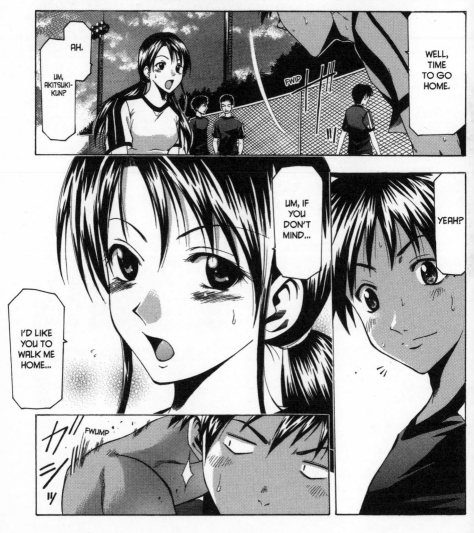

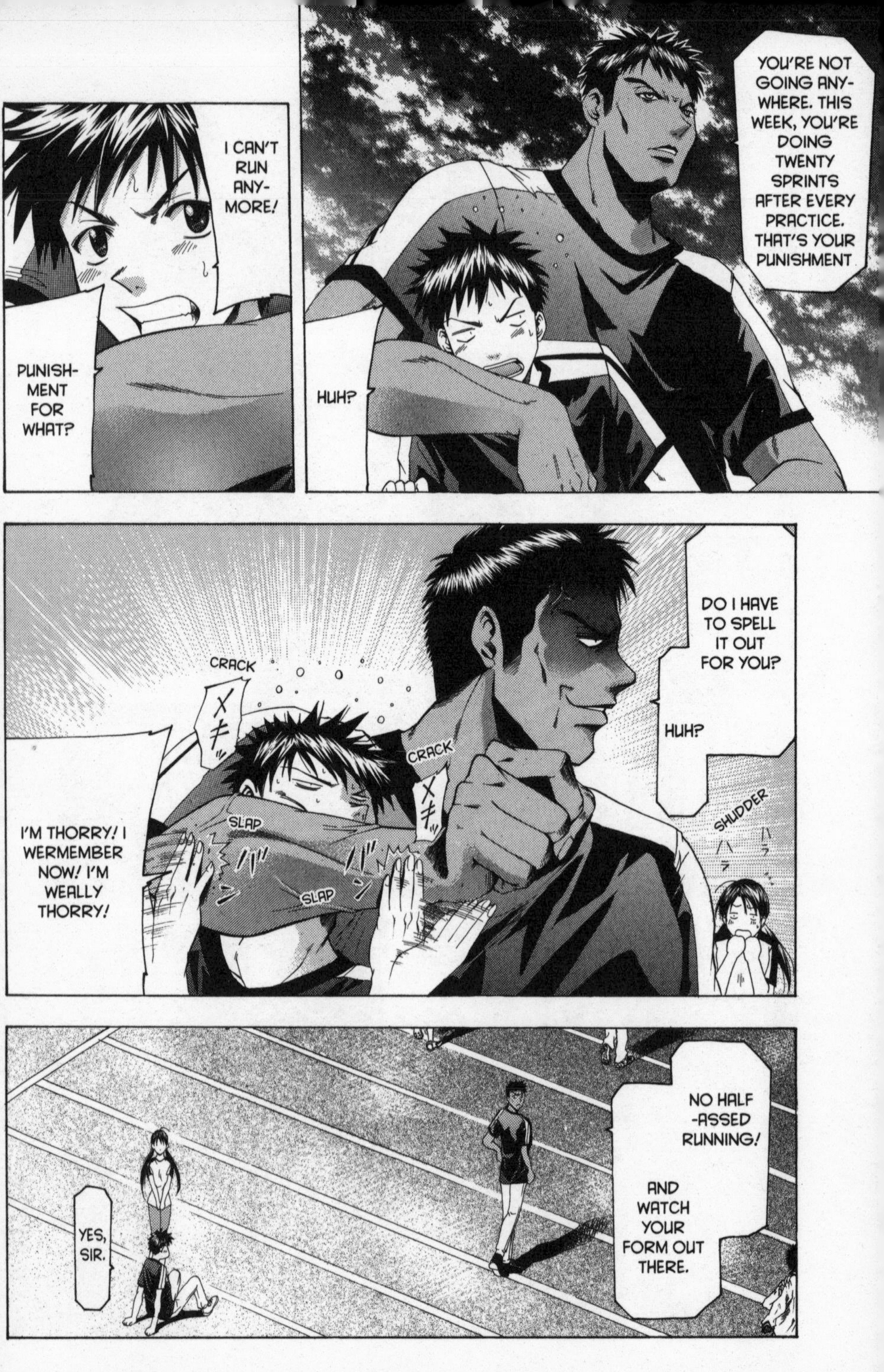
YOU'RE NOT GOING ANYWHERE. THIS WEEK, YOU'RE DOING TWENTY SPRINTS AFTER EVERY PRACTICE. THAT'S YOUR PUNISHMENT
HUH?
I CAN'T RUN ANYMORE!
PUNISHMENT FOR WHAT?
DO I HAVE TO SPELL IT OUT FOR YOU?
HUH?
SHUDDER
CRACK
CRACK
SLAP
SLAP
I'M THORRY! I WERMEMBER NOW! I'M WEALLY THORRY!
NO HALF-ASSED RUNNING!
AND WATCH YOUR FORM OUT THERE.
YES, SIR.

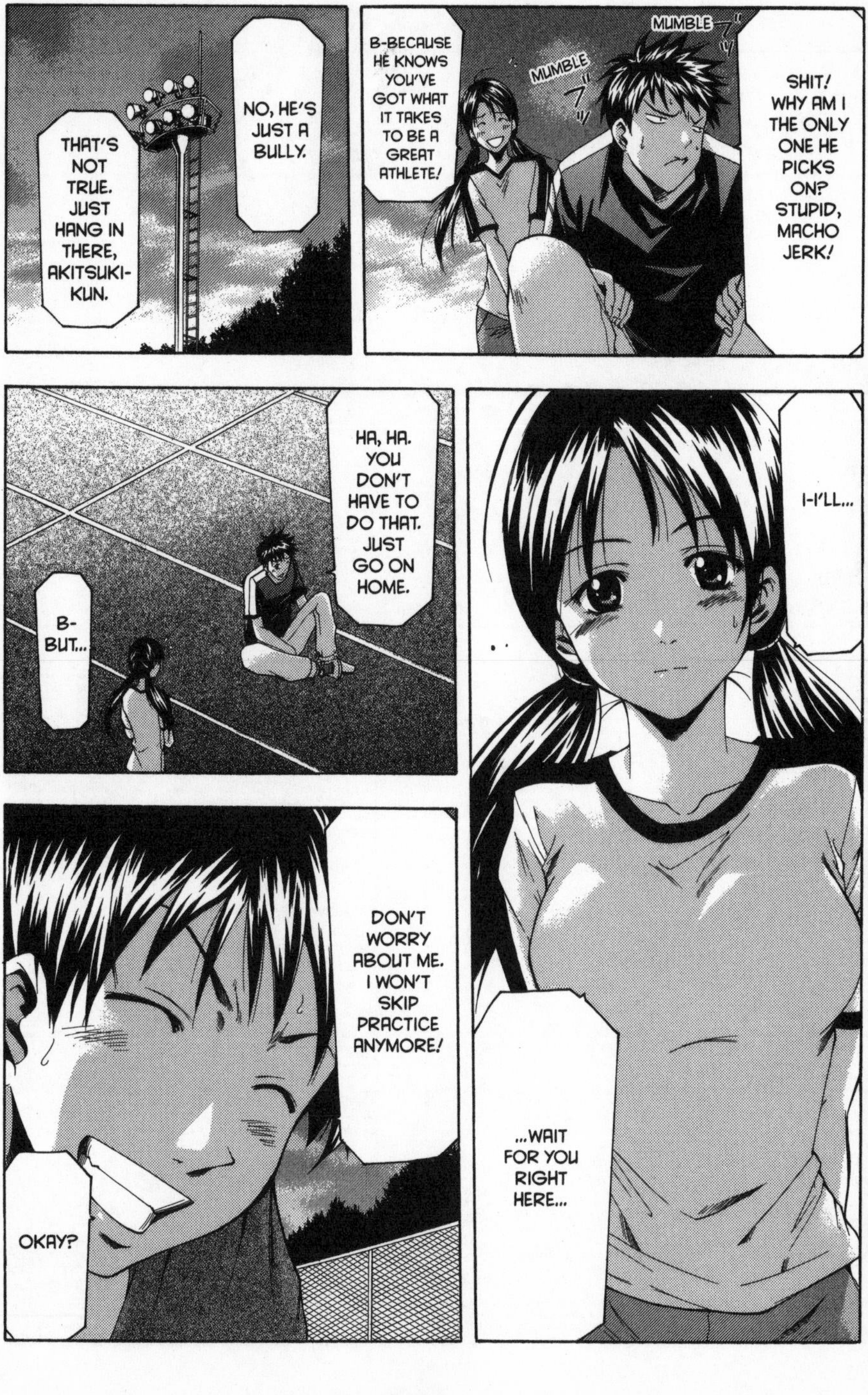
MUMBLE
SHIT! WHY AM I THE ONLY ONE HE PICKS ON? STUPID, MACHO JERK!
MUMBLE
B-BECAUSE HE KNOWS YOU'VE GOT WHAT IT TAKES TO BE A GREAT ATHLETE!
NO, HE'S JUST A BULLY.
THAT'S NOT TRUE. JUST HANG IN THERE, AKITSUKI-KUN.
I-I'LL...
...WAIT FOR YOU RIGHT HERE...
HA, HA. YOU DON'T HAVE TO DO THAT. JUST GO ON HOME.
B-BUT...
DON'T WORRY ABOUT ME. I WON'T SKIP PRACTICE ANYMORE!
OKAY?

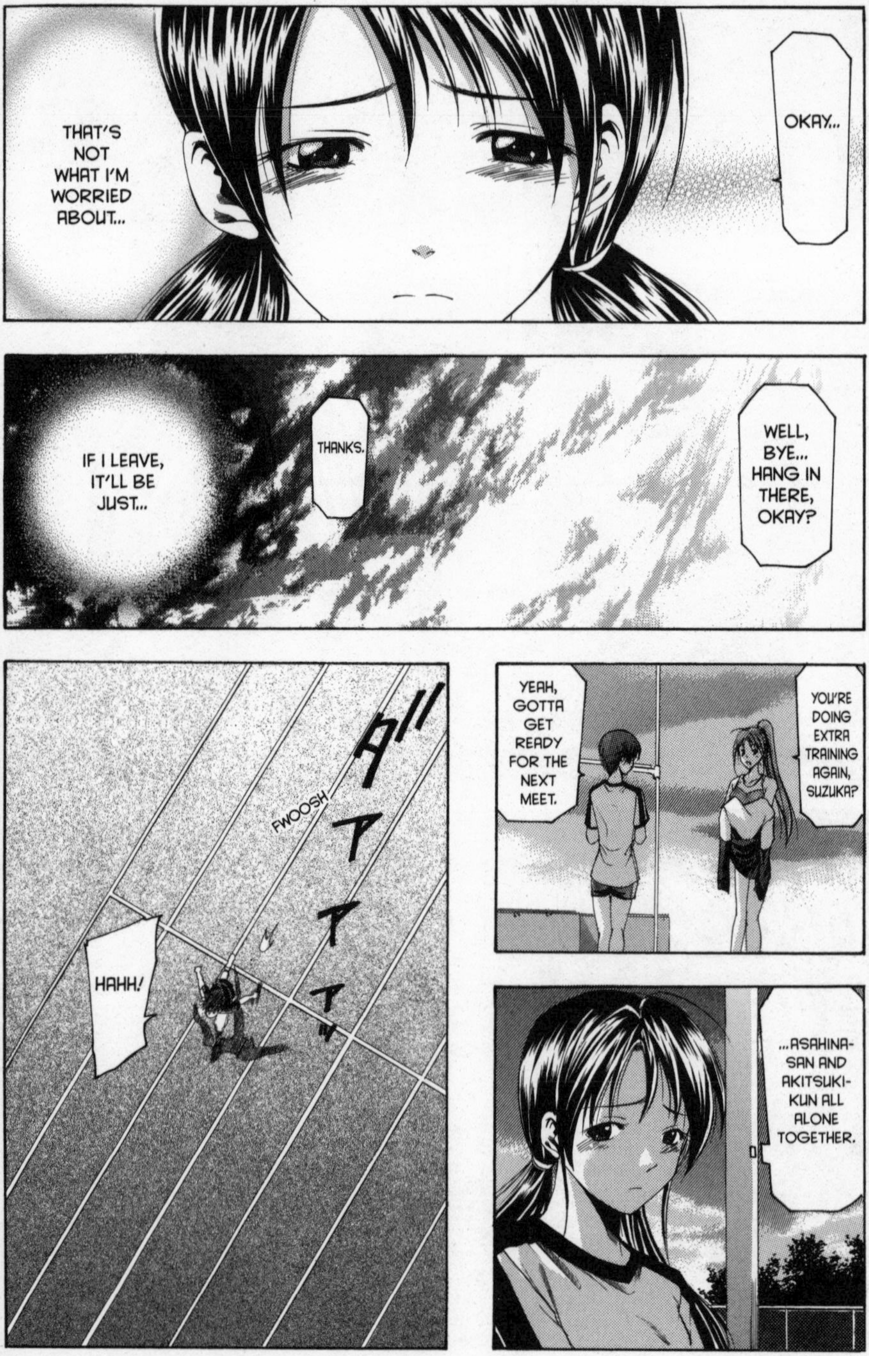
OKAY...
THAT'S NOT WHAT I'M WORRIED ABOUT...
WELL, BYE... HANG IN THERE, OKAY?
THANKS.
IF I LEAVE, IT'LL BE JUST...
YOU'RE DOING EXTRA TRAINING AGAIN, SUZUKA?
YEAH, GOTTA GET READY FOR THE NEXT MEET.
...ASAHINA-SAN AND AKITSUKI-KUN ALL ALONE TOGETHER.
ダァァァッ
FWOOSH
HAHH!

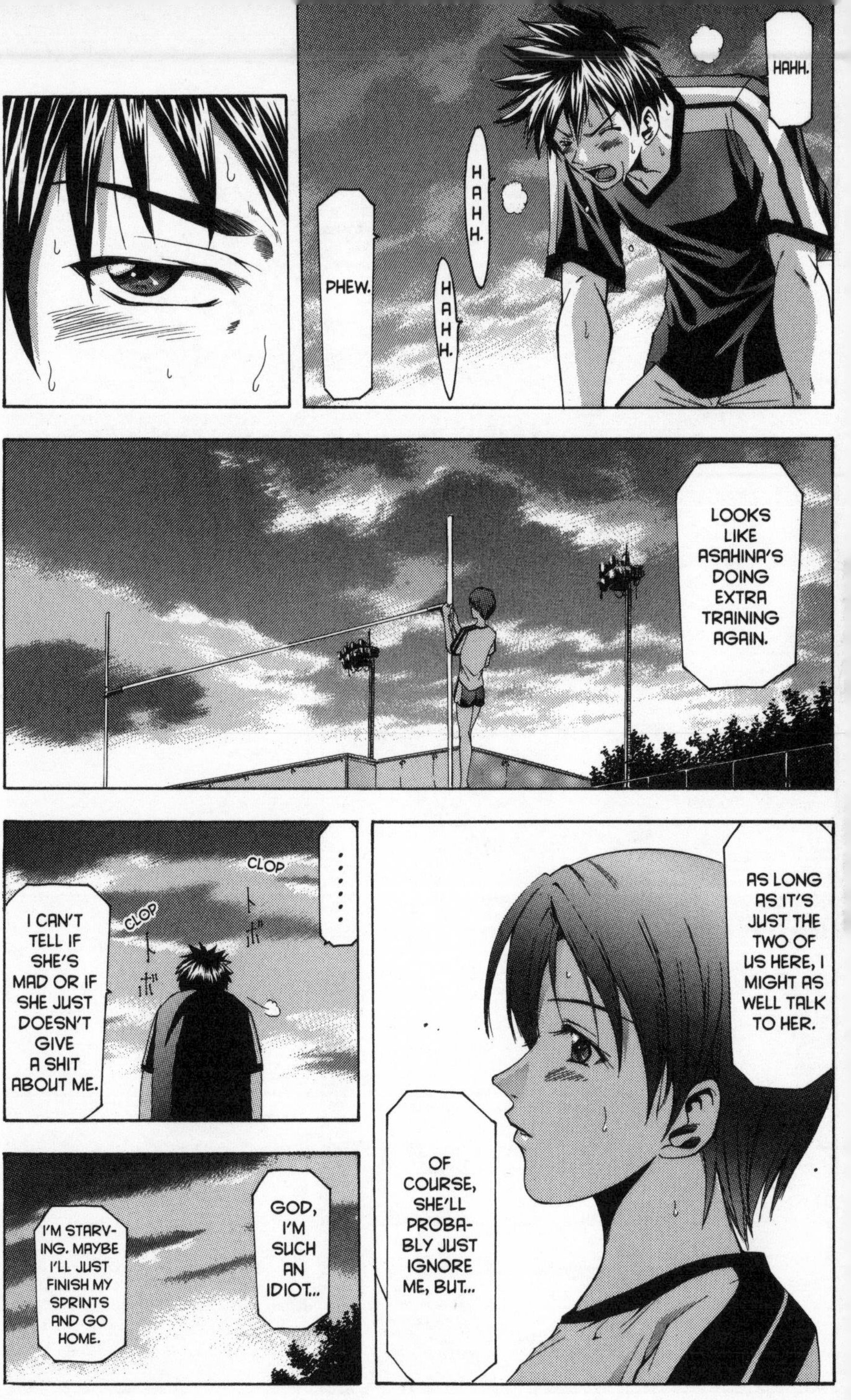
HAHH.
HAHH.
HAHH.
PHEW.
LOOKS LIKE ASAHINA'S DOING EXTRA TRAINING AGAIN.
AS LONG AS IT'S JUST THE TWO OF US HERE, I MIGHT AS WELL TALK TO HER.
OF COURSE, SHE'LL PROBABLY JUST IGNORE ME, BUT...
......
CLOP
CLOP
I CAN'T TELL IF SHE'S MAD OR IF SHE JUST DOESN'T GIVE A SHIT ABOUT ME.
GOD, I'M SUCH AN IDIOT...
I'M STARVING. MAYBE I'LL JUST FINISH MY SPRINTS AND GO HOME.

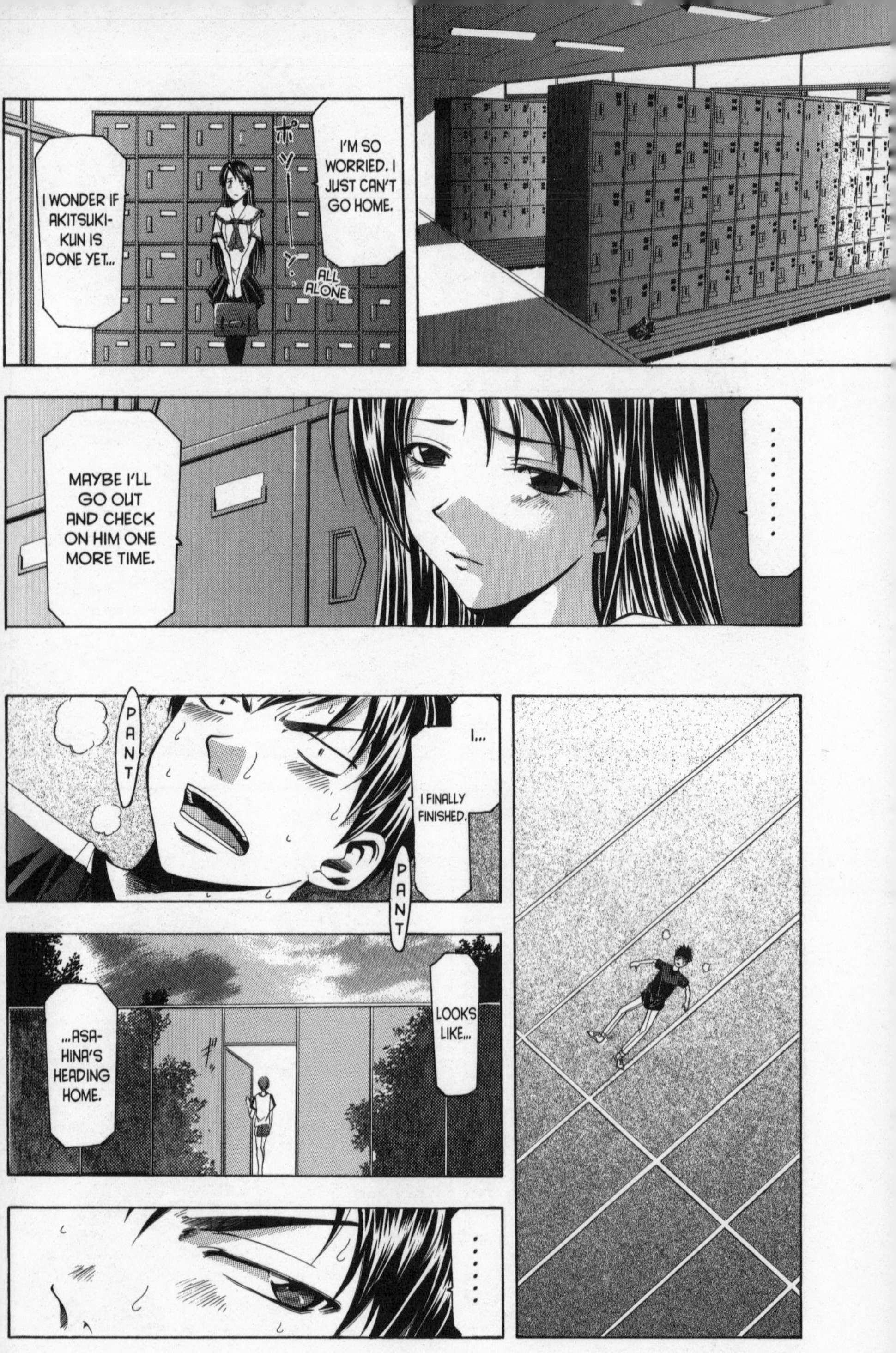
I'M SO WORRIED. I JUST CAN'T GO HOME.
ALL ALONE
I WONDER IF AKITSUKI-KUN IS DONE YET...
......
MAYBE I'LL GO OUT AND CHECK ON HIM ONE MORE TIME.
I...
I FINALLY FINISHED.
PANT
PANT
LOOKS LIKE...
...ASAHINA'S HEADING HOME.
......

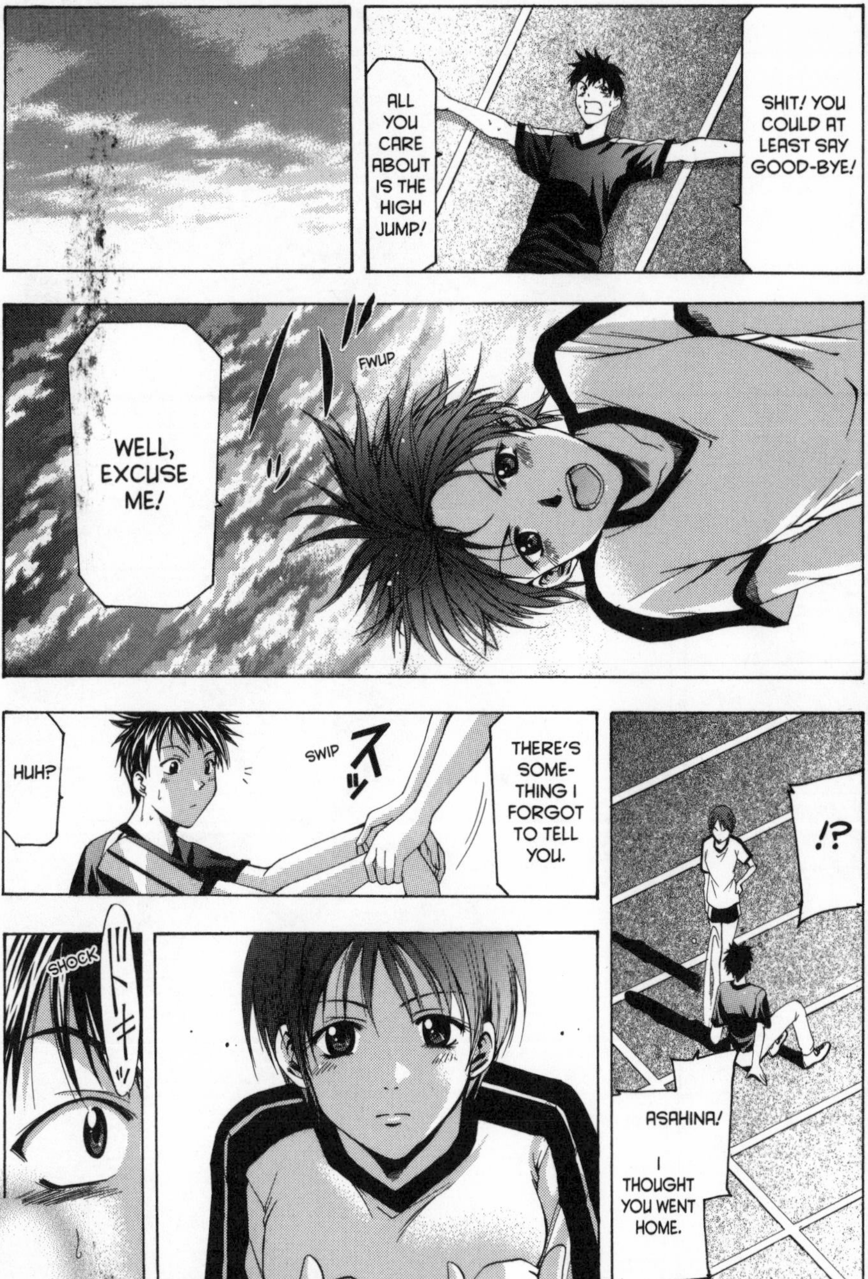
SHIT! YOU COULD AT LEAST SAY GOOD-BYE!
ALL YOU CARE ABOUT IS THE HIGH JUMP!
FWUP
WELL, EXCUSE ME!
!?
ASAHINA!
I THOUGHT YOU WENT HOME.
THERE'S SOME-THING I FORGOT TO TELL YOU.
SWIP
HUH?
SHOCK
WHAT?

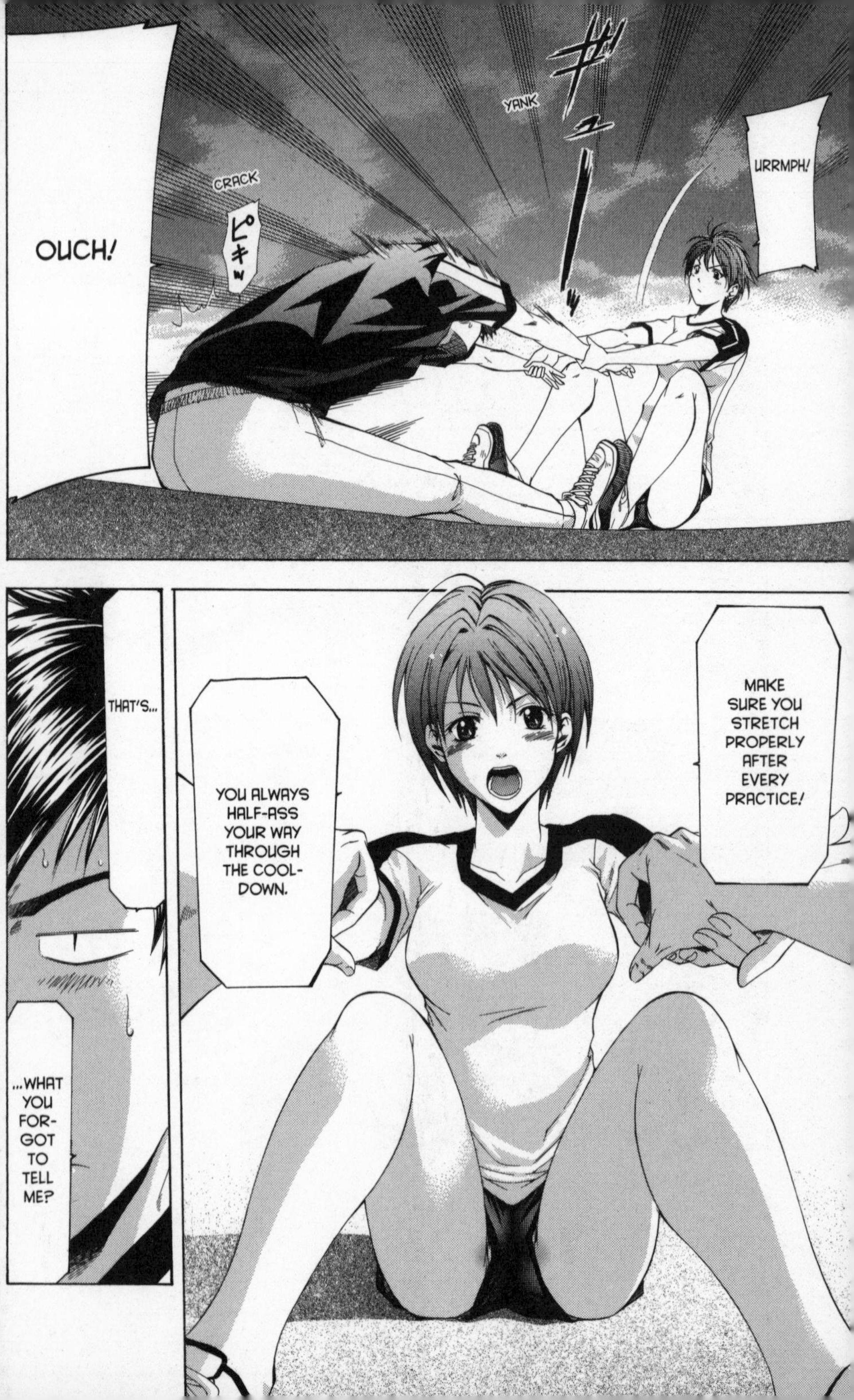
URRMPH!
ギュー
YANK
ピキッ
CRACK
OUCH!
MAKE SURE YOU STRETCH PROPERLY AFTER EVERY PRACTICE!
YOU ALWAYS HALF-ASS YOUR WAY THROUGH THE COOL-DOWN.
THAT'S...
...WHAT YOU FOR-GOT TO TELL ME?

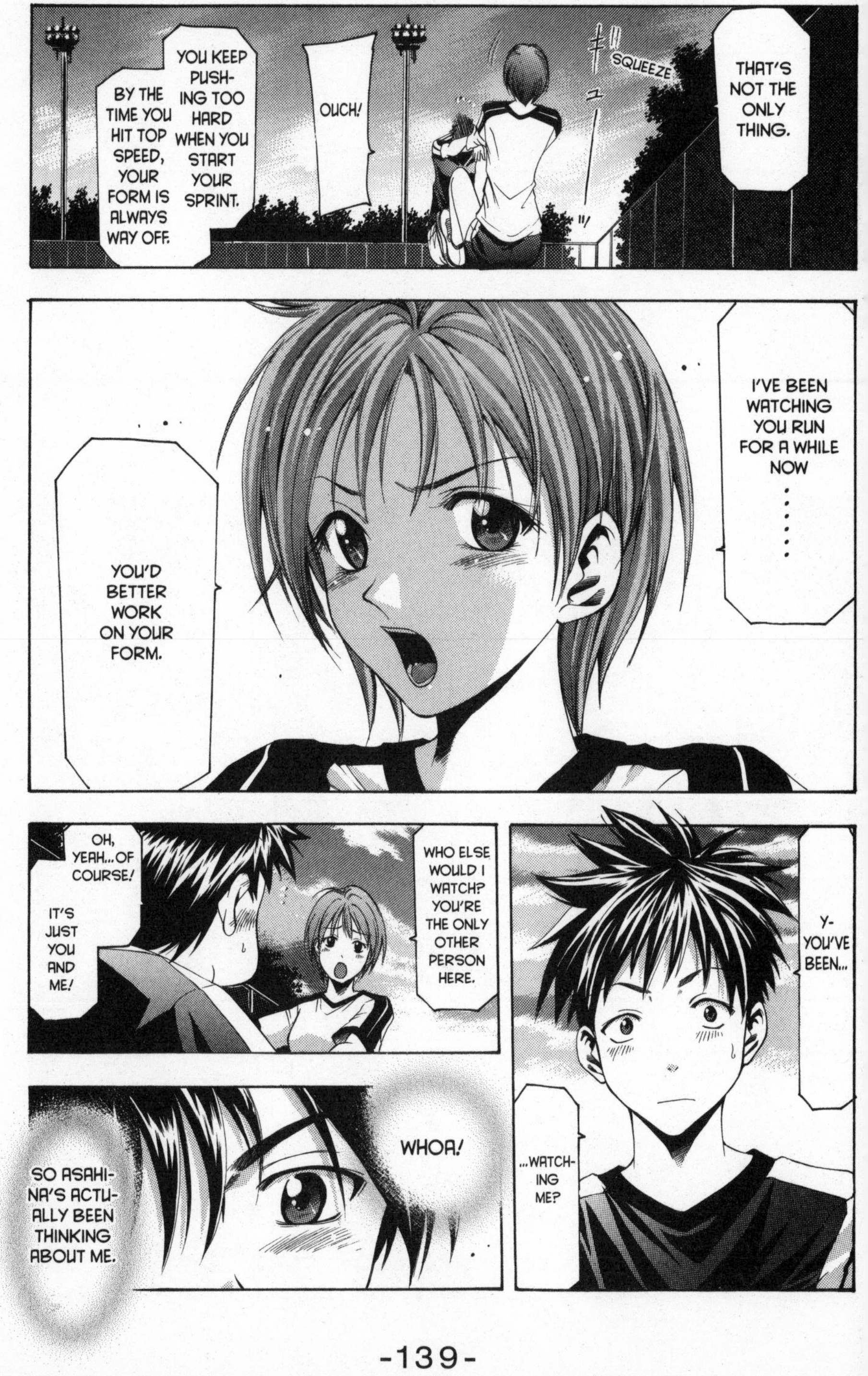
THAT'S NOT THE ONLY THING.
SQUEEZE
OUCH!
YOU KEEP PUSHING TOO HARD WHEN YOU START YOUR SPRINT.
BY THE TIME YOU HIT TOP SPEED, YOUR FORM IS ALWAYS WAY OFF.
I'VE BEEN WATCHING YOU RUN FOR A WHILE NOW......
YOU'D BETTER WORK ON YOUR FORM.
Y-YOU'VE BEEN...
...WATCHING ME?
WHO ELSE WOULD I WATCH? YOU'RE THE ONLY OTHER PERSON HERE.
OH, YEAH...OF COURSE!
IT'S JUST YOU AND ME!
WHOA!
SO ASAHINA'S ACTUALLY BEEN THINKING ABOUT ME.

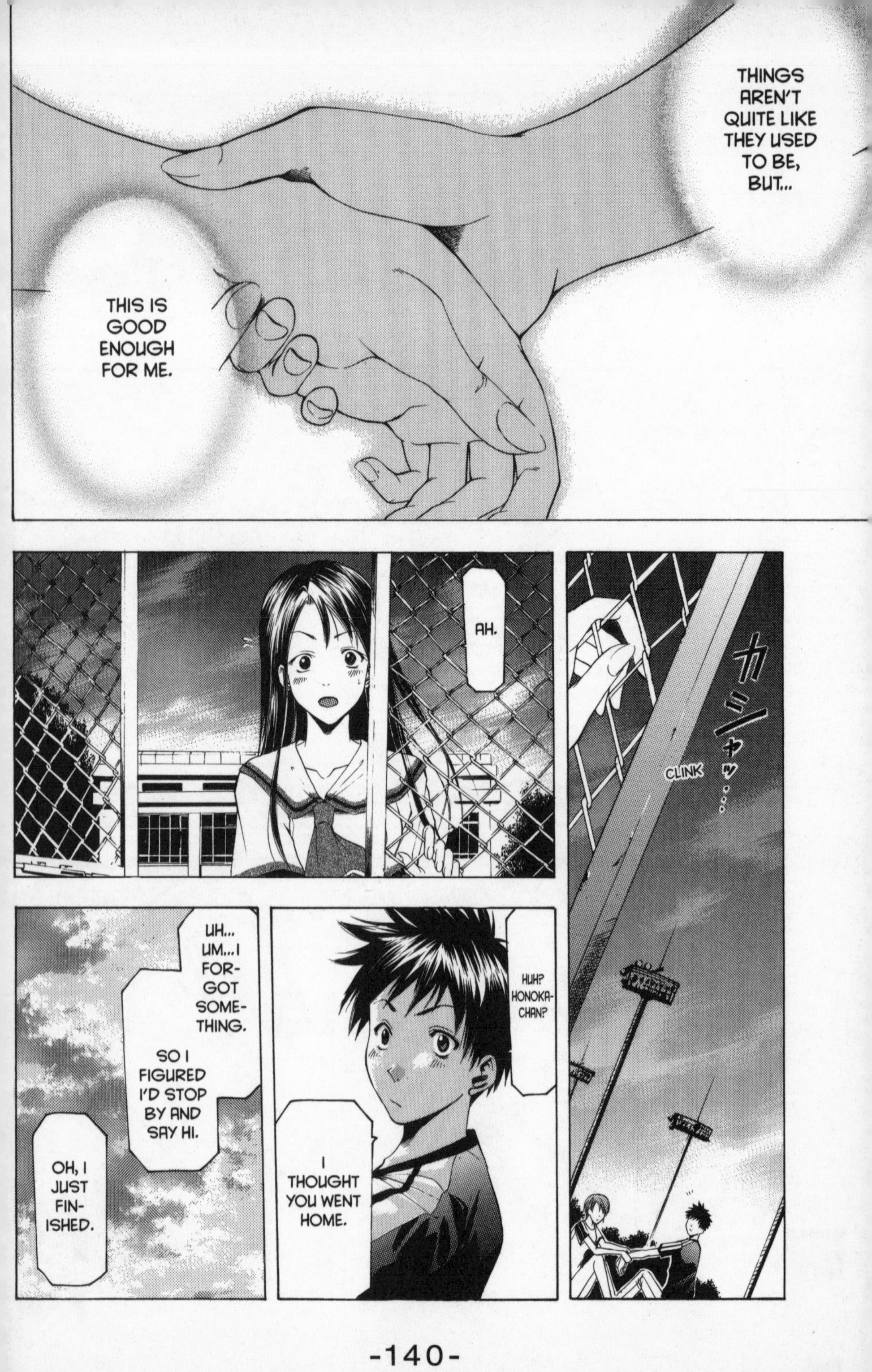
THINGS AREN'T QUITE LIKE THEY USED TO BE, BUT...
THIS IS GOOD ENOUGH FOR ME.
カシャッ...
CLINK
AH.
HUH? HONOKA-CHAN?
I THOUGHT YOU WENT HOME.
UH... UM...I FOR-GOT SOME-THING.
SO I FIGURED I'D STOP BY AND SAY HI.
OH, I JUST FIN-ISHED.

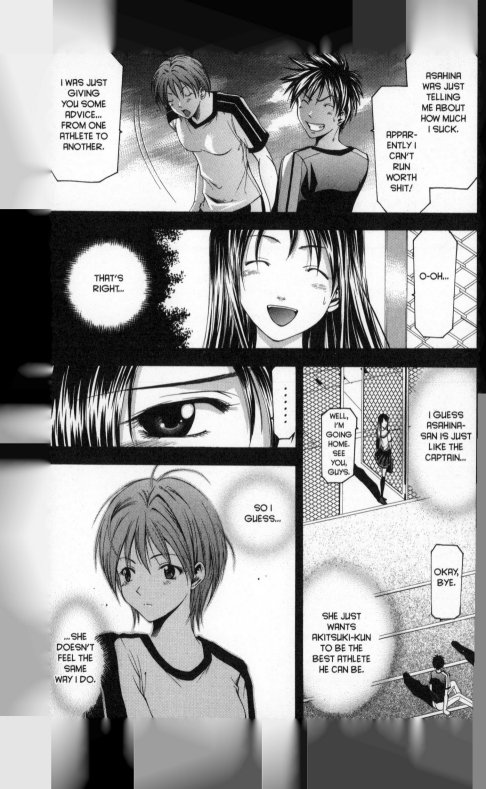

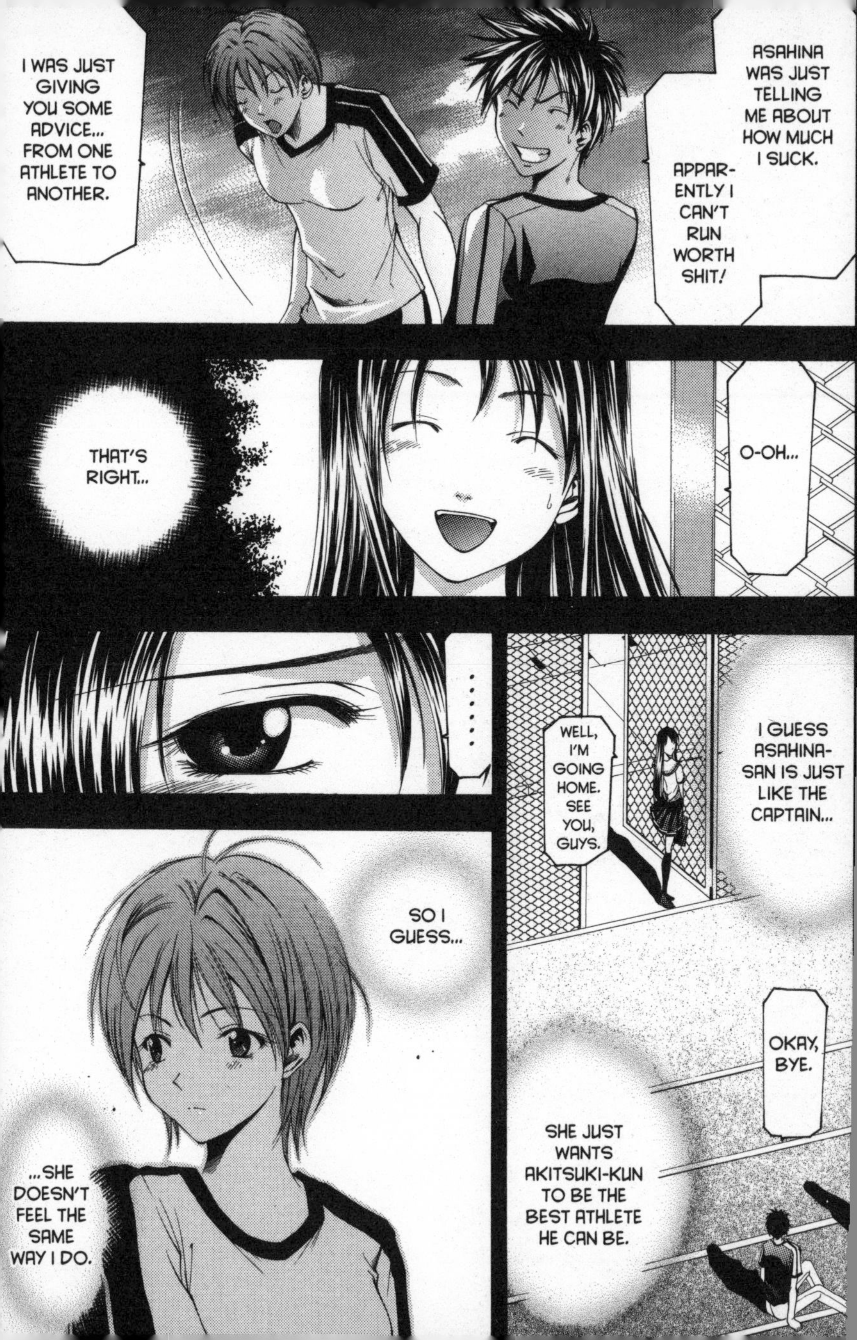
ASAHINA WAS JUST TELLING ME ABOUT HOW MUCH I SUCK.
APPARENTLY I CAN'T RUN WORTH SHIT!
I WAS JUST GIVING YOU SOME ADVICE... FROM ONE ATHLETE TO ANOTHER.
O-OH...
THAT'S RIGHT...
I GUESS ASAHINA-SAN IS JUST LIKE THE CAPTAIN...
WELL, I'M GOING HOME. SEE YOU, GUYS.
......
OKAY, BYE.
SHE JUST WANTS AKITSUKI-KUN TO BE THE BEST ATHLETE HE CAN BE.
SO I GUESS...
...SHE DOESN'T FEEL THE SAME WAY I DO.

CHARACTER PROFILE NO. 11

KAZUKI TSUDA
(DIED AT AGE 15)

DATE OF BIRTH—SEPTEMBER 29 (LIBRA)
HEIGHT—5'7"
WEIGHT—140 LBS
BLOOD TYPE—B

LIKES
•SUZUKA
•TRACK
•RAW EGGS

DISLIKES
•FORMALITIES
•ANYTHING HARD
•BITTER VEGETABLES

MOTTO—PROBLEMS BEGET SOLUTIONS

The take-down of weapon allows insight into the interesting technique

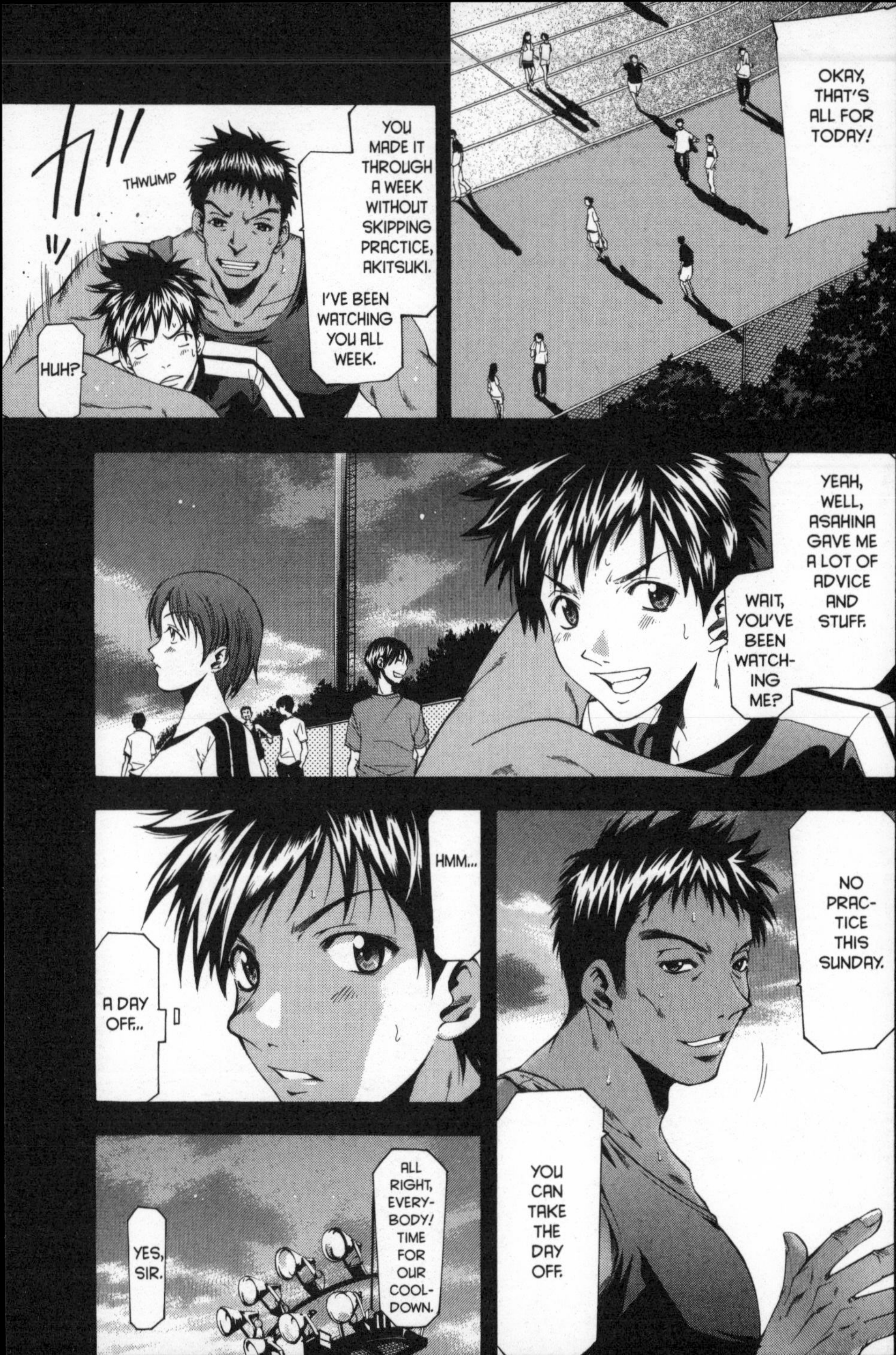
OKAY, THAT'S ALL FOR TODAY!
THWUMP
YOU MADE IT THROUGH A WEEK WITHOUT SKIPPING PRACTICE, AKITSUKI.
I'VE BEEN WATCHING YOU ALL WEEK.
HUH?
YEAH, WELL, ASAHINA GAVE ME A LOT OF ADVICE AND STUFF.
WAIT, YOU'VE BEEN WATCHING ME?
NO PRACTICE THIS SUNDAY.
YOU CAN TAKE THE DAY OFF.
HMM...
A DAY OFF...
ALL RIGHT, EVERYBODY! TIME FOR OUR COOL-DOWN.
YES, SIR.

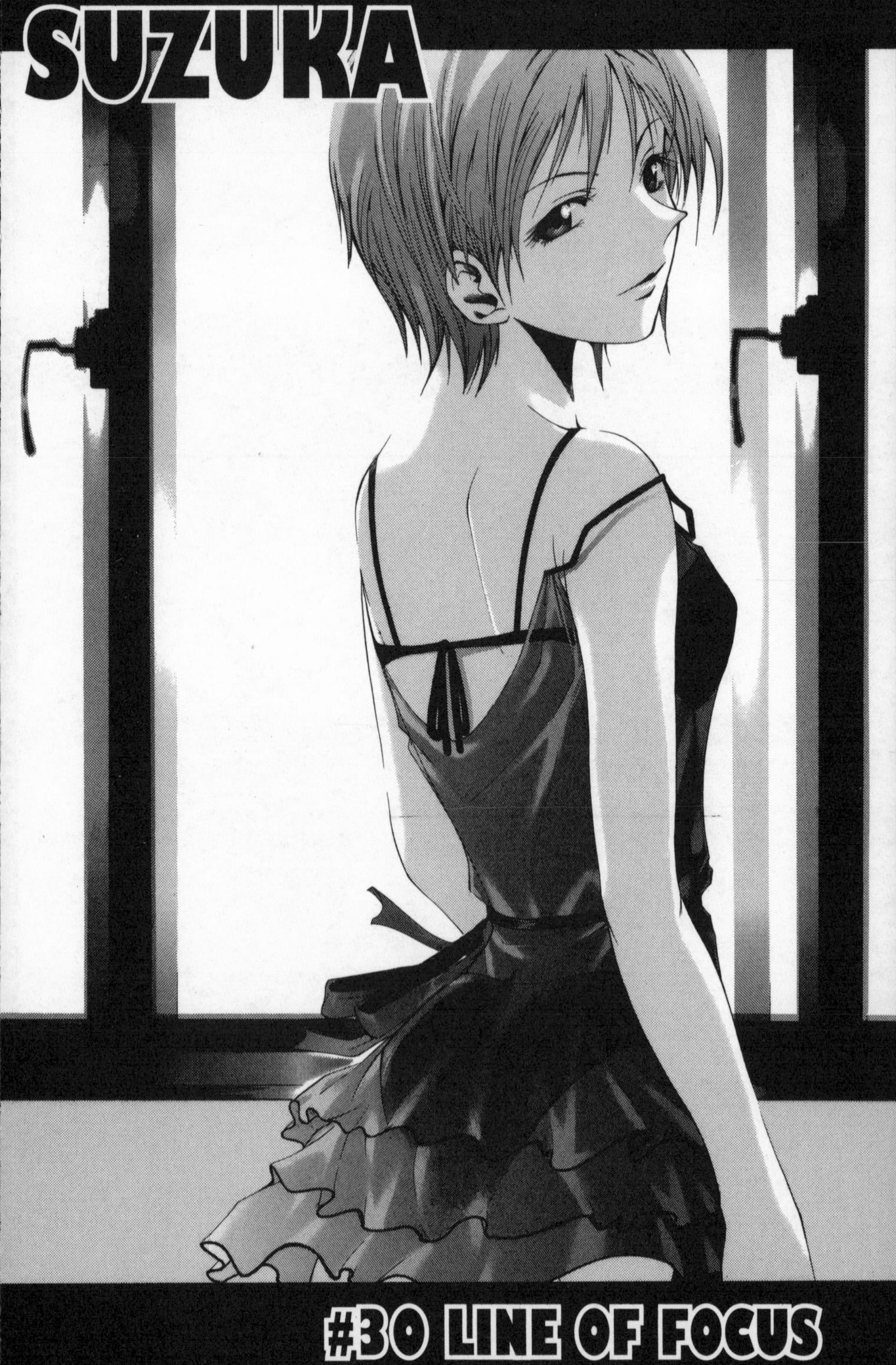
SUZUKA
#30 LINE OF FOCUS

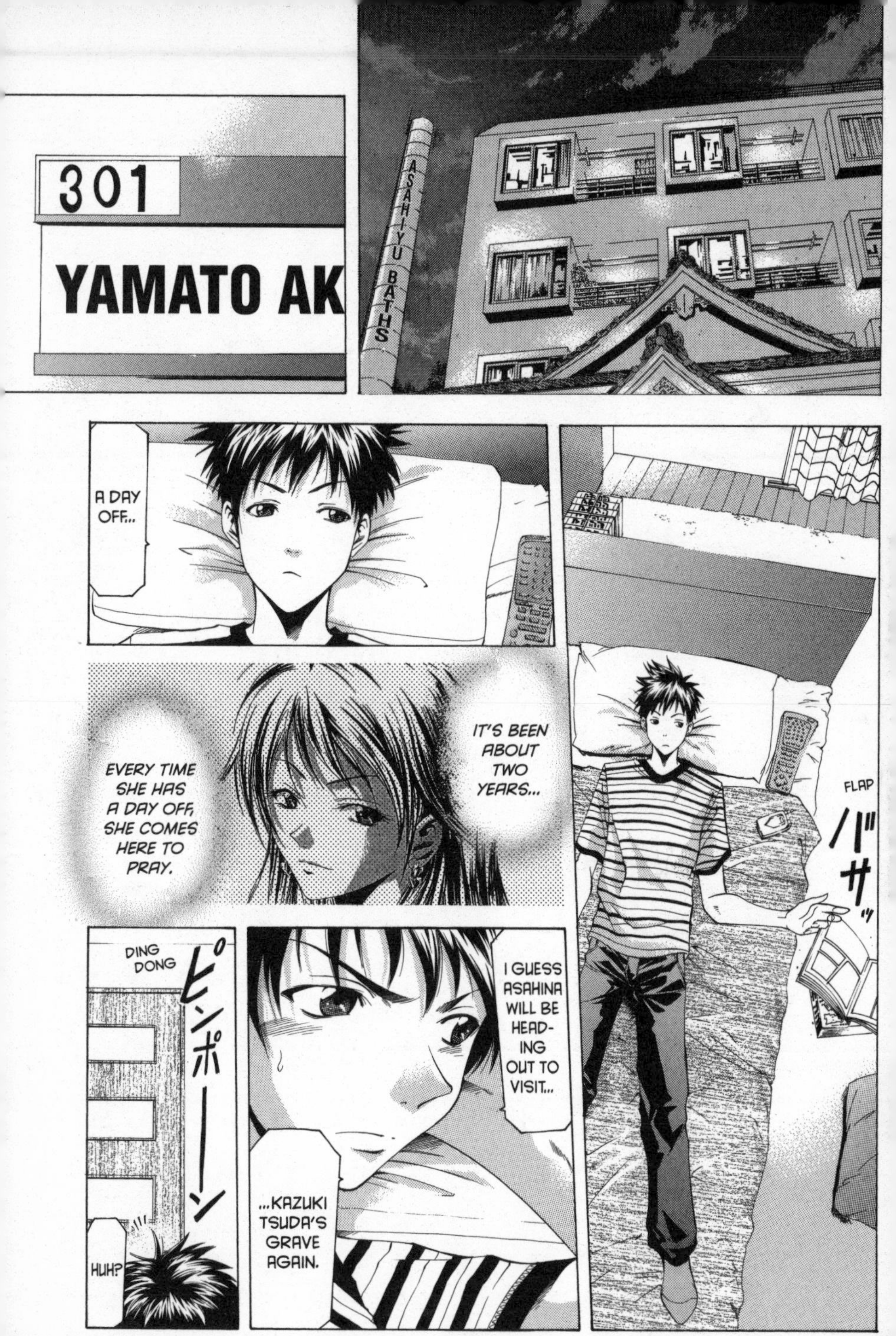
ASAHIYU BATHS
301
YAMATO AK
FLAP
バサッ
A DAY OFF...
IT'S BEEN ABOUT TWO YEARS...
EVERY TIME SHE HAS A DAY OFF, SHE COMES HERE TO PRAY.
I GUESS ASAHINA WILL BE HEAD-ING OUT TO VISIT...
...KAZUKI TSUDA'S GRAVE AGAIN.
DING DONG
ピンポーン
HUH?

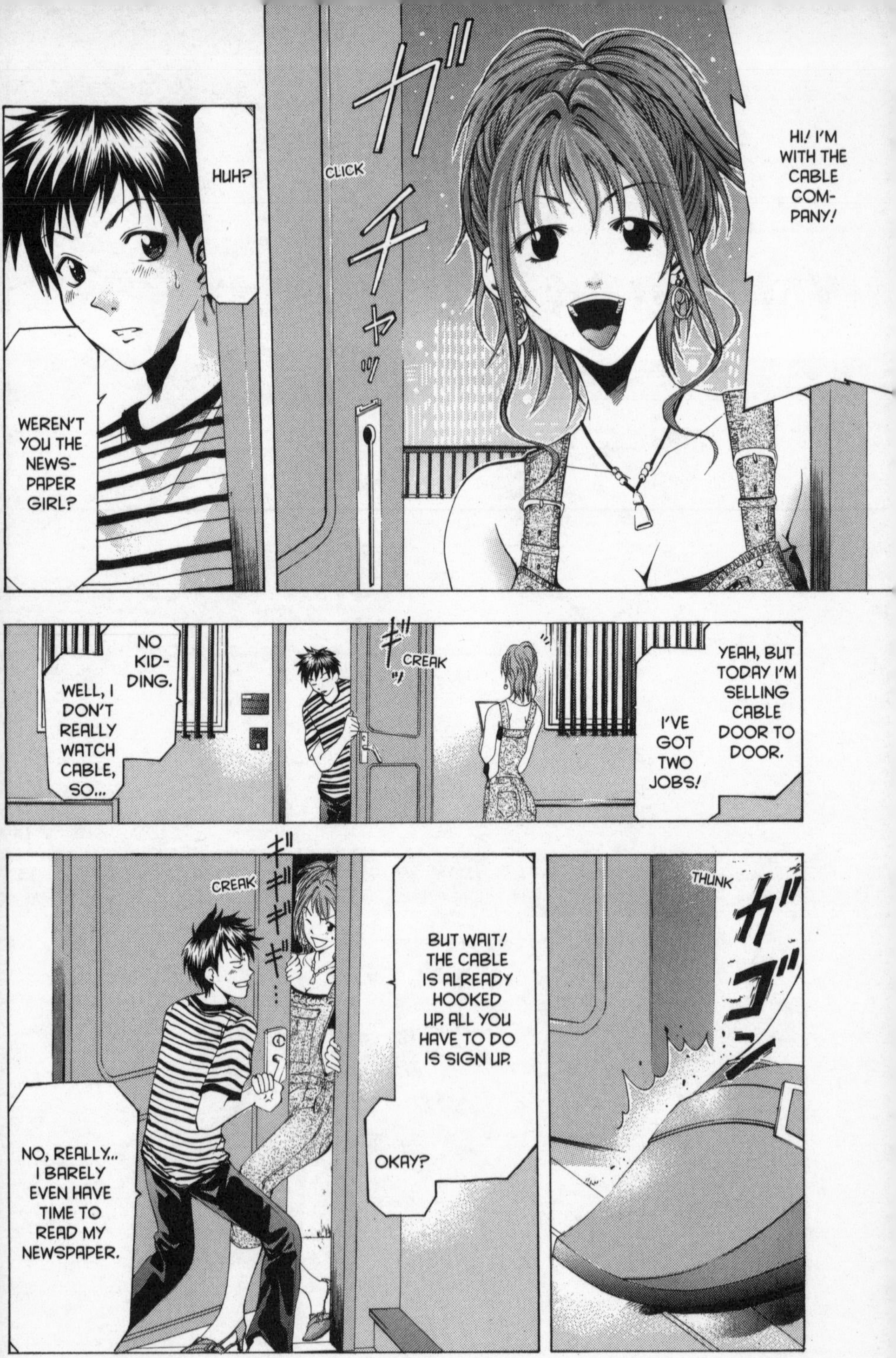
HI! I'M WITH THE CABLE COMPANY!
ガチャッ
CLICK
HUH?
WEREN'T YOU THE NEWSPAPER GIRL?
YEAH, BUT TODAY I'M SELLING CABLE DOOR TO DOOR.
I'VE GOT TWO JOBS!
ギッ
CREAK
NO KIDDING.
WELL, I DON'T REALLY WATCH CABLE, SO...
ガゴン
THUNK
BUT WAIT! THE CABLE IS ALREADY HOOKED UP. ALL YOU HAVE TO DO IS SIGN UP.
OKAY?
ギギギギ…
CREAK
NO, REALLY... I BARELY EVEN HAVE TIME TO READ MY NEWSPAPER.

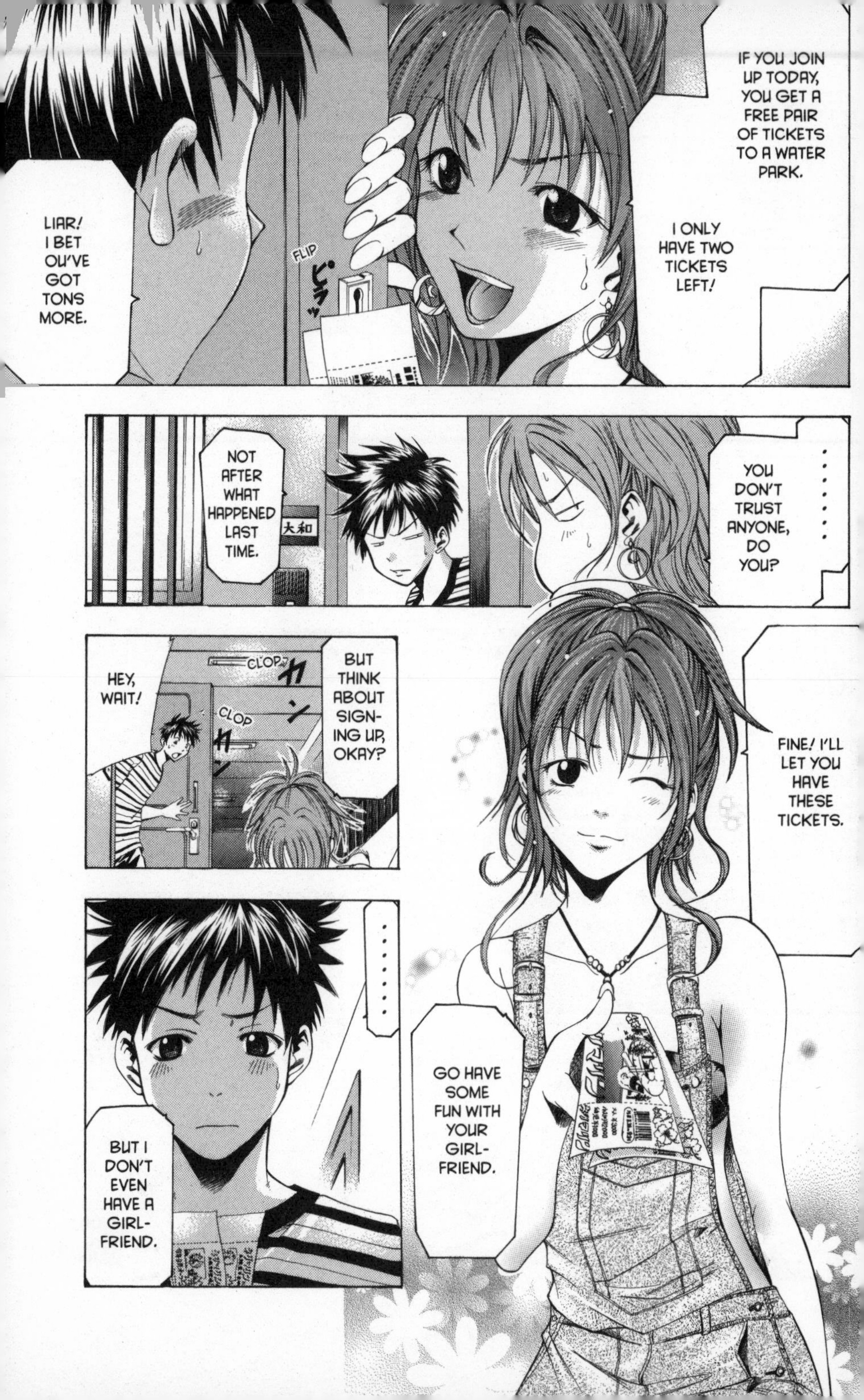
IF YOU JOIN UP TODAY, YOU GET A FREE PAIR OF TICKETS TO A WATER PARK.
I ONLY HAVE TWO TICKETS LEFT!
FLIP
ピラッ
LIAR! I BET OU'VE GOT TONS MORE.
......
YOU DON'T TRUST ANYONE, DO YOU?
NOT AFTER WHAT HAPPENED LAST TIME.
大和
FINE! I'LL LET YOU HAVE THESE TICKETS.
GO HAVE SOME FUN WITH YOUR GIRLFRIEND.
BUT THINK ABOUT SIGNING UP, OKAY?
CLOP
CLOP
HEY, WAIT!
......
BUT I DON'T EVEN HAVE A GIRLFRIEND.

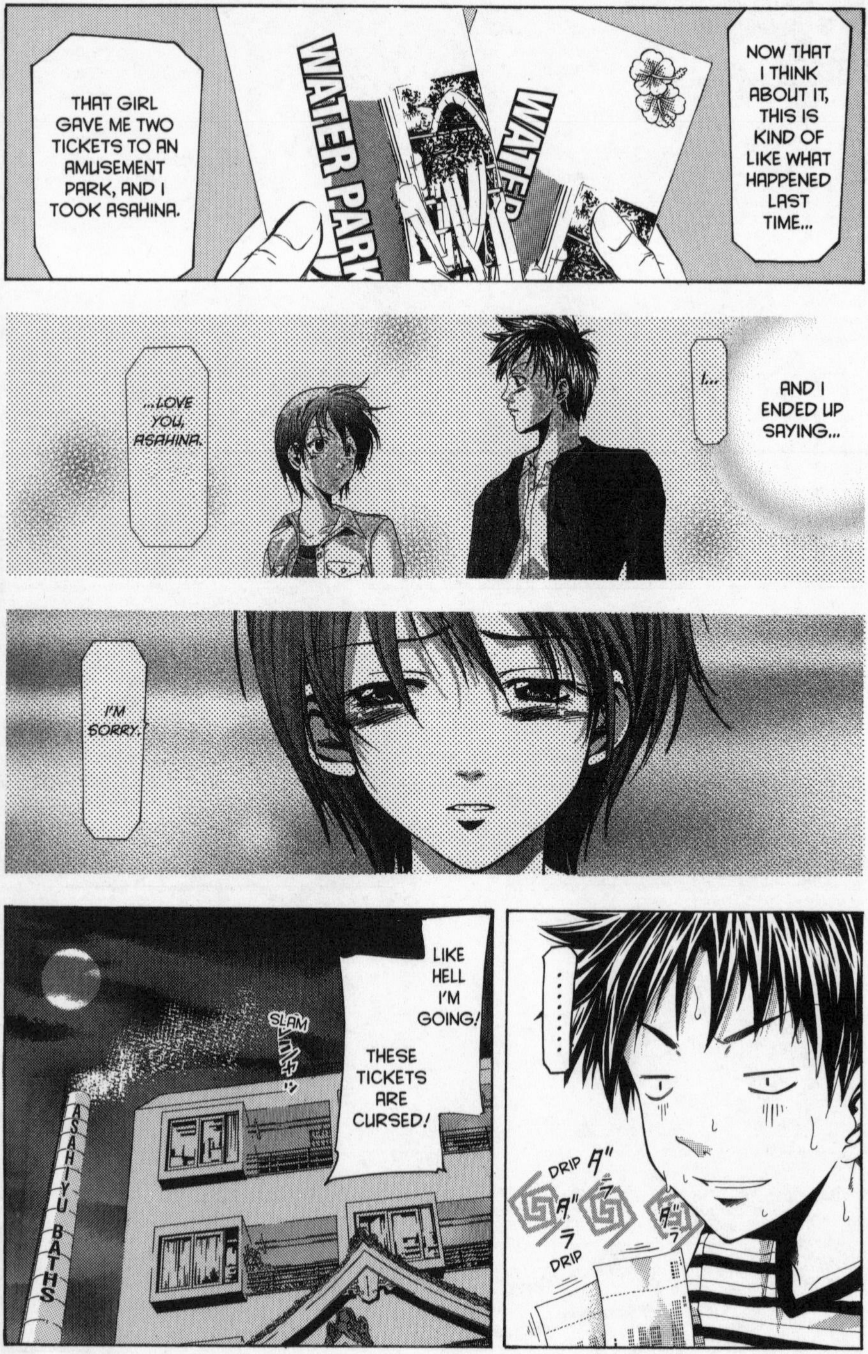
NOW THAT I THINK ABOUT IT, THIS IS KIND OF LIKE WHAT HAPPENED LAST TIME...
WATER
WATER PARK
THAT GIRL GAVE ME TWO TICKETS TO AN AMUSEMENT PARK, AND I TOOK ASAHINA.
AND I ENDED UP SAYING...
I...
...LOVE YOU, ASAHINA.
I'M SORRY.
......
DRIP
DRIP
LIKE HELL I'M GOING!
THESE TICKETS ARE CURSED!
SLAM
ASAHIYU BATHS

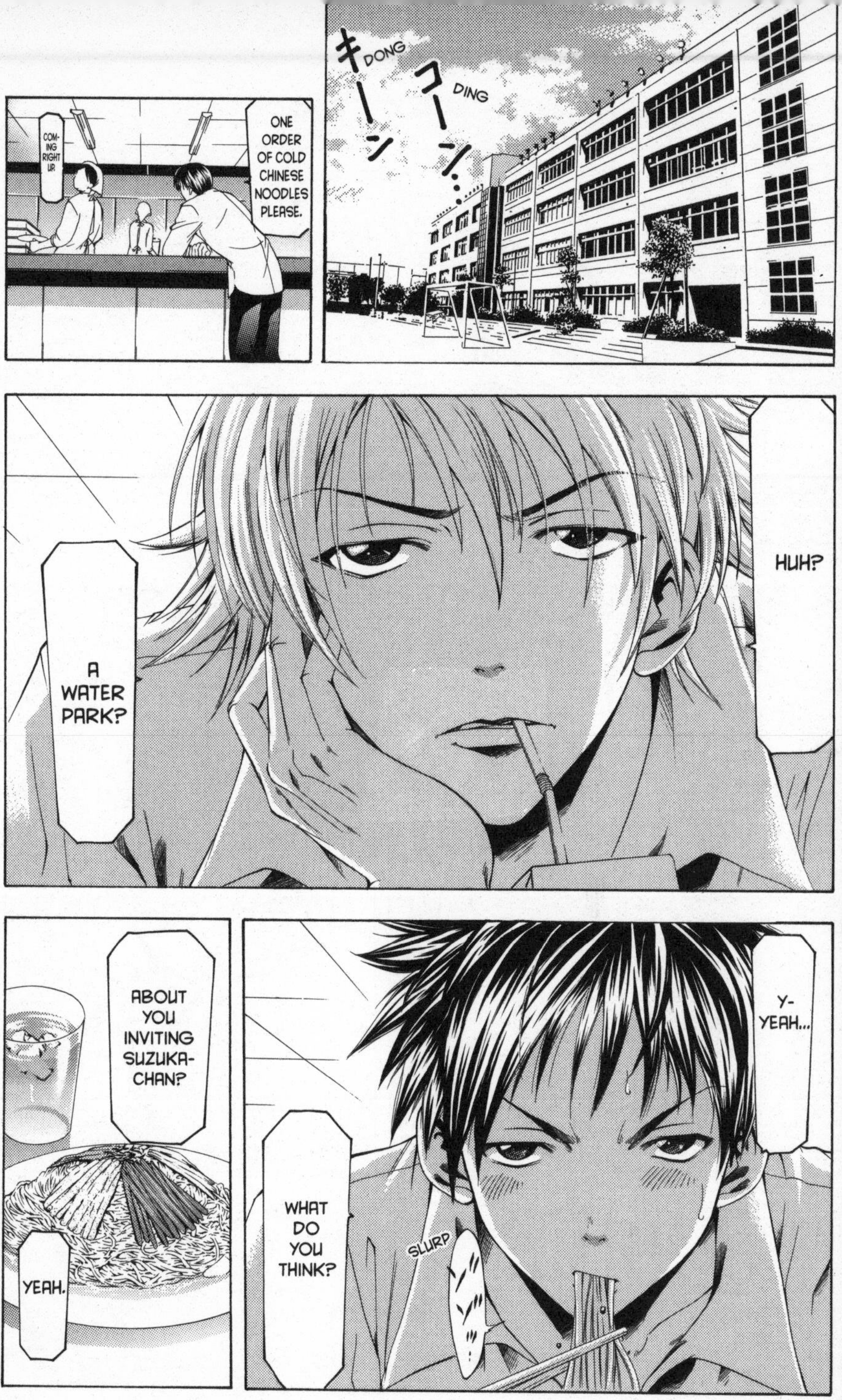
キーン
DONG
コーン
DING
ONE ORDER OF COLD CHINESE NOODLES PLEASE.
COMING RIGHT UP.
HUH?
A WATER PARK?
Y-YEAH...
SLURP
WHAT DO YOU THINK?
ABOUT YOU INVITING SUZUKA-CHAN?
YEAH.

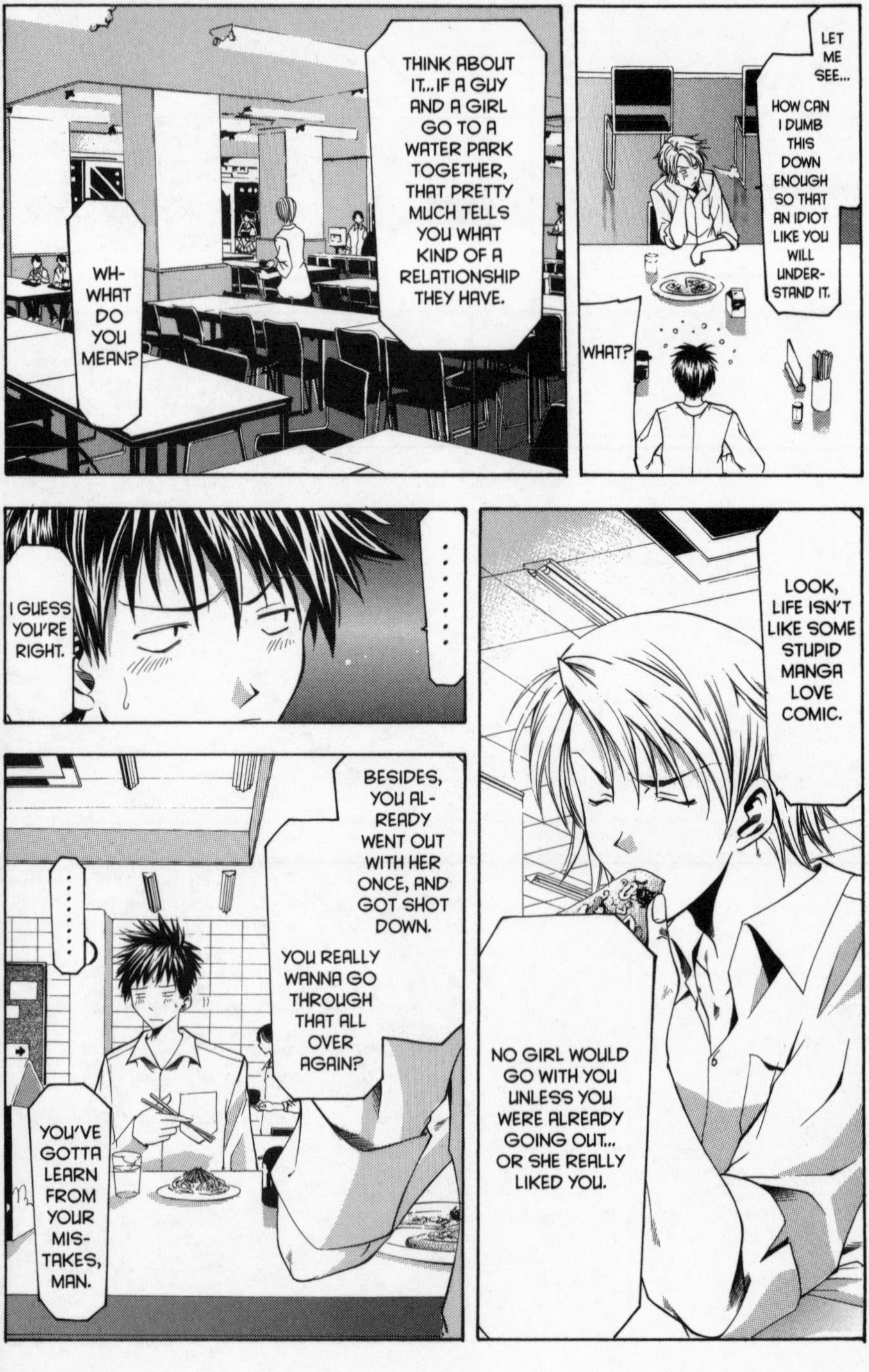
LET ME SEE...
HOW CAN I DUMB THIS DOWN ENOUGH SO THAT AN IDIOT LIKE YOU WILL UNDER-STAND IT.
WHAT?
THINK ABOUT IT...IF A GUY AND A GIRL GO TO A WATER PARK TOGETHER, THAT PRETTY MUCH TELLS YOU WHAT KIND OF A RELATIONSHIP THEY HAVE.
WH-WHAT DO YOU MEAN?
LOOK, LIFE ISN'T LIKE SOME STUPID MANGA LOVE COMIC.
NO GIRL WOULD GO WITH YOU UNLESS YOU WERE ALREADY GOING OUT... OR SHE REALLY LIKED YOU.
......
I GUESS YOU'RE RIGHT.
BESIDES, YOU AL-READY WENT OUT WITH HER ONCE, AND GOT SHOT DOWN.
YOU REALLY WANNA GO THROUGH THAT ALL OVER AGAIN?
......
YOU'VE GOTTA LEARN FROM YOUR MIS-TAKES, MAN.

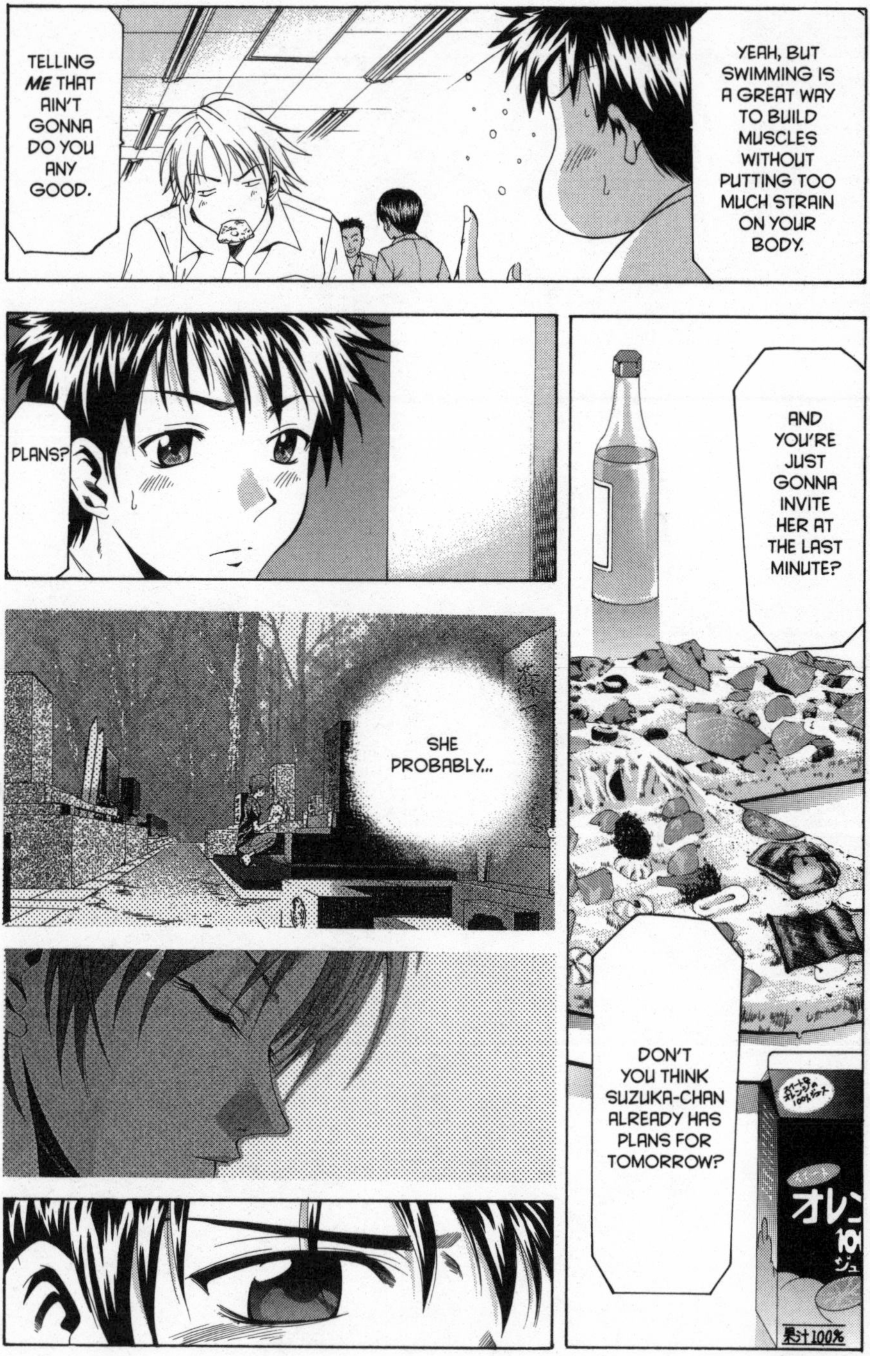
YEAH, BUT SWIMMING IS A GREAT WAY TO BUILD MUSCLES WITHOUT PUTTING TOO MUCH STRAIN ON YOUR BODY.
TELLING *ME* THAT AIN'T GONNA DO YOU ANY GOOD.
AND YOU'RE JUST GONNA INVITE HER AT THE LAST MINUTE?
DON'T YOU THINK SUZUKA-CHAN ALREADY HAS PLANS FOR TOMORROW?
果汁100%
PLANS?
SHE PROBABLY...

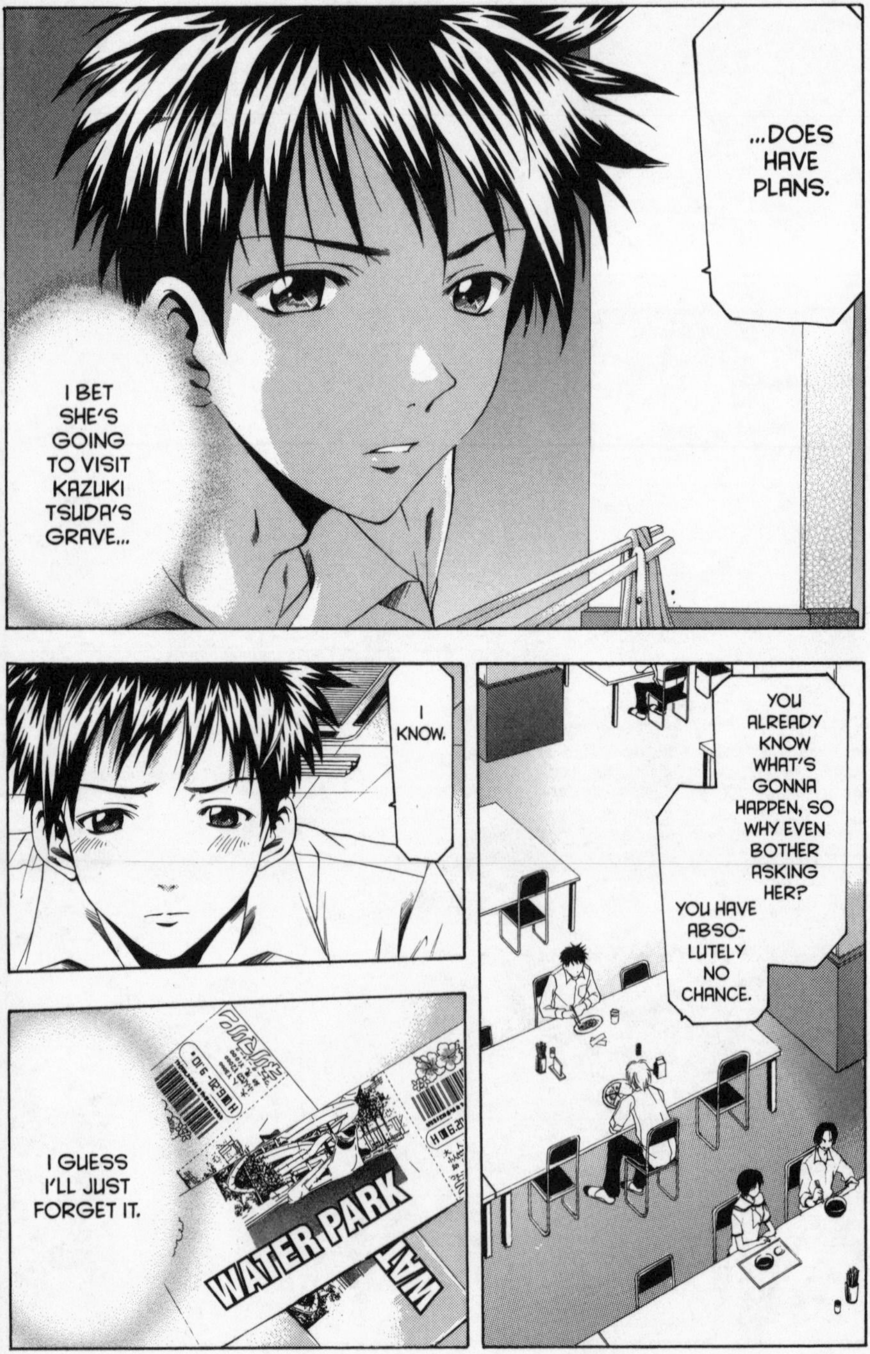
...DOES HAVE PLANS.
I BET SHE'S GOING TO VISIT KAZUKI TSUDA'S GRAVE...
YOU ALREADY KNOW WHAT'S GONNA HAPPEN, SO WHY EVEN BOTHER ASKING HER?
YOU HAVE ABSO-LUTELY NO CHANCE.
I KNOW.
I GUESS I'LL JUST FORGET IT.
WATER PARK

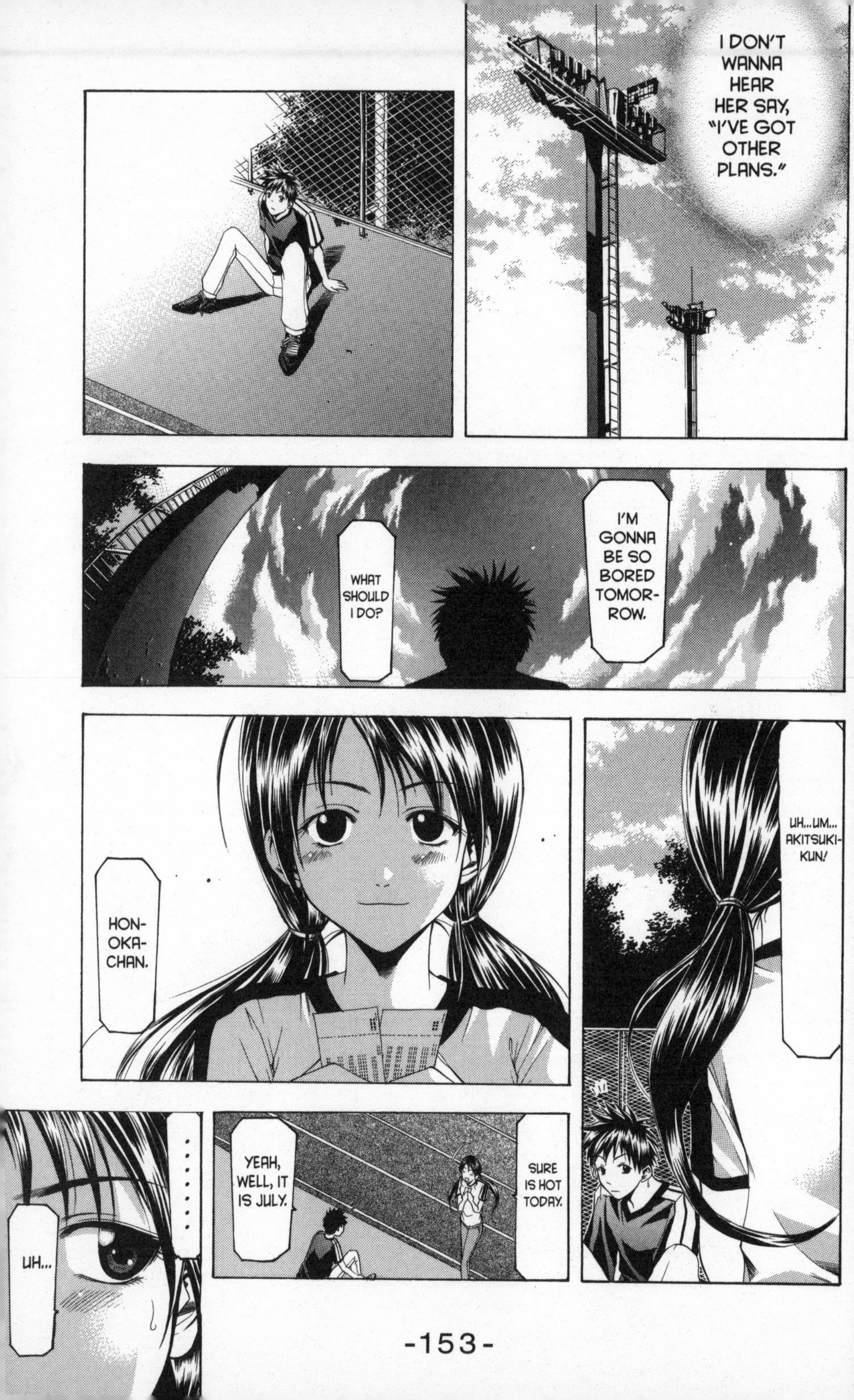

I DON'T WANNA HEAR HER SAY, "I'VE GOT OTHER PLANS."
I'M GONNA BE SO BORED TOMOR-ROW.
WHAT SHOULD I DO?
UH...UM... AKITSUKI-KUN!
HON-OKA-CHAN.
SURE IS HOT TODAY.
YEAH, WELL, IT IS JULY.
......
UH...

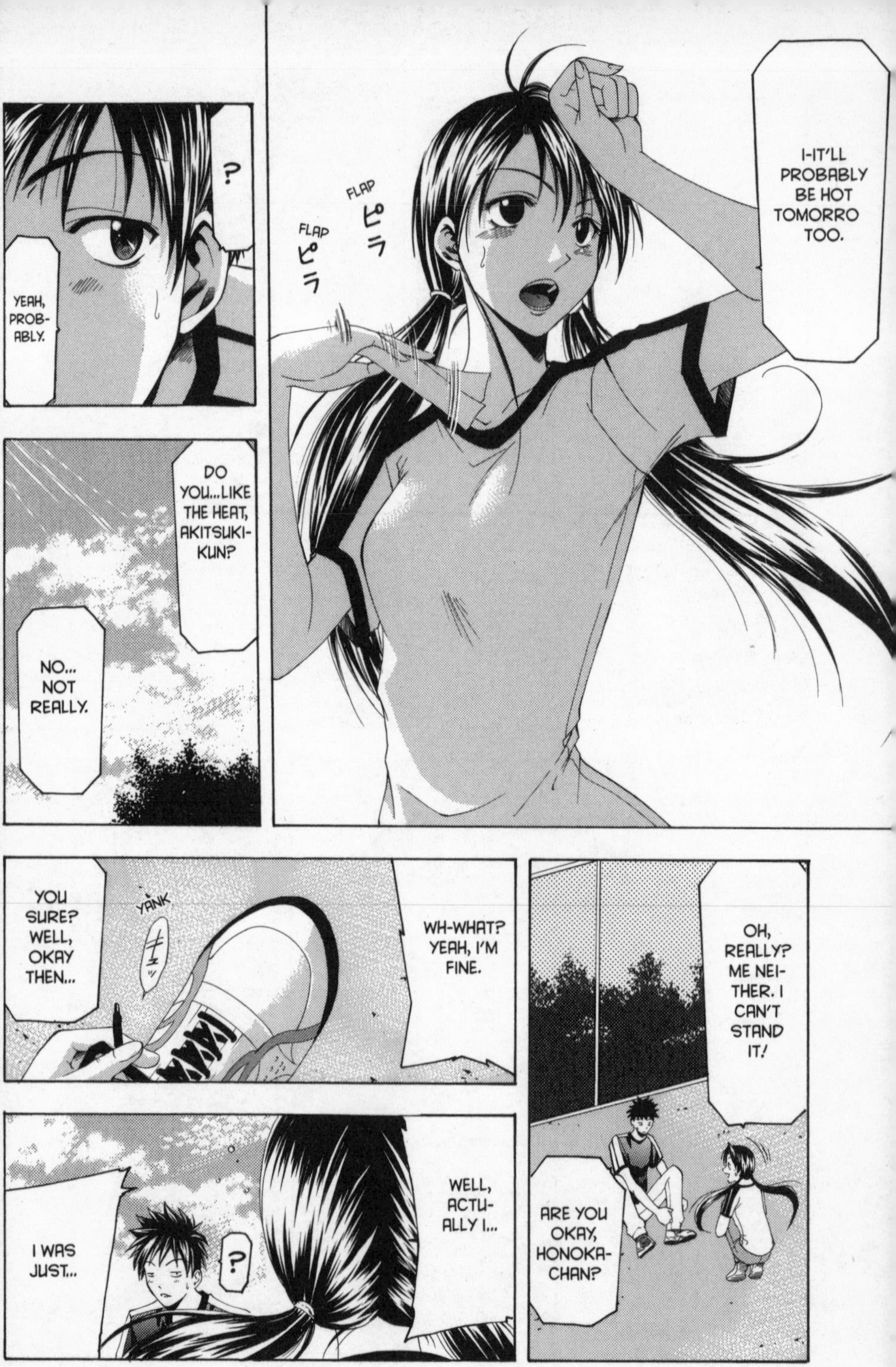
I-IT'LL PROBABLY BE HOT TOMORRO TOO.
FLAP
ピラ
FLAP
ピラ
?
YEAH, PROB-ABLY.
DO YOU...LIKE THE HEAT, AKITSUKI-KUN?
NO... NOT REALLY.
OH, REALLY? ME NEI-THER. I CAN'T STAND IT!
ARE YOU OKAY, HONOKA-CHAN?
WH-WHAT? YEAH, I'M FINE.
YANK
ギュッ
YOU SURE? WELL, OKAY THEN...
WELL, ACTU-ALLY I...
?
I WAS JUST...

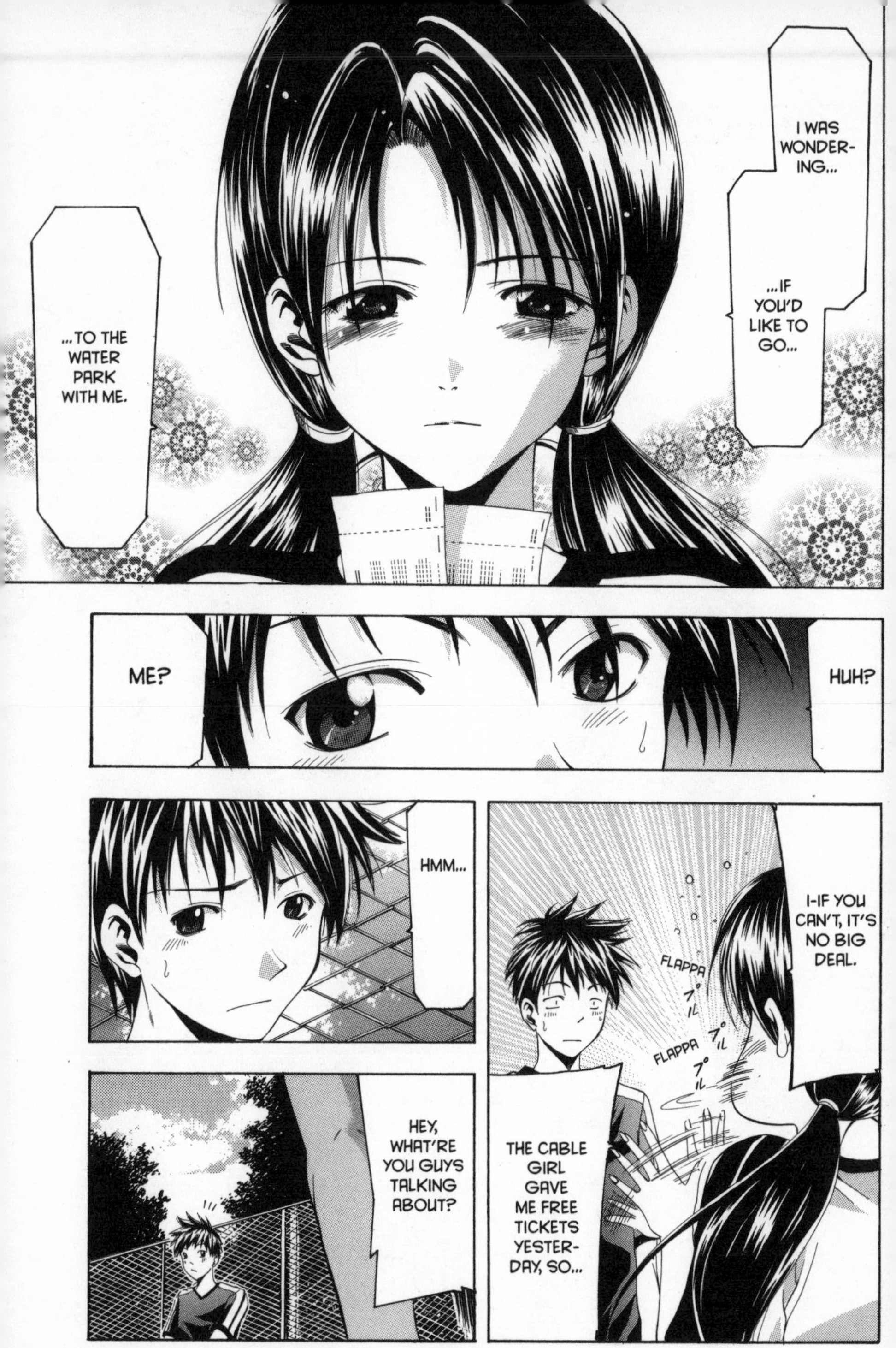
I WAS WONDER-ING...
...IF YOU'D LIKE TO GO...
...TO THE WATER PARK WITH ME.
HUH?
ME?
I-IF YOU CAN'T, IT'S NO BIG DEAL.
FLAPPA
プル
FLAPPA
プル
THE CABLE GIRL GAVE ME FREE TICKETS YESTER-DAY, SO...
HMM...
HEY, WHAT'RE YOU GUYS TALKING ABOUT?

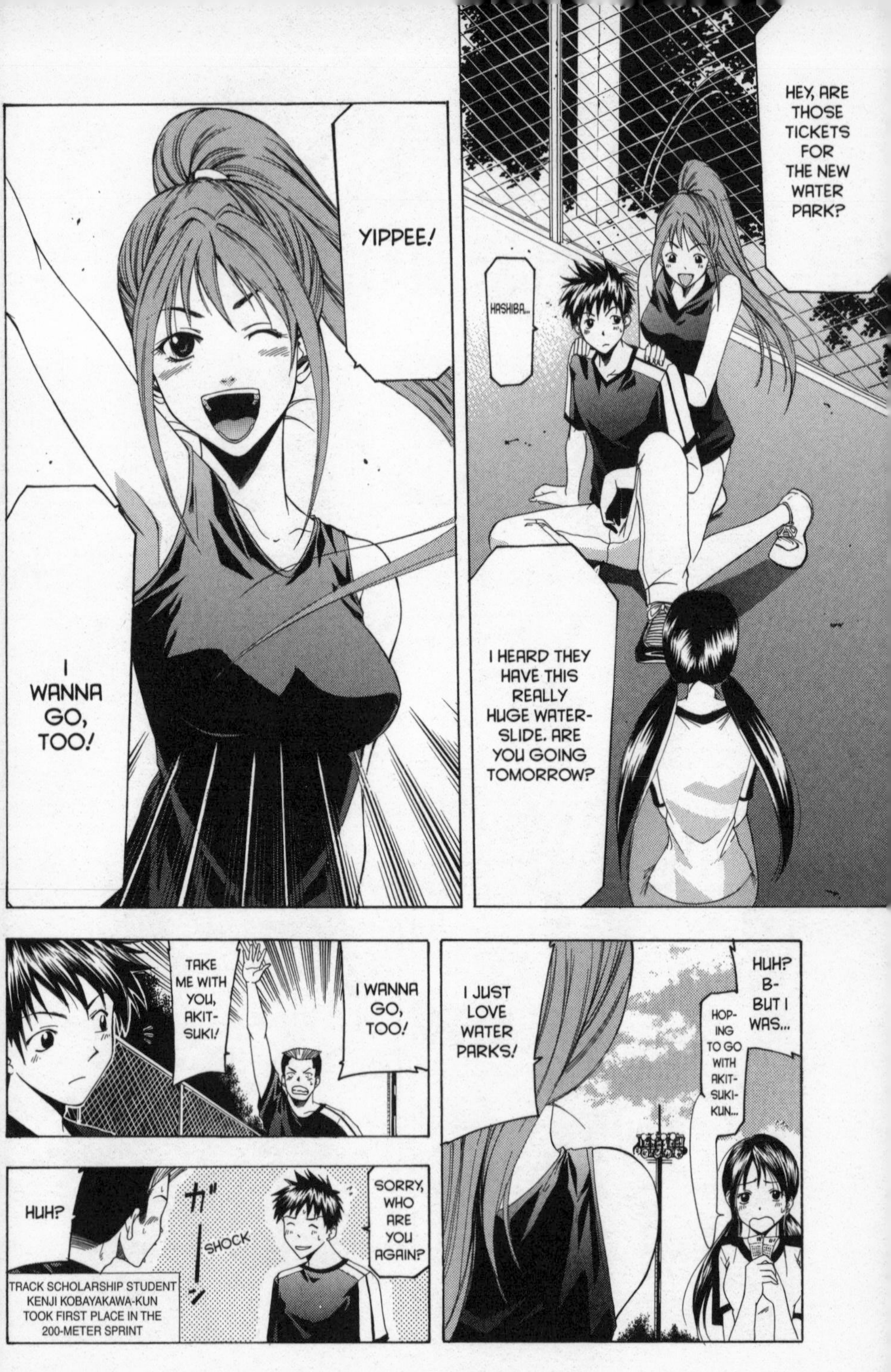
HEY, ARE THOSE TICKETS FOR THE NEW WATER PARK?
HASHIBA...
I HEARD THEY HAVE THIS REALLY HUGE WATER-SLIDE. ARE YOU GOING TOMORROW?
YIPPEE!
I WANNA GO, TOO!
HUH? B-BUT I WAS...
HOPING TO GO WITH AKIT-SUKI-KUN...
I JUST LOVE WATER PARKS!
I WANNA GO, TOO!
TAKE ME WITH YOU, AKIT-SUKI!
SORRY, WHO ARE YOU AGAIN?
SHOCK
HUH?
TRACK SCHOLARSHIP STUDENT KENJI KOBAYAKAWA-KUN TOOK FIRST PLACE IN THE 200-METER SPRINT

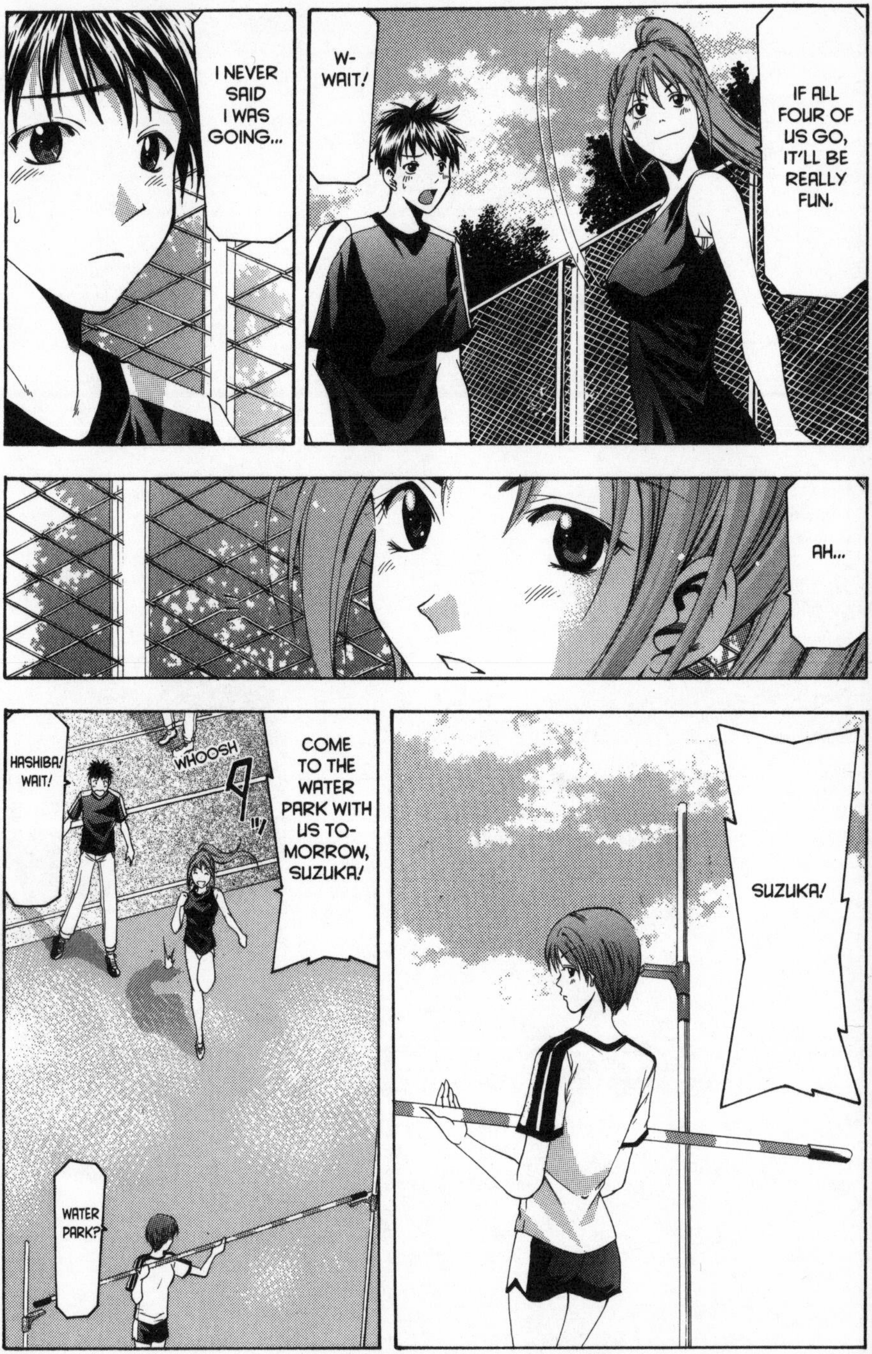
IF ALL FOUR OF US GO, IT'LL BE REALLY FUN.
W-WAIT!
I NEVER SAID I WAS GOING...
AH...
SUZUKA!
COME TO THE WATER PARK WITH US TO-MORROW, SUZUKA!
WHOOSH
HASHIBA! WAIT!
WATER PARK?

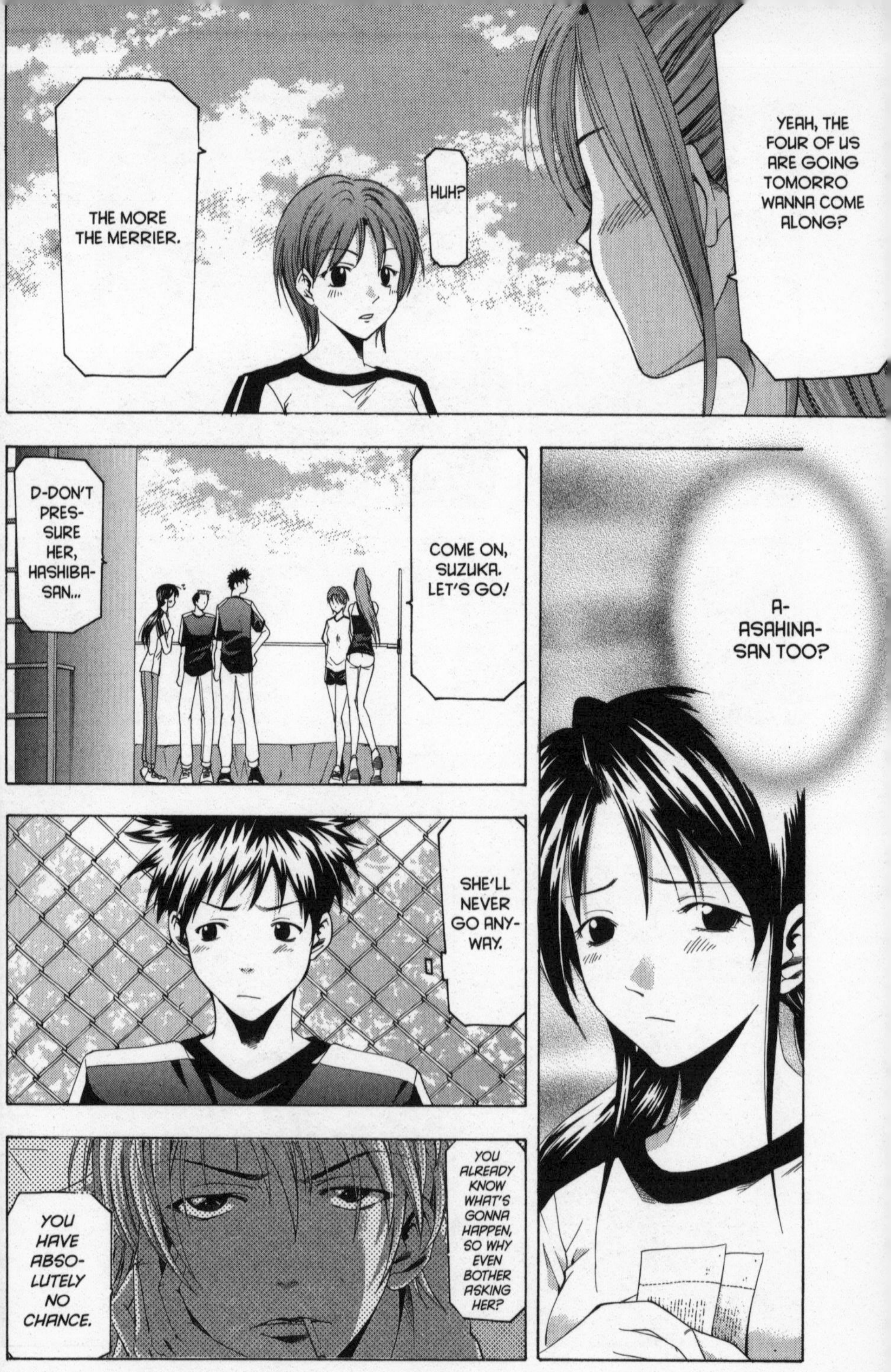
YEAH, THE FOUR OF US ARE GOING TOMORRO WANNA COME ALONG?
HUH?
THE MORE THE MERRIER.
A-ASAHINA-SAN TOO?
COME ON, SUZUKA. LET'S GO!
D-DON'T PRES-SURE HER, HASHIBA-SAN...
SHE'LL NEVER GO ANY-WAY.
YOU ALREADY KNOW WHAT'S GONNA HAPPEN, SO WHY EVEN BOTHER ASKING HER?
YOU HAVE ABSO-LUTELY NO CHANCE.

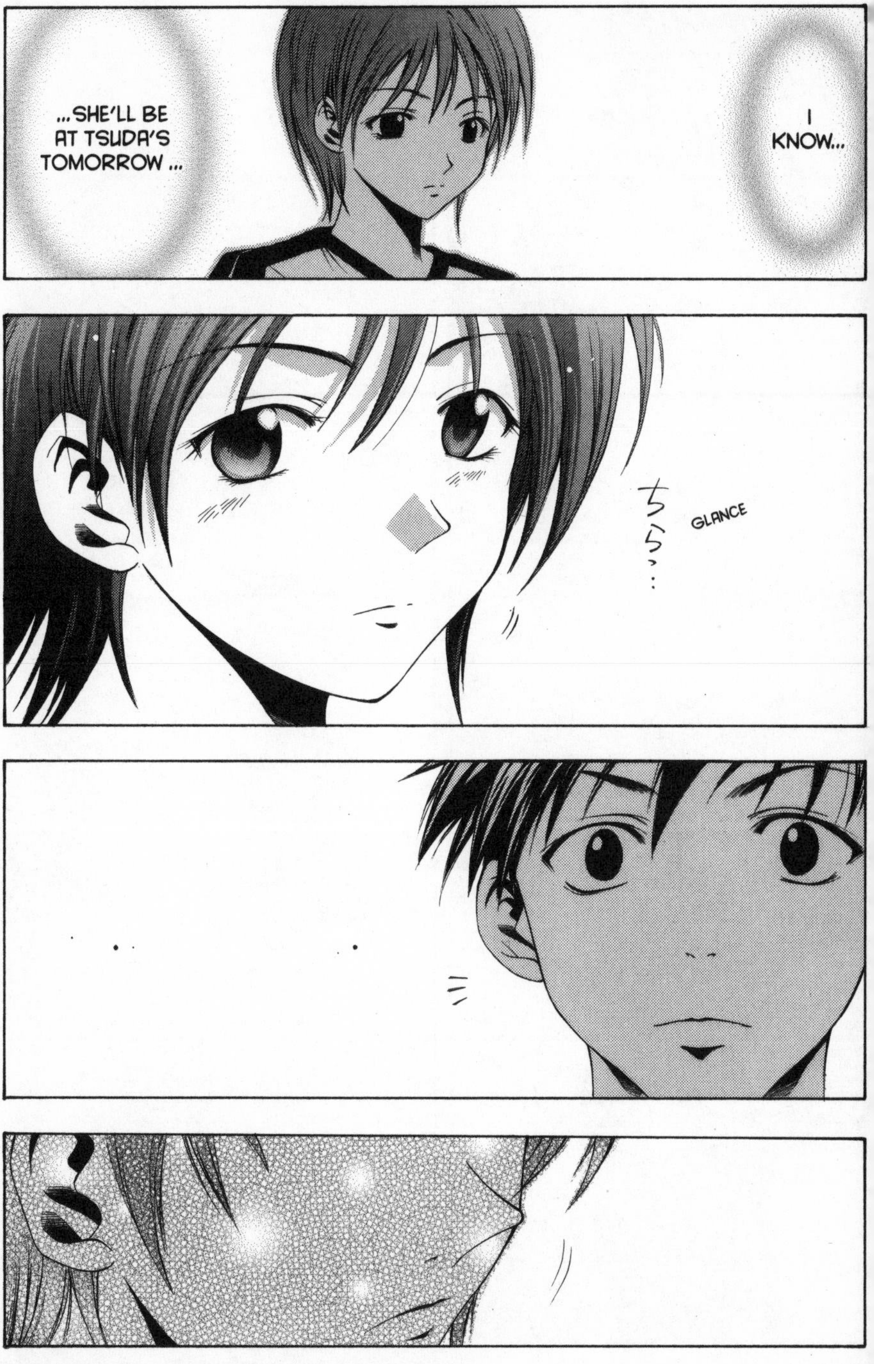
I KNOW...
...SHE'LL BE AT TSUDA'S TOMORROW ...
ちら…
GLANCE

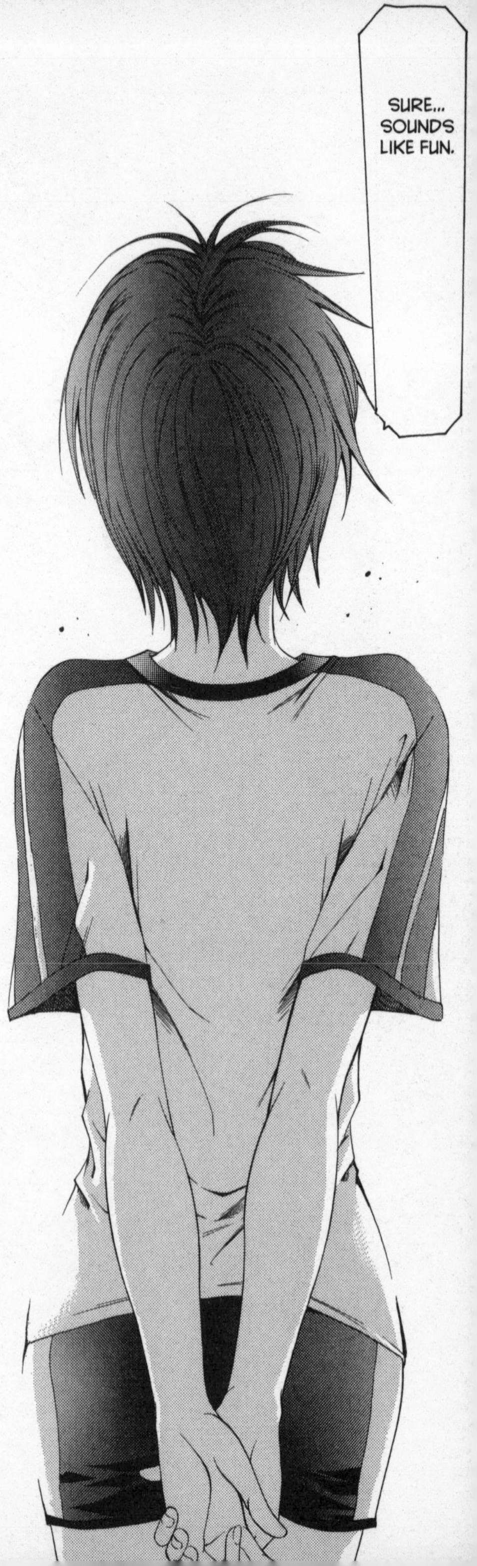
SURE... SOUNDS LIKE FUN.

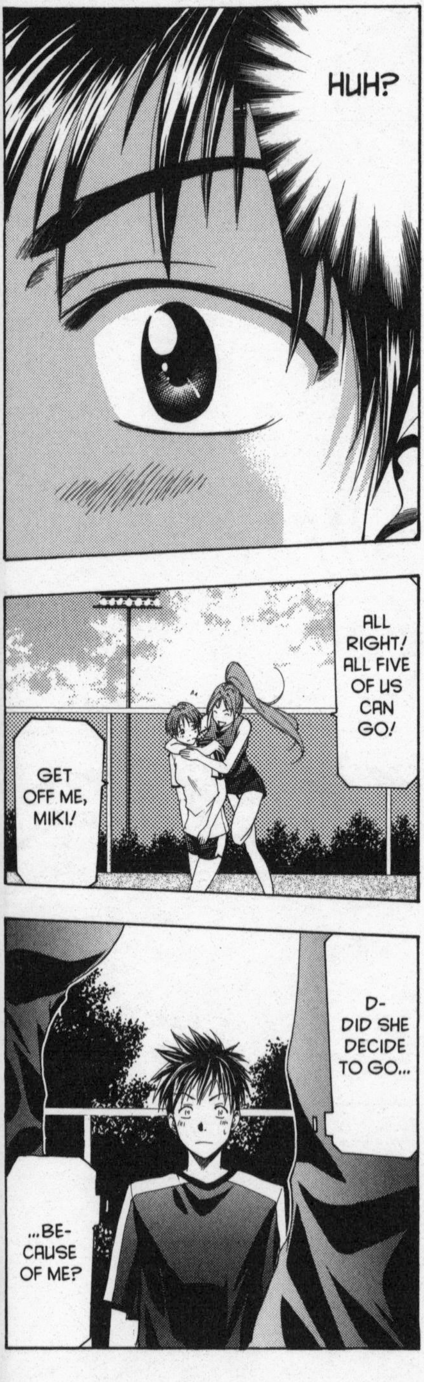
HUH?
ALL RIGHT! ALL FIVE OF US CAN GO!
GET OFF ME, MIKI!
D- DID SHE DECIDE TO GO...
...BE- CAUSE OF ME?

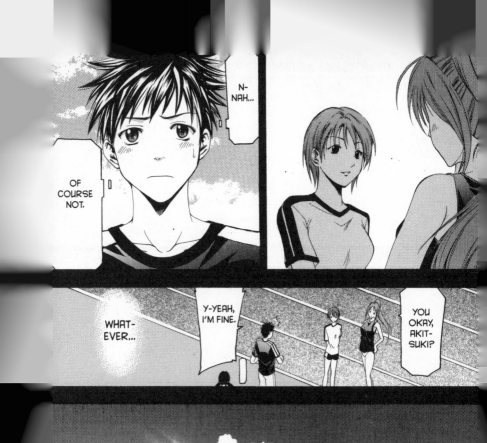

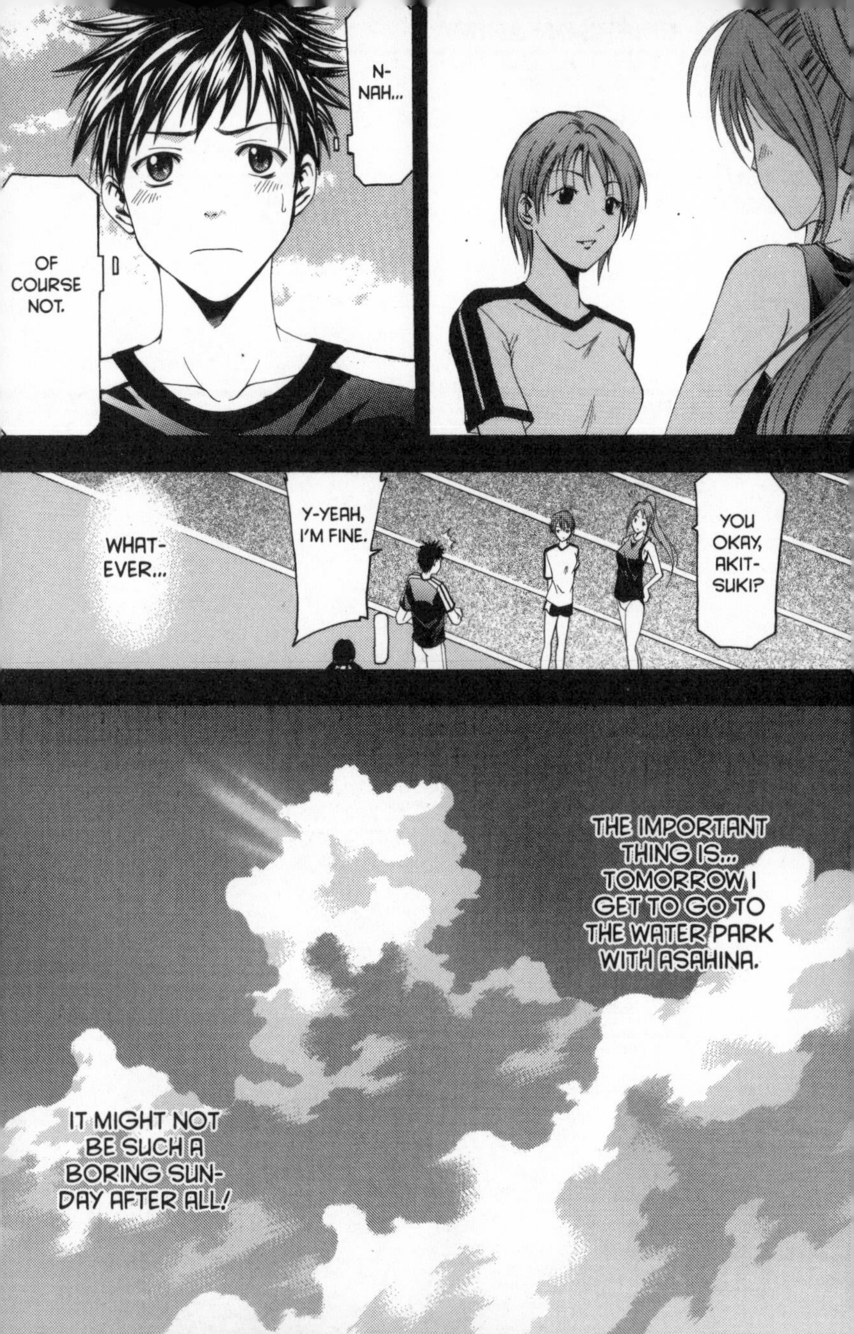
N-NAH...
OF COURSE NOT.
YOU OKAY, AKITSUKI?
Y-YEAH, I'M FINE.
WHATEVER...
THE IMPORTANT THING IS... TOMORROW I GET TO GO TO THE WATER PARK WITH ASAHINA.
IT MIGHT NOT BE SUCH A BORING SUNDAY AFTER ALL!

CHARACTER PROFILE NO. 12

EMERSON ARIMA
(HIGH SCHOOL SOPHOMORE)

DATE OF BIRTH—JULY 7 (CANCER)
HEIGHT—5'9"
WEIGHT—158 LBS
BLOOD TYPE—A

LIKES
- TRACK
- FISH *AQUA PAZZA*
- *SHIROI KOIBITO* COOKIES

DISLIKES
- KAZUKI TSUDA
- BEING TOLD WHAT TO DO
- PICKLES

GOAL—TO RUN THE 100-METER DASH IN UNDER TEN SECONDS

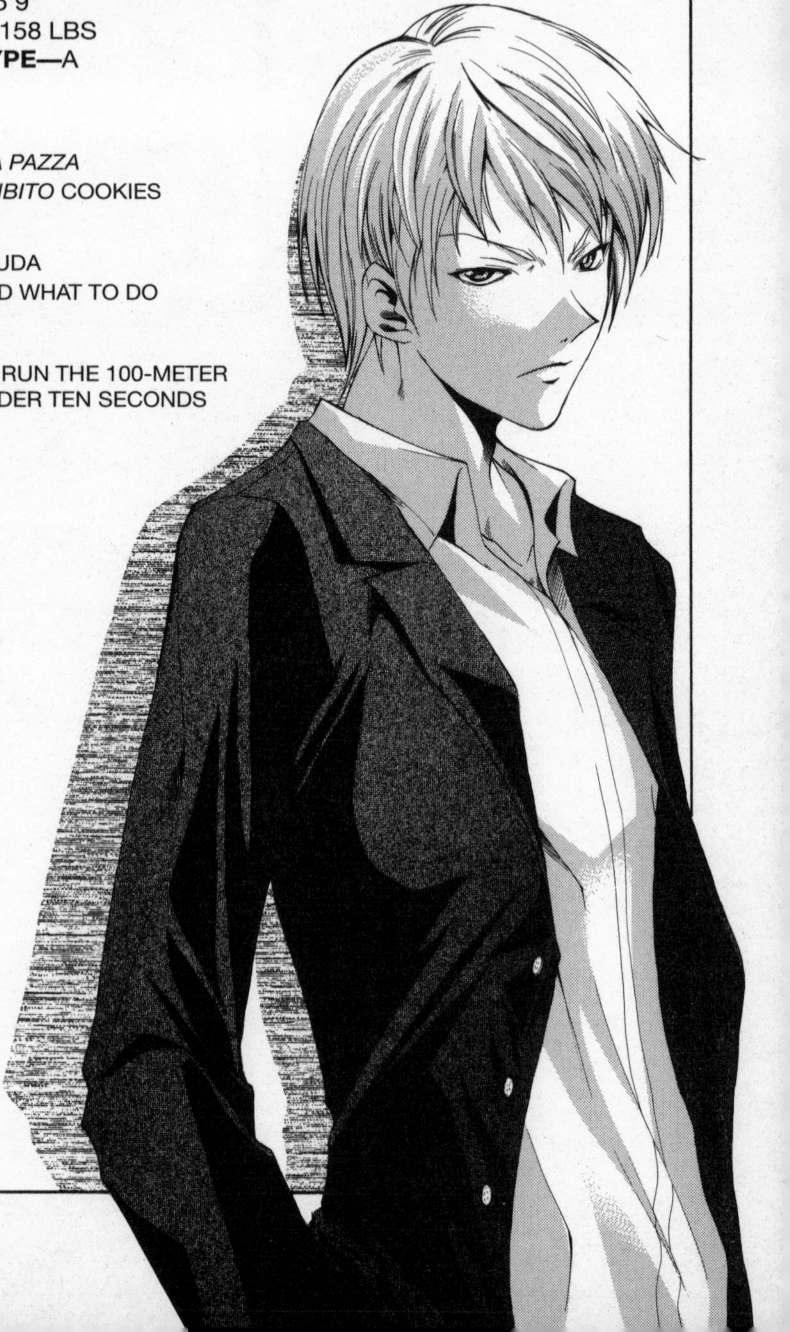

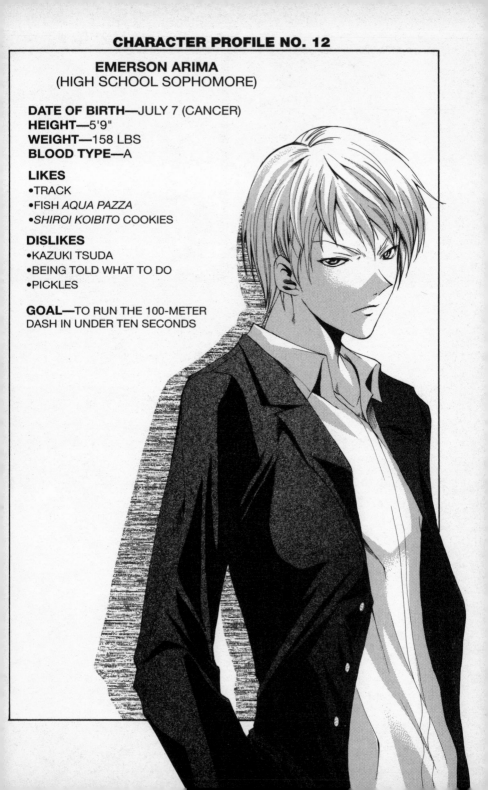

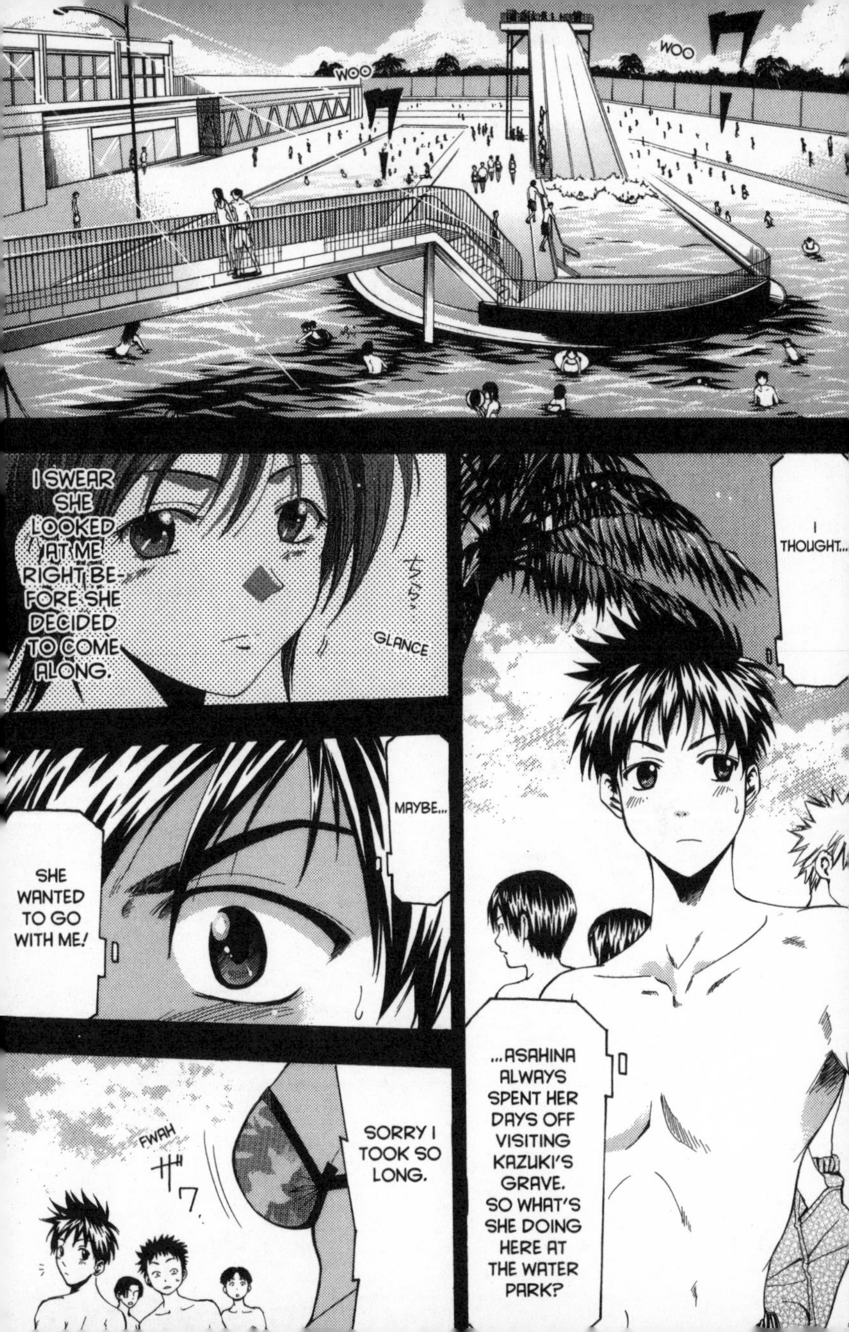
WOO
WOO
I THOUGHT...
...ASAHINA ALWAYS SPENT HER DAYS OFF VISITING KAZUKI'S GRAVE. SO WHAT'S SHE DOING HERE AT THE WATER PARK?
I SWEAR SHE LOOKED AT ME RIGHT BEFORE SHE DECIDED TO COME ALONG.
GLANCE
MAYBE...
SHE WANTED TO GO WITH ME!
SORRY I TOOK SO LONG.
FWAH

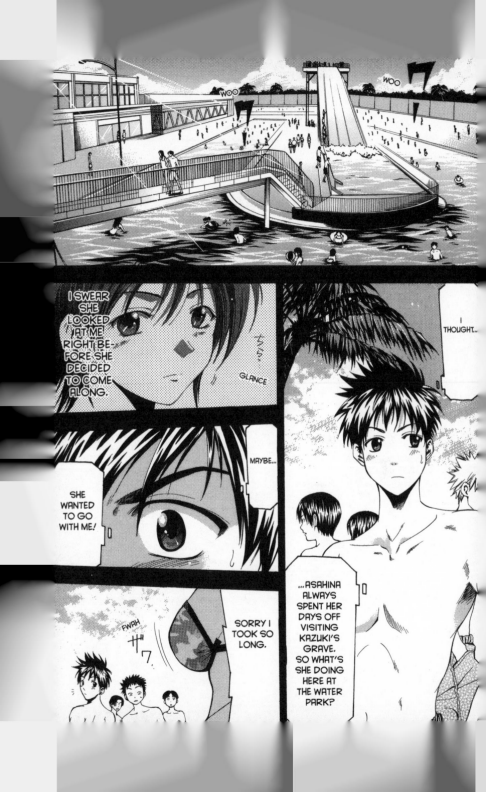

SUZUKA

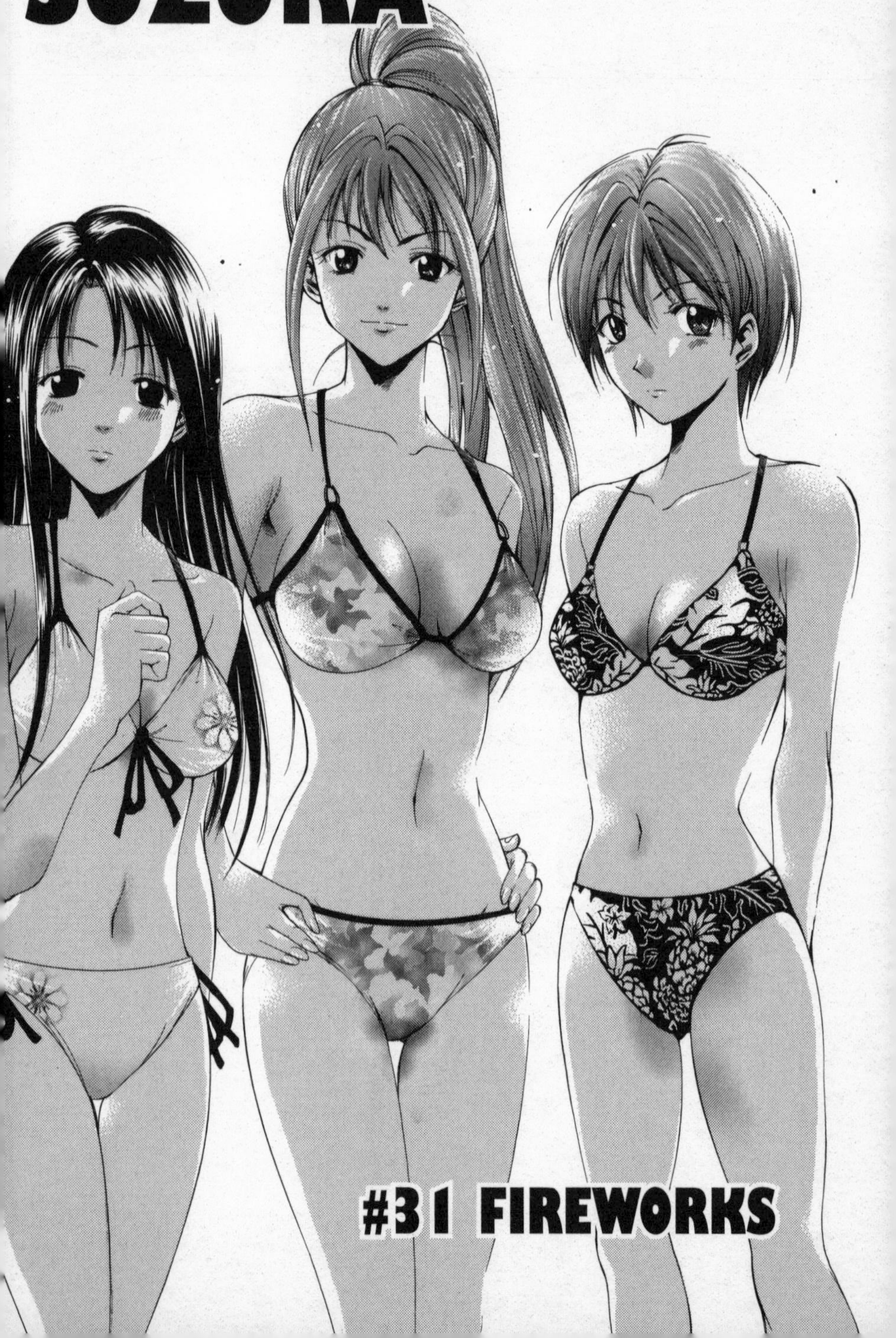

#31 FIREWORKS

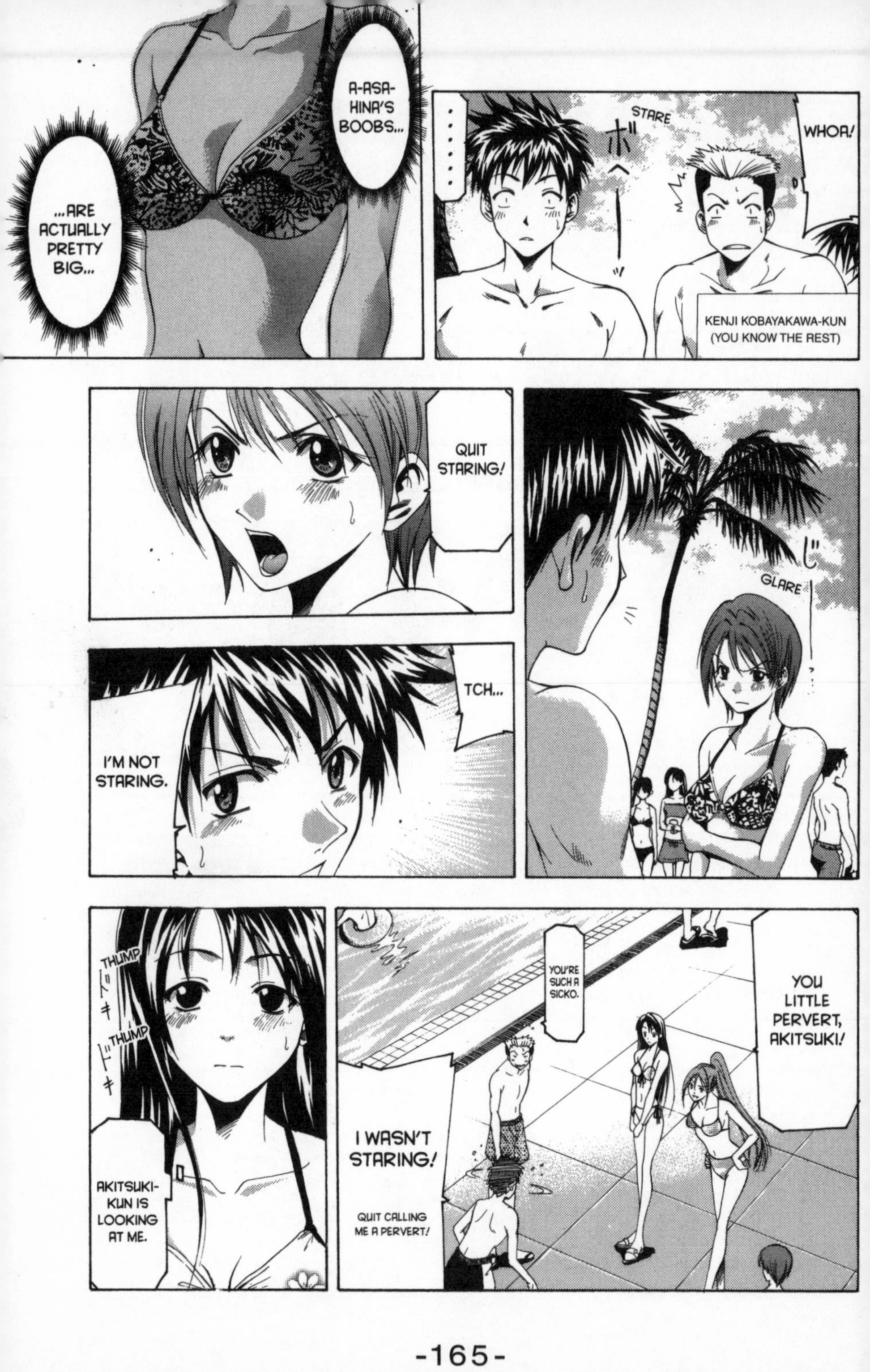
WHOA!
STARE
......
KENJI KOBAYAKAWA-KUN (YOU KNOW THE REST)
A-ASA-HINA'S BOOBS...
...ARE ACTUALLY PRETTY BIG...
GLARE
QUIT STARING!
TCH...
I'M NOT STARING.
YOU LITTLE PERVERT, AKITSUKI!
YOU'RE SUCH A SICKO.
I WASN'T STARING!
QUIT CALLING ME A PERVERT!
THUMP
THUMP
AKITSUKI-KUN IS LOOKING AT ME.

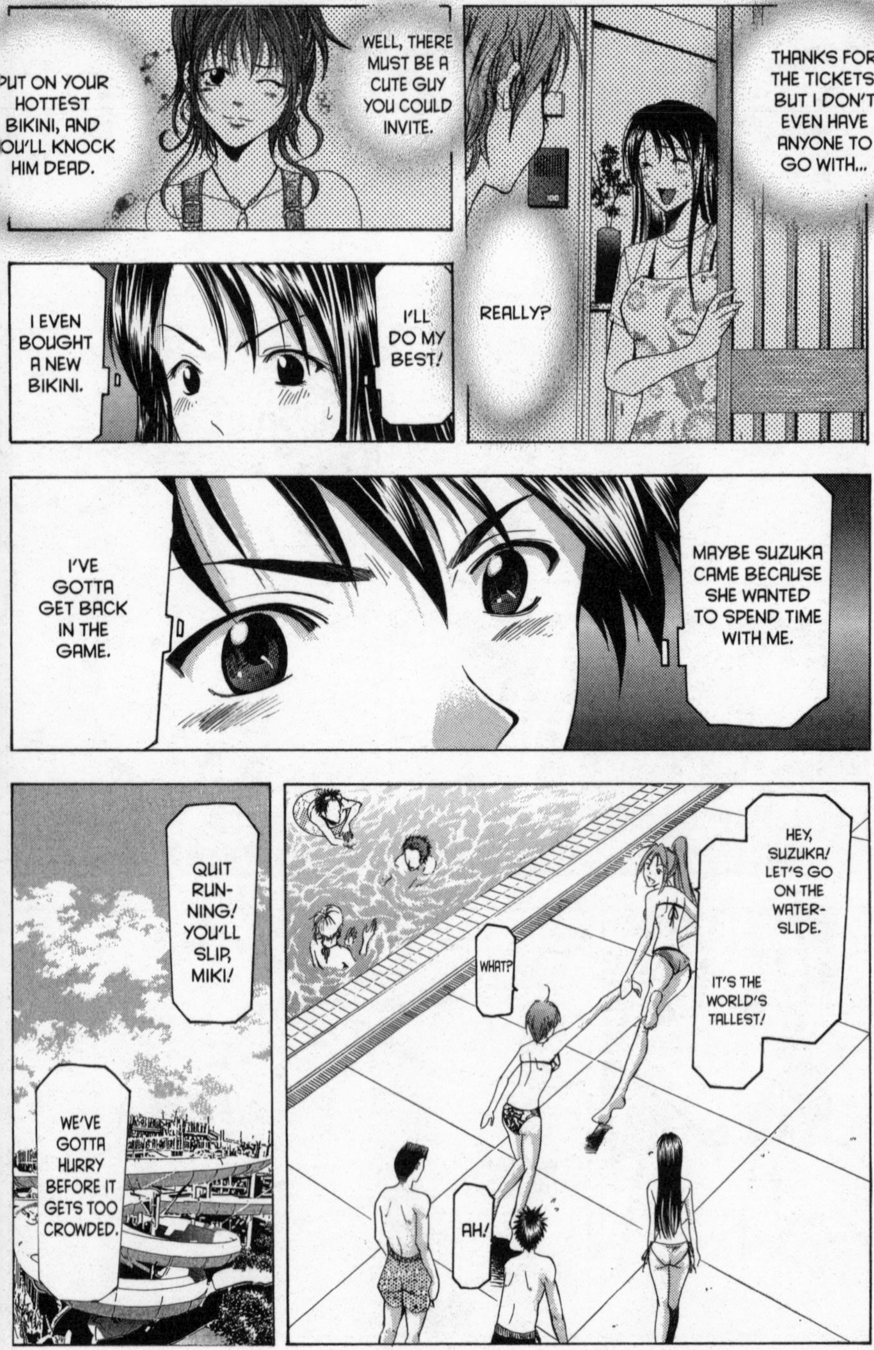

THANKS FOR THE TICKETS, BUT I DON'T EVEN HAVE ANYONE TO GO WITH...
REALLY?
WELL, THERE MUST BE A CUTE GUY YOU COULD INVITE.
UT ON YOUR HOTTEST BIKINI, AND OU'LL KNOCK HIM DEAD.
I'LL DO MY BEST!
I EVEN BOUGHT A NEW BIKINI.
MAYBE SUZUKA CAME BECAUSE SHE WANTED TO SPEND TIME WITH ME.
I'VE GOTTA GET BACK IN THE GAME.
HEY, SUZUKA! LET'S GO ON THE WATER-SLIDE.
IT'S THE WORLD'S TALLEST!
WHAT?
AH!
QUIT RUN-NING! YOU'LL SLIP, MIKI!
WE'VE GOTTA HURRY BEFORE IT GETS TOO CROWDED.

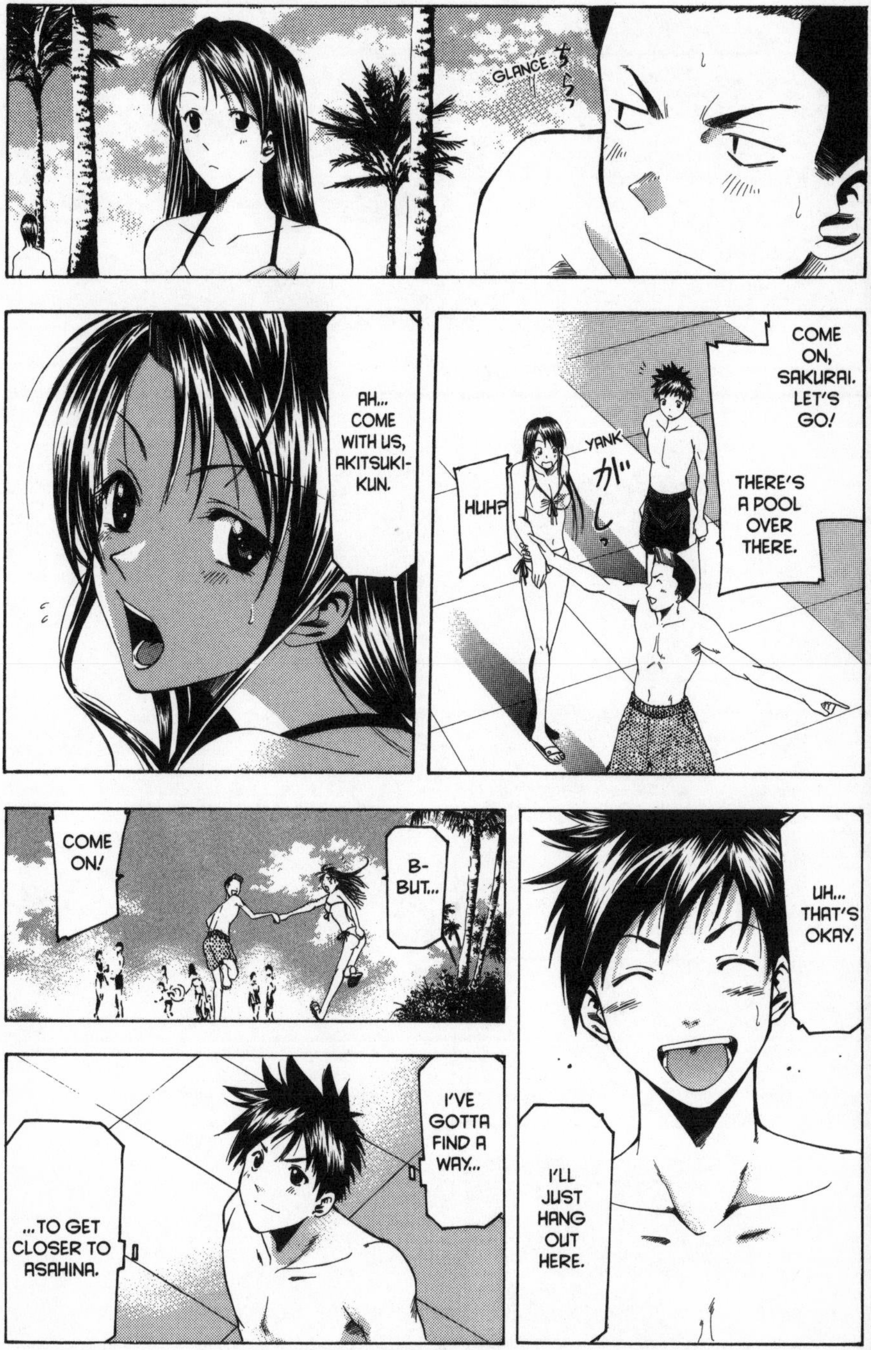
GLANCE
ちらっ
COME ON, SAKURAI. LET'S GO!
THERE'S A POOL OVER THERE.
YANK
がしっ
HUH?
AH... COME WITH US, AKITSUKI-KUN.
UH... THAT'S OKAY.
I'LL JUST HANG OUT HERE.
B-BUT...
COME ON!
I'VE GOTTA FIND A WAY...
...TO GET CLOSER TO ASAHINA.

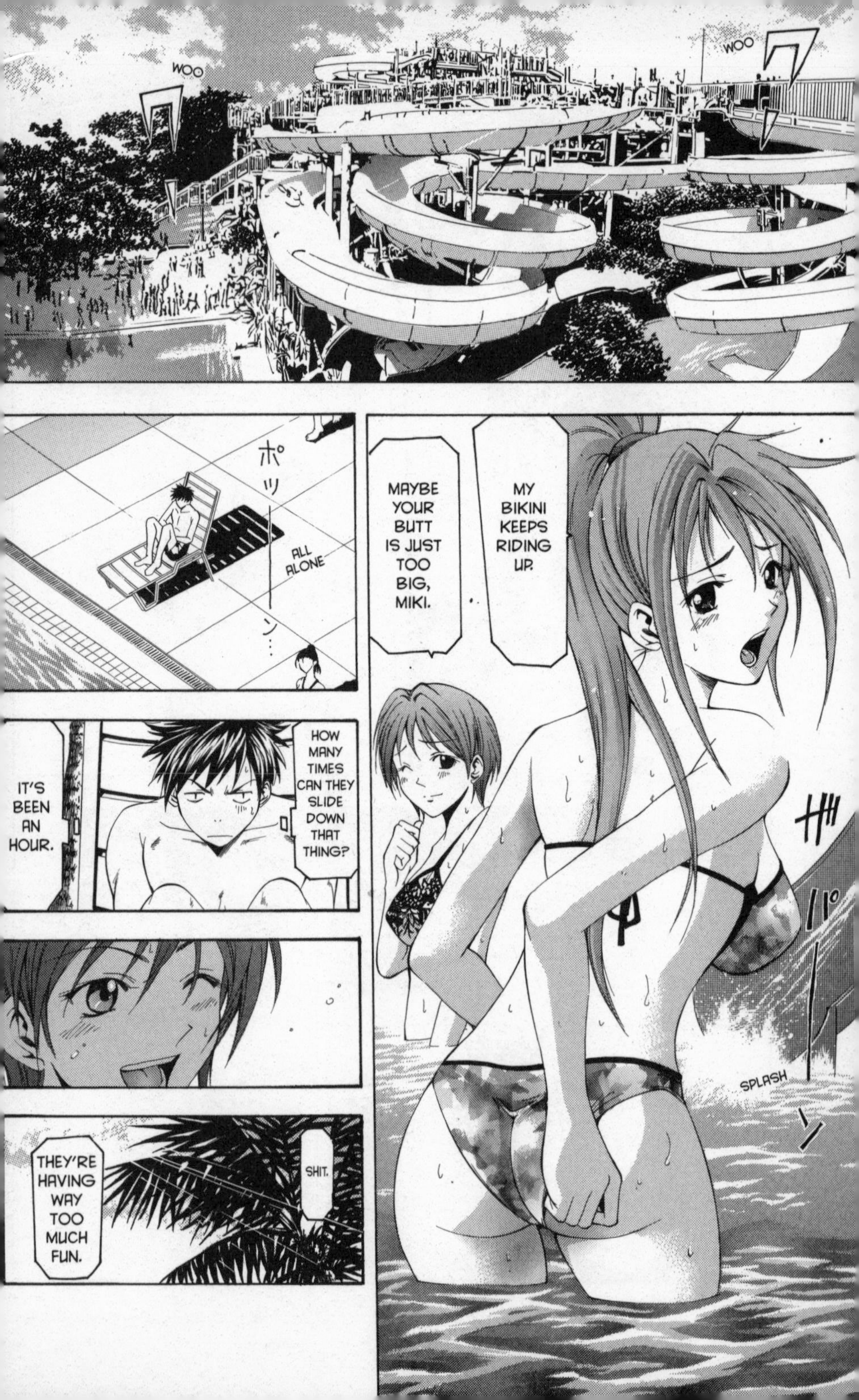
WOO
WOO
MY BIKINI KEEPS RIDING UP.
MAYBE YOUR BUTT IS JUST TOO BIG, MIKI.
ザ
パーン
SPLASH
ポツーン…
ALL ALONE
HOW MANY TIMES CAN THEY SLIDE DOWN THAT THING?
IT'S BEEN AN HOUR.
SHIT.
THEY'RE HAVING WAY TOO MUCH FUN.

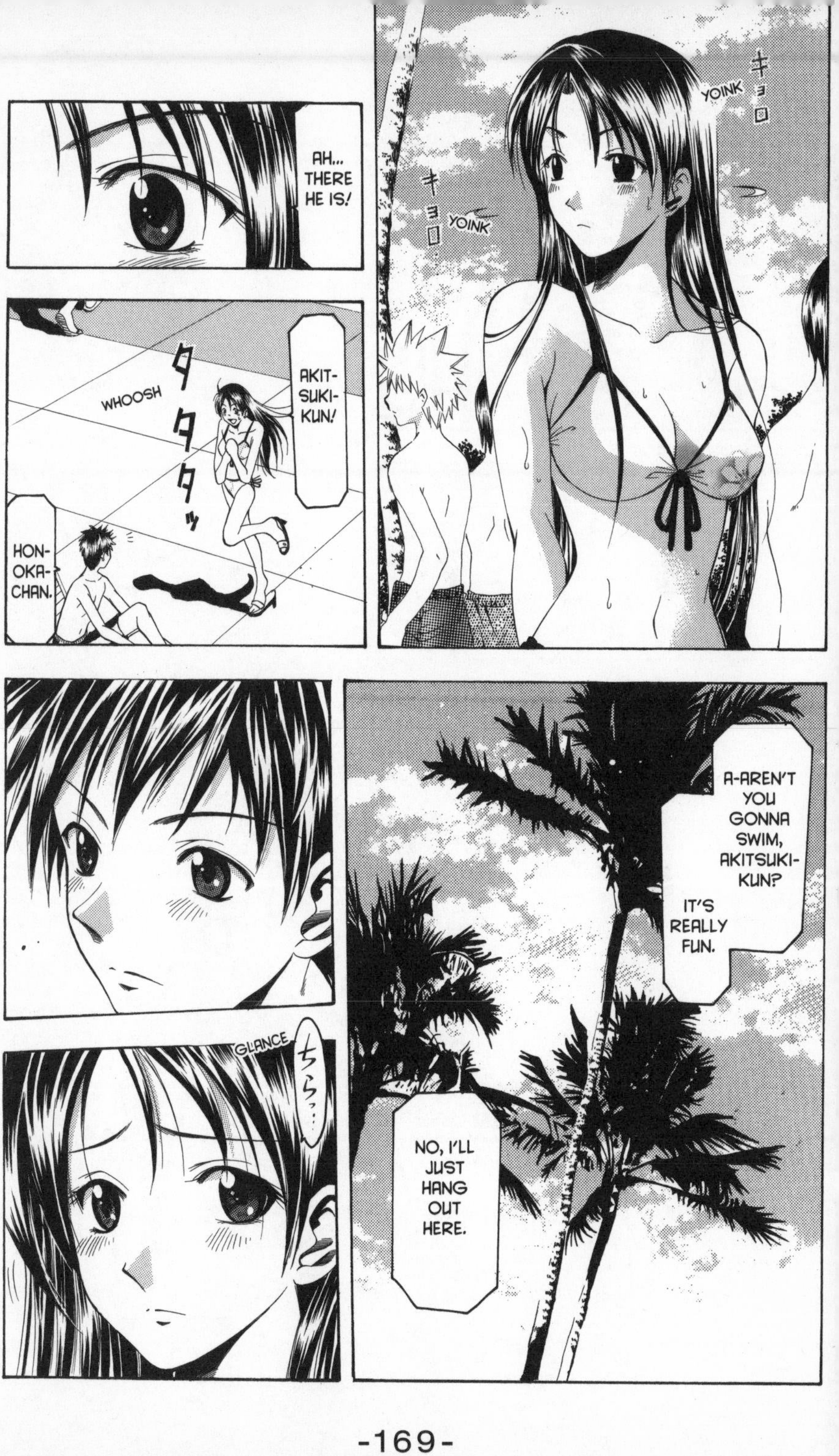
キョロ
YOINK
キョロ
YOINK
AH... THERE HE IS!
AKIT-SUKI-KUN!
タタタッ
WHOOSH
HON-OKA-CHAN.
A-AREN'T YOU GONNA SWIM, AKITSUKI-KUN?
IT'S REALLY FUN.
NO, I'LL JUST HANG OUT HERE.
...
ちらっ…
GLANCE

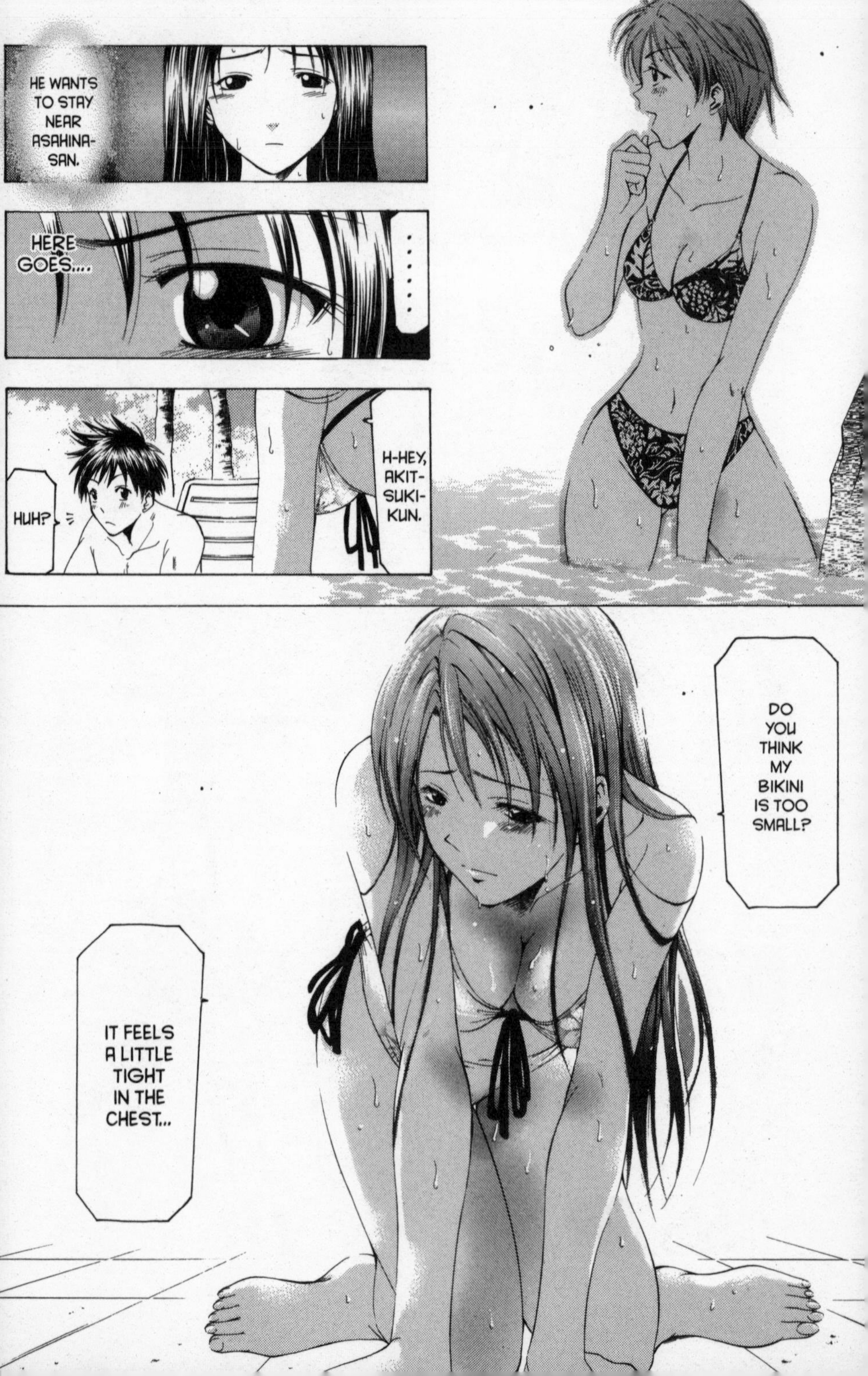
HE WANTS TO STAY NEAR ASAHINA-SAN.
......
HERE GOES....
H-HEY, AKITSUKI-KUN.
HUH?
DO YOU THINK MY BIKINI IS TOO SMALL?
IT FEELS A LITTLE TIGHT IN THE CHEST...

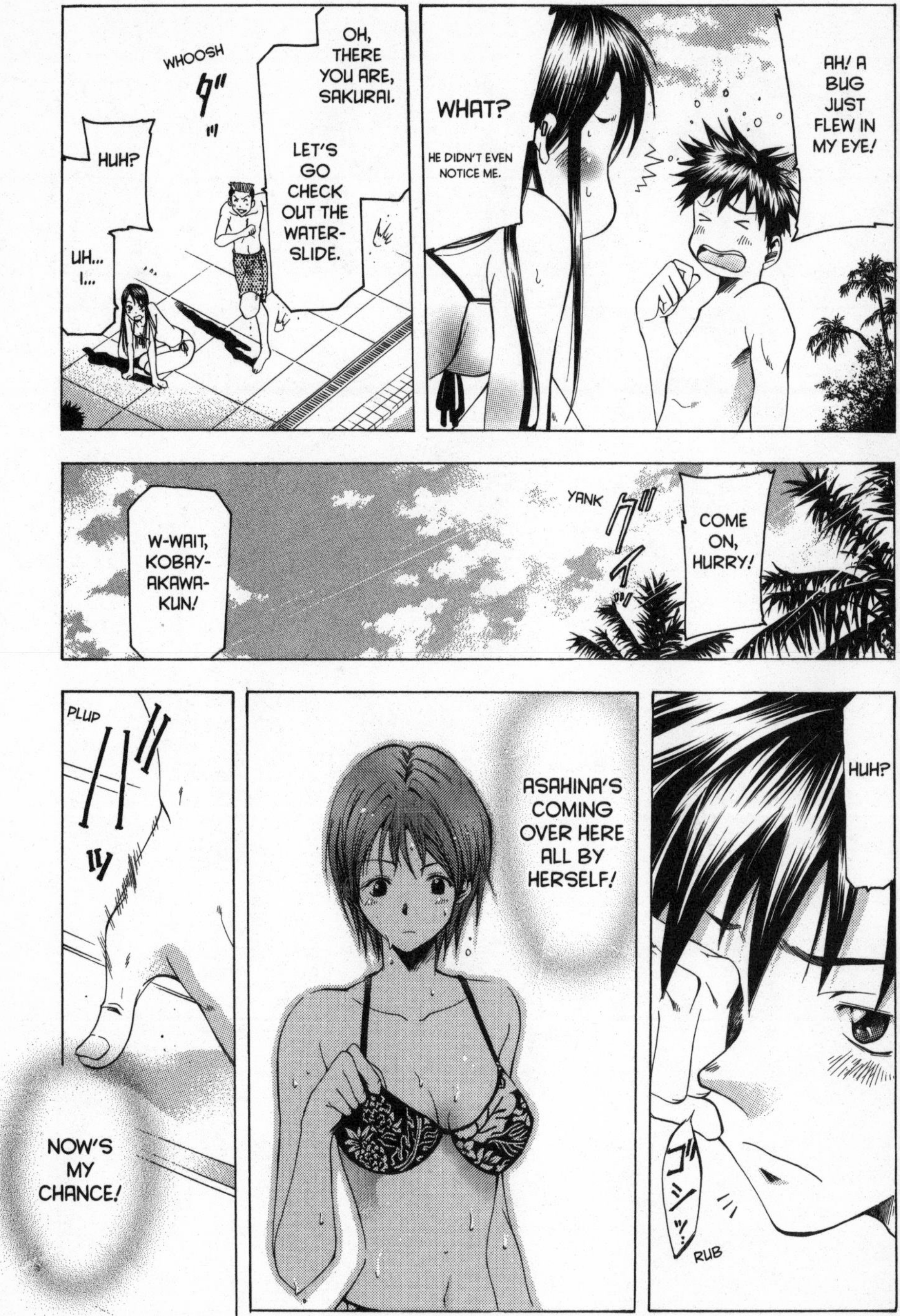
AH! A BUG JUST FLEW IN MY EYE!
WHAT?
HE DIDN'T EVEN NOTICE ME.
OH, THERE YOU ARE, SAKURAI.
LET'S GO CHECK OUT THE WATER-SLIDE.
WHOOSH
HUH?
UH... I...
COME ON, HURRY!
YANK
W-WAIT, KOBAY-AKAWA-KUN!
HUH?
RUB
ASAHINA'S COMING OVER HERE ALL BY HERSELF!
PLUP
NOW'S MY CHANCE!

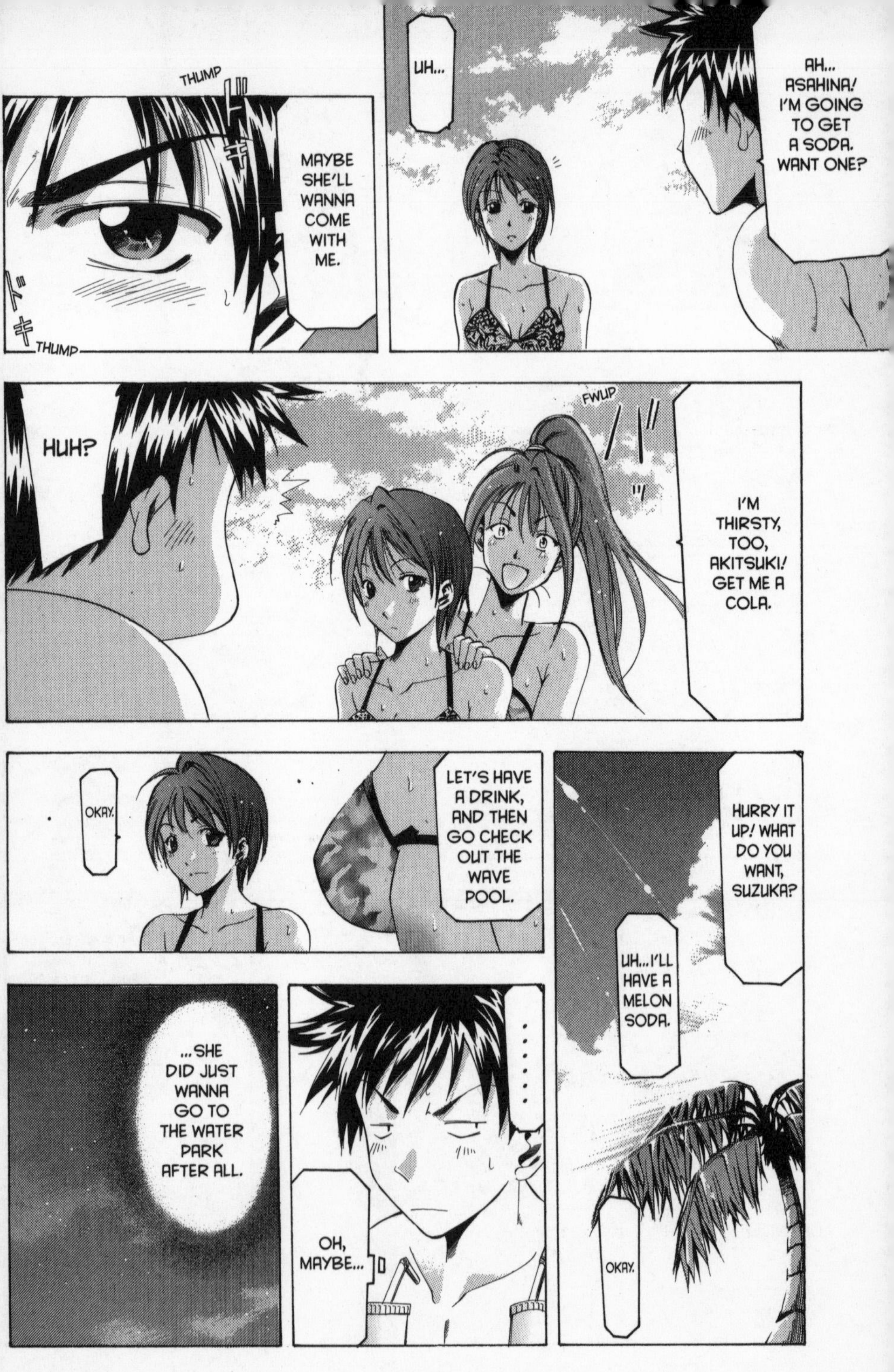
AH... ASAHINA! I'M GOING TO GET A SODA. WANT ONE?
UH...
THUMP
MAYBE SHE'LL WANNA COME WITH ME.
THUMP
I'M THIRSTY, TOO, AKITSUKI! GET ME A COLA.
FWUP
HUH?
HURRY IT UP! WHAT DO YOU WANT, SUZUKA?
UH...I'LL HAVE A MELON SODA.
OKAY.
LET'S HAVE A DRINK, AND THEN GO CHECK OUT THE WAVE POOL.
OKAY.
......
OH, MAYBE...
...SHE DID JUST WANNA GO TO THE WATER PARK AFTER ALL.

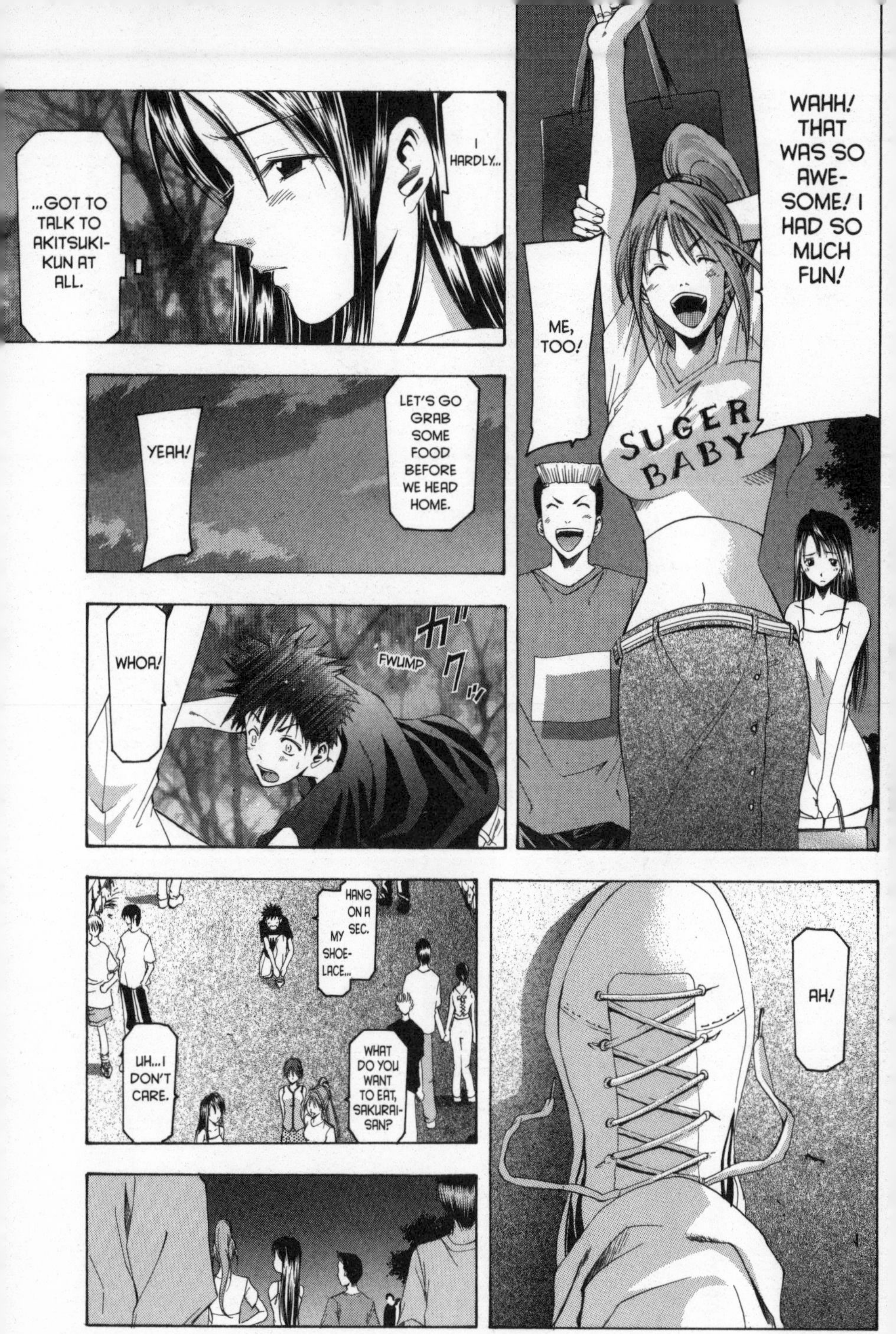
WAHH! THAT WAS SO AWE-SOME! I HAD SO MUCH FUN!
ME, TOO!
I HARDLY...
...GOT TO TALK TO AKITSUKI-KUN AT ALL.
LET'S GO GRAB SOME FOOD BEFORE WE HEAD HOME.
YEAH!
ガクッ
FWUMP
WHOA!
AH!
HANG ON A SEC. MY SHOE-LACE...
WHAT DO YOU WANT TO EAT, SAKURAI-SAN?
UH...I DON'T CARE.

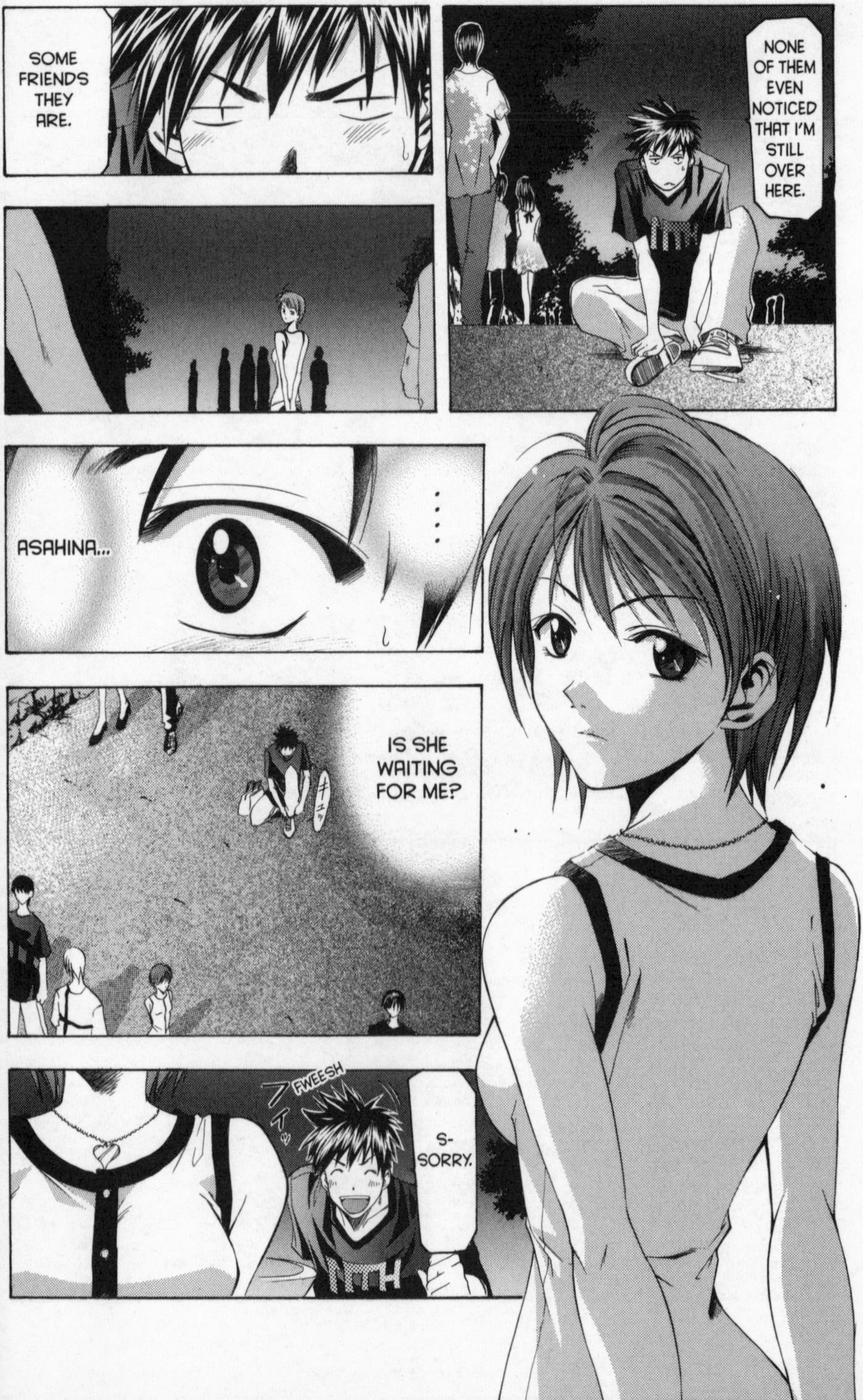
NONE OF THEM EVEN NOTICED THAT I'M STILL OVER HERE.
SOME FRIENDS THEY ARE.
....
ASAHINA...
IS SHE WAITING FOR ME?
S- SORRY.
FWEESH

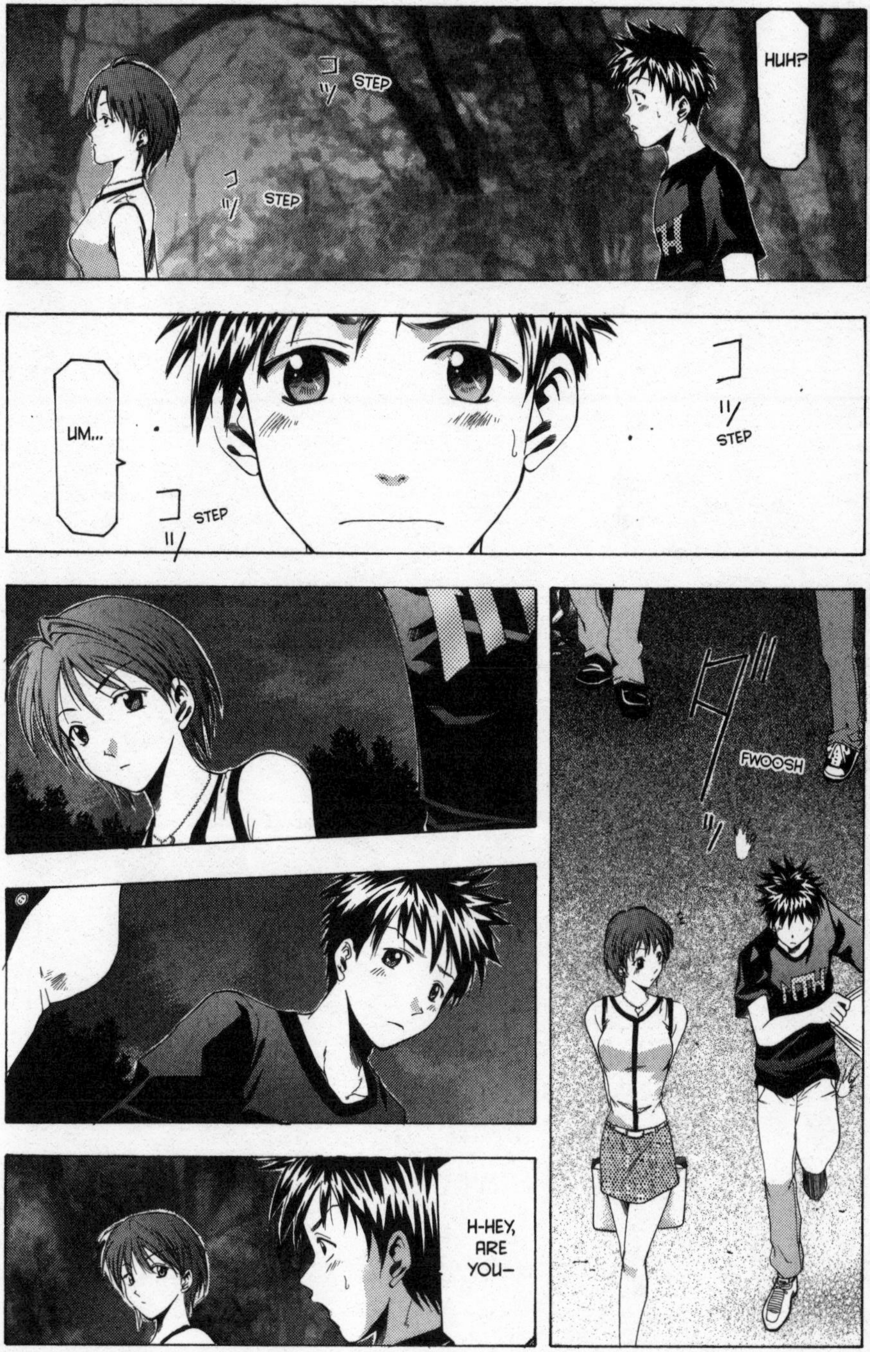
HUH?
コツ
STEP
コツ
STEP
コツ
STEP
UM...
コツ
STEP
ダッ
FWOOSH
H-HEY, ARE YOU—

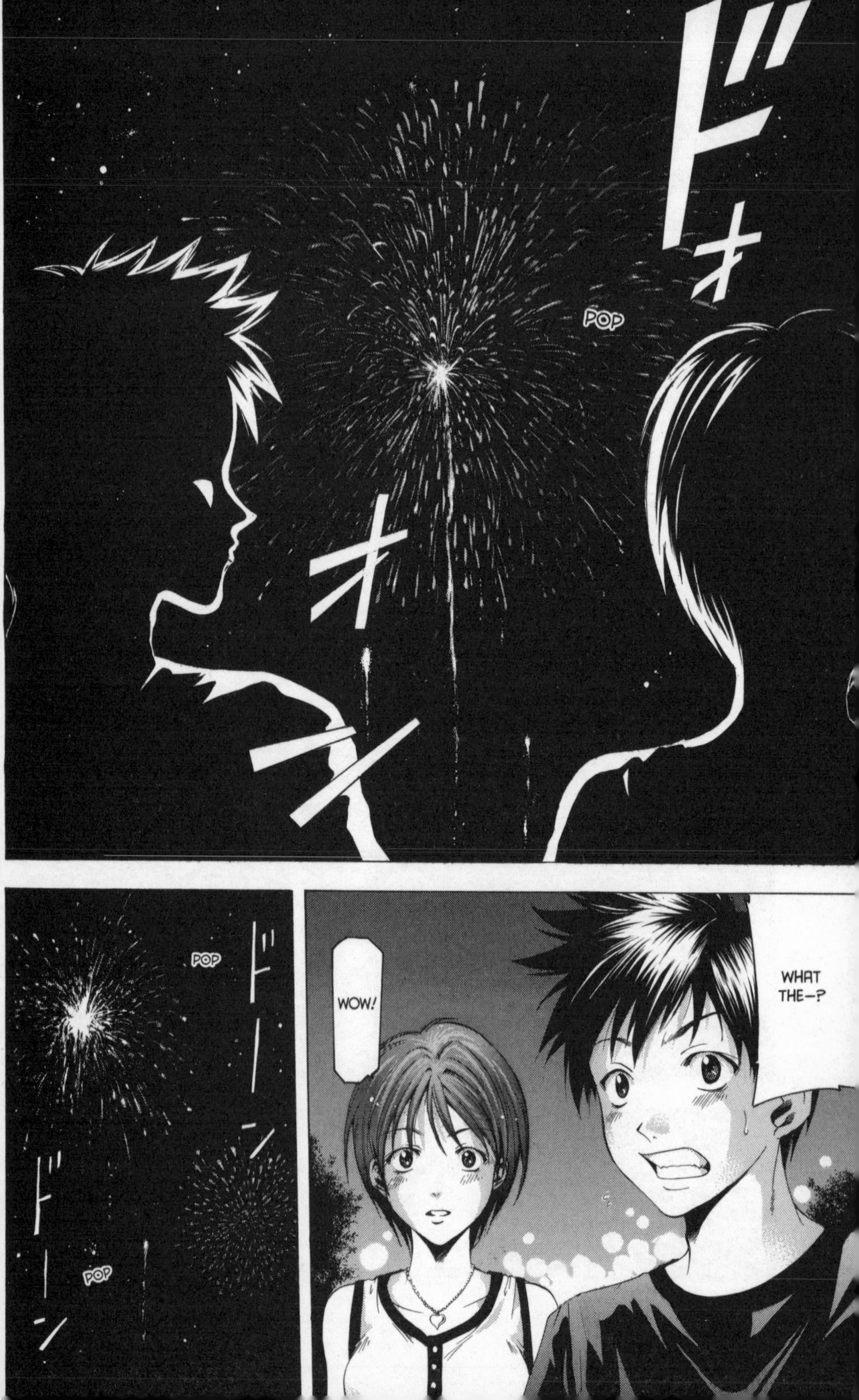
ドォォン
POP
WHAT THE—?
WOW!
ドーン
POP
ドーン
POP

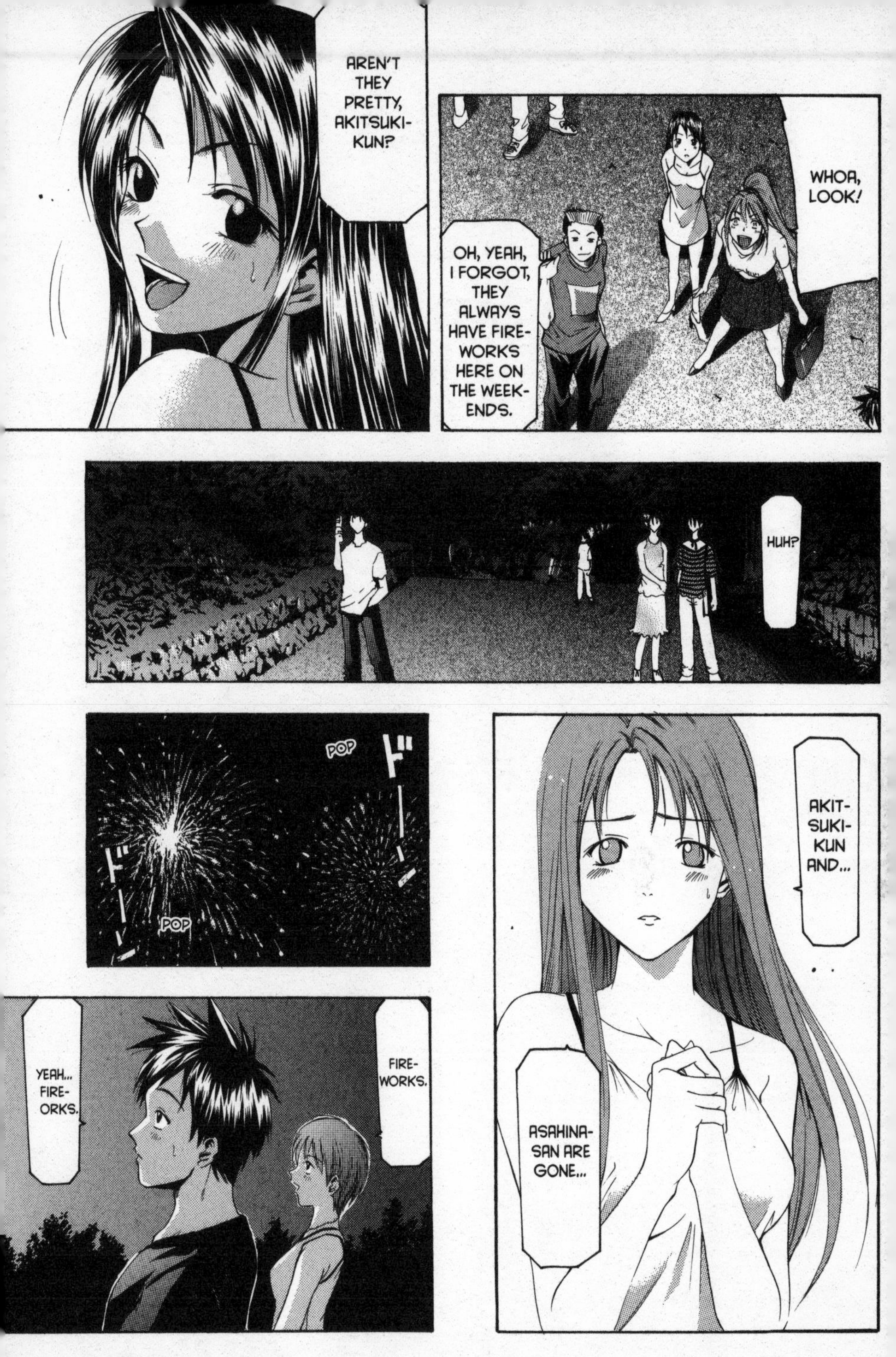
WHOA, LOOK!
OH, YEAH, I FORGOT, THEY ALWAYS HAVE FIRE-WORKS HERE ON THE WEEK-ENDS.
AREN'T THEY PRETTY, AKITSUKI-KUN?
HUH?
AKIT-SUKI-KUN AND...
ASAHINA-SAN ARE GONE...
POP
ドーー
ドーー
POP
FIRE-WORKS.
YEAH... FIRE-ORKS.

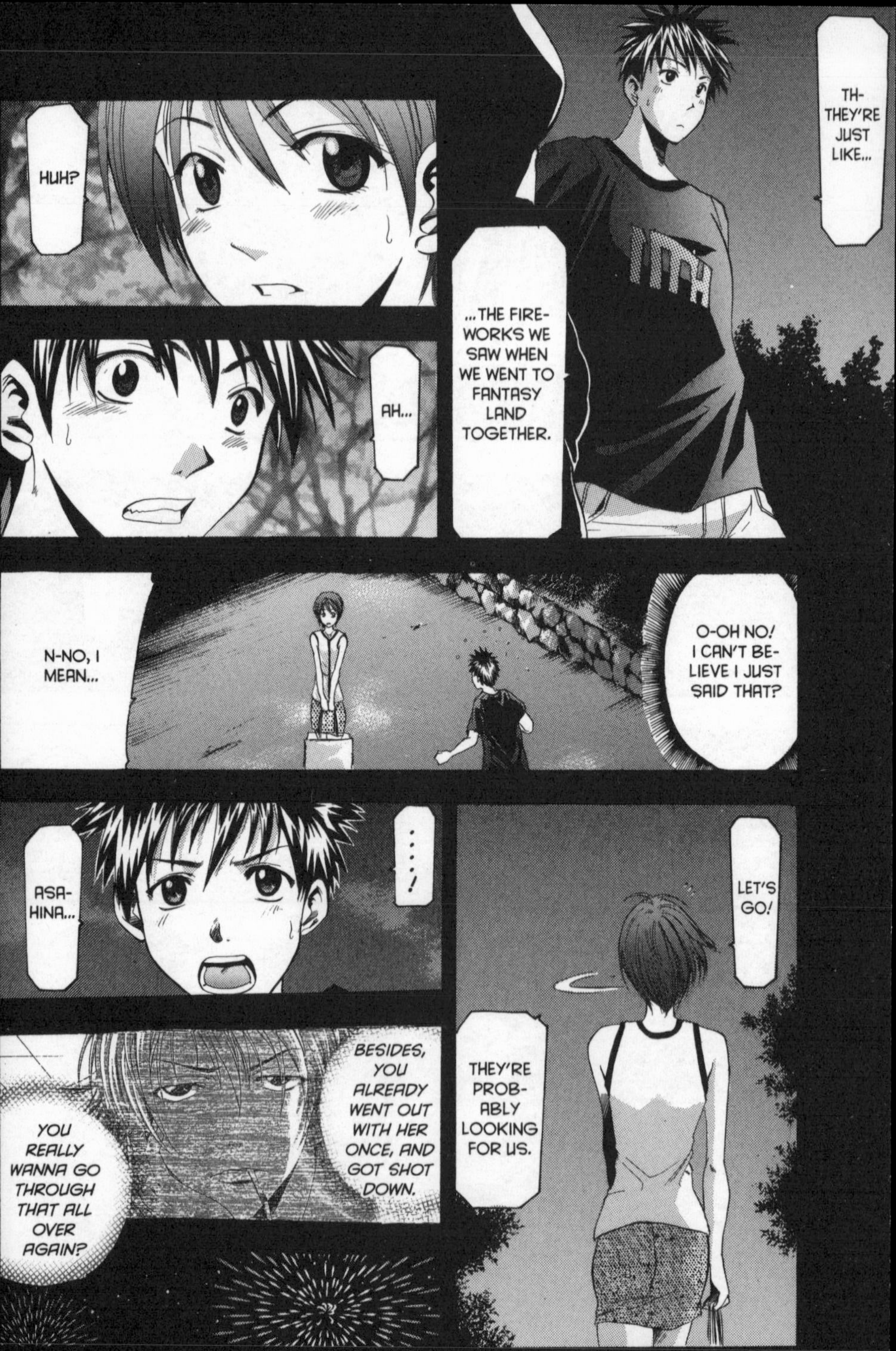
TH- THEY'RE JUST LIKE...
...THE FIRE-WORKS WE SAW WHEN WE WENT TO FANTASY LAND TOGETHER.
HUH?
AH...
O-OH NO! I CAN'T BE-LIEVE I JUST SAID THAT?
N-NO, I MEAN...
LET'S GO!
THEY'RE PROB-ABLY LOOKING FOR US.
....!
ASA-HINA...
BESIDES, YOU ALREADY WENT OUT WITH HER ONCE, AND GOT SHOT DOWN.
YOU REALLY WANNA GO THROUGH THAT ALL OVER AGAIN?

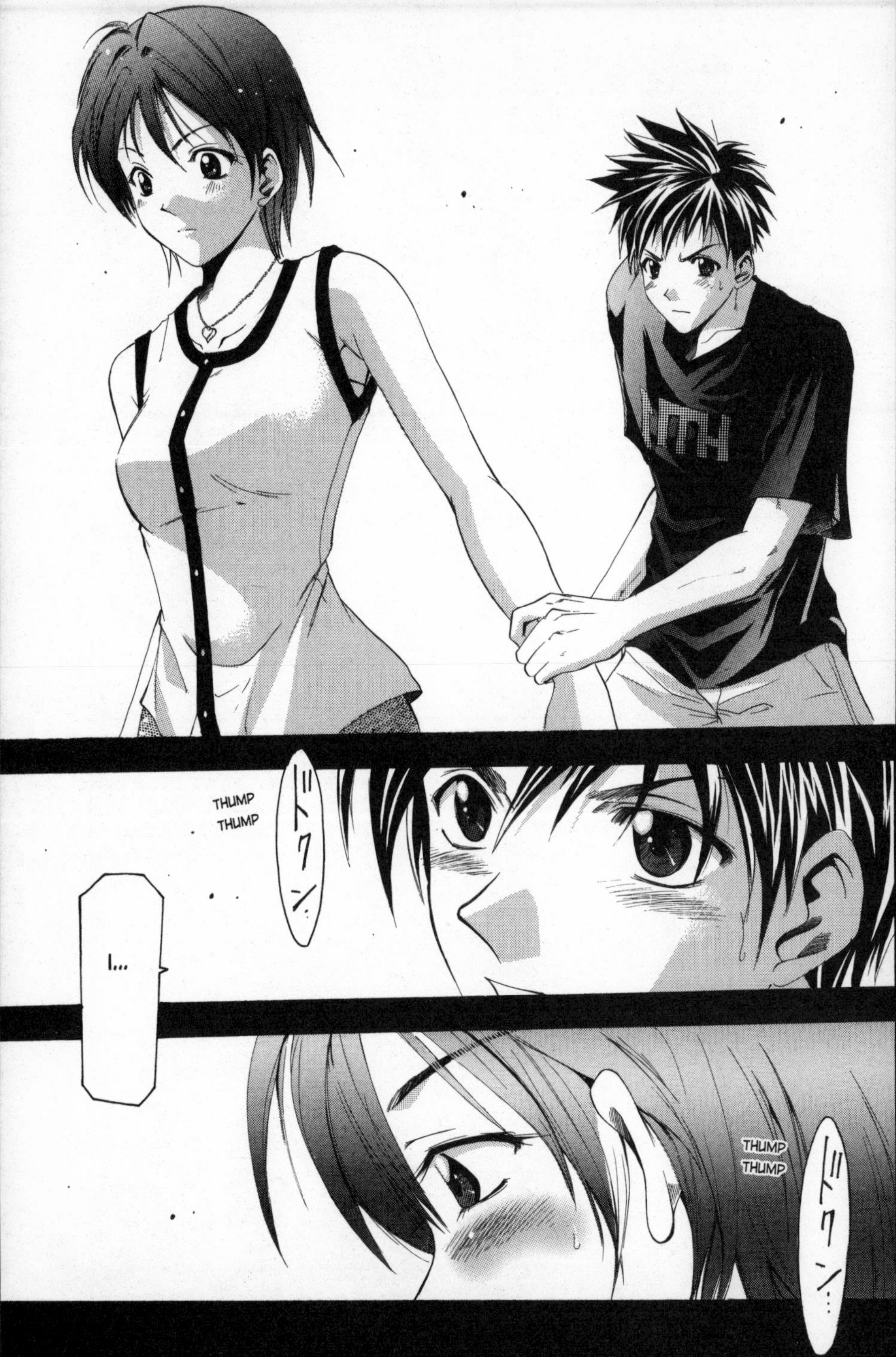

ドクン…
THUMP THUMP
I...
ドクン…
THUMP THUMP

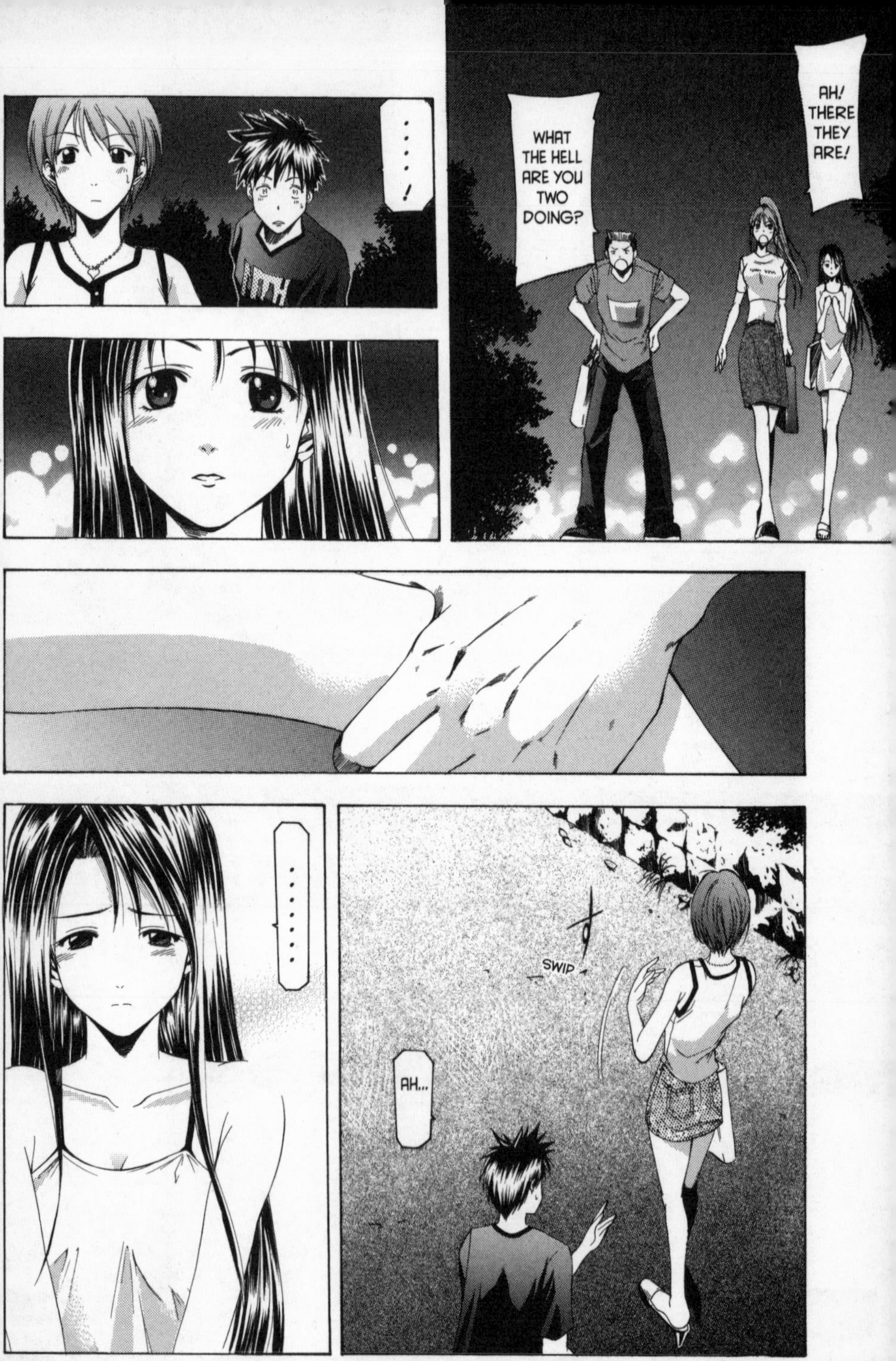
AH! THERE THEY ARE!
WHAT THE HELL ARE YOU TWO DOING?
....!
SWIP
AH...
....

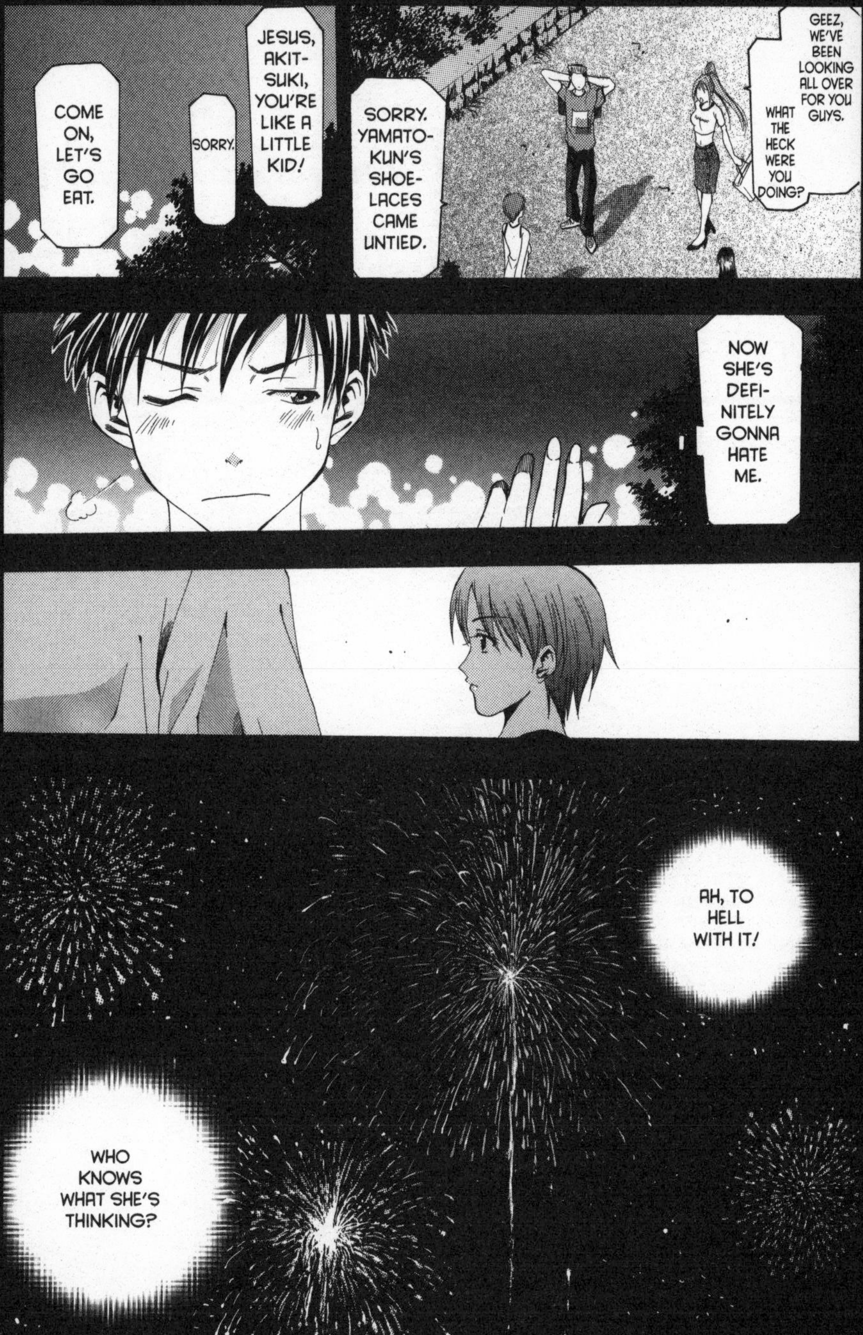
GEEZ, WE'VE BEEN LOOKING ALL OVER FOR YOU GUYS.
WHAT THE HECK WERE YOU DOING?
SORRY. YAMATO-KUN'S SHOE-LACES CAME UNTIED.
JESUS, AKIT-SUKI, YOU'RE LIKE A LITTLE KID!
SORRY.
COME ON, LET'S GO EAT.
NOW SHE'S DEFI-NITELY GONNA HATE ME.
AH, TO HELL WITH IT!
WHO KNOWS WHAT SHE'S THINKING?

CONTINUED IN VOLUME 5

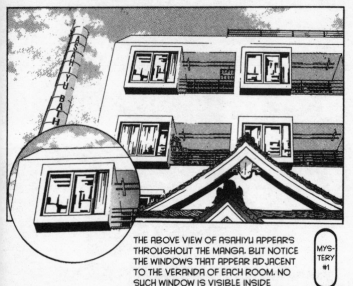

BONUS MANGA–S.M.R. (SUZUKA MYSTERY REPORT)

THE MYSTERIES OF THE ASAHIYU LADIES APARTMENT COMPLEX

ASAHIYU BATH

MYSTERY #1

THE ABOVE VIEW OF ASAHIYU APPEARS THROUGHOUT THE MANGA. BUT NOTICE THE WINDOWS THAT APPEAR ADJACENT TO THE VERANDA OF EACH ROOM. NO SUCH WINDOW IS VISIBLE INSIDE YAMATO'S ROOM. WHAT ON EARTH ARE THESE WINDOWS?

IT IS A MYSTERY INDEED.

MYSTERY #2

THE BOTTOM PANELS SHOW THE ROOMS OF YAMATO, SUZUKA, AND THE LANDLADY. WHY DOES EACH ROOM HAVE THE EXACT SAME CLOCK? IT SEEMS UNLIKELY THAT THEY EACH, COINCIDENTALLY, PURCHASED THE SAME CLOCK. PERHAPS WE SHOULD ASSUME THAT THIS IS THE STANDARD ASAHIYU "WELCOME GIFT" GIVEN TO ALL NEW TENANTS.

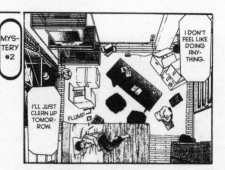

I DON'T FEEL LIKE DOING ANYTHING.
I'LL JUST CLEAN UP TOMORROW.
FLUMP

☆ YAMATO'S ROOM – YOU CAN'T SEE THE WINDOW.

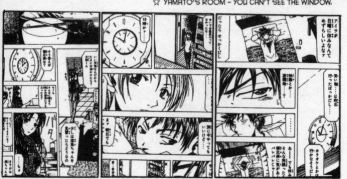

THE PANEL ON THE RIGHT SHOWS YAMATO AND SUZUKA LEAVING FOR SCHOOL. BASED ON WHAT WE SEE IN THIS DRAWING, ONE WOULD ASSUME THAT THEIR ROOMS ARE LAID OUT IN THE MANNER SHOWN IN THE DIAGRAM BELOW.

MYSTERY #3

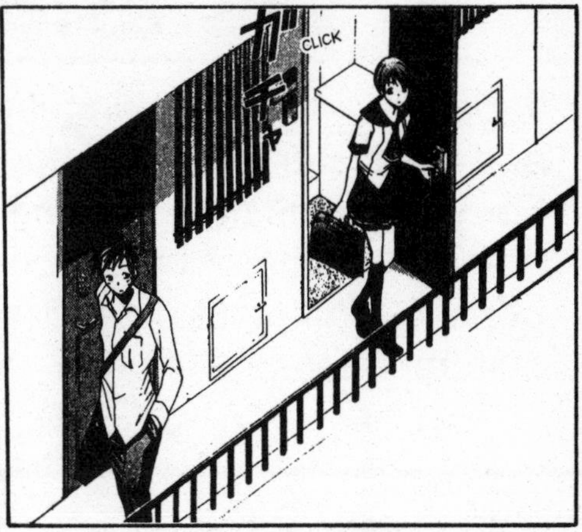
ガチャ
CLICK

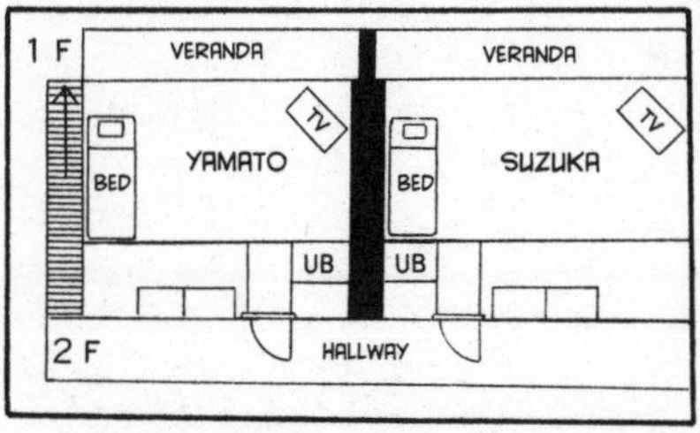
1 F
VERANDA
VERANDA
TV
YAMATO
BED
TV
SUZUKA
BED
UB
UB
2 F
HALLWAY

☆

HOWEVER, THROUGHOUT THE STORY, WE SEE YAMATO CRAWLING THROUGH THE HOLE IN THE WALL TO ENTER SUZUKA'S ROOM. THE HOLE IS SITUATED NEAR YAMATO'S BED, AND WHEN YAMATO GOES THROUGH THE HOLE, HE FINDS HIMSELF NEXT TO SUZUKA'S TV. ACCORDING TO THE DIAGRAM, CRAWLING THROUGH THE HOLE SHOULD PUT YAMATO RIGHT SMACK-DAB IN THE STAIRWELL.

PERHAPS THIS HOLE PASSES THROUGH ANOTHER DIMENSION TO END UP CONNECTING TO SUZUKA'S ROOM. WHO KNOWS, THE NEXT TIME YAMATO STEPS THROUGH THAT HOLE HE MIGHT END UP IN A WHOLE DIFFERENT WORLD.

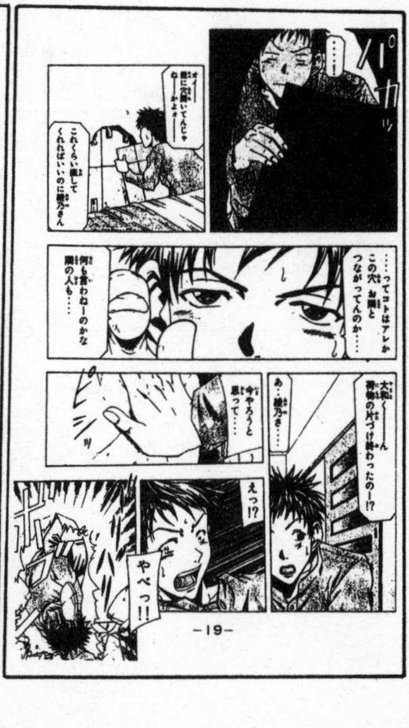
パカッ
……!
オイ〜 壁に穴開いてんじゃねーかよォ〜
これくらい直してくれればいいのに綾乃さん
…ってコトはアレか この穴お隣とつながってんのか……
何も言わねーのかな隣の人も……
大和く〜〜ん 荷物の片づけ終わったの〜!?
あ…綾乃さ……
今やろうと思って……
ピシッ
えっ!?
やべっ!!
-19-

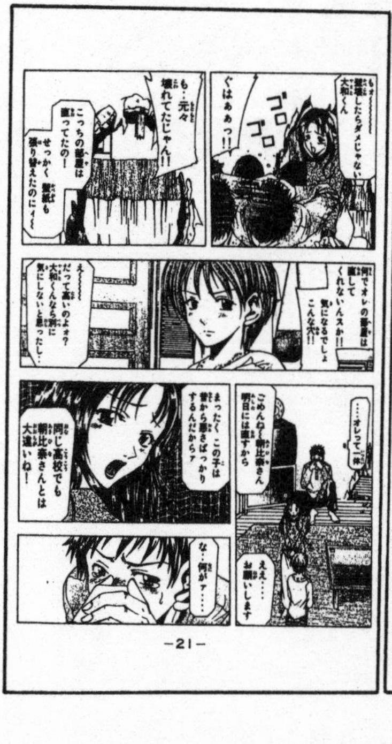
もォ〜〜〜 破壊したらダメじゃない大和くん
ゴロゴロ
ぐはぁぁっ!!
も…元々壊れてたじゃん!!
こっちの部屋は直ってたの! せっかく壁紙も張り替えたのにィ〜
何でオレの部屋は直してくれないんスか!! 気になるでしょ こんな穴!!
え〜〜〜 だって高いのよォ? 大和くんなら別に気にしないと思ったし…
……オレって一体
ごめんね〜朝比奈さん 明日には直すから
まったく この子は昔から悪さばっかりするんだからァ
同じ高校でも朝比奈さんとは大違いね!
ええ……お願いします
な…何がァ…
-21-

RESEARCH BY THE SEO DANDY STUDIO

Translation Notes

Japanese is a tricky language for most Westerners, and translation is often more an art than a science. For your edification and reading pleasure, here are notes on some of the places where we could have gone in a different direction or where a Japanese cultural reference is used.

Suzukaze, page 5

The second character in Suzuka's name can be read as *ka* or *kaze*. *Kaze* means wind, so Kazuki jokingly calls Suzuka by the nickname Suzukaze.

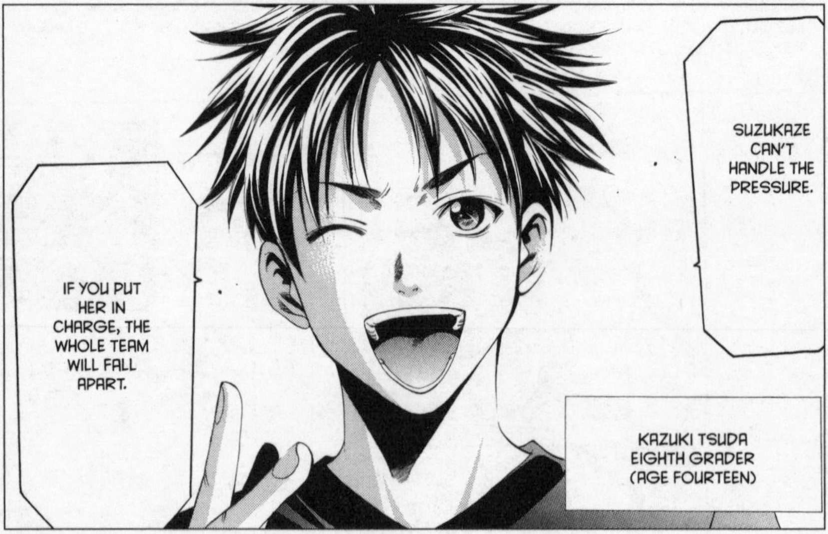
SUZUKAZE CAN'T HANDLE THE PRESSURE.
KAZUKI TSUDA EIGHTH GRADER (AGE FOURTEEN)
IF YOU PUT HER IN CHARGE, THE WHOLE TEAM WILL FALL APART.

Prefectural meet, page 6

Japan is divided into numerous prefectures that function something like states do in the United States.

K fest and Shou-xxx-kan, page 22

K fest probably stands for Kodansha Fest. Kodansha is the Japanese publisher of *Suzuka.* Shou-xxx-kan is probably a reference to one of Kodansha's publishing competitors, Shougakkan. Shougakkan publishes manga and children's books. This was probably a dinosaur exhibit for kids that was sponsored by the publisher.

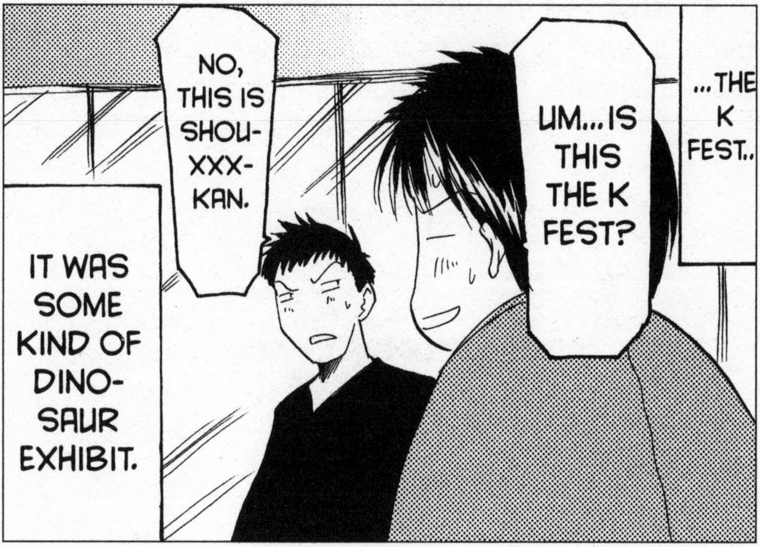
...THE K FEST..
UM...IS THIS THE K FEST?
NO, THIS IS SHOU-XXX-KAN.
IT WAS SOME KIND OF DINO-SAUR EXHIBIT.

Cicadas, page 117

The loud chirping of the cicadas marks Japan's hot, humid summers.

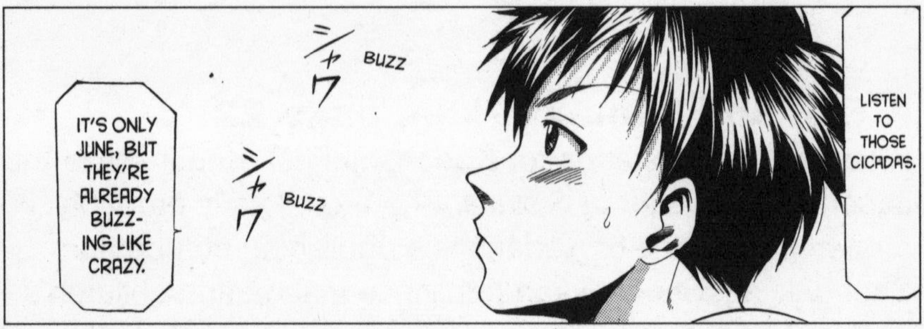
LISTEN TO THOSE CICADAS.
BUZZ
BUZZ
IT'S ONLY JUNE, BUT THEY'RE ALREADY BUZZ-ING LIKE CRAZY.

Cold Chinese noodles, page 149

Yamato is ordering *hiyashi chuuka* or cold Chinese-style noodles. This dish features noodles topped with cucumber, eggs, ham, and a sweet-and-sour sauce. It's a popular summer dish.

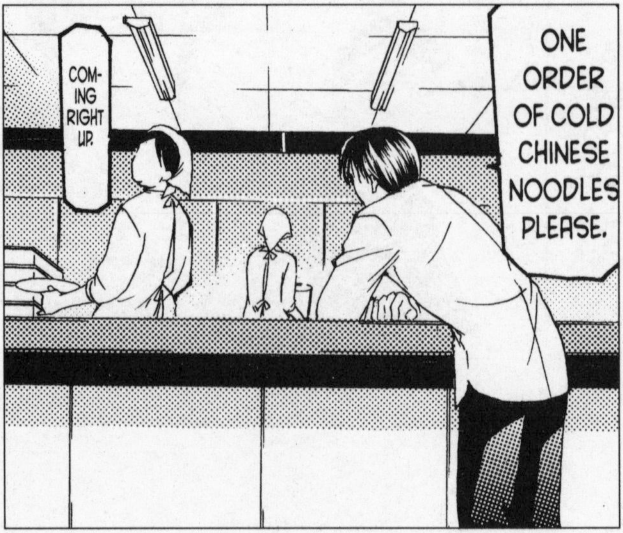
ONE ORDER OF COLD CHINESE NOODLES PLEASE.
COM-ING RIGHT UP.

Aqua pazza and *shiroi koibito*, page 162

Aqua pazza is an Italian style of cooking fish. The fish is cooked in a broth of salted water with garlic and spices and then served in the broth. *Shiroi koibito* is a famous kind of cream-filled cookie from the Hokkaido region of Japan.

CHARACTER PROFILE NO. 12

EMERSON ARIMA
(HIGH SCHOOL SOPHOMORE)

DATE OF BIRTH—JULY 7 (CANCER)
HEIGHT—5'9"
WEIGHT—158 LBS
BLOOD TYPE—A

LIKES
• TRACK
• FISH *AQUA PAZZA*
• *SHIROI KOIBITO* COOKIES

DISLIKES
• KAZUKI TSUDA
• BEING TOLD WHAT TO DO
• PICKLES

GOAL—TO RUN THE 100-METER DASH IN UNDER TEN SECONDS

Preview of Volume 5

We're pleased to present you with a preview of *Suzuka*, Volume 5. This volume will be available on August 28, 2007.

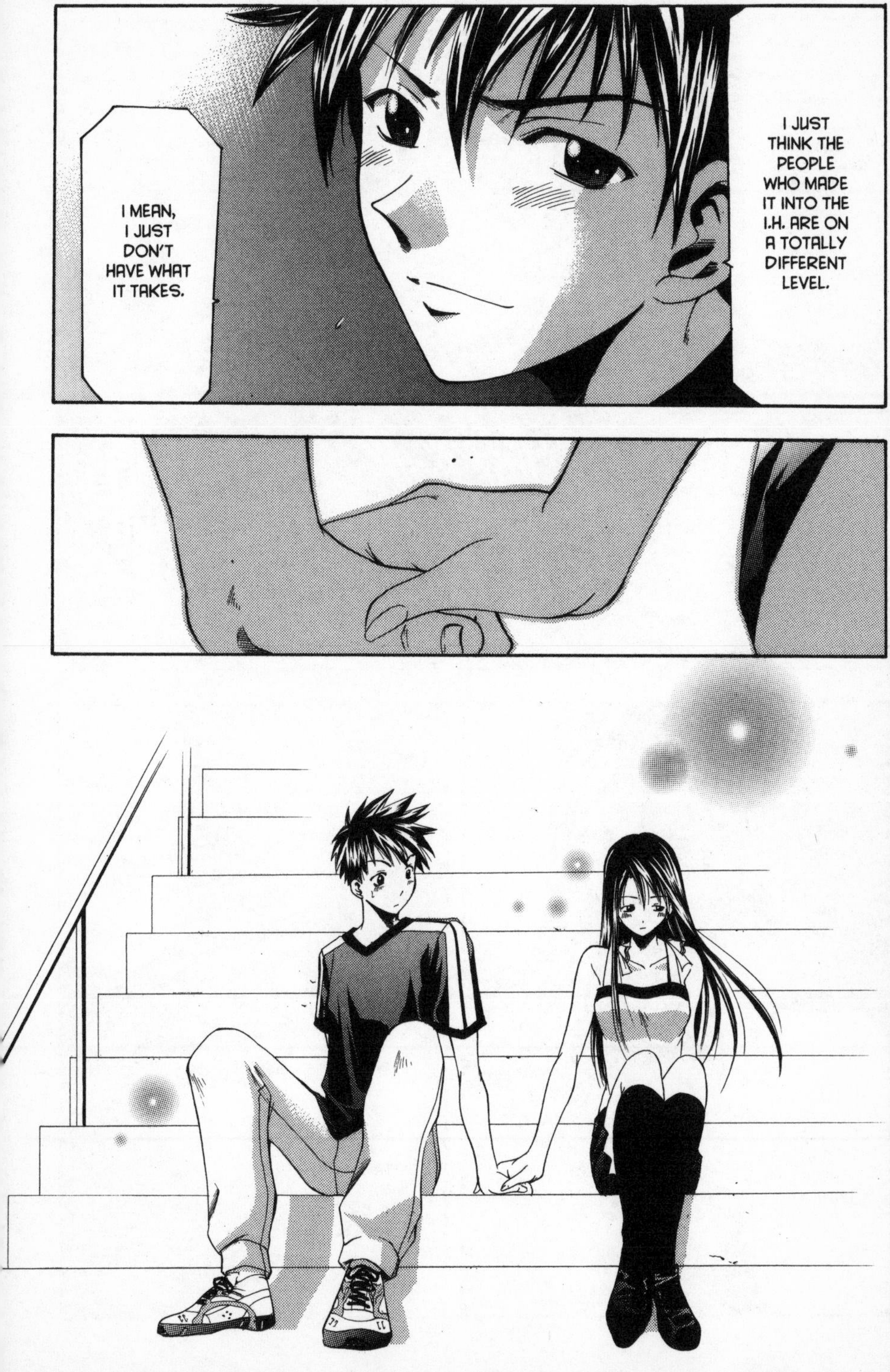
I JUST THINK THE PEOPLE WHO MADE IT INTO THE I.H. ARE ON A TOTALLY DIFFERENT LEVEL.
I MEAN, I JUST DON'T HAVE WHAT IT TAKES.

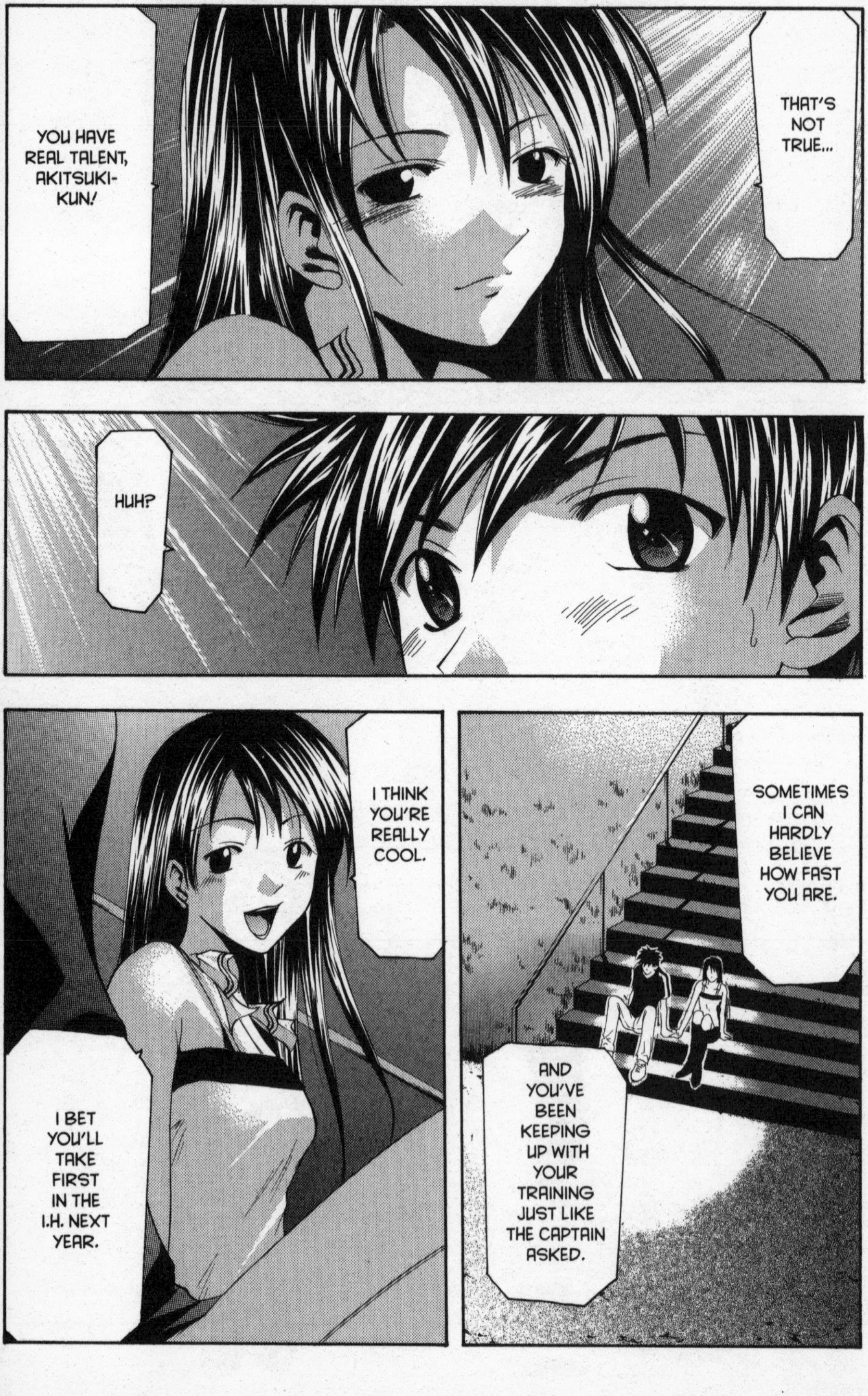
THAT'S NOT TRUE...
YOU HAVE REAL TALENT, AKITSUKI-KUN!
HUH?
SOMETIMES I CAN HARDLY BELIEVE HOW FAST YOU ARE.
AND YOU'VE BEEN KEEPING UP WITH YOUR TRAINING JUST LIKE THE CAPTAIN ASKED.
I THINK YOU'RE REALLY COOL.
I BET YOU'LL TAKE FIRST IN THE I.H. NEXT YEAR.

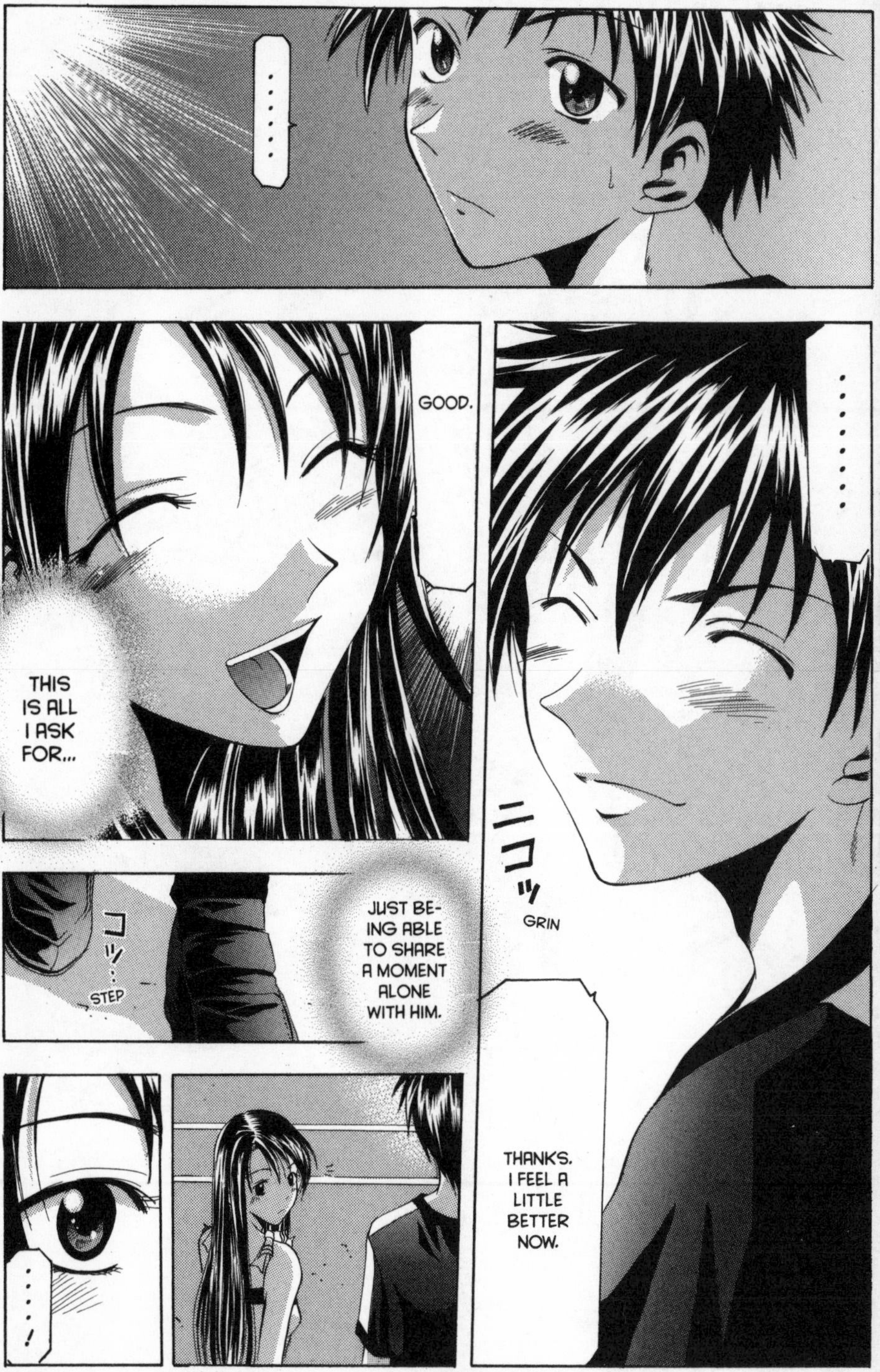
......
......
ニコッ
GRIN
THANKS. I FEEL A LITTLE BETTER NOW.
GOOD.
THIS IS ALL I ASK FOR...
JUST BE-ING ABLE TO SHARE A MOMENT ALONE WITH HIM.
コツ...
STEP
....!

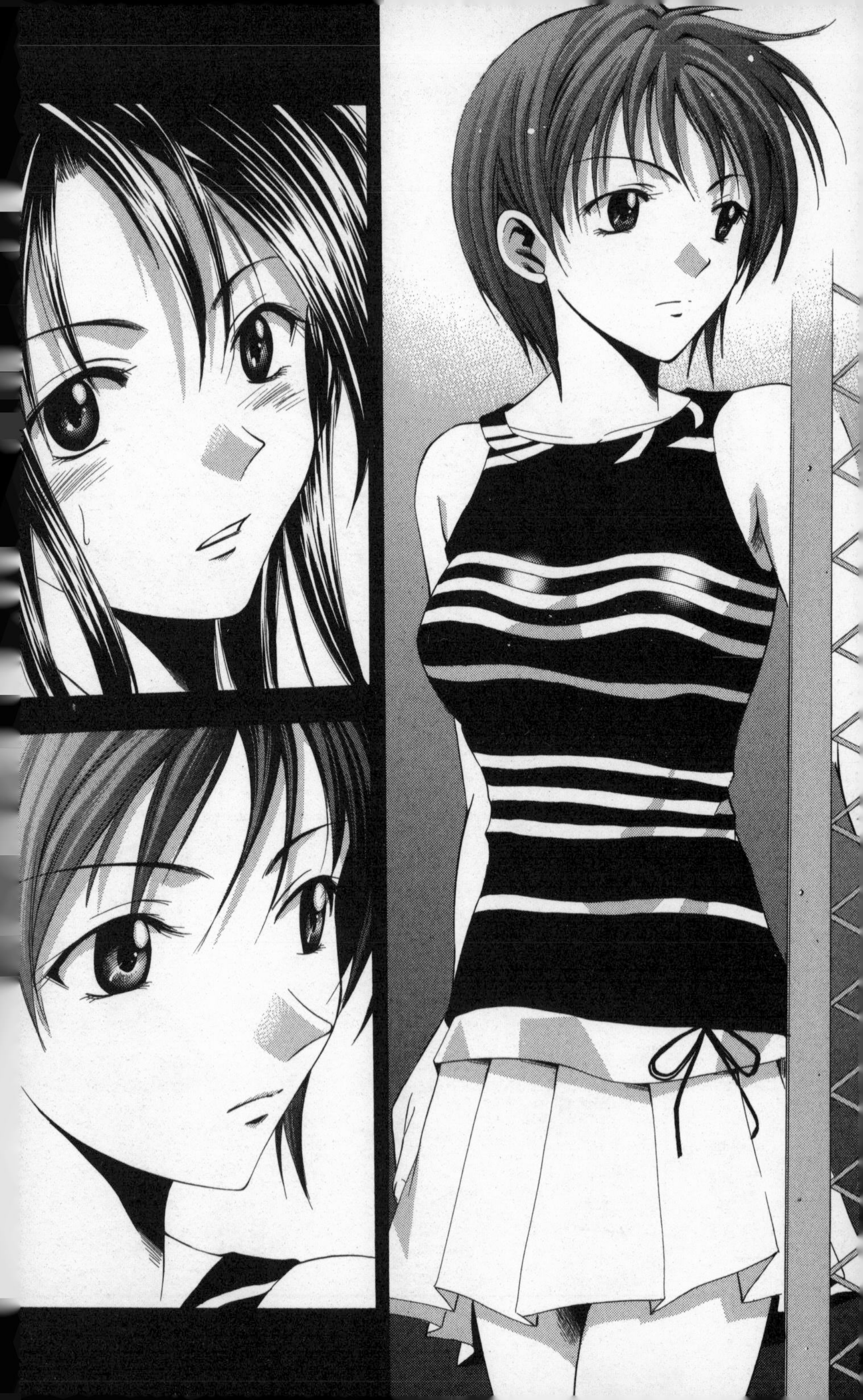

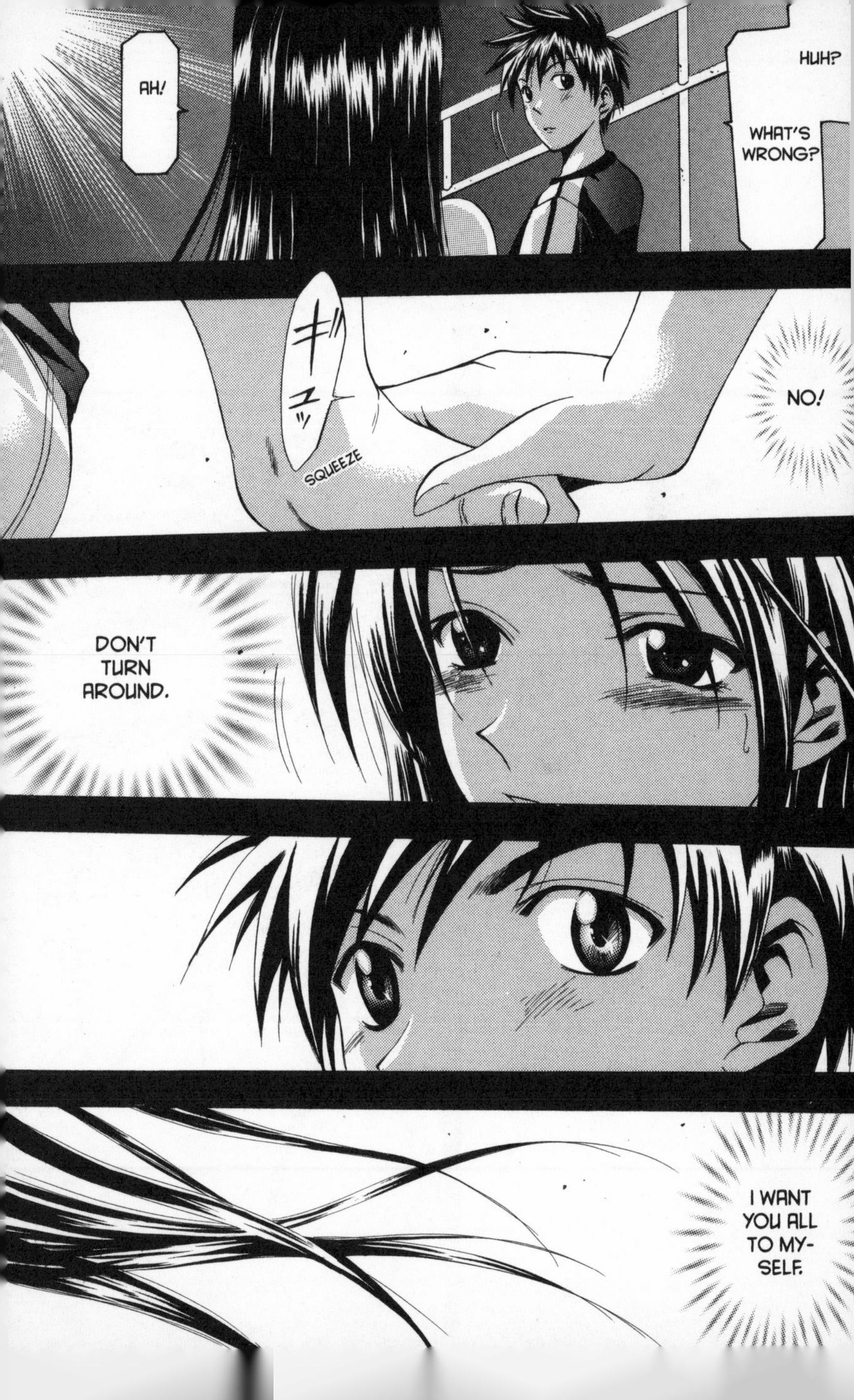
HUH?
WHAT'S WRONG?
AH!
NO!
ギュッ
SQUEEZE
DON'T TURN AROUND.
I WANT YOU ALL TO MY-SELF.

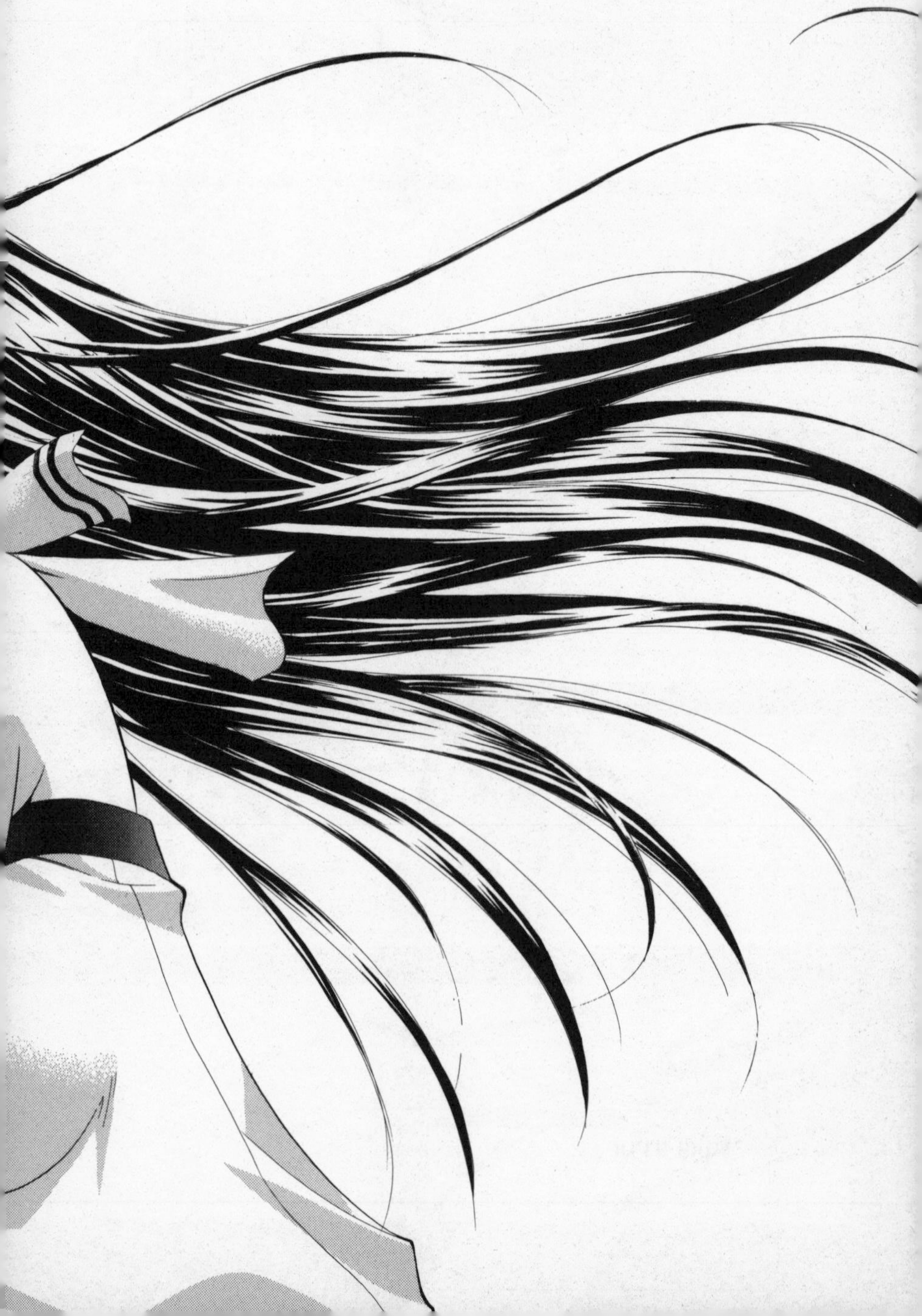

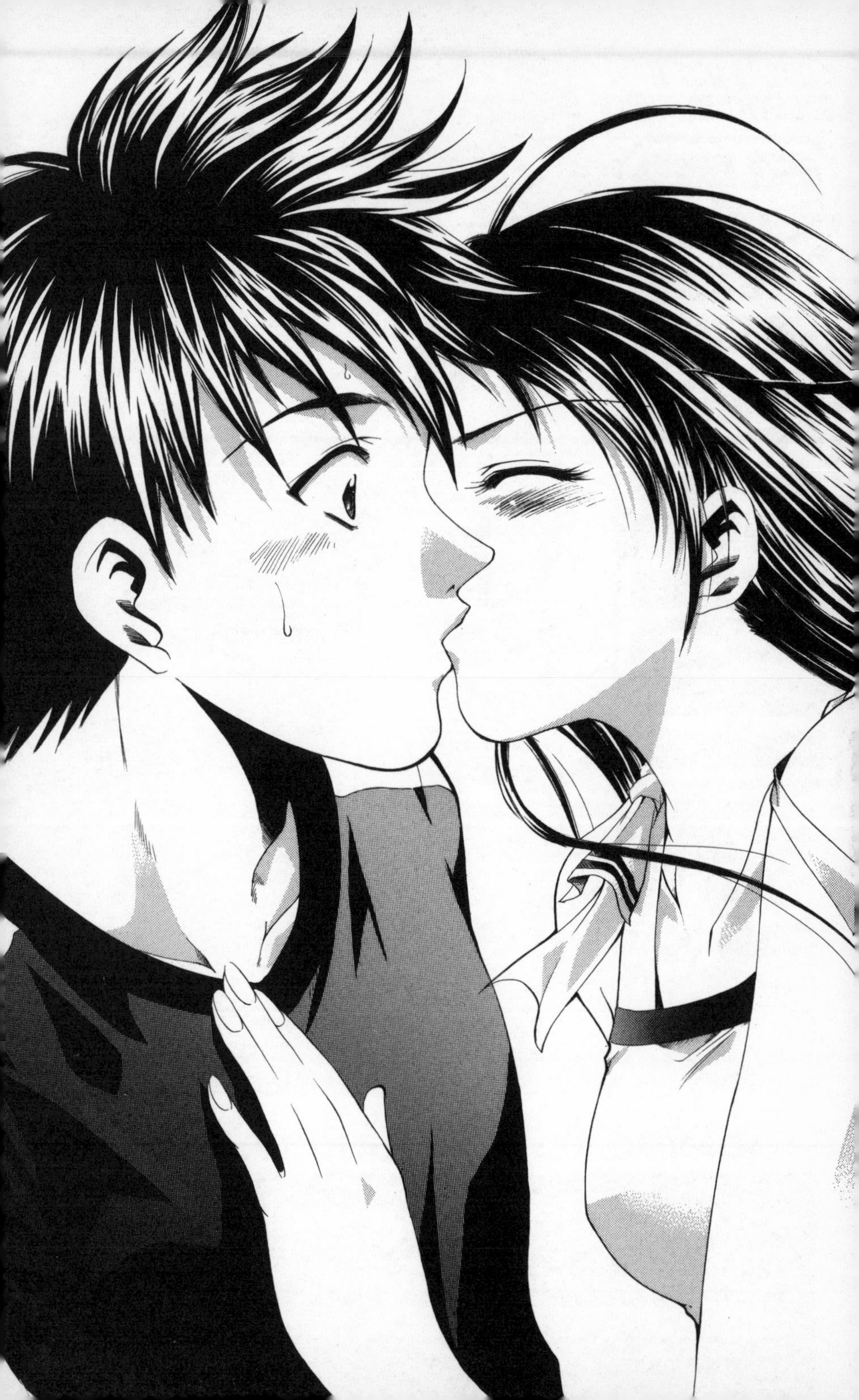

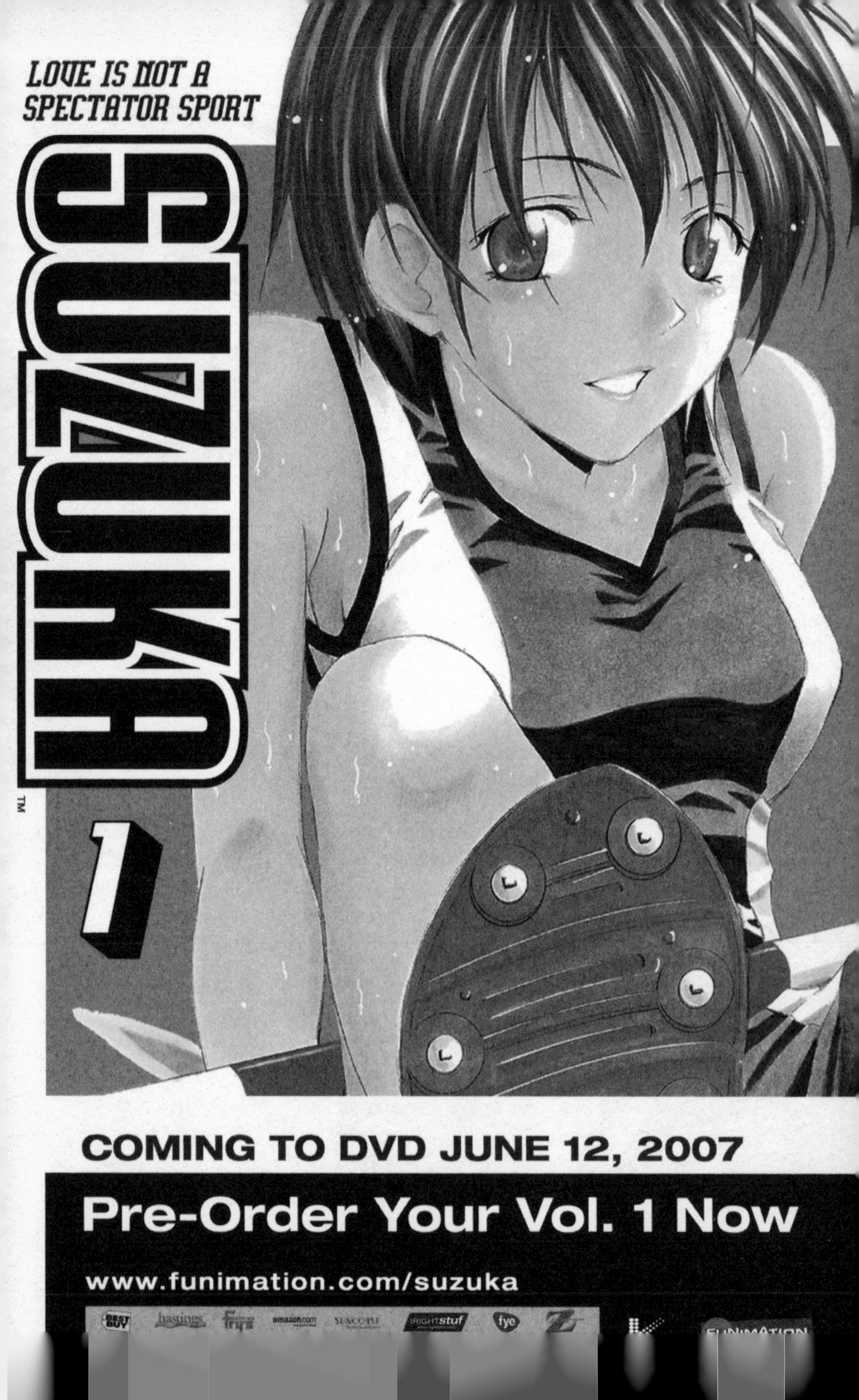
LOVE IS NOT A SPECTATOR SPORT
SUZUKA™
1
COMING TO DVD JUNE 12, 2007
Pre-Order Your Vol. 1 Now
www.funimation.com/suzuka

by Toshihiko Kobayashi

I LOVE YUU

Poor 16-year-old Mugi Tadano is left heartbroken after his girl-friend moves away. A summer job at his friend Kazuki's beachside snack bar/hotel seems like the perfect way to get his mind off the breakup. Soon Kazuki sets Mugi up on a date with a girl named Yuu, who's supposed to be...well...a little less than perfect. But when Yuu arrives, she's not the monster that either of the boys had imagined. In fact, Yuu is about the cutest girl that Mugi has ever seen. But after Mugi accidentally walks in on Yuu while she's in the bath, Yuu is furious. When Mugi goes to apologize the next day, he learns that Yuu has left the island. Mugi vows to search high and low for her, but will he ever see the beautiful Yuu again?

Ages: 16 +

Special extras in each volume! Read them all!

VISIT WWW.DELREYMANGA.COM TO:
• View release date calendars for upcoming volumes
• Sign up for Del Rey's free manga e-newsletter
• Find out the latest about new Del Rey Manga series

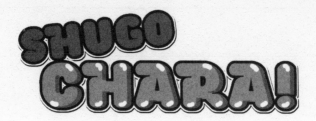

SHUGO CHARA!

PEACH-PIT

Creators of *Dears* and *Rozen Maiden*

Everybody at Seiyo Elementary thinks that stylish and super-cool Amu has it all. But nobody knows the *real* Amu, a shy girl who wishes she had the courage to truly be herself. Changing Amu's life is going to take more than wishes and dreams—it's going to take a little magic! One morning, Amu finds a surprise in her bed: three strange little eggs. Each egg contains a Guardian Character, an angel-like being who can give her the power to be someone new. With the help of her Guardian Characters, Amu is about to discover that her true self is even more amazing than she ever dreamed.

PEACH-PIT
CREATORS OF DEARS AND ROZEN MAIDEN
SHUGO CHARA!
1

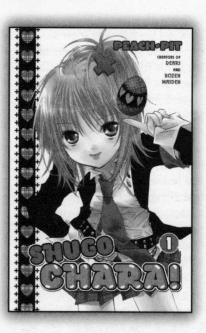

Special extras in each volume! Read them all!

VISIT WWW.DELREYMANGA.COM TO:

- Read sample pages
- View release date calendars for upcoming volumes
- Sign up for Del Rey's free manga e-newsletter
- Find out the latest about new Del Rey Manga series

RATING T AGES 13+

DEL REY MANGA デルレイ

The Otaku's Choice

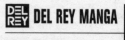

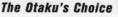

Basilisk

ORIGINAL STORY BY FŪTARO YAMADA
MANGA BY MASAKI SEGAWA

THE BATTLE BEGINS

The Iga clan and the Kouga clan have been sworn enemies for more than four hundred years. Only the Hanzo Hattori truce has kept the two families from all-out war. Now, under the order of Shogun Ieyasu Tokugawa, the truce has been dissolved. Ten ninja from each clan must fight to the death in order to determine who will be the next Tokugawa Shogun. The surviving clan will rule for the next thousand years.

But not all the clan members are in agreement. Oboro of the Iga clan and Gennosuke of the Kouga clan have fallen deeply in love. Now these star-crossed lovers have been pitted against each other. Can their romance conquer a centuries-old rivalry? Or is their love destined to end in death?

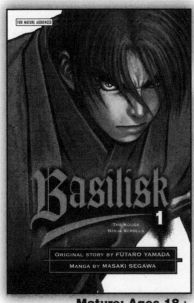

Mature: Ages 18 +

Special extras in each volume! Read them all!

VISIT WWW.DELREYMANGA.COM TO:
- Read sample pages
- View release date calendars for upcoming volumes
- Sign up for Del Rey's free manga e-newsletter
- Find out the latest about new Del Rey Manga series

HIROYUKI TAMAKOSHI

JUST ONE OF THE GIRLS

A whole new Gacha Gacha story line begins! Akira Hatsushiba is just your typical, average high school kid . . . until a glitch in a Gacha Gacha video game changes his life forever. Now, every time Akira sneezes, his entire body undergoes a gender-bending switcheroo! That's right, Akira is always just an *achoo* away from getting in touch with his feminine side. But it's not all bad. Akira has had a crush on Yurika Sakuraba ever since he first laid eyes on her. He's always been too shy, but now that he can change into a girl, Akira finally has a chance to get close to Yurika. Being a girl certainly has its advantages!

Special extras in each volume! Read them all!

VISIT WWW.DELREYMANGA.COM TO:
- Read sample pages
- View release date calendars for upcoming volumes
- Sign up for Del Rey's free manga e-newsletter
- Find out the latest about new Del Rey Manga series

RATING M AGES 18+

 **DEL REY MANGA**

The Otaku's Choice

TOMARE!
[STOP!]

You are going the wrong way!

Manga is a completely different
type of reading experience.

To start at the *beginning,* go to the *end!*

That's right! Authentic manga is read the traditional Japanese
way—from right to left. Exactly the *opposite* of how American
books are read. It's easy to follow: Just go to the other end of
the book, and read each page—and each panel—from right side
to left side, starting at the top right. Now you're experiencing
manga as it was meant to be.